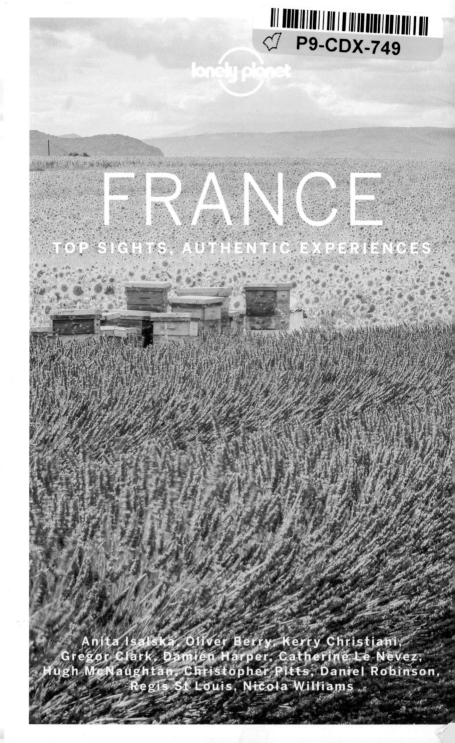

lonely planet

FRANCE

TOP SIGHTS, AUTHENTIC EXPERIENCES

Anita Isalska, Oliver Berry, Kerry Christiani,
Gregor Clark, Damien Harper, Catherine Le Nevez,
Hugh McNaughtan, Christopher Pitts, Daniel Robinson,
Regis St Louis, Nicola Williams

Contents

Rotterdam
NORTH SEA
Bruges
Antwerp
Düsseldorf
Erfurt
Dunkirk
Calais
BRUSSELS
Cologne
Bonn
Lille
Liège
BELGIUM
Lens
Arras
Frankfurt-am-Main
Mainz
SOMME
Amiens
St-Quentin
LUXEMBOURG
GERMANY
Beauvais
CHAMPAGNE p137
Chantilly
Reims
Verdun
Metz
Épernay
Stuttgart
PARIS p35
Nancy
ALSACE
Strasbourg
Baccarat
Chartres
LORRAINE
Troyes
Seine
Chaumont
Épinal
Colmar
Rhine
BURGUNDY
Auxerre
Châtillon-sur-Seine
Belfort
Blois
Basel
Zürich
Dijon
Vézèlay
Besançon
VADUZ
LA SOLOGNE
CÔTE D'OR
BERN
Beaune
Autun
SWITZERLAND
Lausanne
JURA
Guéret
Mâcon
Geneva
Vichy
Annecy
Chamonix
LYON p155
Bergamo
Thiers
Como
Aix-les-Bains
Clermont-Ferrand
Chambéry
FRENCH ALPS p257
Milan
Vienne
St-Étienne
MASSIF CENTRAL
FRENCH ALPS
Brive-la-Gaillarde
Grenoble
Turin
ITALY
Le Puy-en-Velay
Alpe-d'Huez
Sestriere
Valence
Briançon
Figeac
Vaison-la-Romaine
Genoa
NICE p193
PROVENCE p173
Albi
Castellane
Avignon
LANGUEDOC
Nîmes
MONACO
Montpellier
Arles
Aix-en-Provence
Cannes
Antibes
PROVENCE
Narbonne
MARSEILLES p223
ST-TROPEZ p211
Carcassonne
Toulon
ROUSILLON
LIGURIAN SEA
Bastia
Perpignan
Calvi
Collioure
CORSICA
Porto
Cargèse
MEDITERRANEAN SEA
Ajaccio
Girona
Bonifacio
Barcelona

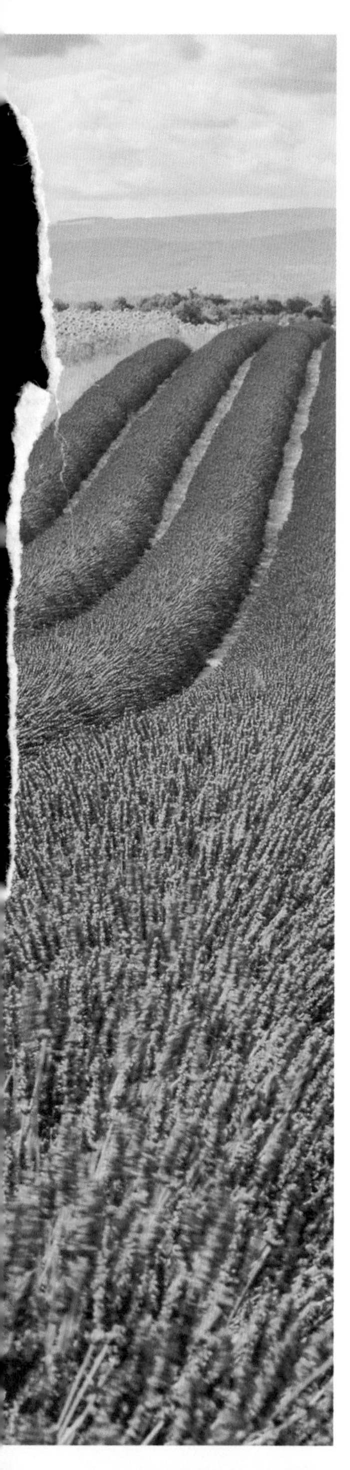

Welcome to France

Vineyards, lavender fields and romantic châteaux... France woos travellers with iconic landmarks and seduces with its unfalteringly familiar culture, woven around cafe terraces, village-square markets and lace-curtained bistros with the plat du jour chalked on the board.

France is a land of languid moments embued with soul. French *art de vivre* (art of living) transforms simple, everyday rituals into unforgettable moments, be it a coffee in the Parisian cafe where Sartre and de Beauvoir met to philosophise, a stroll through the lily-clad gardens Monet painted, or a walk on a beach in Brittany scented with the subtle infusion of language, music and mythology brought by 5th-century Celtic invaders.

Food is of enormous importance to the French: breakfasting on warm croissants from the *boulangerie* (bakery), stopping off at Parisian bistros, and market shopping are all second nature – and it would be rude to refuse.

The *terroir* (land) of France weaves a varied journey from Brittany and Normandy's cliffs and sand dunes to the piercing blue sea of the French Riviera. Outdoor action is what France's lyrical landscape demands – and there's something for everybody. Whether you end up walking barefoot across wave-rippled sand to Mont St-Michel, riding a cable car to glacial panoramas above Chamonix or cartwheeling down Europe's highest sand dune, France does not disappoint. Its great outdoors is thrilling, with endless opportunities and adventure. *Allez!*

> *French* art de vivre *(art of living) transforms simple, everyday rituals into unforgettable moments*

Fields of lavender and sunflowers, Provence (p173)

0 200 km
0 100 miles
CARDIFF
ENGLAND
LONDON
Southampton
Dover
Plymouth
Bournemouth
Brighton
English Channel
(La Manche)
Dieppe
Cherbourg
Honfleur
Bayeux
Caen
Paimpol
St-Malo
NORMANDY p101
Brest
Morlaix
Dinan
Carhaix-
Plouguer
Alençon
Quimper
Rennes
Le Mans
BRITTANY p121
Concarneau
LOIRE VALLEY
Carnac
Vannes
Angers
Loire
Tours
Nantes
Poitiers
ATLANTIC
OCEAN
La Rochelle
Cognac
Limoges
Soulac-
sur-Mer
Bay of
Biscay
Périgueux
BORDEAUX p241
St-Émilion
Arcachon
Cahors
Avilés
Gijón
Oviedo
San
Sebastián
Bayonne
Toulouse
Bilbao
Pau
St-Jean
Pied de
Port
Tarbes
Lourdes
Ponferrada
León
Vitoria
Pamplona
PYRENEES
Logroño
SPAIN
Valladolid
Zaragoza

Arc de Triomphe (p55), Paris

Plan Your Trip
France's Top 12

ANMBPH/SHUTTERSTOCKK ©

Paris

Romance and culture in the City of Light

The cloud-piercing Eiffel Tower, Arc de Triomphe, gargoyled Notre Dame cathedral, lamplit bridges spanning the Seine...Paris (p35) has countless famous landmarks and the French capital more than lives up to its hype. Think sweeping vistas across grand boulevards, world-class art museums, monuments evoking glorious histories, buzzing cafe pavement terraces and a bevy of city bistros. Take the time to absorb, embrace and enjoy. Left: View from Notre Dame's Gargoyles Gallery (p45); Right: Street dining, St-Germain (p69)

1

MATT MUNRO/LONELY PLANET ©

RICHARD SEMIK/SHUTTERSTOCK ©

YURI TURKOV/SHUTTERSTOCK ©

Loire Valley

Châteaux plucked straight from a fairy tale

If it's pomp and architectural splendour you're after, this regal valley is the place to linger. Flowing for more than 1000km, the Loire (p79) is one of France's last *fleuves sauvages* (untamed rivers) and its banks provide a 1000-year snapshot of French high society. Climb the stairway to the rooftop of Château de Chambord, admire art at Château de Chenonceau, and wander the gardens of Château de Villandry. Top: Château de Villandry (p88); Bottom: Château de Chambord (p82)

2

SARANYA33/SHUTTERSTOCK ©

Normandy

Emotional histories in northern France

This coastal chunk of northern France has a rich and often brutal past, brought to life by the island monastery of Mont St-Michel; the Bayeux Tapestry, world-famous for its cartoon scenes of 11th-century life; and the transfixing cemeteries and memorials along the D-Day beaches. Normandy (p101) is also a pastoral land of butter and soft cheeses, a kingdom where creamy Camembert, cider, fiery apple brandy and super-fresh seafood entice. Mont St-Michel (p104)

3

Brittany

Cider, crêpes and the great outdoors

With its wild coastline, islands stitched together with craggy coastal paths, medieval towns and forests laced in Celtic lore and legend, this is a land for explorers. Pedalling past open fields dotted with megaliths gives a poignant reminder of the ancient inhabitants of Brittany (p121), while St-Malo promises visitors pure drama – especially on a sunset stroll along its historic ramparts. Throw back a cider, bite into a sweet crêpe, and rev up your sense of Breton adventure. St-Malo (p126)

Champagne

The heart and soul of French bubbly

Nothing quite fulfils the French dream like easy day hikes through neat rows of vineyards, exquisite picture-postcard villages and a gold-stone riverside hamlet. This is Champagne (p137), the land of French bubbly. Known-brand Champagne houses in the main towns of Reims and Épernay are famed the world over. But much of Champagne's finest liquid gold is created by passionate, small-scale vignerons (winegrowers) in drop-dead-gorgeous villages – rendering the region's scenic driving routes the loveliest way of tasting fine bubbly amid rolling vineyards. Hot-air ballooning above Montagne de Reims (p147)

BORIS STROUJKO/SHUTTERSTOCK ©

MIKI STUDIO/SHUTTERSTOCK ©

Lyon

Gastronomic capital of France

In France's food capital (p155), gastronauts will be in seventh heaven: from tripe and pike dumplings to frogs' legs and grilled carp, there are plenty of culinary adventures to be had. Savouring dishes in *bouchons* (small bistros) creates unforgettable memories – as do the Roman amphitheatres of Fourvière, the Unesco-listed streets of Vieux Lyon, the *traboules* (secret passageways), and the audacious modern architecture of Confluence. Frogs' legs with garlic butter

6

Provence

7

Lavender fields and lazy lunches

Sip pastis (aniseed-flavoured aperitif) over *pétanque* (boules) on the village square, mingle over buckets of herbs and tangy olives at the weekly market, hunt for truffles, taste Côtes de Provence rosé and congratulate yourself on arriving in Provence (p173). This region in France's south calls for slow travel – be it motoring past lavender fields and chestnut forests, cycling through apple-green vineyards or hopping between hilltop villages. Strawberries at a Provençal market (p180)

Nice

Vibrant street life meets year-round sunshine

Undisputed queen of the Riviera's shimmering seas, idyllic beaches and lush hills, Nice (p193) is one of France's smartest urban hang-outs. Its old town is gorgeous, its street markets buzz and its people know how to party. Take the dramatic trio of coastal roads, impossible to drive along without conjuring up the glitz of Riviera high life. Marvel at it all over true *salade niçoise, socca* (chickpea pancakes) or *tourte de blettes* (chard, raisin and pine nut pie). Cours Saleya flower market (p196), Vieux Nice

DANIEL NICHOLSON/DANIELNICHOLSON/500PX ©

CHRISTIAN MUELLER/
SHUTTERSTOCK ©

St-Tropez

Glamorous Riviera fishing port with star power

In summer, sizzling St-Tropez (p211) is the French Riviera's hang-out of choice for celebrities and party aficionados, but it's strangely quiet the rest of the year. In August, arrive by car, and you'll sit for hours in a bottleneck and curse the old fishing port; arrive by boat and love it forever. Indisputable assets: brilliant sandy beaches, couture boutiques, gourmet food shops, galleries and nightclubs on the sand.

Marseille

Cultural fusion by the Mediterranean

Grit and grandeur coexist in Marseille (p223), a multicultural port city with a pedigree stretching back to classical Greece. Marseille's heart is the vibrant Vieux Port, mast-to-mast with yachts and pleasure boats. Uphill is ancient Le Panier, the oldest section of the city, stylish République and the Joliette area, centred on totemic Cathédrale de Marseille Notre Dame de Major. Top: Vieux Port (p231); Bottom left: Basilique Notre Dame de la Garde (p230); Bottom right: Le Panier (p228)

10

Bordeaux

11

Wine capital hemmed by sun-drenched vineyards

Bordeaux (p241) is synonymous with some of France's finest wine. *Dégustation* (tasting) is part of life, from aged *premiers crus* to the *vin nouveau* opened at festivals after the autumn harvest. Paired with the city's exceptional dining scene – traditional kitchens, neo-bistros, fusion restaurants – there is no tastier marriage. Beyond this, Bordeaux is a blend of 18th-century savoir-faire, millennial high-tech and urban street life. Vineyards around St-Émilion (p254)

French Alps

12

Pure adrenaline on the roof of Europe

These mighty mountains, mirror lakes and crevasse-scarred glaciers form one of Europe's true epics. Crowned by Mont Blanc (4810m), the Alps (p257) show no mercy in their outdoor-action overload. Europe's biggest and most prestigious ski resorts are here. In summer they melt into meadow-draped hiking country. Aiguille du Midi (p260)

Plan Your Trip
Need to Know

When to Go

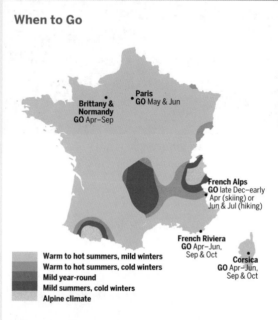

Paris
GO May & Jun

Brittany & Normandy
GO Apr–Sep

French Alps
GO late Dec–early Apr (skiing) or Jun & Jul (hiking)

French Riviera
GO Apr–Jun, Sep & Oct

Corsica
GO Apr–Jun, Sep & Oct

Warm to hot summers, mild winters
Warm to hot summers, cold winters
Mild year-round
Mild summers, cold winters
Alpine climate

High Season (Jul & Aug)

- Queues at big sights and on roads, especially August.
- Christmas, New Year and Easter all busy.
- Late December to March is high season in ski resorts.
- Book accommodation and tables in the best restaurants well in advance.

Shoulder (Apr–Jun & Sep)

- Hotel rates drop in the south and other hot spots.
- Spring brings warm weather, flowers, local produce.
- Autumn's *vendange* (grape harvest) is reason to visit.

Low Season (Oct–Mar)

- Prices up to 50% less than high season.
- Sights, attractions and restaurants open fewer days.
- Hotels and restaurants in quiet rural regions are closed.

Currency

Euro (€)

Language

French

Visas

Generally not required for stays of up to 90 days (or at all for EU nationals); some nationalities need a Schengen visa (p307).

Money

ATMs at every airport, most train stations and on every second street corner in towns and cities. Visa, MasterCard and Amex widely accepted.

Mobile Phones

European and Australian phones work, but only American cells with 900 and 1800 MHz networks are compatible; check with your provider before leaving home. Use a French SIM card to make cheaper calls with a French number.

Time

Central European Time (GMT/UTC plus one hour)

Daily Costs

Budget: less than €130

- Dorm bed: €18–30
- Double room in a budget hotel: €90
- Admission to many attractions first Sunday of month: free
- Lunch *menus* (set meals): less than €20

Midrange: €130–220

- Double room in a midrange hotel: €90–190
- Lunch *menus* in gourmet restaurants: €20–40

Top End: over €220

- Double room in a top-end hotel: €190–350
- Top restaurant dinner: *menu* €65, à la carte €100–150

Useful Websites

France.fr (www.france.fr) Official country website.

France 24 (www.france24.com/en/france) French news in English.

Paris by Mouth (www.parisbymouth.com) Dining and drinking; one-stop site for where and how to eat in the capital with plenty of the latest openings.

David Lebovitz (www.davidlebovitz.com) American pastry chef in Paris and author of several French cook books; insightful postings and great France-related articles shared on his Facebook page.

French Word-a-Day (http://french-word-a-day.typepad.com) Fun language learning.

Lonely Planet (www.lonelyplanet.com/france) Destination information, hotel bookings, traveller forum and more.

Opening Hours

Opening hours vary throughout the year. We list high-season opening hours, but remember that they often decrease in shoulder and low seasons.

Banks 9am to noon and 2pm to 5pm Monday to Friday or Tuesday to Saturday

Bars 7pm to 1am

Cafes 7am to 11pm

Clubs 10pm to 3am, 4am or 5am Thursday to Saturday

Restaurants Noon to 2.30pm and 7pm to 11pm six days a week

Shops 10am to noon and 2pm to 7pm Monday to Saturday

Arriving in France

Aéroport de Charles de Gaulle (p76; Paris) Trains, buses and RER suburban trains run to Paris' city centre every 15 to 30 minutes from 5am to 11pm, after which night buses kick in (12.30am to 5.30am). It's a €55/50 flat fare for a 30-minute taxi ride to right-/left-bank central Paris.

Aéroport d'Orly (p76; Paris) Linked to central Paris by Orlyval rail then RER or bus every 15 minutes between 5am and 11pm. Or T7 tram to Villejuif–Louis Aragon then metro to the centre. The 25-minute journey by taxi costs €35/30 to right-/left-bank central Paris.

Getting Around

Transport in France is comfortable, quick, usually reliable and reasonably priced.

Train State-owned SNCF (p314), France's rail network, is first class, with extensive coverage and frequent departures.

Car Away from cities and large towns (where it's hard to park) a car comes into its own. Cars can be hired at airports and train stations. Drive on the right. Be aware of France's potentially hazardous 'priority to the right' rule.

Bus Cheaper and slower than trains. Useful for remote villages not serviced by trains.

Bicycle Certain regions – Loire Valley, Brittany, Provence's Luberon – beg to be explored on two wheels, with dedicated cycling paths, some along canal towpaths or between fruit orchards and vineyards.

For more on **getting around**, see p309 

Plan Your Trip
Hot Spots for...

PREMIER PHOTO/SHUTTERSTOCK ©

French Cuisine

Gourmet appetites know no bounds in France, a paradise for food lovers with its varied regional cuisines, open-air markets and local gusto for dining well. Bon appétit!

Lyon's Bouchons (p158)
Unofficial gastronomic capital adored for its *bouchons* (small bistros) serving no-nonsense Lyonnais cuisine.

Best Bistro (p168)
Feisty sausages and fish dumplings at Le Poêlon d'Or.

Provençal Markets (p180)
Fresh fish quayside in Marseille, cherries and olives... Provençal *marchés* showcase the best produce.

Best Buys (p182)
Cheese, honey and sweet *berlingots* in Carpentras.

Normandy Seafood (p114)
Brittany is famous for cider and crêpes but don't miss the market-fresh seafood.

Freshest Oysters (p114)
Slurp oysters at Rouen's Bar à Huîtres.

BELLENA/SHUTTERSTOCK ©

Art & Architecture

Literature, music, painting, cinema: France's vast artistic heritage is the essence of French art de vivre (art of living).

Paris Galleries (p62)
Impressionists at the Musée d'Orsay, Monet's water lilies and the *Mona Lisa:* Paris boasts world-class art.

Louvre Masterpieces (p40)
Mind-blowing art in the Louvre's Denon Wing.

Belle Époque Nice (pictured; p193)
From beach-side art deco palace to belle époque folly, seaside town Nice oozes old-world opulence.

Photo Op (p196)
Dazzling baroque churches light up Nice's Old Town.

Chic St-Tropez (p211)
Côte d'Azur glamour comes alive when this fishing port is bathed in a pure golden light.

Modern Art (p218)
Musée de l'Annonciade's pointillist, Fauvist and cubist art.

Outdoor Activities

From extreme sports beneath snowy Mont Blanc to kayaking tours along the sunny south coast, France's dramatically varied landscapes offer adventures of all shapes and sizes.

EO NAYA/SHUTTERSTOCK ©

Chamonix Peaks (p262)
In the French Alps, the birthplace of mountaineering is heaven on earth for hikers and skiers.

Daredevil Run (p263)
Legendary Vallée Blanche with an off-piste guide.

Kayaking Les Calanques (p226)
Bijou rocky coves lace the shore east of Marseille and kayaking is the best way to enjoy them up close.

Secret Coves (p227)
Tackle the three-hour trail to reach 'God's Finger'.

Dune du Pilat (pictured; p246)
Climb Europe's largest sand dune for a coastal panorama. Enjoy great surfing at nearby beaches.

Perfect Timing (p247)
Guided dune walks at sunset run by the Espace Accueil.

Wine Tasting

Viticulture in France is an ancient art and tradition. From tastings at cellars to watching the grape harvest, French wine culture demands to be sipped and savoured.

FREEPROD33/SHUTTERSTOCK ©

Champagne Routes (pictured; p144)
These gourmet drives are scenic journeys around beautiful villages and vineyard cellars packed with bubbly.

Bubbly Tours (p140)
Delve into the cellars of swish Moët & Chandon.

Bordeaux Wine Tasting (p244)
Bordeaux has the perfect climate for producing well-balanced reds.

Best Tasting (p248)
Exploratory tours and smart tastings at La Cité du Vin.

Loire Vineyards (p94)
Reds, whites and crémants (sparkling wines) are available to sip at more than 320 cellars.

Perfect Pairings (p94)
Match wines with cheeses at Amboise's market.

Plan Your Trip
Essential France

Activities

From strolling Parisian parks to scaling Alpine peaks, fresh-air activities are part of the French lifestyle. There are 3427km of coastline along which to kayak, swim and stroll, the French have been die-hard hikers for centuries, and anyone who can flits off for the weekend to ski or snowboard.

Spring and autumn are best for walking and cycling in Provence and the French Riviera, which swelter in summer. In the French Alps, summer is short and sweet (mid-June to September) while ski season runs from mid-December into April.

Shopping

Paris is the obvious place to shop, with its fashion houses, historic department stores and international chains. Lovely as they are, designer goods probably aren't any cheaper than at home. Shop for a snip of the usual price at France's *soldes* (sales), by law held twice a year for three weeks in January and again in July.

Non-EU residents can claim a value-added tax (VAT) refund on same-day purchases over €175, providing the goods are for personal consumption and are being personally transported home; retailers have details.

Take your own bag to local markets and supermarkets. With the exception of the odd haggle at the market, little bargaining goes on.

Eating

The freshness of ingredients, regional variety and range of cooking methods in France is phenomenal. Adopt the local culinary pace: breakfast is a tartine (slice of baguette with butter and jam) and *un café* (espresso), long milky *café au lait* or – especially for kids – hot chocolate. In French homes, coffee and hot chocolate are drunk from a cereal bowl – perfect bread-dunking terrain. Croissants are a weekend treat.

Déjeuner (lunch) translates as an *entrée* (starter) and *plat* (main course) with wine. *Goûter*, an afternoon snack, is devoured

PETR KOVALENKOV/SHUTTERSTOCK ©

with particular relish by French children (a slab of milk chocolate inside a wedge of baguette is a traditional favourite). Dinner, generally with wine and often ending with cheese and/or dessert, is a more languid affair.

A *menu* in French is a two- or three-course meal at a fixed price – by far the best-value dining, with most bistros chalking the day's *menu* on a board.

Drinking & Nightlife

From traditional neighbourhood cafes to cutting-edge cocktail bars, drinking options abound. The line between a cafe, *salon de thé* (tearoom), bistro, brasserie, bar and *bar à vins* (wine bar) is blurred. A cafe that's quiet mid-afternoon might have DJ sets in the evening and dancing later on.

The *apéro* (aperitif) is sacred. Urban cafes and bars get packed out from around 5pm as locals relax over *kir* (white wine with blackcurrant syrup), beer or red wine. At weekends, leisurely noon-time *apéro* is equally acceptable.

★ Best Cafe Culture

Beans on Fire, Paris (p72)

L'Instant, Lyon (p169)

Les Deux Magots, Paris (p74)

Bar des 13 Coins, Marseille (p236)

La Movida, Nice (p197)

Entertainment

Catching a performance in Paris, Lyon or Marseille is a treat. French and international opera, ballet and theatre companies and cabaret dancers take to the stage in fabled venues, and a flurry of artists form fascinating fringe art scenes. Cinemas show films in French and sometimes in their original language (including English) with French subtitles ('VO'; *version originale*).

From left: Promenade des Anglais (p202), Nice; Les Deux Magots (p74), Paris

Plan Your Trip
Month by Month

KARL ALLGAEUER/SHUTTERSTOCK ©

January

With New Year festivities done and dusted, head to the Alps. Crowds on the slopes thin out once school's back, but January remains busy. On the Mediterranean, mild winters are wonderfully serene in a part of France that's madly busy the rest of the year.

Truffle Season

No culinary product is more aromatic or decadent than black truffles. Hunt them in Provence – the season runs late December to March, but January is the prime month.

Vive le Ski!

Grab your skis, hit the slopes. Most resorts in the Alps open mid- to late December, and some stay open into late April.

February

Crisp cold weather in the mountains – lots of blue skies now – translates as ski season in top gear. Alpine resorts get mobbed by families during the February school holidays and accommodation is at its priciest.

Nice Carnival

Nice makes the most of its mild climate with this crazy Lenten carnival (www.nicecarnival.com). As well as parade and costume shenanigans, merrymakers pelt each other with blooms during the legendary flower battles.

April

Dedicated ski fiends can carve glaciers in the highest French ski resorts until mid-April or later at highest altitudes. Then it's off with the ski boots and on with the hiking gear as peach and almond trees flower pink against a backdrop of snowcapped peaks.

Fête de la Transhumance

During the ancient Fête de la Transhumance in April or May, shepherds walk their flocks of sheep up to green summer pastures; St-Rémy de Provence's fest is the best known.

Above: Truffles

A.CHAILAN/OTCN ©

May

There is no lovelier month to travel in France, as the first melons ripen in Provence and outdoor markets burst with new-found colour.

May Day

No one works on 1 May, a national holiday that incites summer buzz, with *muguets* (lilies of the valley) sold at roadside stalls and given to friends for good luck.

☆ Monaco Grand Prix

Formula One's glamorous rip around the streets of one of the world's most glam countries (www.grand-prix-monaco.com).

June

As midsummer approaches, the festival pace quickens alongside a rising temperature gauge, which tempts the first bathers into the sea.

★ Best Festivals

Nice Carnival, February

Monaco Grand Prix, May

Festival d'Avignon, July

Route du Champagne en Fête, August

Fête des Lumières, December

☆ Fête de la Musique

Orchestras, crooners, buskers and bands fill streets with free music during France's vibrant nationwide celebration of music on 21 June (www.fetedelamusique.culture.fr).

☆ Paris Jazz Festival

No festival better evokes the brilliance of Paris' interwar jazz age than this annual fest (http://parisjazzfestival.paris.fr) in the Parc Floral de Paris.

Above: Nice Carnival

July

If fields of lavender are your heart's desire, now is the time to catch them flowering in Provence. But you won't be the only one. School's out for the summer, showering the country with tourists, traffic and too many *complet* (full) signs strung in hotel windows.

☆ Tour de France

The world's most prestigious cycling race ends on Paris' av des Champs-Élysées on the third or fourth Sunday of July, but you can catch it across France in the two weeks before then – the route changes each year but the French Alps are a hot spot.

Bastille Day

Join the French in celebrating the storming of the Bastille on 14 July 1789 – country-wide there are firework displays, balls, processions, parades and lots of hoo-ha all round.

Festival d'Avignon

Rouse your inner thespian with Avignon's legendary performing-arts festival. Street acts in its fringe fest are as inspired as those on official stages.

August

It's that crazy summer month when the French join everyone else on holiday. Paris, Lyon and other big cities empty; traffic jams at motorway toll booths test the patience of a saint; and temperatures soar. Avoid. Or don your party hat and join the crowd!

Festival Interceltique de Lorient

Celtic culture is the focus of this festival when hundreds of thousands of Celts from Brittany and abroad flock to Lorient to celebrate just that.

Route du Champagne en Fête

There's no better excuse for a flute or three of bubbly than during the first weekend in August when Champagne toasts its vines and vintages with the Route du Champagne en Fête. Free tastings, cellar visits, music and dancing.

☆ Festival Jazz en Ville

Concerts and jam sessions featuring big names from the international jazz scene in the Breton town of Vannes; late July or early August.

September

As sun-plump grapes hang heavy on darkened vines and that August madness drops off as abruptly as it began, a welcome tranquillity falls across autumnal France. This is the start of the *vendange* (grape harvest).

☆ Mating Season

Nothing beats getting up at dawn to watch mating stags, boar and red deer at play. Observatory towers are hidden in woods around Château de Chambord.

October

The days become shorter, the last grapes are harvested and the first sweet chestnuts fall from trees. With the changing of the clocks on the last Sunday of the month, there's no denying it's winter.

☆ Nuit Blanche

In one last-ditch attempt to stretch out what's left of summer, Paris museums, monuments, cultural spaces, bars and clubs rock around the clock during Paris' so-called White Night, aka one fabulous all-nighter!

December

Days are short and it's cold everywhere bar the south of France. But there are Christmas school holidays and festive celebrations to bolster sun-deprived souls, not to mention some season-opening winter skiing in the highest-altitude Alpine resorts from mid-December.

☆ Fête des Lumières

France's biggest and best light show, on and around 8 December, transforms the streets and squares of Lyon into an open stage.

Plan Your Trip
Get Inspired

ANA CANDIDA/SHUTTERSTOCK ©

Read

A Moveable Feast (Ernest Hemingway; 1964) Beautiful evocation of 1920s Paris.

Life: A User's Manual (Georges Perec; 1978) Intricately structured novel about an apartment block's inhabitants.

Everybody Was So Young (Amanda Vaill; 1995) The French Riviera in the roaring twenties.

The Horseman on the Roof (Jean Giono; 1951) An Italian exile in 1830s Provence, ravaged by a cholera epidemic.

Paris (Edward Rutherford; 2013) Eight centuries of Parisian history.

The Hundred-Foot Journey (Richard C Morais; 2010) Culinary warfare in a remote French village.

Watch

Cyrano de Bergerac (1990) Glossy version of the classic, with Gérard Depardieu.

La Haine (Hate; 1995) Mathieu Kassovitz' prescient take on social tensions in modern Paris.

Bienvenue Chez Les Ch'tis (2008) Satirical comedy about France's north–south divide.

Aurore (I Got Life!; 2017) A heart-warming French comedy about a mother's lot.

La Môme (La Vie en Rose; 2007) Story of singer Édith Piaf starring French actor Marion Cotillard.

Hugo (2011) Martin Scorsese's Oscar-winning adventure of an orphan boy who tends clocks at a Paris train station.

Listen

Le Début de la Suite (Bénabar; 2018) Modern French *chansons*.

Je Veux (Zaz; 2010) Acoustic hit from former Montmartre busker Zaz (aka Isabelle Geffroy), fusing jazz, soul and *chanson*.

Personne d'Autre (Françoise Hardy; 2018) Mellow and reflective; the 24th album by one of France's greatest 1960s, yé-yé-era pop singers.

Barbara (Barbara; 1964) To buy, simply to listen to 'Le Mal de Vivre'.

Scarifications (Abd al Malik; 2015) Hip hop by Franco-Congolese rapper and slam-poet.

L'Enfant Sauvage (Gojira; 2012) France's biggest name in heavy metal.

Above: Cathédrale Notre Dame de Paris (p44), Paris

Plan Your Trip
Five-Day Itineraries

Cross Channel

Snug on the English Channel (La Manche to the French), the wind-buffeted, dramatic coastline of northern France welcomes visitors with fierce regional pride and passion (not to mention cider, seafood and a whole host of intriguing coastal sights and capers).

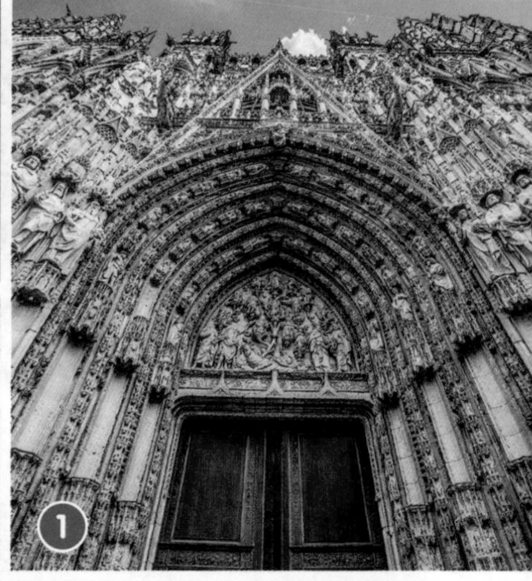

1 **Rouen** (p111) Explore Rouen's medieval town, Gothic cathedral and buzzing bistros and bars.
🚗 2 hrs to Bayeux

2 **Bayeux** (p108) Pore over battle-torn history portrayed in the Bayeux Tapestry and experience the D-Day landing beaches.
🚗 1½ hrs to Mont St-Michel

3 **Mont St-Michel** (p104) Marvel at sea-splashed Mont St-Michel and go back in time in the abbey.
🚗 2½ hrs to Carnac

4 **Carnac** (p132) Get off the beaten track with wild Breton coastline, historic towns and mystical prehistoric relics.

French Allure

Be it a long weekend or a short holiday, France's capital city is a hot date any time of year. What makes it even more wonderful is the green and utterly picturesque trail of elegant Renaissance châteaux and sparkling wine that unfurls within an hour of the city.

1 **Paris** (p35) Play the romantic atop the Eiffel Tower, sashay through parks and galleries, and stroll by the Seine.
1¼–2¾ hrs to Épernay

2 **Épernay** (p152) Spend two days touring cellars and tasting bubbly in some of the world's most celebrated Champagne houses.
1½ hrs to Blois

3 **Blois** (p90) Flit west to romance, Renaissance-style, in beautiful gardens and châteaux fit for a fairy-tale.

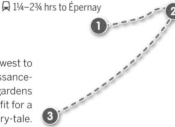

FROM LEFT: MIKI STUDIO/SHUTTERSTOCK ©; SAMOT/SHUTTERSTOCK ©

Plan Your Trip
10-Day Itinerary

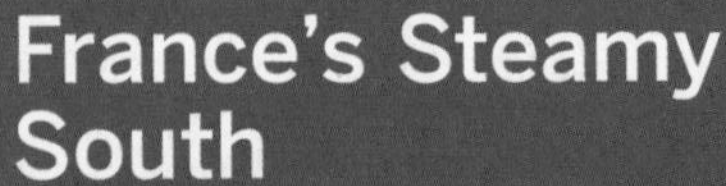

France's Steamy South

The sun-baked south exceeds expectations with its beaches, cutting-edge museums, captivating food culture and glitzy Riviera resorts. For outdoor enthusiasts, its picture-postcard lavender fields, vineyards, mountains and dazzling azure sea demand action.

Roussillon (p178) Duck inland to spend four days exploring hilltop villages, hiking red rock and dining exceedingly well in the Lubéron.

CHRISTIAN MUELLER/SHUTTERSTOCK ©

Nice (p193) Meet the queen of the French Riviera as she preens in a pageant of belle époque palaces, charming neighbourhoods and dazzling shores. 🚗 1¾ hrs to St-Tropez

St-Tropez (p211) On day five, move to this glamorous fishing port where millionaire yachts jostle for space with street artists.
🚗 2½ hrs to Roussillon

Two-Week Itinerary

Food Lover's Fortnight

Cruising around the country's tastiest destinations inspires culinary adventure and much mingling with gourmet-inclined locals. Spring and early summer are brilliant for markets bursting with fresh produce.

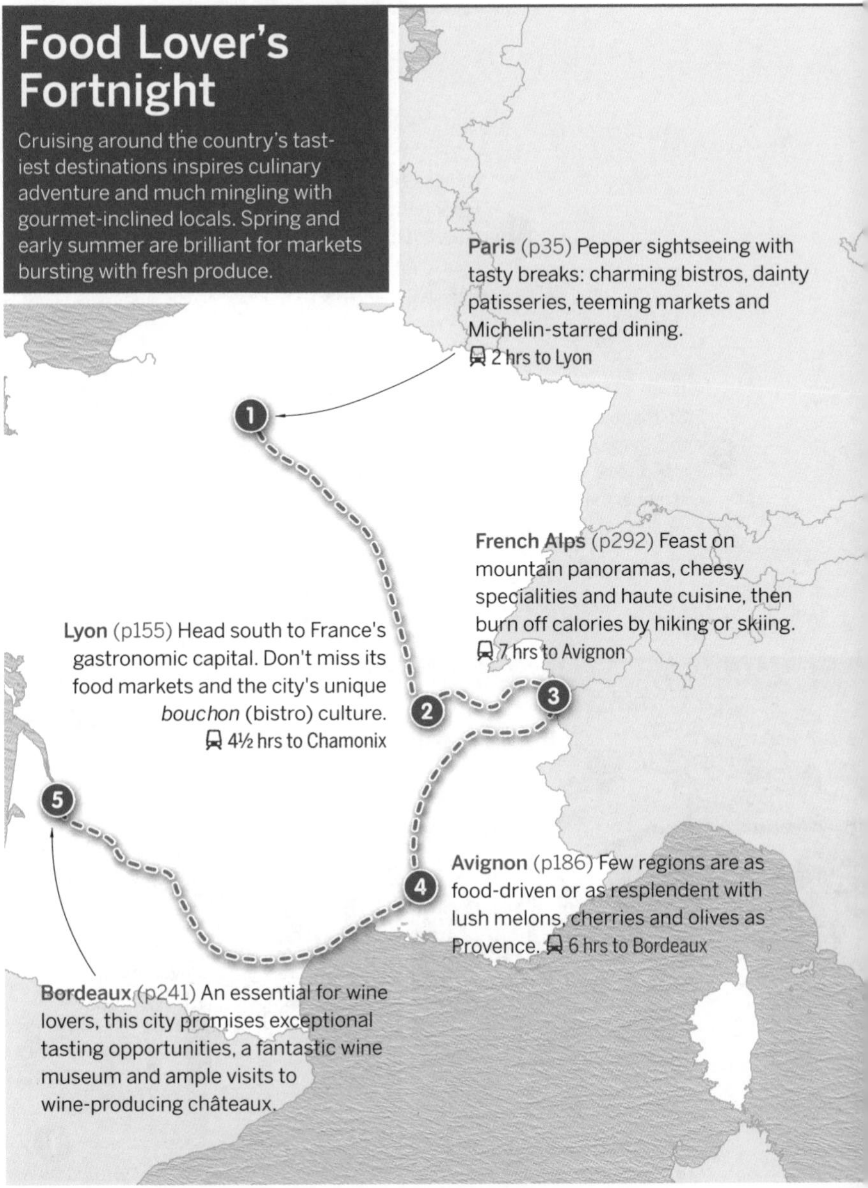

1 Paris (p35) Pepper sightseeing with tasty breaks: charming bistros, dainty patisseries, teeming markets and Michelin-starred dining.
2 hrs to Lyon

2 Lyon (p155) Head south to France's gastronomic capital. Don't miss its food markets and the city's unique *bouchon* (bistro) culture.
4½ hrs to Chamonix

3 French Alps (p292) Feast on mountain panoramas, cheesy specialities and haute cuisine, then burn off calories by hiking or skiing.
7 hrs to Avignon

4 Avignon (p186) Few regions are as food-driven or as resplendent with lush melons, cherries and olives as Provence. 6 hrs to Bordeaux

5 Bordeaux (p241) An essential for wine lovers, this city promises exceptional tasting opportunities, a fantastic wine museum and ample visits to wine-producing châteaux.

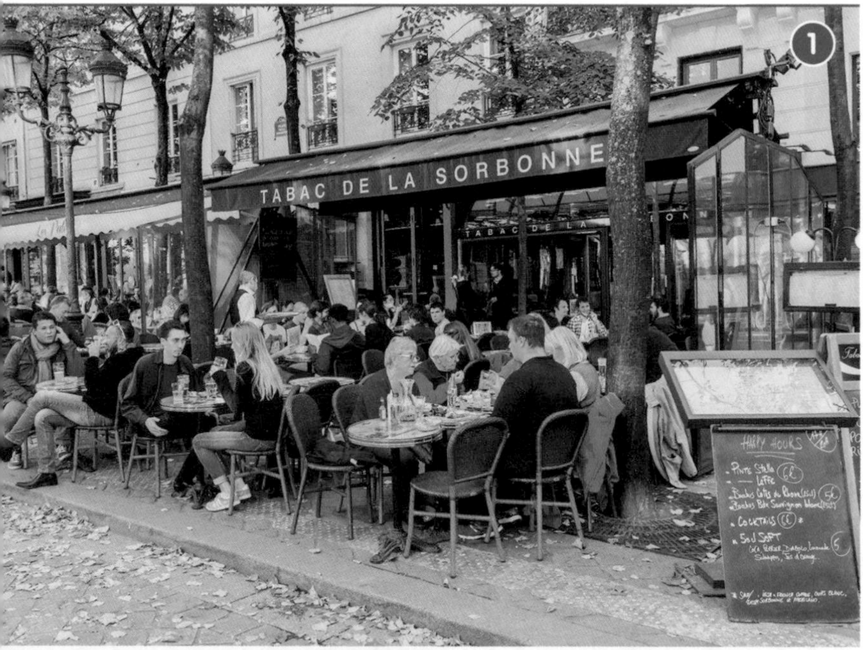

tomme fermière
la pièce 12€
les deux 20€
tommette
de chèvre
3

5

Plan Your Trip
Family Travel

MIHASTOCK/SHUTTERSTOCK ©

Be it the kid-friendly *capital extraordinaire* or rural hinterland, France spoils families with its rich mix of cultural sights, activities and entertainment. To get the most out of travelling *en famille,* plan ahead.

Savvy parents can find kid-appeal in most sights in France, must-sees included: skip the formal guided tour of Mont St-Michel and hook up with a walking guide to lead you and the children barefoot across the sand to the abbey; trade the daytime queues at the Eiffel Tower for a tour after dark with teens; don't dismiss wine tasting in Provence outright – rent bicycles and turn it into a family bike ride instead. The opportunities are endless.

Museums & Monuments

Many Paris museums organise creative *ateliers* (workshops) for children, parent-accompanied or solo. Workshops are themed, require booking, last 1½ to two hours, and cost €5 to €20 per child. French children have no school on Wednesday afternoons, so most workshops happen Wednesday afternoons, weekends and daily during school holidays. Most cater for kids aged seven to 14 years, although in Paris art activities at the Louvre start at four years and at the Musée d'Orsay, five years.

Countrywide, when buying tickets at museums and monuments, ask about children's activity sheets – most have something to hook kids. Another winner is to arm your gadget-mad child (from six years) with an audioguide. Older children can check out what apps a museum or monument might have for smartphones and tablets.

Entertainment

Tourist offices can tell you what's on – and the repertoire is impressive: puppet shows alfresco, children's theatres, children's films at cinemas Wednesday afternoons and weekends, street buskers, illuminated monuments after dark, an abundance of music festivals and so on. Sure winners are the *son et lumière* (sound-and-light) shows

JULIA KUZNETSOVA/SHUTTERSTOCK ©

projected on some châteaux and cathedral façades. Outstanding after-dark illuminations that never fail to enchant include Paris' Eiffel Tower and Marseille's MuCEM.

Dining Out

Children's *menus* (fixed meals at a set price) are common, although anyone in France for more than a few days will soon tire of the ubiquitous spaghetti bolognaise or *saucisse* (sausage), or *steak haché* (beef burger) and *frites* (fries) followed by ice cream that most feature. Don't be shy in asking for a half-portion of an adult main – restaurants generally oblige. Ditto in budget and midrange places to ask for a plate of *pâtes au beurre* (pasta with butter) for fussy or very young eaters.

It is perfectly acceptable to dine *en famille* after dark providing the kids don't run wild. Few restaurants open their doors, however, before 7.30pm or 8pm, making brasseries and cafes – many serve food continuously from 7am or 8am until midnight – more appealing for families with younger children. Some restaurants have high chairs and supply paper and pens for children to draw with while waiting for their meal.

Baby requirements are easily met. The choice of infant formula, soy and cow's milk, nappies (diapers) and jars of baby food in supermarkets and pharmacies is similar to any developed country, although opening hours are more limited (few shops open Sunday). Organic *(bio)* baby food is harder to find.

★ Best Energy-Burners

Skiing, French Alps (p262)

Canoeing, Pont du Gard, Provence (p185)

Aiguille du Midi, Chamonix (p260)

Beaches, Brittany (p131)

From left: Lavender fields, Provence (p173); Hiking, Chamonix (p266)

CATARINA BELOVA/SHUTTERSTOCK ©

Climb the iconic Eiffel Tower (p38)

PARIS

In This Chapter

Paris at a Glance...

Paris has a timeless familiarity, with instantly recognisable architectural icons, memorable cuisine and chic boutiques. Dining is a quintessential part of the Parisian experience – at bistros, Michelin-starred restaurants, boulangeries (bakeries) and street markets. Its art repository is one of the best, showcasing priceless treasures in palatial museums.

Paris' real magic lies in the unexpected: hidden parks, small unsung museums and sun-spangled cafe terraces where you can watch Parisian life unfold. Meanwhile, a new wave of multimedia galleries, creative wine bars and design shops are making the City of Light even more exciting...

Two Days in Paris

Start early with the **Louvre** (p40), which could easily consume a whole day. Linger for a drink on rue Montmartre, then head to the late-opening **Centre Pompidou** (p57).

On day two, climb the mighty **Arc de Triomphe** (p55) and stroll the **Champs-Élysées**. Admire art and awesome architecture at the **Musée du Quai Branly** (p54). Sunset is the best time to ascend the **Eiffel Tower** (p38).

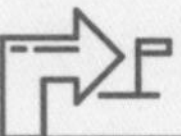

Four Days in Paris

Day three, start early at **Notre Dame** (p44) and nearby **Sainte-Chapelle** (p61), crossing the Pont St-Louis to buy a **Berthillon** (p68) ice cream. Swoon over the magnificent **Musée d'Orsay** (p62) and laze in the **Jardin du Luxembourg** (p55). Day four, head to hilltop **Sacré-Cœur** (p57) and stroll the shaded towpaths of **Canal St-Martin** (p60). Sailing schedules permitting, hop on a **canal cruise** (p64).

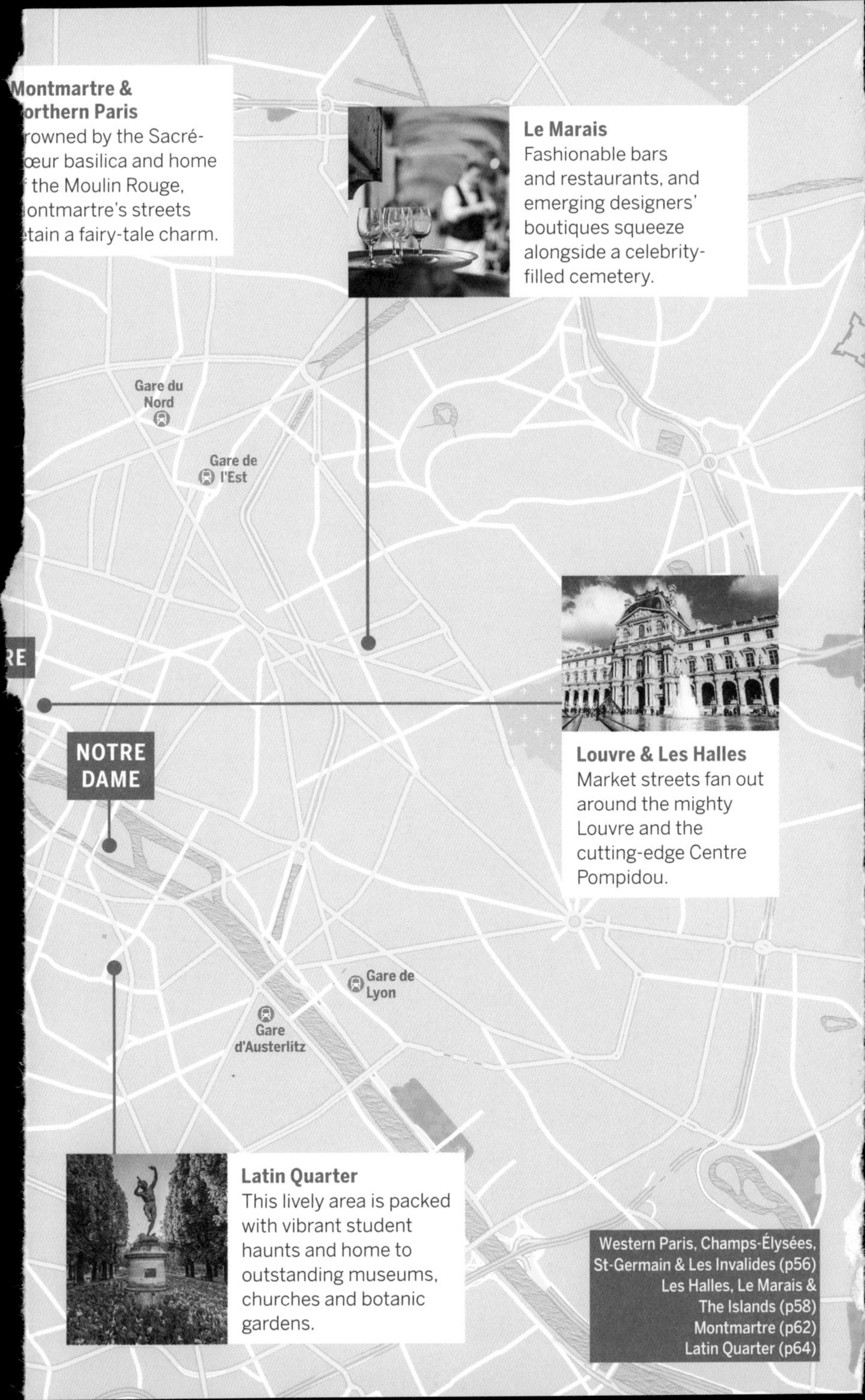

Montmartre & Northern Paris
Crowned by the Sacré-Cœur basilica and home of the Moulin Rouge, Montmartre's streets retain a fairy-tale charm.

Le Marais
Fashionable bars and restaurants, and emerging designers' boutiques squeeze alongside a celebrity-filled cemetery.

Gare du Nord

Gare de l'Est

Louvre & Les Halles
Market streets fan out around the mighty Louvre and the cutting-edge Centre Pompidou.

RE

NOTRE DAME

Gare de Lyon

Gare d'Austerlitz

Latin Quarter
This lively area is packed with vibrant student haunts and home to outstanding museums, churches and botanic gardens.

Western Paris, Champs-Élysées, St-Germain & Les Invalides (p56)
Les Halles, Le Marais & The Islands (p58)
Montmartre (p62)
Latin Quarter (p64)

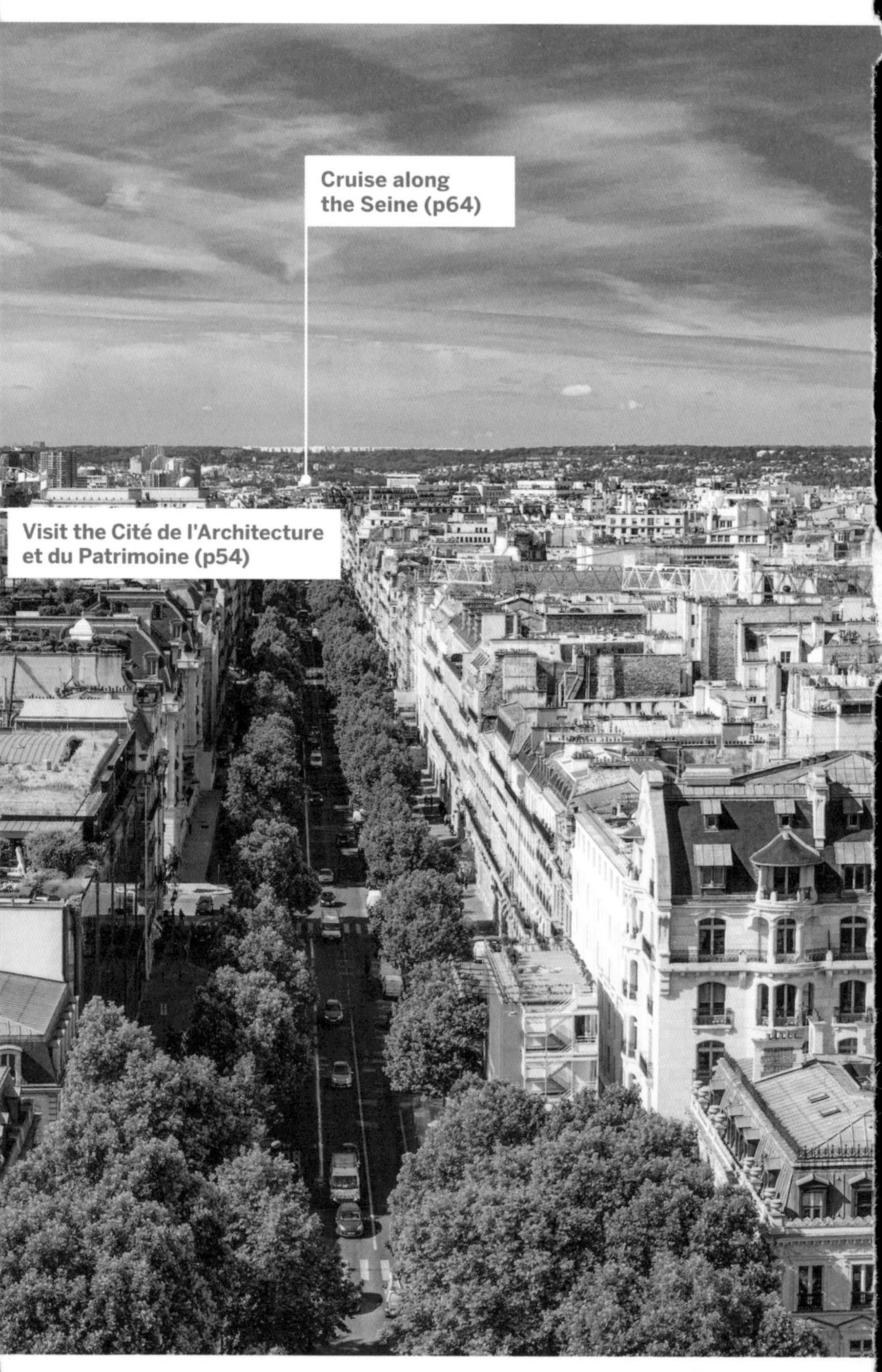
Cruise along
the Seine (p64)
Visit the Cité de l'Architecture
et du Patrimoine (p54)

Stroll through Paris' lush green parks (p55)

Champs-Élysées & Grands Boulevards
Paris' grandest avenue, art nouveau department stores and a 19th-century opera house.

N
C
C
o
M
re

Gare St-Lazare

Eiffel Tower & Western Paris
This is where you can find the city's symbolic tower and major museums.

EIFFEL TOWER

Seine

LOUVI

Jardin du Luxembourg

Gare Montparnasse

Cimetière du Montparnasse

(13km)

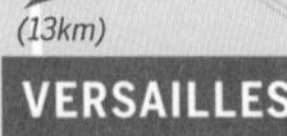

0 2 km
0 1 mile

St-Germain & Les Invalides
Literary buffs, antique collectors and fashionistas flock to this legendary cafe-filled neighbourhood.

Basilique du Sacré-Cœur (p57), Montmartre

Arriving in Paris

Charles de Gaulle Airport Trains (RER), buses and night buses to the city centre cost €6 to €17; taxi €50 to €55.

Orly Airport Trains (Orlyval then RER), buses and night buses to the city centre €8.70 to €13.25; T7 tram to Villejuif–Louis Aragon then metro to centre (€3.80); taxi €30 to €35.

Gare du Nord train station Within central Paris; served by metro (€1.90).

Where to Stay

Paris' wealth of accommodation spans all budgets, but it's often *complet* (full) well in advance. Reservations are recommended year-round and essential during the warmer months (April to October) and all public and school holidays. Although marginally cheaper, accommodation outside central Paris is invariably a false economy given travel time and costs. Choose somewhere within Paris' 20 *arrondissements* (city districts).

Eiffel Tower

No one could imagine Paris today without it. But Gustave Eiffel only constructed this elegant, 320m-tall signature spire as a temporary exhibit for the 1889 World's Fair. Climb it to admire Paris laid out at your feet.

It took 300 workers, 2.5 million rivets and two years of nonstop labour to assemble. Upon completion the tower became the tallest human-made structure in the world (324m or 1063ft) – a record held until the completion of the Chrysler Building in New York (1930). A symbol of the modern age, it faced massive opposition from Paris' artistic and literary elite, and the 'metal asparagus', as some Parisians snidely called it, was originally slated to be torn down in 1909. It was spared only because it proved an ideal platform for the transmitting antennas needed for the newfangled science of radiotelegraphy.

1st Floor

Of the tower's three floors, the 1st floor (57m) has the most space but the least impressive views. The glass-enclosed

Great For...

☑ Don't Miss

A glass of bubbly in the top-floor Champagne Bar (open noon to 5.15pm and 6.15pm to 10.45pm).

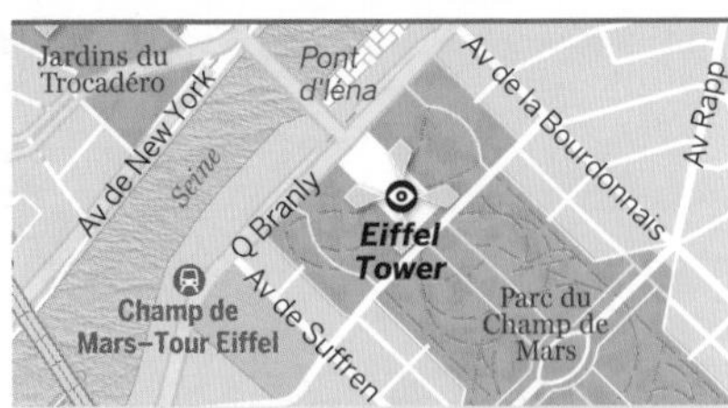

Need to Know

Map p56; ☎08 92 70 12 39; www.toureiffel.paris; Champ de Mars, 5 av Anatole France, 7e; adult/child lift to top €25/6.30, lift to 2nd fl €16/4, stairs to 2nd fl €10/2.50; ⏰9am-12.45am mid-Jun–Aug, 9.30am-11.45pm, Sep–mid-Jun; Ⓜ Bir Hakeim or RER Champ de Mars–Tour Eiffel

Take a Break

Dine brasserie style at 1st-floor **58 Tour Eiffel** (☎01 76 70 04 86; www.restaurants-toureiffel.com; menus lunch €37.20, dinner €93.70-113.70; ⏰11.30am-4.30pm & 6.30-11pm; 🖋👪).

★ Top Tip

Cut queues by buying lift tickets ahead online; print or display on a smartphone.

Pavillon Ferrié – open since summer 2014 – houses an immersion film along with a small cafe and souvenir shop, while the outer walkway features a discovery circuit to help visitors learn more about the tower's ingenious design. Check out the sections of glass flooring that proffer a dizzying view of the ant-like people walking on the ground far below.

2nd Floor

Views from the 2nd floor (115m) are the best – impressively high but still close enough to see the details of the city below. Telescopes and panoramic maps placed around the tower pinpoint locations in Paris and beyond. Story windows give an overview of the lifts' mechanics, and the vision well allows you to gaze through glass panels to the ground.

Top Floor

Views from the wind-buffeted top floor (276m) stretch up to 60km on a clear day, though at this height the panoramas are more sweeping than detailed. Afterwards peep into Gustave Eiffel's restored top-level office where lifelike wax models of Eiffel and his daughter Claire greet Thomas Edison. To access the top floor, take a separate lift on the 2nd floor (closed during heavy winds).

Nightly Sparkles

Every hour on the hour, the entire tower sparkles for five minutes with 20,000 6-watt lights. They were first installed for Paris' millennium celebration in 2000 – it took 25 mountain climbers five months to install the bulbs and 40km of electrical cords. For the best view of the light show, head across the Seine to the Jardins du Trocadéro.

TAKASHI IMAGES/SHUTTERSTOCK ©

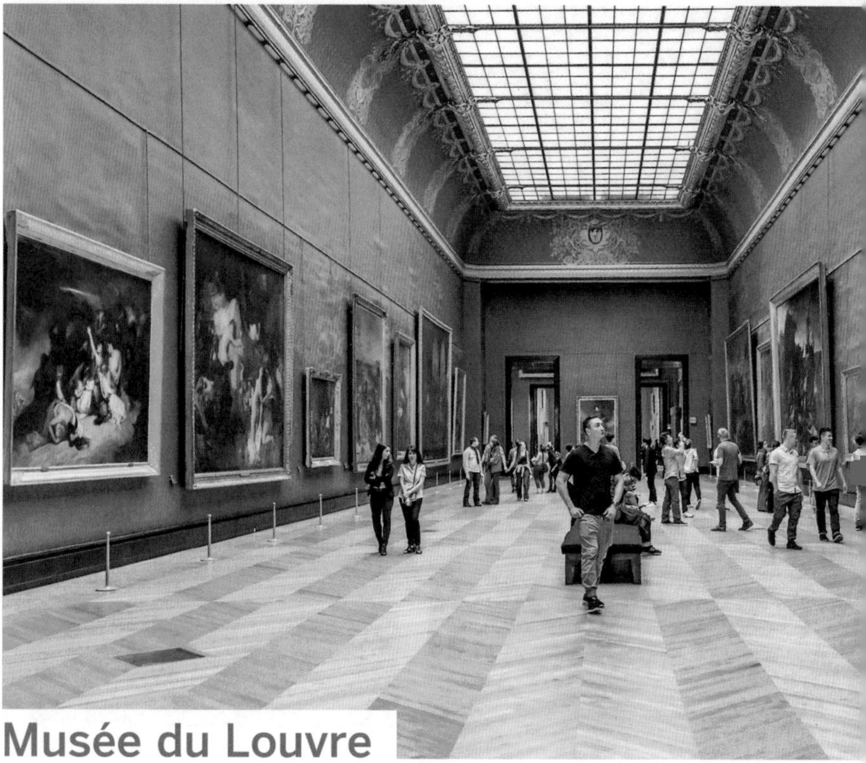

Musée du Louvre

Few art galleries are as prized or daunting as the Musée du Louvre, Paris' pièce de résistance. One of the world's largest and most diverse museums, it showcases an unbelievable 35,000-odd works of art. It would take nine months to glance at every piece.

Great For...

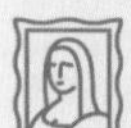

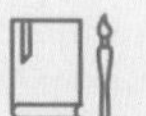

☑ Don't Miss

Da Vinci's bewitching *Mona Lisa;* the Mesopotamian and Egyptian collections.

The Louvre today rambles over four floors and through three wings: the **Sully Wing** creates the four sides of the Cour Carrée (literally 'Square Courtyard') at the eastern end of the complex; the **Denon Wing** stretches 800m along the Seine to the south; and the northern **Richelieu Wing** skirts rue de Rivoli. The building started life as a fortress built by Philippe-Auguste in the 12th century – medieval remnants are still visible on the lower ground floor (Sully). In the 16th century it became a royal residence and after the Revolution, in 1793, it was turned into a national museum.

Priceless Antiquities

Both **Mesopotamia** (ground floor, Richelieu) and **Egypt** (ground and 1st floors, Sully) are well represented in the Louvre; seek out the *Code of Hammurabi* (Room

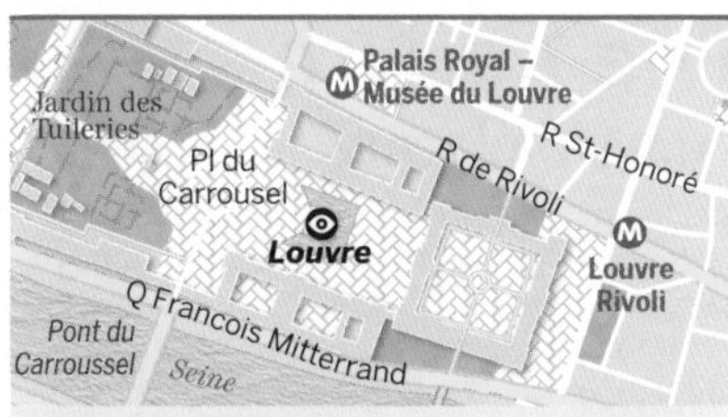

Need to Know

Map p56; ☎01 40 20 53 17; www.louvre.fr; rue de Rivoli & quai des Tuileries, 1er; adult/child €15/free; ⊙9am-6pm Mon, Thu, Sat & Sun, to 9.45pm Wed & Fri; MPalais Royal–Musée du Louvre

Take a Break

Picnic in the Jardin des Tuileries (p55) or enjoy secret **Maison Maison** (Map p58; ☎09 67 82 07 32; www.facebook.com/maison maisonparis; opposite 16 quai du Louvre, 1er; 2-/3-course lunch menu €20/25, small plates €7-16; ⊙10am-2am Wed-Sun, 6pm-2am Tue; MPont Neuf).

★ Top Tip

The longest queues are usually outside the Grande Pyramide; use the Carrousel du Louvre entrance (99 rue de Rivoli or direct from the metro) instead.

3, ground floor, Richelieu) and *The Seated Scribe* (Room 22, 1st floor, Sully). Room 12 (ground floor, Sully) holds impressive friezes and an enormous **two-headed-bull column** from the Darius Palace in ancient Iran, while an enormous seated **statue of Pharaoh Ramesses II** highlights the temple room (Room 12, Sully).

The lower ground floor culminates with the world's most famous armless duo, the **Venus de Milo** (Room 16, ground floor, Sully) and the **Winged Victory of Samothrace** (top of Daru staircase, 1st floor, Denon).

French & Italian Masterpieces

The **1st floor of the Denon Wing**, where the *Mona Lisa* is found, is easily the most popular. Rooms 75 through 77 are hung with monumental French paintings: look for the *Consecration of the Emperor Napoléon I* (David), *The Raft of the Medusa* (Géricault) and *Grande Odalisque* (Ingres).

Rooms 1, 3, 5 and 8 are also must-visits, filled with classic works by **Renaissance** masters (Raphael, Titian, Uccello, Botticini). Contemplate Botticelli's graceful frescoes (Room 1) and the superbly detailed *Wedding Feast at Cana* (Room 6).

Mona Lisa

Easily the Louvre's most admired work is Leonardo da Vinci's *La Joconde* (in French; *La Gioconda* in Italian), the lady with that enigmatic smile known as *Mona Lisa* (Room 6, 1st floor, Denon). *Mona* (*monna* in Italian) is a contraction of *madonna*, and Gioconda is the feminine form of the surname Giocondo. Infrared technology has confirmed *her* identity as Lisa Gherardini (1479–1542).

The Louvre

A HALF-DAY TOUR

Successfully visiting the Louvre is a fine art. Its complex labyrinth of galleries and staircases spiralling across three wings and four floors renders discovery a snakes-and-ladders experience. Initiate yourself with this three-hour itinerary – a playful mix of *Mona Lisa*–obvious and up-to-the-minute unexpected.

Arriving in the newly renovated **1 Cour Napoléon** beneath IM Pei's glass pyramid, pick up colour-coded floor plans at an information stand, then ride the escalator up to the Sully Wing and swap passport or credit card for a multimedia guide (there are limited descriptions in the galleries) at the wing entrance.

The Louvre is as much about spectacular architecture as masterful art. To appreciate this, zip up and down Sully's Escalier Henri II to admire **2 Venus de Milo**, then up parallel Escalier Henri IV to the palatial displays in **3 Cour Khorsabad**. Cross Room 1 to find the escalator up to the 1st floor and the opulent **4 Napoléon III apartments**. Next traverse 25 consecutive galleries (thank you, floor plan!) to flip conventional contemplation on its head with Cy Twombly's **5 The Ceiling**, and the hypnotic **6 Winged Victory of Samothrace**, which brazenly insists on being admired from all angles. End with the impossibly famous **7 Raft of the Medusa**, **8 Mona Lisa** and **9 Virgin & Child**.

TOP TIPS

➡ Don't even consider entering the Louvre's maze of galleries without a floor plan, free from the information desk in the Hall Napoléon.

➡ The Denon Wing is always packed; visit on late nights (Wednesday or Friday) or trade Denon in for the notably quieter Richelieu Wing.

➡ Tickets to the Louvre are valid for the whole day, meaning that you can nip out for lunch.

BRIAN KINNEY / SHUTTERSTOCK ©

Napoléon III Apartments
1st Floor, Richelieu
Napoléon III's gorgeous gilt apartments were built from 1854 to 1861, featuring an over-the-top decor of gold leaf, stucco and crystal chandeliers that reaches a dizzying climax in the Grand Salon and State Dining Room.

LOUVRE AUDITORIUM

Classical-music concerts are staged several times a week at the Louvre Auditorium (off the main entrance hall). Don't miss the Thursday lunchtime concerts featuring emerging composers and musicians. The season runs from September to April or May, depending on the concert series.

Mona Lisa
Room 6, 1st Floor, Denon
No smile is as enigmatic or bewitching as hers. Da Vinci's diminutive *La Joconde* hangs opposite the largest painting in the Louvre – sumptuous, fellow Italian Renaissance artwork *The Wedding at Cana*.

The Raft of the Medusa

Room 77, 1st Floor, Denon

Decipher the politics behind French romanticism in Théodore Géricault's *Raft of the Medusa.*

Cour Khorsabad

Ground Floor, Richelieu

Time travel with a pair of winged human-headed bulls to view some of the world's oldest Mesopotamian art. **DETOUR»** Night-lit statues in Cour Puget.

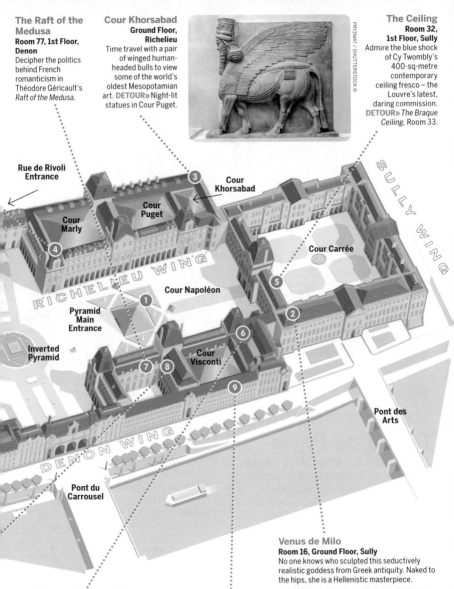

PRYZMAT / SHUTTERSTOCK ©

The Ceiling

Room 32, 1st Floor, Sully

Admire the blue shock of Cy Twombly's 400-sq-metre contemporary ceiling fresco – the Louvre's latest, daring commission. **DETOUR»** *The Braque Ceiling*, Room 33.

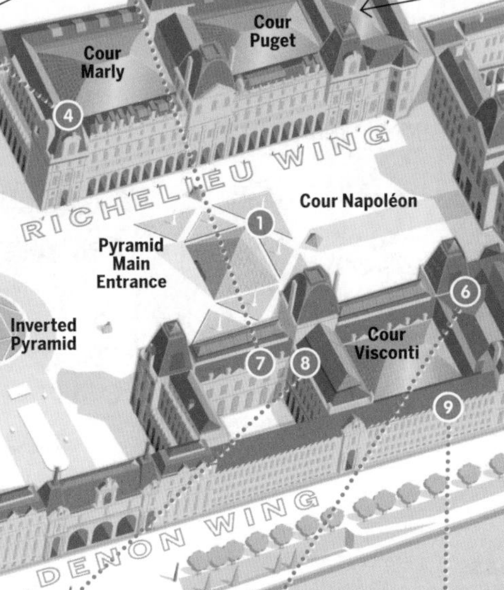

PRYZMAT / SHUTTERSTOCK ©

Winged Victory of Samothrace

Escalier Daru, 1st Floor, Sully

Draw breath at the aggressive dynamism of this headless, handless Hellenistic goddess. **DETOUR»** The razzle-dazzle of the Apollo Gallery's crown jewels.

Virgin & Child

Grande Galerie, 1st Floor, Denon

In the spirit of artistic devotion save the Louvre's most famous gallery for last: a feast of Virgin-and-child paintings by Da Vinci, Raphael, Domenico Ghirlandaio, Giovanni Bellini and Francesco Botticini.

Venus de Milo

Room 16, Ground Floor, Sully

No one knows who sculpted this seductively realistic goddess from Greek antiquity. Naked to the hips, she is a Hellenistic masterpiece.

TUTTI FRUTTI / SHUTTERSTOCK ©

Cathédrale Notre Dame de Paris

Paris' mighty cathedral is a masterpiece of French Gothic architecture. Highlights include its three spectacular rose windows, treasury and expansive views from the top of its bell towers.

Great For...

☑ Don't Miss

An evening concert at the cathedral; program online at www.musique-sacree-notredamedeparis.fr.

Paris' most visited unticketed sight, with more than 14 million visitors per year, is a wonder of French Gothic architecture. Its interior accommodates 6000 worshippers. Enter the magnificent forest of ornate **flying buttresses** that encircle the cathedral chancel and support its walls and roof.

Rose Windows

The three rose windows colouring the cathedral's vast 127m-by-48m interior are its most spectacular feature. Admire a 10m-wide window over the western façade above the organ – one of the largest in the world, with 7800 pipes (900 of which have historical classification), 111 stops, five 56-key manuals and a 32-key pedalboard – and the window on the northern side of the transept (virtually unchanged since the 13th century).

North rose window

PAL TERAVAGIMOV PHOTOGRAPHY/GETTY IMAGES ©

Bell Towers

A constant queue marks the entrance to the **Tours de Notre Dame** (www.tours-notre-dame-de-paris.fr), the cathedral's bell towers. Climb the 400-odd spiralling steps to the top of the western façade of the North Tower, where gargoyles grimace and grin on the rooftop **Galerie des Chimères** (Gargoyles Gallery). These statues divert rainwater from the roof to prevent masonry damage, and, purportedly, ward off evil spirits.

Bible of the Poor

The statues above the three main portals were once brightly coloured to make them more effective as a *Biblia pauperum* ('Bible of the poor') to help the illiterate faithful understand Old Testament stories, the Passion of the Christ and the lives of the saints.

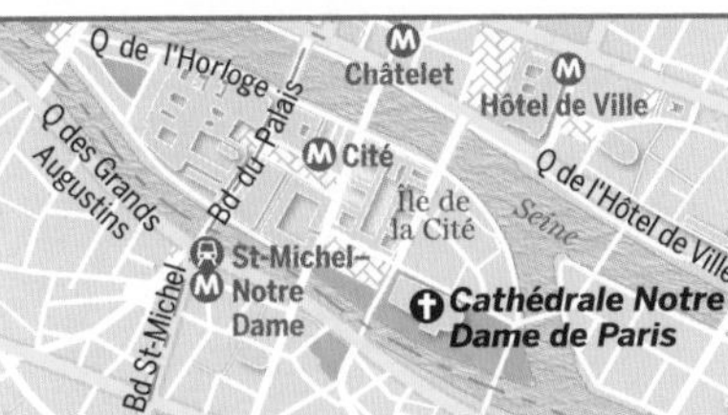

Need to Know

Map p58; ☎01 42 34 56 10, towers 01 53 10 07 00; www.notredamedeparis.fr; 6 Parvis Notre Dame – place Jean-Paul-II, 4e; cathedral free, adult/child towers €10/free, treasury €5/3; ⏲cathedral 7.45am-6.45pm Mon-Fri, to 7.15pm Sat & Sun, towers 10am-6.30pm Sun-Thu, 10am-11pm Fri & Sat Jul & Aug, 10am-6.30pm Apr-Jun & Sep, 10am-5.30pm Oct-Mar, treasury 9.45am-5.30pm; MCité

Take a Break

Pop across to Île St-Louis for brunch, cocktails or anything in between at **Café Saint Régis** (Map p58; ☎01 43 54 59 41; www.cafesaintregisparis.com; 6 rue Jean du Bellay, 4e; breakfast & snacks €3.50-15.50, mains €18-32; ⏲6.30am-2am, kitchen 8am-midnight; 📶; MPont Marie).

★ Top Tip

Free 45-minute English-language tours take place at 2pm Wednesday to Friday, and at 2.30pm Monday, Tuesday and Saturday.

Treasury

The *trésor* (treasury) is a dazzling treasure chest of sacred jewels in the cathedral's southeastern transept. The **Ste-Couronne** (Holy Crown) is purportedly the wreath of thorns placed on Jesus' head before he was crucified.

Easier to admire are the wonderful **Les Camées des Papes** (Papal cameos). Sculpted in shell with incredible finesse and framed in silver, the 268-piece collection depicts every pope in miniature from St Pierre to the present day, ending with Pope Benoit XVI.

Fountain of Apollo

S-F/SHUTTERSTOCK ©

Château de Versailles

This monumental, 700-room palace and sprawling estate, with its gardens, fountains, ponds and canals, is a Unesco World Heritage–listed wonder situated an easy 40-minute train ride from central Paris.

Great For...

☑ Don't Miss

Summertime 'dancing water' displays set to music by Baroque- and classical-era composers.

Amid magnificently landscaped formal gardens, this splendid and enormous palace was built in the mid-17th century during the reign of Louis XIV – the Roi Soleil (Sun King) – to project the absolute power of the French monarchy, which was then at the height of its glory. The château has undergone relatively few alterations since its construction, though almost all the interior furnishings disappeared during the Revolution and many of the rooms were rebuilt by Louis-Philippe (r 1830–48).

Exquisite Architecture

Some 30,000 workers and soldiers toiled on the structure, the bills for which all but emptied the kingdom's coffers.

Work began in 1661 under the guidance of architect Louis Le Vau (Jules Hardouin-Mansart took over from Le Vau in the mid-1670s); painter and interior designer

Palace gate depicting the Sun King, Louis XIV

VALEKSTUDIO/SHUTTERSTOCK ©

Parc de Versailles
Bd de la Reine
Versailles–Rive Droite
R des Réservoirs
Château de Versailles
Av de St-Cloud
Rte de St-Cyr
Av de Paris
Versailles-Château–Rive Gauche

Need to Know

01 30 83 78 00; www.chateauversailles.fr; place d'Armes; adult/child passport ticket incl estate-wide access €20/free, with musical events €27/free, palace €18/free except during musical events; 9am-6.30pm Tue-Sun Apr-Oct, to 5.30pm Tue-Sun Nov-Mar; RER Versailles-Château–Rive Gauche

Take a Break

Nearby rue de Satory is lined with restaurants and cafes.

★ Top Tip

Arrive early morning and avoid busy Tuesday, Saturday and Sunday.

Charles Le Brun; and landscape artist André Le Nôtre, whose workers flattened hills, drained marshes and relocated forests as they laid out the **gardens** (free except during musical events; gardens 8am-8.30pm Apr-Oct, to 6pm Nov-Mar, park 7am-8.30pm Apr-Oct, 8am-6pm Nov-Mar), ponds and fountains.

Le Brun and his hundreds of artisans decorated every moulding, cornice, ceiling and door of the interior with the most luxurious and ostentatious of appointments: frescoes, marble, gilt and woodcarvings, many with themes and symbols drawn from Greek and Roman mythology. The King's Suite of the Grands Appartements du Roi et de la Reine (King's and Queen's State Apartments), for example, includes rooms dedicated to Hercules, Venus, Diana, Mars and Mercury. The opulence reaches its peak in the Galerie des Glaces (Hall of Mirrors), a 75m-long ballroom with 17 huge mirrors on one side and, on the other, an equal number of windows looking out over the gardens and the setting sun.

Guided Tours

To access areas that are otherwise off limits and to learn more about Versailles' history, prebook a 90-minute **guided tour** (01 30 83 77 88; www.chateauversailles.fr; tours €10, plus palace entry; English-language tours 9.30am Tue-Sun) of the Private Apartments of Louis XV and Louis XVI and the Opera House or Royal Chapel.

The current €400 million restoration program is the most ambitious yet, and until it's completed in 2020, a part of the palace is likely to be clad in scaffolding.

The château is situated in the leafy, bourgeois suburb of Versailles, about 22km southwest of central Paris. Take RER C5 (return €7.10, 40 minutes, frequent) from Paris' Left Bank RER stations to Versailles-Château–Rive Gauche station.

Versailles

A DAY IN COURT

Visiting Versailles – even just the State Apartments – may seem overwhelming at first, but think of it as a house where people ate, drank, worked, slept and conspired and you'll be on the right path.

Some two decades into his long reign, Louis XIV began turning his father's hunting lodge into a palace large enough to house his entire court (to keep closer tabs on the 6000-strong army of courtiers). Sparing no expense, the Sun King employed the greatest artists and craftspeople of the day and by 1682 he'd created the most extravagant dormitory in history.

The royal schedule was as accurate and predictable as a Swiss watch. By following this itinerary of rooms you can recreate the king's day, starting with the 1 **King's Bedchamber** and the 2 **Queen's Bedchamber**, where the royal couple was roused at about the same time. The royal procession then leads through the 3 **Hall of Mirrors** to the 4 **Royal Chapel** for morning Mass and returns to the 5 **Council Chamber** for late-morning meetings with ministers. After lunch the king might ride or hunt or visit the 6 **King's Library**. Later he could join courtesans for an 'apartment evening' starting from the 7 **Hercules Drawing Room** or play billiards in the 8 **Diana Drawing Room** before supping at 10pm.

VERSAILLES BY NUMBERS

Rooms 700 (11 hectares of roof)

Windows 2153

Staircases 67

Gardens and parks 800 hectares

Trees 200,000

Fountains 50 (with 620 nozzles)

Paintings 6300 (measuring 11km laid end to end)

Statues and sculptures 2100

Objets d'art and furnishings 5000

Visitors 5.3 million per year

Queen's Bedchamber
Chambre de la Reine
The queen's life was on constant public display and even the births of her children were watched by crowds of spectators in her own bedchamber. **DETOUR »** The Guardroom, with a dozen armed men at the ready.

LUNCH BREAK

Contemporary French cuisine at Alain Ducasse's restaurant Ore, or a picnic in the park.

Hercules Drawing Room
Salon d'Hercule
This salon, with its stunning ceiling fresco of the strong man, gave way to the State Apartments, which were open to courtiers three nights a week. **DETOUR»** Apollo Drawing Room, used for formal audiences and as a throne room.

Hall of Mirrors

Galerie des Glaces

The solid-silver candelabra and furnishings in this extravagant hall, devoted to Louis XIV's successes in war, were melted down in 1689 to pay for yet another conflict. **DETOUR»** The antithetical Peace Drawing Room, adjacent.

King's Bedchamber

Chambre du Roi

The king's daily life was anything but private and even his *lever* (rising) at 8am and *coucher* (retiring) at 11.30pm would be witnessed by up to 150 sycophantic courtiers.

Council Chamber

Cabinet du Conseil

This chamber, with carved medallions evoking the king's work, is where the monarch met his various ministers (state, finance, religion etc) depending on the days of the week.

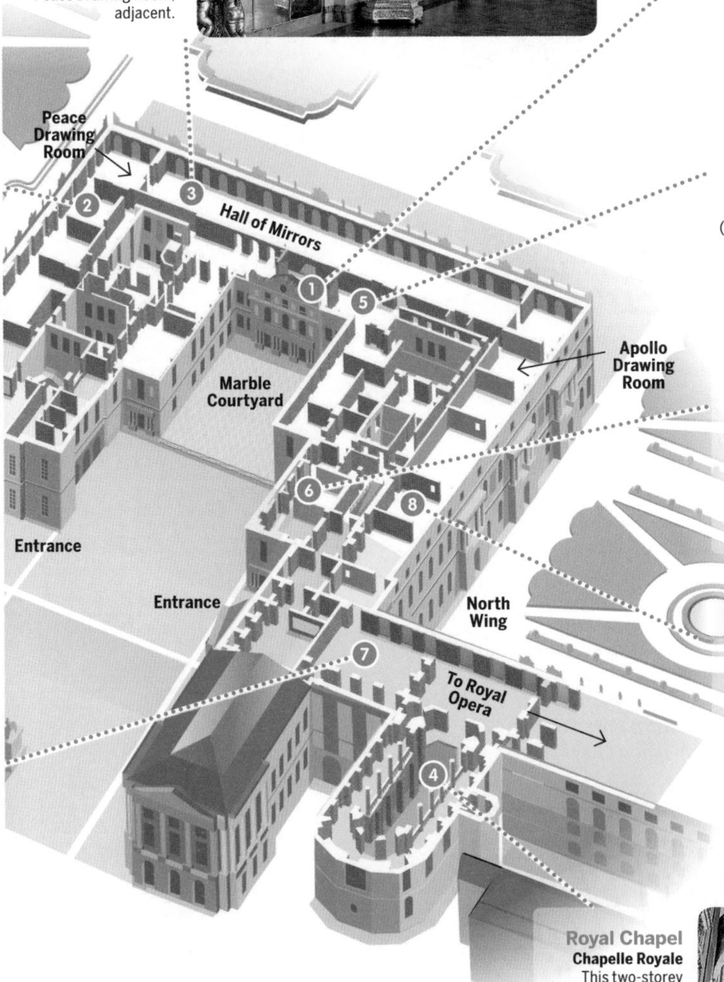

Peace Drawing Room

2

3

Hall of Mirrors

1

5

Marble Courtyard

Apollo Drawing Room

6

8

Entrance

Entrance

North Wing

7

To Royal Opera

4

King's Library

Bibliothèque du Roi

The last resident, bibliophile Louis XVI, loved geography and his copy of *The Travels of James Cook* (in English, which he read fluently) is still on the shelf here.

Diana Drawing Room

Salon de Diane

With walls and ceiling covered in frescoes devoted to the mythical huntress, this room contained a large billiard table reserved for Louis XIV, a keen player.

Royal Chapel

Chapelle Royale

This two-storey chapel (with gallery for the royals and important courtiers, and the ground floor for the B-list) was dedicated to St Louis, patron of French monarchs. **DETOUR»** The sumptuous Royal Opera.

SAVVY SIGHTSEEING

Avoid Versailles on Monday (closed), Tuesday (Paris' museums close, so visitors flock here) and Sunday, the busiest day. Also, book tickets online so you don't have to queue.

Arty Montmartre

This walk takes you through the heart of hilltop Montmartre where artists lived, worked and partied hard in the 19th century. With its ivy-clad buildings, steep narrow lanes and celebrity cafe terraces used as film sets, this is cinematic Paris at its best.

Start Ⓜ Abbesses
Distance 1km
Duration One hour

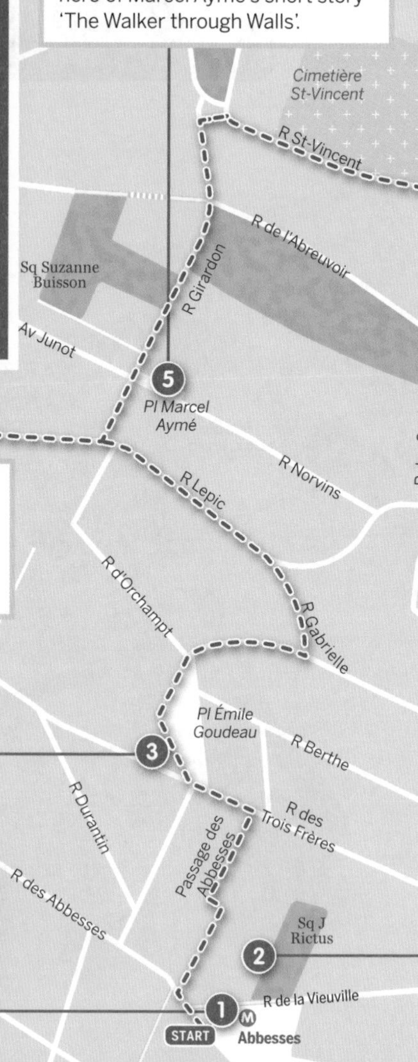

5 See a man pop out of a stone wall on place Marcel Aymé. **Le Passe-Muraille** portrays Dutilleul, hero of Marcel Aymé's short story 'The Walker through Walls'.

4 In 1876 windmill **Moulin Blute Fin**, on rue Lepic, became an open-air dance hall, immortalised by Renoir in his 1876 tableau *Bal du Moulin de la Galette.*

3 On place Émile Goudeau see **Le Bateau Lavoir** studios of Max Jacob, Amedeo Modigliani and Pablo Picasso, who painted *Les Demoiselles d'Avignon* (1907) here.

1 Admire Hector Guimard's iconic art nouveau metro entrance (1900) on **place des Abbesses**.

6 Don't miss the mural of a rabbit jumping out of a cooking pot by caricaturist André Gill, decorating the façade of celebrated cabaret **Au Lapin Agile**.

7 Pocket-sized vineyard, **Clos Montmartre**, dates from 1933. Its 2000 vines produce an average of 800 bottles of wine each October.

8 Uphill is Montmartre's oldest building, the 17th-century manor house and one-time home to painters Renoir, Utrillo and Raoul Dufy that's now **Musée de Montmartre** (www.museedemontmartre.fr).

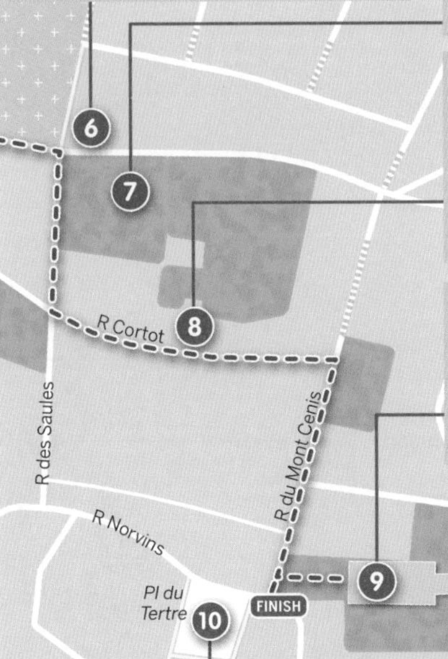

9 In 1534 the 12th-century **Église St-Pierre de Montmartre** witnessed the founding of the Jesuits, who met in the crypt under the guidance of Ignatius of Loyola.

Basilique du Sacré Cœur

R Lamarck

Take a Break... Hardware Société (p72) Great for coffee, breakfast or lunch.

10 Lap up the local life on **place du Tertre**, packed with buskers, portrait artists, cafe terraces and crowds of tourists.

2 Learn 'I love you!' in another language or 10 with **Le Mur des je t'aime**, a work of art in tiny gated park, Sq Jehan Rictus, off place des Abbesses.

0 100 m
0 0.05 miles

Medieval Marais

While Henri IV was busy having place Royale (today's place des Vosges) built, aristocrats were commissioning gold-brick *hôtels particuliers* – beautiful Renaissance mansions that lend Le Marais a particular architectural harmony.

Start rue François Miron Ⓜ St-Paul
Distance 2km
Duration 1½ hours

5 Dip into **Musée Cognacq-Jay** (www.cognacq-jay.paris.fr), inside Hôtel de Donon, to ogle at the collection of Ernest Cognacq (1839–1928) and his wife.

4 Stride along rue Pavée where Henri II's legitimised daughter lived in late-Renaissance mansion **Hôtel Lamoignon** at No 24.

Take a Break... Le Loir dans La Théière (www.leloirdanslatheiere.com) A dozen types of tea and excellent savoury tarts.

1 Walk south on rue du Prévôt to rue Charlemagne. At 7 rue de Jouy admire majestic **Hôtel d'Aumont**, built in 1648 for a king's councillor.

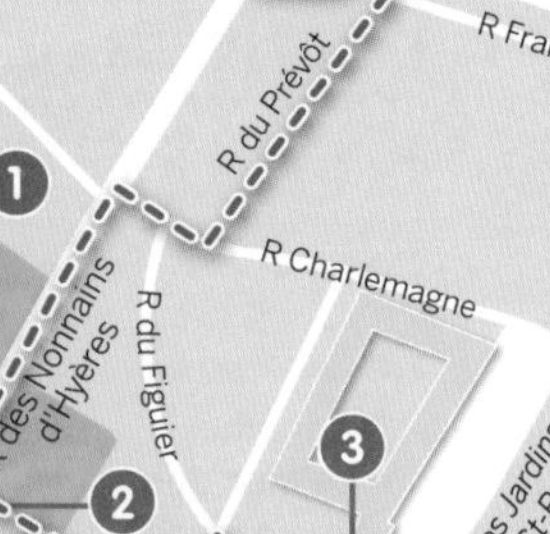

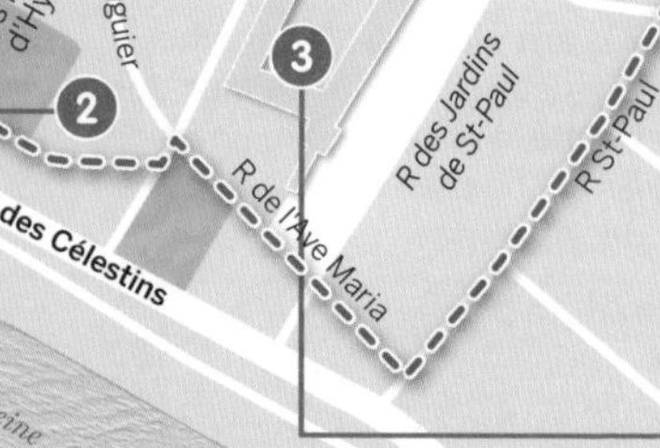

2 Snap geometric gardens and a neo-Gothic turret at **Hôtel de Sens** (1 rue du Figuier), begun around 1475 for the lucky archbishops of Sens and restored in 1930.

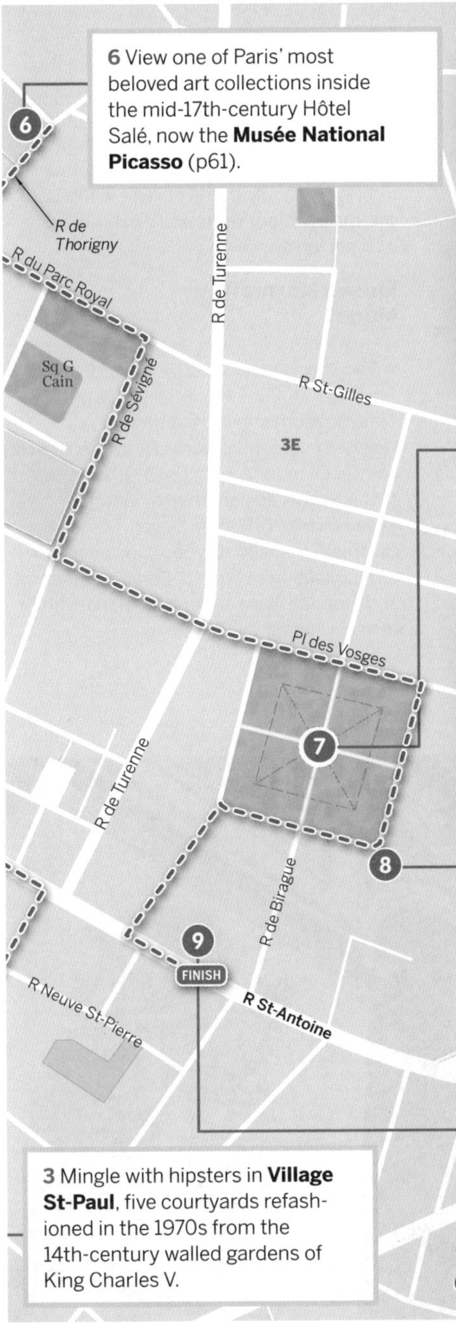

6 View one of Paris' most beloved art collections inside the mid-17th-century Hôtel Salé, now the **Musée National Picasso** (p61).

Classic Photo No square in Paris demands to be photographed quite like Place des Vosges.

7 Flop on a bench or the grassy lawns of Paris' oldest city square, **place des Vosges**, and contemplate its exquisite architectural symmetry.

8 At No 6 **Maison de Victor Hugo** (www.maisonsvictorhugo.paris.fr), inside elegant Hôtel de Rohan-Guéménée, is where the celebrated novelist and poet once lived.

9 Duck beneath the arch in the southwest corner of place des Vosges and fall instantly in love with the beautifully decorated Renaissance courtyards of **Hôtel de Sully** (www.hotel-de-sully.fr).

3 Mingle with hipsters in **Village St-Paul**, five courtyards refashioned in the 1970s from the 14th-century walled gardens of King Charles V.

R de Thorigny
R du Parc Royal
R de Turenne
Sq G Cain
R de Sévigné
R St-Gilles
3E
Pl des Vosges
R de Turenne
R de Birague
FINISH
R Neuve St-Pierre
R St-Antoine
N
0 — 200 m
0 — 0.1 miles

SIGHTS

Eiffel Tower & Western Paris

Cité de l'Architecture et du Patrimoine — Museum

(Map p56; www.citechaillot.fr; 1 place du Trocadéro et du 11 Novembre, 16e; adult/child €8/free; 11am-7pm Wed & Fri-Sun, to 9pm Thu; MTrocadéro) This mammoth 23,000-sq-metre space is an ode on three floors to French architecture. The highlight is the light-filled ground floor with a beautiful collection of plaster and wood *moulages* (casts) of cathedral portals, columns and gargoyles. Replicas of murals and stained glass originally created for the 1878 Exposition Universelle are on display on the upper floors. Views of the Eiffel Tower are equally monumental.

Musée du Quai Branly — Museum

(Map p56; 01 56 61 70 00; www.quaibranly.fr; 37 quai Branly, 7e; adult/child €10/free; 11am-7pm Tue, Wed & Sun, 11am-9pm Thu-Sat; MAlma Marceau or RER Pont de l'Alma) A tribute to the diversity of human culture, Musée du Quai Branly's highly inspiring overview of indigenous and folk art spans four main sections – Oceania, Asia, Africa and the Americas. An impressive array of masks, carvings, weapons, jewellery and more make up the body of the rich collection, displayed in a refreshingly unorthodox interior without rooms or high walls. Look out for excellent temporary exhibitions and performances.

Musée Marmottan Monet — Gallery

(01 44 96 50 33; www.marmottan.fr; 2 rue Louis Boilly, 16e; adult/child €11/7.50; 10am-6pm Tue, Wed & Fri-Sun, to 9pm Thu; MLa Muette) This museum showcases the world's largest collection of works by impressionist painter Claude Monet (1840–1926) – about 100 – as well as paintings by Gauguin, Sisley, Pissarro, Renoir, Degas, Manet and Berthe Morisot. It also contains an important collection of French, English, Italian and Flemish illuminations from the 13th to 16th centuries.

Arc de Triomphe

T. OZAIR/SHUTTERSTOCK ©

Champs-Élysées & Grands Boulevards

Arc de Triomphe — Landmark

(Map p56; www.paris-arc-de-triomphe.fr; place Charles de Gaulle, 8e; viewing platform adult/child €12/free; 10am-11pm Apr-Sep, to 10.30pm Oct-Mar; M Charles de Gaulle–Étoile) If anything rivals the Eiffel Tower (p38) as the symbol of Paris, it's this magnificent 1836 monument to Napoléon's victory at Austerlitz (1805), which he commissioned the following year. The intricately sculpted triumphal arch stands sentinel in the centre of the Étoile (Star) roundabout. From the viewing platform on top of the arch (50m up via 284 steps and well worth the climb) you can see the dozen avenues.

Palais Garnier — Historic Building

(Map p56; 08 92 89 90 90; www.operadeparis.fr; cnr rues Scribe & Auber, 9e; self-guided tours adult/child €12/8, guided tours adult/child €15.50/8.50; self-guided tours 10am-5pm, guided tours 11am & 2.30pm; M Opéra) The fabled 'phantom of the opera' lurked in this opulent opera house designed in 1860 by Charles Garnier (then an unknown 35-year-old architect). Reserve a spot on a 90-minute English-language guided tour, or visit on your own (audioguides available; €5). Don't miss the Grand Staircase and gilded auditorium with red velvet seats, a massive chandelier and Chagall's ceiling mural. Also worth a peek is the museum, with posters, costumes, backdrops, original scores and other memorabilia.

Grand Palais — Gallery

(Map p56; 01 44 13 17 17; www.grandpalais.fr; 3 av du Général Eisenhower, 8e; adult/child €14/free; 10am-8pm Thu-Mon, to 10pm Wed; M Champs-Élysées–Clemenceau) Erected for the 1900 Exposition Universelle (World's Fair), the Grand Palais today houses several exhibition spaces beneath its huge 8.5-tonne art nouveau glass roof. Some of Paris' biggest shows (Renoir, Chagall, Turner) are held in the **Galeries Nationales**, lasting three to four months. Hours, prices and exhibition dates vary significantly for all galleries. Reserving a ticket online for any show is strongly advised. Note that the Grand Palais will close for renovations from late 2020 to mid-2024.

Parisian Parks

For apartment-dwelling locals, the city's parks are a backyard where they can stroll in style or enjoy cheese and wine.

The **Jardin du Luxembourg** (Map p64; www.senat.fr/visite/jardin; hours vary; M Mabillon, St-Sulpice, Rennes, Notre Dame des Champs, RER Luxembourg) is an oasis of formal terraces, chestnut groves and lush lawns. Napoléon dedicated the 23 gracefully laid-out hectares to the children of Paris, and many Parisians spent their childhood prodding 1920s wooden **sailboats** (rental per 30min €4; 11am-6pm Apr-Oct) with long sticks on the octagonal Grand Bassin.

The 28-hectare **Jardin des Tuileries** (Map p56; rue de Rivoli, 1er; 7am-9pm Apr-late Sep, 7.30am-7.30pm late Sep-Mar; M Tuileries, Concorde) was laid out in its present form in 1664 by André Le Nôtre, architect of the gardens at Versailles. It's filled with fountains, ponds and sculptures, and is now part of the Banks of the Seine Unesco World Heritage Site.

The **Jardin du Palais Royal** (Map p56; www.domaine-palais-royal.fr; 2 place Colette, 1er; 8am-10.30pm Apr-Sep, to 8.30pm Oct-Mar; M Palais Royal–Musée du Louvre) is perfect for a picnic, or shopping in the trio of beautiful arcades that frame it. However, it's the southern end, with sculptor Daniel Buren's 260 black-and-white striped columns, that has become the garden's signature feature.

Elegant **Parc Monceau** (35 bd de Courcelles, 8e; 7am-10pm May-Aug, to 9pm Sep, to 8pm Oct-Apr; M Monceau) has an Egyptian-style pyramid, a bridge modelled on Venice's Rialto, a Renaissance arch and a Corinthian colonnade. There are puppet shows and a carousel.

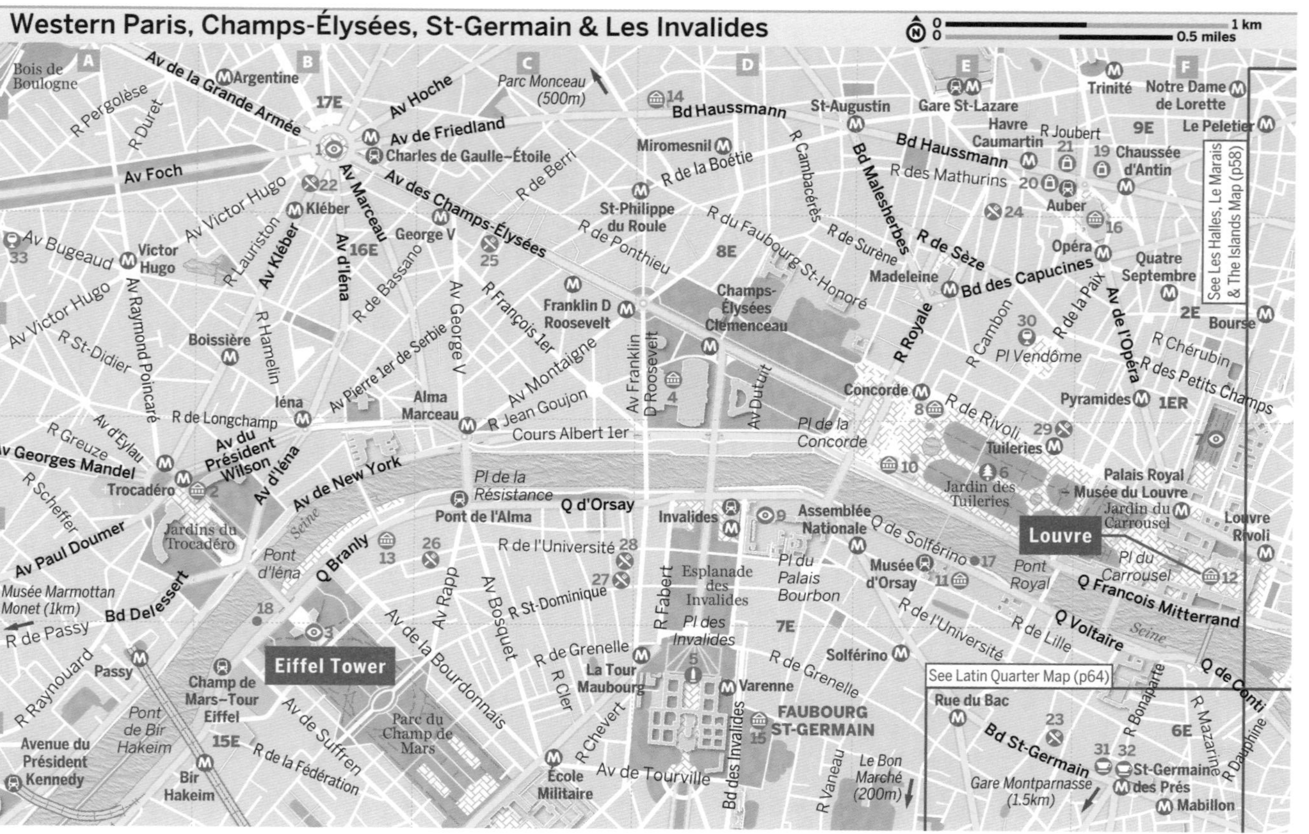
Western Paris, Champs-Élysées, St-Germain & Les Invalides
0 1 km
0 0.5 miles
See Les Halles, Le Marais & The Islands Map (p58)
See Latin Quarter Map (p64)
Parc Monceau (500m)
Musée Marmottan Monet (1km)
Le Bon Marché (200m)
Gare Montparnasse (1.5km)
Eiffel Tower
Louvre
Bois de Boulogne
Jardins du Trocadéro
Parc du Champ de Mars
Jardin des Tuileries
Esplanade des Invalides
FAUBOURG ST-GERMAIN
Av des Champs-Élysées
Av de la Grande Armée
Av Foch
Bd Haussmann
Bd St-Germain
Bd Malesherbes
Bd des Capucines
Av de l'Opéra
R de Rivoli
Cours Albert 1er
Q d'Orsay
Q Voltaire
Q Francois Mitterrand
Seine

Western Paris, Champs-Élysées, St-Germain & Les Invalides

Sights

1 Arc de Triomphe B1
2 Cité de l'Architecture et du Patrimoine.... B3
3 Eiffel Tower B4
Galerie des Galeries .... (see 19)
4 Grand Palais.......... D2
5 Hôtel des Invalides.......... D4
6 Jardin des Tuileries.......... E3
7 Jardin du Palais Royal F3
8 Jeu de Paume E2
9 Ministère des Affaires Étrangères D3
10 Musée de l'Orangerie.......... E3
11 Musée d'Orsay.......... E3
12 Musée du Louvre.......... F3
13 Musée du Quai Branly B3
14 Musée Jacquemart-André.......... D1
15 Musée Rodin D4
16 Palais Garnier F2

Activities, Courses & Tours

17 Paris Canal Croisières E3
18 Vedettes de Paris.......... B3

Shopping

19 Galeries Lafayette.......... F1
20 Galeries Lafayette – Home & Gourmet..... E1
21 Galeries Lafayette – Men's Store.......... E1
Galeries Lafayette Fashion Show.......... (see 19)

Eating

58 Tour Eiffel.......... (see 3)
22 Bustronome B1
23 Clover.......... E4
24 Helmut Newcake E1
25 Ladurée.......... C2
Lafayette Gourmet.......... (see 20)
Le Jules Verne.......... (see 3)
26 Les Deux Abeilles.......... C3
27 Restaurant David Toutain C3
28 Tomy & Co.......... C3
29 Uma E3

Drinking & Nightlife

30 Bar Hemingway E2
31 Café de Flore.......... F4
32 Les Deux Magots F4
33 St James Paris.......... A2

Entertainment

Palais Garnier.......... (see 16)
Palais Garnier Box Office.......... (see 16)

Louvre & Les Halles

Centre Pompidou Museum

(Map p58; ☎01 44 78 12 33; www.centrepompidou.fr; place Georges Pompidou, 4e; museum, exhibitions & panorama adult/child €14/free, panorama only ticket €5/free; ⏲11am-9pm Wed-Mon; Ⓜ Rambuteau) Renowned for its radical architectural statement, the 1977-opened Centre Pompidou brings together galleries and cutting-edge exhibitions, hands-on workshops, dance performances, cinemas and other entertainment venues, with street performers and fanciful fountains outside. Don't miss the spectacular Parisian panorama from the rooftop.

Musée de l'Orangerie Museum

(Map p56; ☎01 44 77 80 07; www.musee-orangerie.fr; place de la Concorde, 1er; adult/child €9/free; ⏲9am-6pm Wed-Mon; Ⓜ Concorde) Monet's extraordinary cycle of eight enormous *Decorations des Nymphéas* (Water Lilies) occupies two huge oval rooms purpose-built in 1927 on the artist's instructions. The lower level houses more of Monet's impressionist works and many by Sisley, Renoir, Cézanne, Gauguin, Picasso, Matisse and Modigliani, as well as Derain's *Arlequin et Pierrot*.

Montmartre & Northern Paris

Basilique du Sacré-Cœur Basilica

(Map p62; ☎01 53 41 89 00; www.sacre-coeur-montmartre.com; Parvis du Sacré-Cœur; basilica free, dome adult/child €6/4, cash only; ⏲basilica 6am-10.30pm, dome 8.30am-8pm May-Sep, 9am-5pm Oct-Apr; Ⓜ Anvers, Abbesses) Begun in 1875 in the wake of the Franco-Prussian War and the chaos of the Paris Commune, Sacré-Cœur is a symbol of the former struggle between the conservative Catholic old guard and the secular, republican radicals. It was finally consecrated in 1919, standing in contrast to the bohemian lifestyle that surrounded it. The view over Paris from its parvis is breathtaking. Avoid walking up the steep hill by using a regular metro ticket aboard the **funicular** (www.ratp.fr; place St-Pierre, 18e; ⏲6am-12.45am) to the **upper station** (rue du Cardinal Dubois, 18e).

Les Halles, Le Marais & The Islands

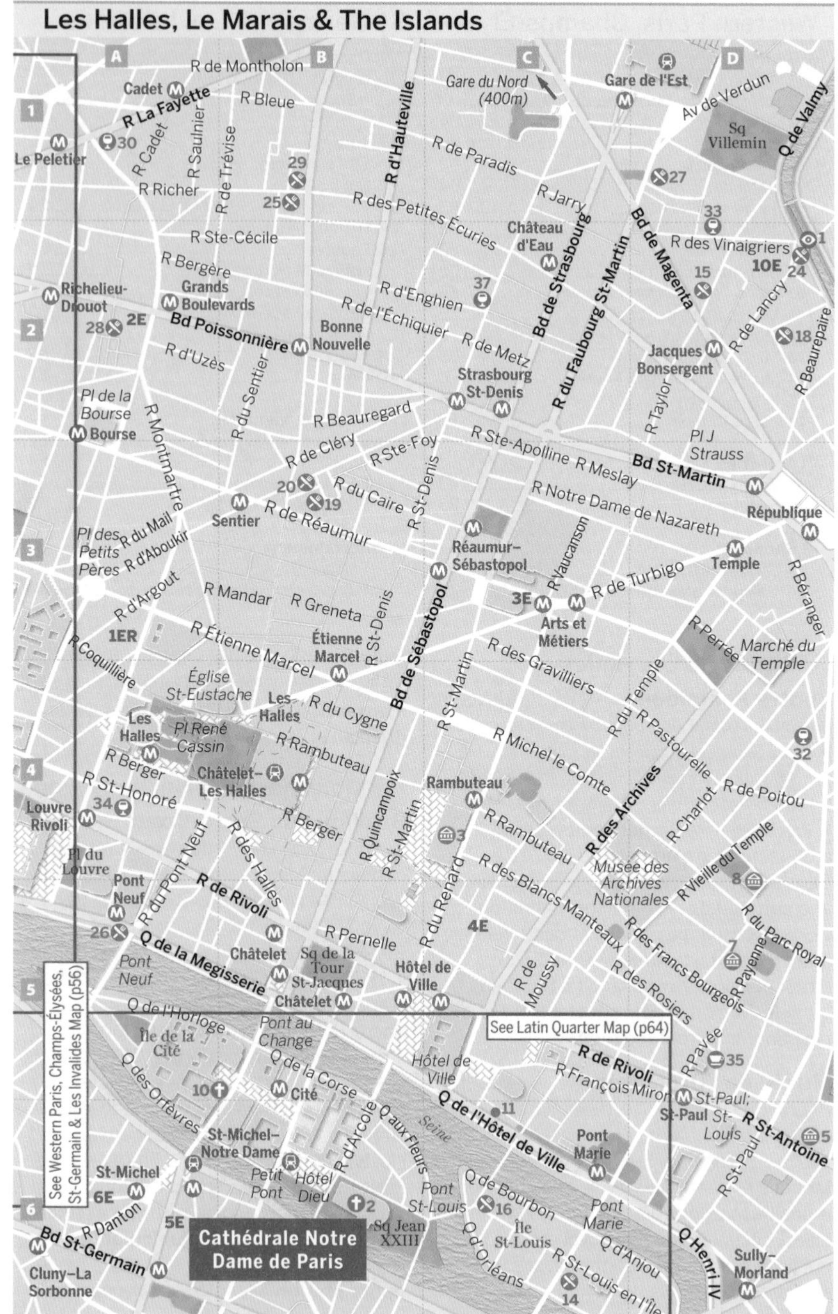

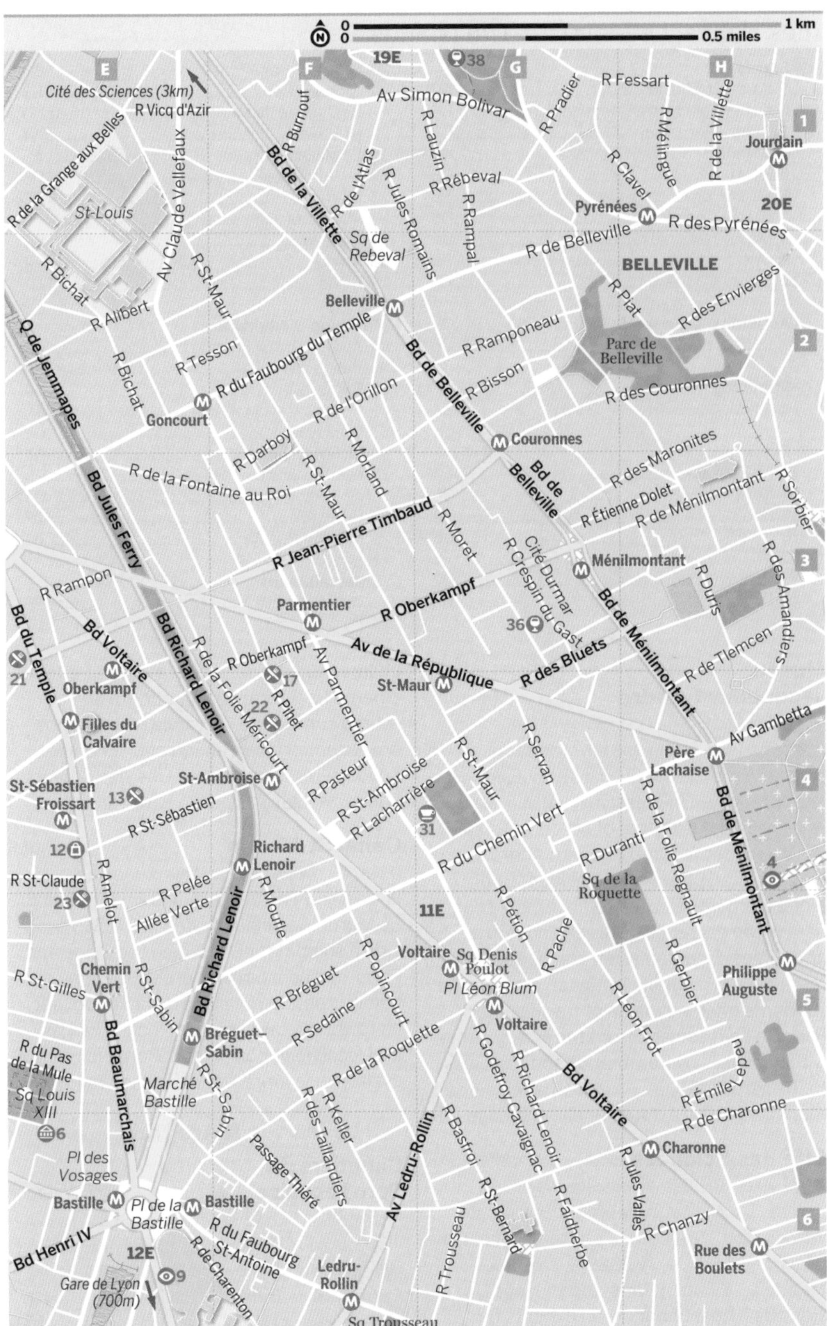

0
0
1 km
0.5 miles
E
F
G
H
19E
38
Cité des Sciences (3km)
R Vicq d'Azir
R Burnouf
Av Simon Bolivar
R Pradier
R Fessart
1
Jourdain
R Mélingue
R de la Villette
R Clavel
R de la Grange aux Belles
Av Claude Vellefaux
Bd de la Villette
R de l'Atlas
R Lauzin
R Jules Romains
R Rébeval
St-Louis
Sq de Rebeval
R Rampal
Pyrénées
20E
R des Pyrénées
R de Belleville
R Bichat
R St-Maur
BELLEVILLE
R Piat
R des Envierges
Belleville
R Alibert
R du Faubourg du Temple
Q de Jemmapes
R Ramponeau
2
Parc de Belleville
R Tesson
Bd de Belleville
R Bichat
R Bisson
R des Couronnes
Goncourt
R de l'Orillon
R Darboy
R Morland
Couronnes
R des Maronites
R de la Fontaine au Roi
R St-Maur
Bd de Belleville
R Sorbier
Bd Jules Ferry
R Étienne Dolet
R de Ménilmontant
R Jean-Pierre Timbaud
R Moret
Cité Durmar
R Crespin du Gast
Ménilmontant
3
R des Amandiers
R Rampon
R Duris
Parmentier
R Oberkampf
Bd du Temple
Bd Voltaire
Bd Richard Lenoir
36
Bd de Ménilmontant
R de la Folie Méricourt
R Oberkampf
Av de la République
R des Bluets
R de Tlemcen
21
Oberkampf
17
Av Parmentier
St-Maur
22
R Pihet
Av Gambetta
Filles du Calvaire
R St-Maur
R Servan
Père Lachaise
St-Sébastien Froissart
St-Ambroise
R Pasteur
R St-Ambroise
R Lacharrière
4
13
R St-Sébastien
R de la Folie Regnault
31
R du Chemin Vert
12
Richard Lenoir
R Duranti
R St-Claude
R Amelot
R Pelée
R Moufle
Sq de la Roquette
4
23
Allée Verte
R Pétion
11E
R Pache
Bd Richard Lenoir
R Popincourt
Voltaire
Sq Denis Poulot
R St-Gilles
Chemin Vert
R St-Sabin
R Bréguet
Pl Léon Blum
Philippe Auguste
Voltaire
R Gerbier
R Léon Frot
5
Bd Beaumarchais
Bréguet-Sabin
R Sedaine
R Godefroy Cavaignac
R Richard Lenoir
R du Pas de la Mule
R de la Roquette
Bd Voltaire
R Émile Lepeu
Sq Louis XIII
Marché Bastille
R St-Sabin
R des Taillandiers
R Keller
R de Charonne
6
Av Ledru-Rollin
R Basfroi
Charonne
Pl des Vosges
Passage Thiéré
R Jules Vallès
R St-Bernard
R Faidherbe
Bastille
Pl de la Bastille
Bastille
R Trousseau
R Chanzy
6
Bd Henri IV
R du Faubourg St-Antoine
Rue des Boulets
12E
R de Charenton
Ledru-Rollin
9
Gare de Lyon (700m)
Sq Trousseau

Les Halles, Le Marais & The Islands

Sights
1 Canal St-Martin D2
2 Cathédrale Notre Dame de Paris B6
3 Centre Pompidou C4
4 Cimetière du Père Lachaise H4
5 Hôtel de Sully D6
6 Maison de Victor Hugo E6
7 Musée Cognacq-Jay D5
8 Musée National Picasso D4
9 Opéra Bastille E6
10 Sainte-Chapelle B5

Activities, Courses & Tours
11 La Cuisine Paris C6

Shopping
12 Merci E4

Eating
13 Au Passage E4
14 Berthillon C6
15 Bob's Juice Bar D2
16 Café Saint Régis C6
17 Chambelland F4
18 Du Pain et des Idées D2
19 Frenchie B3
20 Frenchie Bar à Vins B3
21 Jacques Genin E3
La Cantine de Merci (see 12)
22 La Cave de l'Insolite F4
23 La Maison Plisson E5
24 Le Verre Volé D2
25 L'Office B1
26 Maison Maison A5
27 Marrow D1
28 Noglu A2
29 Richer B1

Drinking & Nightlife
30 Au Général La Fayette A1
31 Beans on Fire G4
32 Candelaria D4
Cinéma Café Merci (see 12)
33 Gravity Bar D2
34 Le Garde Robe A4
35 Le Loir dans La Théière D5
36 Le Perchoir G3
37 Le Syndicat C2
38 Pavillon Puebla G1

Entertainment
Opéra Bastille (see 9)

Musée Jacquemart-André Museum

(Map p56; 01 45 62 11 59; www.musee-jacquemart-andre.com; 158 bd Haussmann, 8e; adult/child €13.50/10.50; 10am-6pm, to 8.30pm Mon during temporary exhibitions; M Miromesnil) The home of art collectors Nélie Jacquemart and Édouard André, this opulent late-19th-century residence combined elements from different eras – seen here in the presence of Greek and Roman antiquities, Egyptian artefacts, period furnishings and portraits by Dutch masters. Its 16 rooms offer a glimpse of the lifestyle of Parisian high society: from the library, hung with canvases by Rembrandt and Van Dyck, to the Jardin d'Hiver – a glass-paned garden room backed by a double-helix staircase.

Cité des Sciences Museum

(01 40 05 80 00; www.cite-sciences.fr; 30 av Corentin Cariou, Parc de la Villette, 19e; per attraction adult/child €12/9; 10am-6pm Tue-Sat, to 7pm Sun, La Géode 10.30am-8.30pm Tue-Sun; M Porte de la Villette) Paris' top museum for kids has a host of hands-on exhibits for children aged two and up, a special-effects cinema La Géode, a planetarium and a retired submarine. Advance reservations are essential for weekend and school holiday visits, and for the Cité des Enfants educative play sessions year-round.

Canal St-Martin Canal

(Map p58; M République, Jaurès, Jacques Bonsergent) The tranquil, 4.5km-long Canal St-Martin was inaugurated in 1825 to provide a shipping link between the Seine and Paris' northeastern suburbs. Emerging from below ground near place de la République, its towpaths take you past locks, bridges and local neighbourhoods. Come for a stroll, cycle, picnic lunch or dusk-time drink.

Le Marais & Around

Cimetière du Père Lachaise Cemetery

(Map p58; 01 55 25 82 10; www.pere-lachaise.com; 16 rue du Repos & 8 bd de Ménilmontant, 20e; 8am-6pm Mon-Fri, from 8.30am Sat, from 9am Sun mid-Mar–Oct, shorter hours Nov–mid-Mar; M Père Lachaise, Gambetta)

Opened in 1804, Père Lachaise is today the world's most visited cemetery. Its 70,000 ornate tombs of the rich and famous form a verdant, 44-hectare sculpture garden. The most visited are those of 1960s rock star Jim Morrison (division 6) and Oscar Wilde (division 89). Pick up cemetery maps at the **conservation office** (Bureaux de la Conservation; ⏰8.30am-12.30pm & 2-5pm Mon-Fri) near the main bd de Ménilmontant entrance. Other notables buried here include composer Chopin, playwright Molière, poet Apollinaire, and writers Balzac, Proust, Gertrude Stein and Colette.

Musée National Picasso — Museum

(Map p58; ☎01 85 56 00 36; www.museepicassoparis.fr; 5 rue de Thorigny, 3e; adult/child €12.50/free; ⏰10.30am-6pm Tue-Fri, from 9.30am Sat & Sun; Ⓜ Chemin Vert, St-Paul) One of Paris' most treasured art collections is showcased inside the mid-17th-century Hôtel Salé, an exquisite private mansion owned by the city since 1964. The Musée National Picasso is a staggering art museum devoted to Spanish artist Pablo Picasso (1881–1973), who spent much of his life living and working in Paris. The collection includes more than 5000 drawings, engravings, paintings, ceramic works and sculptures by the *grand maître* (great master), although they're not all displayed at the same time.

Latin Quarter

Panthéon — Mausoleum

(Map p64; ☎01 44 32 18 00; www.paris-pantheon.fr; place du Panthéon, 5e; adult/child €9/free; ⏰10am-6.30pm Apr-Sep, to 6pm Oct-Mar; Ⓜ Maubert-Mutualité or RER Luxembourg) The Panthéon's stately neoclassical dome is an icon of the Parisian skyline. Its vast interior is an architectural masterpiece: originally an abbey church dedicated to Ste Geneviève and now a mausoleum, it has served since 1791 as the resting place of some of France's greatest thinkers, including Voltaire, Rousseau, Braille and Hugo. A copy of Foucault's pendulum, first hung from the dome in 1851 to demonstrate the rotation of the earth, takes pride of place.

Sparkling Stained Glass

Enshrined within the Palais de Justice (Law Courts), gem-like **Sainte-Chapelle** (Map p58; ☎01 53 40 60 80, concerts 01 42 77 65 65; www.sainte-chapelle.fr; 8 bd du Palais, 1er; adult/child €10/free, joint ticket with Conciergerie €15; ⏰9am-7pm Apr-Sep, to 5pm Oct-Mar; Ⓜ Cité) is Paris' most exquisite Gothic monument. Completed in 1248, just six years after the first stone was laid, the 'Holy Chapel' was conceived by Louis IX to house his personal collection of holy relics, including the famous Holy Crown (now in Notre Dame). The 1113 windows contain Paris' oldest, finest stained glass, at their dazzling best on a sunny day. Free 45-minute guided tours in English depart daily between 11am and 3pm.

Sainte-Chapelle's stained-glass windows

Institut du Monde Arabe — Museum

(Arab World Institute; Map p64; ☎01 40 51 38 38; www.imarabe.org; 1 place Mohammed V, 5e; adult/child €8/4; ⏰10am-6pm Tue-Fri, to 7pm Sat & Sun; Ⓜ Jussieu) The Arab World Institute was jointly founded by France and 18 Middle Eastern and North African nations in 1980, with the aim of promoting cross-cultural dialogue. It hosts temporary exhibitions and a fascinating museum of Arabic culture and history (4th to 7th floors). The stunning building, designed by French architect Jean Nouvel, was inspired by latticed-wood windows *(mashrabiya)* traditional to Arabic architecture.

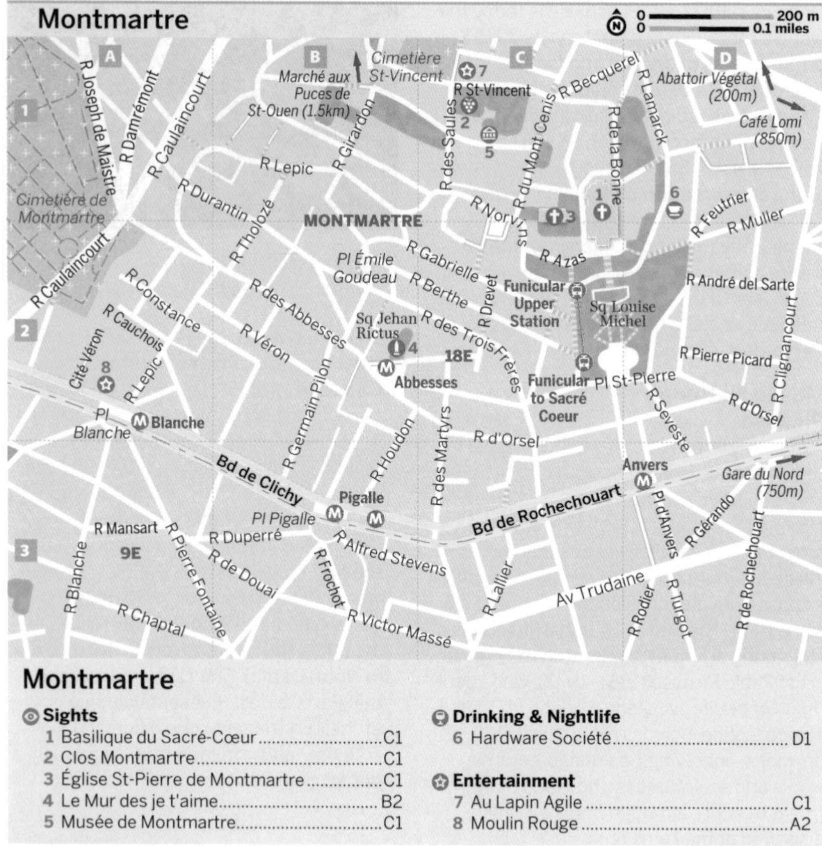

Montmartre

Sights

1 Basilique du Sacré-Cœur C1
2 Clos Montmartre C1
3 Église St-Pierre de Montmartre C1
4 Le Mur des je t'aime B2
5 Musée de Montmartre C1

Drinking & Nightlife

6 Hardware Société D1

Entertainment

7 Au Lapin Agile C1
8 Moulin Rouge A2

Musée National du Moyen Âge — Museum

(Map p64; ☎01 53 73 78 16; www.musee-moyen age.fr; 6 place Paul Painlevé, 5e; adult/child €8/free; ⏰9.15am-5.45pm Wed-Mon; Ⓜ Cluny–La Sorbonne) Undergoing renovation until late 2020, the National Museum of the Middle Ages is considered one of Paris' top small museums. It showcases a series of sublime treasures, from medieval statuary, stained glass and objets d'art to its celebrated series of tapestries, *The Lady with the Unicorn* (1500). Other highlights include ornate 15th-century mansion Hôtel de Cluny and the *frigidarium* (cold room) of an enormous Roman-era bathhouse.

St-Germain & Les Invalides

Musée d'Orsay — Museum

(Map p56; ☎01 40 49 48 14; www.musee-orsay.fr; 1 rue de la Légion d'Honneur, 7e; adult/child €12/free; ⏰9.30am-6pm Tue, Wed & Fri-Sun, to 9.45pm Thu; Ⓜ Assemblée Nationale, RER Musée d'Orsay) The home of France's national collection from the impressionist, postimpressionist and art nouveau movements spanning from 1848 to 1914 is the glorious former Gare d'Orsay railway station – itself an art nouveau showpiece – where a roll-call of masters and their world-famous works are on display.

Top of every visitor's must-see list is the painting collection, centred on the world's largest collection of impressionist and post-impressionist art. Allow time to swoon over masterpieces by Manet, Monet, Cézanne, Renoir, Degas, Pissarro and Van Gogh.

Musée Rodin Museum, Garden

(Map p56; ☎01 44 18 61 10; www.musee-rodin.fr; 79 rue de Varenne, 7e; adult/child €10/free, garden only €4/free; ⏲10am-5.45pm Tue-Sun; Ⓜ Varenne or Invalides) Sculptor, painter, sketcher, engraver and collector Auguste Rodin donated his entire collection to the French state in 1908 on the proviso that it dedicate his former workshop and showroom, the beautiful 1730 Hôtel Biron, to displaying his works. They're now installed not only in the magnificently restored mansion itself, but also in its rose-filled garden – one of the most peaceful places in central Paris and a wonderful spot to contemplate his famous work, *The Thinker*. Prepurchase tickets online to avoid queuing.

Hôtel des Invalides Monument, Museum

(Map p56; www.musee-armee.fr; 129 rue de Grenelle, 7e; adult/child €12/free; ⏲10am-6pm; Ⓜ Varenne, La Tour Maubourg) Flanked by the 500m-long Esplanade des Invalides lawns, Hôtel des Invalides was built in the 1670s by Louis XIV to house 4000 *invalides* (disabled war veterans). On 14 July 1789, a mob broke into the building and seized 32,000 rifles before heading on to the prison at Bastille and the start of the French Revolution.

Admission includes entry to all the Hôtel des Invalides sights (but temporary exhibitions cost extra). Hours for individual sites can vary – check the website for updates.

ACTIVITIES

La Cuisine Paris Cooking

(Map p58; ☎01 40 51 78 18; www.lacuisineparis.com; 80 quai de l'Hôtel de Ville, 4e; 2hr cooking class/walking tours from €69/80; Ⓜ Pont Marie, Hôtel de Ville) Classes in English range from how to make bread and croissants to macarons as well as market classes and gourmet 'foodie walks'.

Musée d'Orsay

Vedettes de Paris — Boating

(Map p56; ☎01 44 18 19 50; www.vedettesde-paris.fr; Port de Suffren, 7e; adult/child €15/7; ⏲11.30am-7.30pm May-Sep, 11.30am-5.30pm Oct-Apr; Ⓜ Bir Hakeim or RER Pont de l'Alma) These one-hour sightseeing cruises on smaller boats are a more intimate experience than the major companies. It runs themed cruises too, including tours for kids.

Paris Canal Croisières — Cruise

(☎01 42 40 96 97; www.pariscanal.com; Parc de la Villette, 19e; adult/child €22/14; ⏲mid-Mar–mid-Nov; Ⓜ Porte de Pantin) Seasonal 2½-hour Seine-and-canal cruises depart from Parc de la Villette and from **quai Anatole France** (Map p56; Ⓜ Solférino, RER Musée d'Orsay) near the Musée d'Orsay.

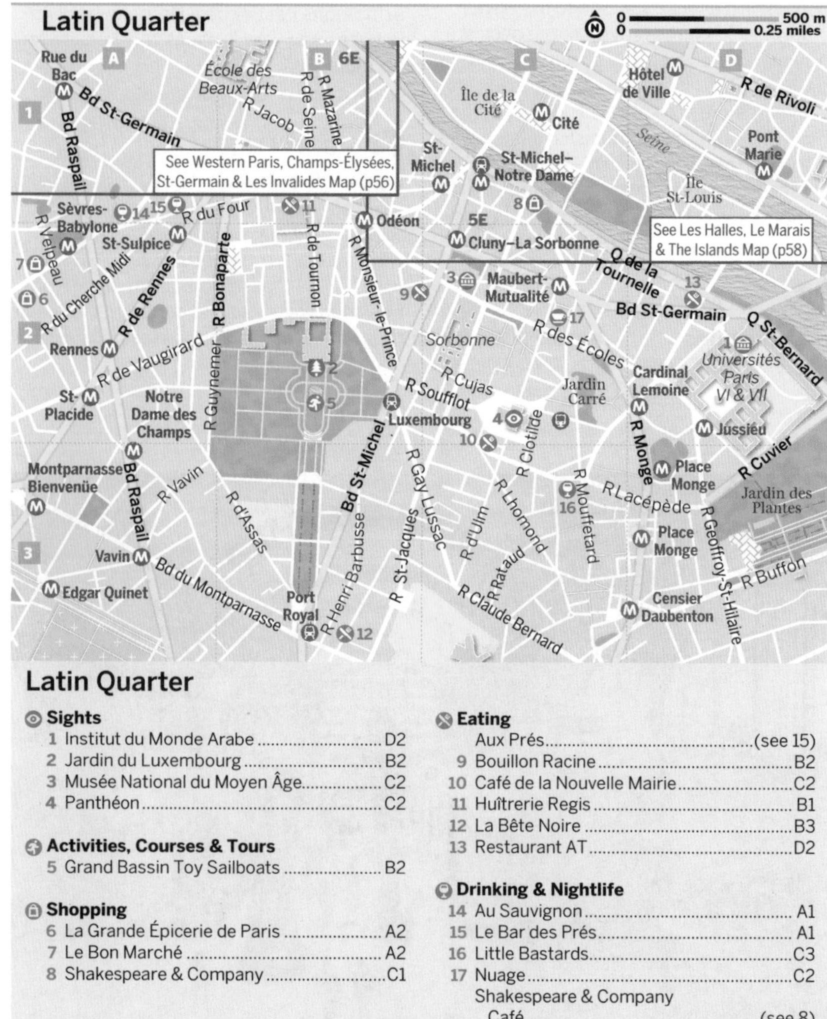

Latin Quarter

Sights
1 Institut du Monde Arabe D2
2 Jardin du Luxembourg B2
3 Musée National du Moyen Âge C2
4 Panthéon C2

Activities, Courses & Tours
5 Grand Bassin Toy Sailboats B2

Shopping
6 La Grande Épicerie de Paris A2
7 Le Bon Marché A2
8 Shakespeare & Company C1

Eating
Aux Prés .... (see 15)
9 Bouillon Racine B2
10 Café de la Nouvelle Mairie C2
11 Huîtrerie Regis B1
12 La Bête Noire B3
13 Restaurant AT D2

Drinking & Nightlife
14 Au Sauvignon A1
15 Le Bar des Prés A1
16 Little Bastards C3
17 Nuage C2
Shakespeare & Company Café .... (see 8)

SHOPPING

Galeries Lafayette Department Store

(Map p56; ☎01 42 82 34 56; http://haussmann.galerieslafayette.com; 40 bd Haussmann, 9e; ⊙9.30am-8.30pm Mon-Sat, 11am-7pm Sun; 📶; Ⓜ Chaussée d'Antin or RER Auber) Grande-dame department store Galeries Lafayette is spread across the main store (its magnificent stained-glass dome is over a century old), men's store and homewares store with a gourmet emporium.

Catch modern art in the 1st-floor **gallery** (☎01 42 82 81 98) FREE, take in a **fashion show** (☎bookings 01 42 82 81 98; ⊙3pm Fri Mar-Jun & Sep-Dec by reservation), ascend to a free, windswept rooftop panorama, or take a break at one of its 24 restaurants and cafes.

Le Bon Marché Department Store

(Map p64; ☎01 44 39 80 00; http://lebon-marche.com; 24 rue de Sèvres, 7e; ⊙10am-8pm Mon-Wed, Fri & Sat, 10am-8.45pm Thu, 11am-8pm Sun; Ⓜ Sèvres-Babylone) Built by Gustave Eiffel as Paris' first department store in 1852, this is the epitome of style, with a superb concentration of men's and women's fashions, homewares, stationery, books and toys. Break for a coffee, afternoon tea with cake or a light lunch at the Rose Bakery tearoom on the 2nd floor.

The icing on the cake is its glorious **food hall** (www.lagrandeepicerie.com; 36 rue de Sèvres, 7e; ⊙8.30am-9pm Mon-Sat, 10am-8pm Sun).

Merci Gifts & Souvenirs

(Map p58; ☎01 42 77 00 33; www.merci-merci.com; 111 bd Beaumarchais, 3e; ⊙10am-7.30pm; Ⓜ St-Sébastien–Froissart) A Fiat Cinquecento marks the entrance to this unique concept store, which donates all its profits to a children's charity in Madagascar. Shop for fashion, accessories, linens, lamps and nifty designs for the home. Complete the experience with a coffee in its hybrid used-bookshop-cafe, a juice at its **Cinéma Café** (Map p58; ⊙11am-2pm Mon-Sat) or lunch in its stylish **La Cantine de Merci** (Map p58; mains €16-21; ⊙10am-7.30pm).

Flea Market Treasure Trove

Spanning 9 hectares, the **Marché aux Puces de St-Ouen** (www.marcheauxpuces-saintouen.com; rue des Rosiers, St-Ouen; ⊙Sat-Mon; Ⓜ Porte de Clignancourt) is a vast flea market, founded in 1870 and said to be Europe's largest. Over 2000 stalls are grouped into 15 *marchés* (markets) selling everything from 17th-century furniture to 21st-century clothing. Each market has different opening hours – check the website for details. There are miles upon miles of 'freelance' stalls; come prepared to spend some time.

Marché aux Puces de St-Ouen
GABRIEL12/SHUTTERSTOCK ©

EATING

Eiffel Tower & Western Paris

Les Deux Abeilles Cafe $

(Map p56; ☎01 45 55 64 04; 189 rue de l'Université, 7e; lunch menu €24, salads €15-20; ⊙9am-7pm Mon-Sat; Ⓜ Alma Marceau or RER Pont d'Alma) There is no lovelier sanctuary from the Eiffel Tower crowds than this old-fashioned tearoom, the elegant love child of a mother-and-daughter team who greet regulars with a *bisou* (kiss). Delicious homemade cakes and *citronnade* (ginger lemonade) aside, the Two Bees cook up quiches, tarts and salads, ensuring every table is full by 1pm. Breakfast and brunch available too.

Bustronome Gastronomy $$$

(Map p56; ☎09 54 44 45 55; www.bustronome.com; 2 av Kléber, 16e; 4-course lunch €65, 6-course

From left: Macarons at Ladurée; Du Pain et des Idées; Bustronome (p65)

dinner €100; ⌚by reservation 12.15pm, 12.45pm, 7.45pm & 8.45pm; ; MKléber, Charles de Gaulle–Étoile) A true moveable feast, Bustronome is a voyage into French gastronomy aboard a glass-roofed bus, with Paris' famous monuments – the Arc de Triomphe, Grand Palais, Palais Garnier, Notre Dame and Eiffel Tower – gliding by as you dine on seasonal creations prepared in the purpose-built vehicle's lower-deck galley. Children's menus for lunch/dinner cost €40/50; vegetarian, vegan and gluten-free menus are available.

Champs-Élysées & Grands Boulevards

Richer Bistro $

(Map p58; www.lericher.com; 2 rue Richer, 9e; mains €17-21; ⌚noon-2.30pm & 7.30-10.30pm; MPoissonière, Bonne Nouvelle) Run by the same team as across-the-street neighbour **L'Office** (Map p58; 01 47 70 67 31; www.office-resto.com; 3 rue Richer, 9e; 2-/3-course lunch menus €22/27, mains €23-29; ⌚noon-2pm & 7.30-10.30pm Mon-Fri), Richer's pared-back, exposed-brick decor is a smart setting for genius creations including smoked-duck-breast ravioli in miso broth, and quince-and-lime cheesecake for dessert. It doesn't take reservations, but it serves snacks and Chinese tea, and has a full bar (open until midnight). Fantastic value.

Ladurée Pastries $$

(Map p56; 01 40 75 08 75; www.laduree.com; 75 av des Champs-Élysées, 8e; pastries from €2.60, mains €18-47, 2-/3-course menu €35/42; ⌚7.30am-11pm Sun-Thu, 7.30am-midnight Fri & Sat; ; MGeorge V) One of Paris' oldest patisseries, Ladurée has been around since 1862 and first created the lighter-than-air, ganache-filled macaron in the 1930s. Its tearoom is the classiest spot to indulge on the Champs.

Louvre & Les Halles

Uma Fusion $$

(Map p56; 01 40 15 08 15; www.uma-restaurant.fr; 7 rue du 29 Juillet, 1er; 2-/3-course lunch €25/29, 7-/9-course dinner €67/82; ⌚12.30-2.30pm & 7.30-10.30pm Mon-Sat; MTuileries) Embark on a culinary voyage at Uma, where

XAVIER TESTELIN/GAMMA-RAPHO VIA GETTY IMAGES ©

chef Lucas Felzine infuses contemporary French sensibilities with Nikkei: Peruvian-Japanese fusion food. The lunch menu comes with two exquisitely prepared starters (think ceviche with daikon radish or smoked duck with lychees); grab a table upstairs to spy on the open kitchen. Mezcal, pisco and vodka cocktails served until 1.30am.

Frenchie Bistro $$$

(Map p58; ☎01 40 39 96 19; www.frenchie-restaurant.com; 5 rue du Nil, 2e; 4-course lunch menu €45, 5-course dinner menu €74, with wine €175; ⏲6.30-11pm Mon-Fri, noon-2.30pm Thu & Fri in summer; Ⓜ Sentier) Tucked down an inconspicuous alley, this tiny bistro with wooden tables and old stone walls is always packed and for good reason: excellent-value dishes are modern, market-driven and prepared with unpretentious flair by French chef Gregory Marchand. Reserve well in advance or arrive early and pray for a cancellation (it does happen). Alternatively, head to **Frenchie Bar à Vins** (Map p58; 6 rue du Nil, 2e; dishes €9-23; ⏲6.30-11pm; Ⓜ Sentier), located just next door.

Montmartre & Northern Paris

Du Pain et des Idées Bakery $

(Map p58; www.dupainetdesidees.com; 34 rue Yves Toudic, 10e; breads €1.20-7, pastries €2.50-6.50; ⏲6.45am-8pm Mon-Fri; Ⓜ Jacques Bonsergent) This traditional bakery with an exquisite interior from 1889 is famed for its naturally leavened bread, orange-blossom brioche and *escargots* (scroll-like 'snails') in four sweet flavours. Its mini savoury *pavés* (breads) flavoured with Reblochon cheese and fig, or goat's cheese, sesame and honey are perfect for lunch on the run. A wooden picnic table sits on the pavement outside.

Abattoir Végétal Vegan $

(61 rue Ramey, 18e; 3-course lunch menu €18, mains €13-16, Sunday brunch adult/child €25/5; ⏲9am-6pm Tue & Wed, 9am-11.45pm Thu & Fri, 10am-11.45pm Sat, 10.30am-4.30pm Sun; 📶🖉; Ⓜ Jules Joffrin) Mint-green wrought-iron chairs and tables line the pavement outside the 'plant slaughterhouse' (it occupies a former butcher shop), while the light, bright interior has bare-bulb downlights, distempered walls and greenery-filled hanging baskets. Each day there's a choice of three

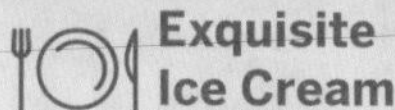

Exquisite Ice Cream

Esteemed **Berthillon** (Map p58; www.berthillon.fr; 29-31 rue St-Louis en l'Île, 4e; 1/2/3/4 scoops takeaway €3/4.50/6/7.50; ⏲10am-8pm Wed-Sun, closed mid-Feb–early Mar & Aug; Ⓜ Pont Marie) is still run by the same family as when it was founded in 1954. Its 70-plus all-natural, chemical-free ice creams include fruit sorbets (pink grapefruit, raspberry and rose) and richer varieties made from fresh milk and eggs: salted caramel, candied Ardèche chestnuts, Armagnac and prunes, to name just a few...

Berthillon
BLUEORANGE STUDIO/SHUTTERSTOCK ©

raw and cooked organic dishes per course, cold-pressed juices and craft beers from Parisian brewery BapBap.

Le Verre Volé Bistro $

(Map p58; ☎01 48 03 17 34; www.leverrevole.fr; 67 rue de Lancry, 10e; mains €11-22, sandwiches €7.90; ⏲bistro 12.30-2.30pm & 7.30-11.30pm, wine bar 10am-2am; 📶; Ⓜ Jacques Bonsergent) The tiny 'Stolen Glass' – a wine shop with a few tables – is one of Paris' most popular wine bar–restaurants, with outstanding natural and unfiltered wines and expert advice. Unpretentious, hearty *plats du jour* are excellent. Reserve in advance for meals, or stop by to pick up a gourmet sandwich (such as mustard-smoked burrata with garlic-pork sausage) and a bottle.

Marrow Bistro $$

(Map p58; ☎09 81 34 57 00; 128 rue du Faubourg St-Martin, 10e; mains €11-19; ⏲6-10pm Tue-Sat, bar to 2am, closed Aug; Ⓜ Gare de l'Est) Hay-smoked quail with peat vinaigrette, grilled octopus and fennel confit, and breaded roast bone marrow are among the adventurous flavour combinations from Hugo Blanchet, who partnered with mixologist Arthur Combe to open this neobistro that's taking Paris' foodie scene by storm. Rough stone walls, blonde wood tables and a small pavement terrace create a relaxed backdrop.

Le Marais & Around

Jacques Genin Pastries $

(Map p58; ☎01 45 77 29 01; www.jacquesgenin.fr; 133 rue de Turenne, 3e; pastries €9; ⏲11am-7pm Tue-Fri & Sun, to 7.30pm Sat; Ⓜ Oberkampf, Filles du Calvaire) Wildly creative *chocolatier* Jacques Genin is famed for his flavoured caramels, *pâtes de fruits* (fruit jellies) and exquisitely embossed *bonbons de chocolat* (chocolate sweets). But what completely steals the show at his elegant chocolate showroom is the *salon de dégustation* (aka tearoom), where you can order a pot of outrageously thick hot chocolate and legendary Genin millefeuille, assembled to order.

La Maison Plisson Cafe, Deli $

(Map p58; www.lamaisonplisson.com; 93 bd Beaumarchais, 3e; mains €8-15; ⏲9.30am-9pm Mon, from 8.30am Tue-Sat, 9.30am-8pm Sun; Ⓜ St-Sébastien–Froissart) Framed by glass-canopied wrought-iron girders, this gourmand's dream incorporates a covered-market-style, terrazzo-floored food hall filled with exquisite, mostly French produce: meat, vegetables, cheese, wine, chocolate, jams, freshly baked breads and much more. If your appetite's whet, its cafe, opening to twin terraces, serves charcuterie, foie gras and cheese planks, bountiful salads and delicacies such as olive-oil-marinated, Noilly Prat–flambéed sardines.

Au Passage Bistro $$

(Map p58; ☎01 43 55 07 52; www.restaurant-aupassage.fr; 1bis passage St-Sébastien, 11e; small plates €9-18, meats to share €25-70; ⏲7-10.30pm Tue-Sat; Ⓜ St-Sébastien-Froissart)

Rising-star chefs continue to make their name at this *petit bar de quartier* (little neighbourhood bar). Choose from a good-value, uncomplicated selection of *petites assiettes* (small tapas-style plates) of cold meats, raw or cooked fish, vegetables and so on, and larger meat dishes such as slow-roasted lamb shoulder or *côte de bœuf* (rib steak) to share. Book ahead.

La Cave de l'Insolite Bistro **$$**

(Map p58; ☎01 53 36 08 33; www.lacavedelinsolite.fr; 30 rue de la Folie Méricourt, 11e; 2-/3-course midweek lunch menus €18/20, mains €18-21; ⊙noon-2.30pm & 7.30-10.30pm Tue-Sat, to 10pm Sun; 📶; Ⓜ St-Ambroise, Parmentier) Brothers Axel and Arnaud, who have worked at some of Paris' top addresses, run this rustic-chic wine bar with barrels, timber tables and a wood-burning stove. Duck pâté with cider jelly, haddock rillettes with lime and endive confit, and beef with mushroom and sweetbread sauce are among the seasonal dishes; its 100-plus hand-harvested wines come from small-scale French vineyards.

Latin Quarter

Café de la Nouvelle Mairie Cafe **$**

(Map p64; ☎01 44 07 04 41; 19 rue des Fossés St-Jacques, 5e; mains €10-20; ⊙8am-midnight Mon-Fri, kitchen noon-2.30pm & 8-10.30pm Mon-Thu, 8-10pm Fri; Ⓜ Cardinal Lemoine) Shhhh… just around the corner from the Panthéon (p61) but hidden away on a small, fountained square, this hybrid cafe-restaurant and wine bar is a tip-top neighbourhood secret, serving natural wines by the glass and delicious seasonal bistro fare from oysters and ribs *(à la française)* to grilled lamb sausage over lentils. It takes reservations for dinner but not lunch – arrive early.

La Bête Noire Mediterranean **$**

(Map p64; ☎06 15 22 73 61; www.facebook.com/labetenoireparis; 58 rue Henri Barbusse, 5e; mains lunch €12-15, dinner €20, brunch €25; ⊙8am-5pm Tue, 8am-11pm Wed-Fri, 9.30am-5.30pm Sat & Sun; 📶🌶; Ⓜ RER Port Royal) Funky music and a small, fashionably minimalist interior with open kitchen ensure bags of soul at this off-the-radar *'cantine gastronomique',* a showcase for the sensational home cooking of passionate chef-owner Maria. Inspired by her Russian-Maltese heritage, she cooks just one meat and one vegetarian dish daily, using seasonal products sourced from local farmers and small producers, washed down with Italian wine.

Restaurant AT Gastronomy **$$$**

(Map p64; ☎01 56 81 94 08; www.atsushitanaka.com; 4 rue du Cardinal Lemoine, 5e; 6-course lunch menu €55, 12-course dinner tasting menu €105; ⊙12.15-2pm & 8-9.30pm Mon-Sat; Ⓜ Cardinal Lemoine) Trained by some of the biggest names in gastronomy (Pierre Gagnaire included), chef Atsushi Tanaka showcases abstract art-like masterpieces incorporating rare ingredients (charred bamboo, kohlrabi turnip cabbage, juniper berry powder, wild purple fennel, Nepalese Timut pepper) in a blank-canvas-style dining space on stunning outsized plates. Ingeniously, dinner menus can be paired with wine (€70) or juice (€45). Reservations essential.

St-Germain & Les Invalides

Bouillon Racine Brasserie **$$**

(Map p64; ☎01 44 32 15 60; www.bouillonracine.com; 3 rue Racine, 6e; 2-course weekday lunch menu €16.90, 3-course menu €35, mains €16-27.50; ⊙noon-11pm; 👪; Ⓜ Cluny-La Sorbonne) Inconspicuously situated in a quiet street, this heritage-listed art nouveau 'soup kitchen', with mirrored walls, floral motifs and ceramic tiling, was built in 1906 to feed market workers. Despite the magnificent interior, the food – inspired by age-old recipes – is no afterthought but superbly executed (stuffed, spit-roasted suckling pig, pork shank in Rodenbach red beer, scallops and shrimps with lobster coulis).

Tomy & Co Gastronomy **$$**

(Map p56; ☎01 45 51 46 93; 22 rue Surcouf, 7e; 2-course lunch menu €27, 3-course/tasting dinner menu €47/68, mains wine pairings €45; ⊙noon-2pm & 7.30-9.30pm Mon-Fri; Ⓜ Invalides) Tomy Gousset's restaurant near Mademoiselle Eiffel has been a sensation since day one.

The French-Cambodian chef works his magic on inspired seasonal dishes using produce from his organic garden. Winter ushers in aromatic black truffles (themed tasting menu €95). The spectacular desserts – chocolate tart with fresh figs, Cambodian palm sugar and fig ice cream anyone? – are equally seasonal. Reservations essential.

Restaurant David Toutain Gastronomy **$$$**

(Map p56; ☎01 45 50 11 10; http://davidtoutain.com; 29 rue Surcouf, 7e; 3-course lunch menu €55, tasting menus €80-140, wine pairings €70-100; ⏰12.30-2pm & 8-10pm Mon, noon-2pm & 8-10pm Tue-Fri; MInvalides) Prepare to be wowed: David Toutain pushes the envelope at his eponymous Michelin-starred restaurant with some of the most creative high-end cooking in Paris. Mystery *dégustation* (tasting) courses include unlikely combinations such as smoked eel in green-apple-and-black-sesame mousse, cauliflower, white chocolate and coconut truffles, or candied celery and truffled rice pudding with artichoke praline. Stunning wine pairings are available.

DRINKING & NIGHTLIFE

Eiffel Tower & Western Paris

St James Paris Bar

(Map p56; www.saint-james-paris.com; 43 av Bugeaud, 16e; ⏰7pm-1am; 📶; MPorte Dauphine) Hidden behind a stone wall, this historic mansion-turned-hotel opens its bar nightly to nonguests – and the setting redefines extraordinary. Winter drinks are in the wood-panelled library; summer drinks are on the impossibly romantic 300-sq-metre garden terrace with giant balloon-shaped gazebos (the first hot-air balloons took flight here). It has over 70 cocktails and an adjoining Michelin-starred restaurant.

Champs-Élysées & Grands Boulevards

Au Général La Fayette Bar

(Map p58; ☎01 47 70 59 08; http://augeneralla fayette.fr; 52 rue la Fayette, 9e; ⏰8am-1am; 📶; MLe Peletier) With its archetypal belle époque decor (brass fittings, polished wood, large murals) and excellent wines by the glass, this old-style brasserie is an atmospheric spot for an afternoon coffee or evening drink.

From left: Helmut Newcake; Bar Hemingway; Restaurant David Toutain; Le Garde Robe

PHOTO 12/ALAMY STOCK PHOTO ©

"CHAMPAGNE"/ALAMY STOCK PHOTO ©

Louvre & Les Halles

Bar Hemingway Cocktail Bar

(Map p56; www.ritzparis.com; Hôtel Ritz Paris, 15 place Vendôme, 1er; ⌚6pm-2am; 📶; Ⓜ Opéra) Black-and-white photos and memorabilia (hunting trophies, old typewriters and framed handwritten letters by the great writer) fill this snug bar inside the Ritz – Hemingway drank here in the 1920s. Head bartender Colin Field mixes monumental cocktails, including three different Bloody Marys made with juice from freshly squeezed seasonal tomatoes.

Le Garde Robe Wine Bar

(Map p58; ☎01 49 26 90 60; 41 rue de l'Arbre Sec, 1er; ⌚12.30-2.30pm & 6.30pm-midnight Tue-Fri, 4.30pm-midnight Mon-Sat; Ⓜ Louvre Rivoli) Le Garde Robe is possibly the world's only bar to serve alcohol alongside a detox menu. While you probably shouldn't come here for the full-on cleansing experience, you can definitely expect excellent, affordable natural wines, a casual atmosphere and a good selection of food, ranging from cheese and charcuterie plates to adventurous

Gourmet Gluten-Free

In a city known for its bakeries, it's only right that gluten-free diners can also tuck in. **Chambelland** (Map p58; ☎01 43 55 07 30; www.chambelland.com; 14 rue Ternaux, 11e; lunch menus €10-12, pastries €2.50-5.50; ⌚9am-8pm Tue-Sat, to 6pm Sun; Ⓜ Parmentier) is a 100% gluten-free bakery creating exquisite cakes, pastries and sourdough loaves and brioches, while takeaway-only **Helmut Newcake** (Map p56; ☎09 81 31 28 31; www.helmutnewcake.com; 28 rue Vignon, 9e; plats du jour €6.80-11.50; ⌚11am-7pm Tue-Sat; Ⓜ Madeleine) has tempting gluten-free eclairs, fondants and cheesecakes, as well as savoury lunches like pizzas and quiches. **Noglu** (Map p58; ☎01 40 26 41 24; www.noglu.fr; 16 passage des Panoramas, 2e; mains €17-21; ⌚noon-3pm Mon-Fri, 11am-4pm Sat, 7.30-10.30pm Tue-Sat; 🌶; Ⓜ Richelieu-Drouot, Grands Boulevards) also operates a gluten-free kitchen and, just across the passage, a bakery.

PETIT PHILIPPE/GETTY IMAGES ©

HEMIS/ALAMY STOCK PHOTO ©

Paris' Best Cafes

Outstanding coffee is guaranteed at innovative **Beans on Fire** (Map p58; www.thebeansonfire.com; 7 rue du Général Blaise, 11e; ⌚8.30am-5pm Mon-Fri, 9.30am-6pm Sat & Sun; 📶; Ⓜ St-Ambroise), a welcoming local cafe, overlooking a park, and collaborative roastery, where movers and shakers on Paris' reignited coffee scene come to roast their beans (ask about two-hour roasting workshops, in English).

Part of the new co-working cafe scene, **Nuage** (Map p64; ☎09 82 39 80 69; www.nuagecafe.fr; 14 rue des Carmes, 5e; per hr/day €5/25; ⌚8.30am-7pm Mon-Fri, 11am-8pm Sat & Sun; 📶; Ⓜ Maubert-Mutualité) lures a loyal following of digital creatives with its cosy, home-like spaces in an old church. Pay by the hour or day.

With its black-and-white floor, Christian Lacroix butterflies fluttering across one wall and perfect love-heart-embossed cappuccinos, **Hardware Société** (Map p62; ☎01 42 51 69 03; 10 rue Lamarck, 18e; ⌚9am-4pm Mon-Fri, 9.30am-4.30pm Sat & Sun; 📶; Ⓜ Château Rouge) is a fine spot near Sacré-Cœur to linger over superb barista-crafted coffee (yes, that's a Slayer espresso machine). This Paris outpost of the Melbourne cafe has bountiful breakfasts and brunches served at marble-topped tables.

options (tuna gravlax with black quinoa and guacamole).

Montmartre & Northern Paris

Le Syndicat Cocktail Bar

(Map p58; www.syndicatcocktailclub.com; 51 rue du Faubourg St-Denis, 10e; ⌚6pm-2am Mon-Sat, from 7pm Sun; Ⓜ Château d'Eau) Plastered top to bottom in peeling posters, an otherwise unmarked façade conceals one of Paris' hottest cocktail bars, but it's no fly-by-night. Le Syndicat's subtitle, Organisation de Défense des Spiritueux Français, reflects its impassioned commitment to French spirits. Ingeniously crafted (and named) cocktails include Saix en Provence (Armagnac, chilli syrup, lime and lavender).

Pavillon Puebla Beer Garden

(Map p58; www.leperchoir.tv; Parc des Buttes Chaumont, 39 av Simon Bolivar, 19e; ⌚6pm-2am Wed-Fri, from noon Sat, noon-10pm Sun; 📶; Ⓜ Buttes Chaumont) Strung with fairy lights, this rustic ivy-draped cottage's two rambling terraces in the Parc des Buttes Chaumont evoke a *guinguette* (old-fashioned outdoor tavern/dance venue), with a 21st-century vibe provided by its Moroccan decor, contemporary furniture, and DJ beats from Thursdays to Saturdays. Alongside mostly French wines and craft beers, cocktails include its signature Spritz du Pavillon (Aperol, Prosecco and soda).

Gravity Bar Cocktail Bar

(Map p58; 44 rue des Vinaigriers, 10e; ⌚6pm-2am Tue-Sat; Ⓜ Jacques Bonsergent) Gravity's stunning wave-like interior, crafted from slats of plywood descending to the curved concrete bar, threatens to distract from the business at hand – serious cocktails, such as Back to My Roots (Provence herb-infused vodka, vermouth, raspberry purée and lemon juice), best partaken in the company of excellent and inventive tapas-style small plates such as clam gnocchi.

Le Marais & Around

Candelaria Cocktail Bar

(Map p58; www.quixotic-projects.com; 52 rue de Saintonge, 3e; ⌚bar 6pm-2am, taqueria noon-10.30pm Sun-Wed, to 11.30pm Thu-Sat; Ⓜ Filles du Calvaire) A lime-green *taqueria* serving homemade tacos, quesadillas and tostadas conceals one of Paris' coolest cocktail bars through an unmarked internal door. Phenomenal cocktails made from agave spirits, including mezcal, are inspired by Central and South America.

EQROY/SHUTTERSTOCK ©

Shakespeare & Company

Le Perchoir Rooftop Bar

(Map p58; ☎01 48 06 18 48; www.leperchoir.tv; 14 rue Crespin du Gast, 11e; ⏲6pm-2am Tue-Fri, from 4pm Sat; 📶; Ⓜ Ménilmontant) Sunset is the best time to head up to this 7th-floor bar for a drink overlooking Paris' rooftops, where DJs spin on Saturday nights. Greenery provides shade in summer; in winter, it's covered by a sail-like canopy and warmed by fires burning in metal drums.

Latin Quarter

Shakespeare & Company Café Cafe

(Map p64; ☎01 43 25 95 95; 2 rue St-Julien le Pauvre, 5e; ⏲9.30am-7pm Mon-Fri, to 8pm Sat & Sun; 📶; Ⓜ St-Michel) 🍃 Instant history was made when this literary-inspired cafe opened in 2015 adjacent to magical bookshop **Shakespeare & Company** (Map p64; ☎01 43 25 40 93; www.shakespeareandcompany.com; 37 rue de la Bûcherie, 5e; ⏲10am-10pm), designed from long-lost sketches to fulfil a dream of late bookshop founder George Whitman from the 1960s. Organic chai tea, turbo-power juices and coffee marry with soups, salads, bagels and pastries.

Little Bastards Cocktail Bar

(Map p64; ☎01 43 54 28 33; www.facebook.com/lilbastards; 5 rue Blainville, 5e; ⏲6pm-2am Mon-Thu, 6pm-4am Fri & Sat; Ⓜ Place Monge) Only house-creation cocktails (€12) are listed on the menu at uberhip Little Bastards – among them Balance Ton Cochon (bacon-infused rum, egg white, lime juice, oak wood–smoked syrup and bitters) and Deep Throat (Absolut vodka, watermelon syrup and Pernod). The bartenders will mix up classics too if you ask.

St-Germain & Les Invalides

Au Sauvignon Wine Bar

(Map p64; ☎01 45 48 49 02; http://ausauvignon.com; 80 rue des Sts-Pères, 7e; ⏲8am-11pm Mon-Sat, 9am-10pm Sun; Ⓜ Sèvres-Babylone) Grab a table in the evening light at this authentic wine bar or head to the bistro interior, with original zinc bar, packed tables and hand-painted ceiling celebrating French viticultural tradition. A plate of *casse-croûtes au pain Poilâne* (toast with ham, pâté, terrine, smoked salmon and foie gras) is the perfect accompaniment.

Les Deux Magots Cafe

(Map p56; ☎01 45 48 55 25; www.lesdeuxmagots.fr; 170 bd St-Germain, 6e; ⊙7.30am-1am; MSt-Germain des Prés) If ever there was a cafe that summed up St-Germain des Prés' early-20th-century literary scene, it's this former hang-out of anyone who was anyone. You'll spend substantially more here than elsewhere to sip *un café* (€4.70) in a wicker-woven bistro chair on the pavement terrace shaded by dark-green awnings and geraniums spilling from window boxes, but it's an undeniable piece of Parisian history.

Le Bar des Prés Cocktail Bar

(Map p64; ☎01 43 25 87 67; www.lebardespres.com; 25 rue du Dragon, 6e; ⊙noon-2.30pm & 7-11pm; MSt-Sulpice) Sake-based craft cocktails and tantalising shared plates (€18 to €24) by a Japanese chef create buzz at the chic cocktail-bar arm of Cyril Lignac's foodie empire on rue du Dragon – his glam, 1950s-styled **bistro** (Map p64; ☎01 45 48 29 68; www.restaurantauxpres.com; 27 rue du Dragon, 6e; 2-/3-course menu €38/49; ⊙noon-2.30pm & 7-11pm) is right next door. The scallops with caramelised miso, avocado and fresh coriander are heavenly, as is the yellow tail sashimi, jellied eel and other sushi.

ENTERTAINMENT

Opéra Bastille Opera

(Map p58; ☎international calls 01 71 25 24 23, within France 08 92 89 90 90; www.operadeparis.fr; 2-6 place de la Bastille, 12e; ⊙box office 11.30am-6.30pm Mon-Sat, 1hr prior to performances Sun; MBastille) Paris' premier opera hall, Opéra Bastille's 2745-seat main auditorium also stages ballet and classical concerts. Online tickets go on sale up to three weeks before telephone or box-office sales (from noon on Wednesdays; online flash sales offer significant discounts). Standing-only tickets (*places débouts;* €5) are available 90 minutes before performances. French-language 90-minute **guided tours** take you backstage.

Palais Garnier Opera, Ballet

(Map p56; place de l'Opéra, 9e; MOpéra) The city's original opera house (p55) is smaller than its Bastille counterpart, but has perfect acoustics. Due to its odd shape, some

Palais Garnier

SONGQUAN DENG/SHUTTERSTOCK ©

seats have limited or no visibility – book carefully. Ticket prices and conditions (including last-minute discounts) are available from the **box office** (Map p56; international calls 01 71 25 24 23, within France 08 92 89 90 90; www.operadeparis.fr; cnr rues Scribe & Auber; 10am-6.30pm Mon-Sat; Opéra). Online flash sales are held from noon on Wednesdays.

INFORMATION

MEDICAL SERVICES

Paris has some 50 hospitals, including the following:

Hôpital Hôtel Dieu (01 42 34 88 19; www.aphp.fr; 1 Parvis Notre Dame – place Jean-Paul-II, 4e; Cité) One of the city's main government-run public hospitals; after 8pm use the emergency entrance on rue de la Cité.

L'Institut Hospitalier Franco-Britannique (IHFB; 01 47 59 59 59; www.ihfb.org; 4 rue Kléber, Levallois-Perret; Anatole France) Private, English-speaking option.

Pharmacies (chemists) are marked by a large illuminated green cross outside. At least one in each neighbourhood is open for extended hours; find a complete night-owl listing on the Paris Convention & Visitors Bureau website (www.parisinfo.com).

Pharmacie Bader (01 43 26 92 66; www.pharmaciebader.com; 10-12 bd St-Michel, 6e; 8.30am-9pm; St-Michel)

Pharmacie de la Mairie (01 42 78 53 58; www.pharmacie-mairie-paris.com; 9 rue des Archives, 4e; 9am-8pm; Hôtel de Ville)

Pharmacie Les Champs (01 45 62 02 41; Galerie des Champs-Élysées, 84 av des Champs-Élysées, 8e; 24hr; George V)

TOURIST INFORMATION

Paris Convention & Visitors Bureau (Paris Office de Tourisme; 01 49 52 42 63; www.parisinfo.com; 29 rue de Rivoli, 4e; 9am-7pm; ; Hôtel de Ville) Paris' main tourist office is at the Hôtel de Ville. It sells tickets for tours and several attractions, plus museum and transport passes.

Life Is a Cabaret

Whirling lines of feather-boa-clad, high-kicking dancers at grand-scale cabarets like the cancan creator, the Moulin Rouge, are a quintessential fixture on Paris' entertainment scene – for everyone but Parisians. Still, the dazzling sets, costumes and dancing guarantee an entertaining evening (or matinee).

Moulin Rouge (Map p62; 01 53 09 82 82; www.moulinrouge.fr; 82 bd de Clichy, 18e; show only from €87, lunch & show from €165, dinner & show from €190; show only 2.45pm, 9pm & 11pm, lunch & show 1.45pm, dinner & show 7pm; Blanche) Immortalised in Toulouse-Lautrec's posters and later in Baz Luhrmann's film, Paris' legendary cabaret twinkles beneath a 1925 replica of its original red windmill. Yes, it's packed with bus-tour crowds. But from the opening bars of music to the last high cancan kick, it's a whirl of fantastical costumes, sets, choreography and Champagne. Book in advance and dress smartly. No entry for children under six years.

Au Lapin Agile (Map p62; 01 46 06 85 87; www.au-lapin-agile.com; 22 rue des Saules, 18e; adult €28, student except Sat €20; 9pm-1am Tue-Sun; Lamarck–Caulaincourt) Named after *Le Lapin à Gill*, a mural of a rabbit jumping out of a cooking pot by caricaturist André Gill, which can still be seen on the western exterior wall, this rustic cabaret venue was favoured by artists and intellectuals in the early 20th century and traditional *chansons* are still performed here.

Moulin Rouge

GETTING THERE & AWAY

AIR

Most international airlines fly to **Aéroport de Charles de Gaulle** (CDG; 01 70 36 39 50; www.parisaeroport.fr), 28km northeast of central Paris. In French the airport is commonly called 'Roissy' after the suburb in which it is located.

Aéroport d'Orly (ORY; 01 70 36 39 50; www.parisaeroport.fr) is 19km south of central Paris, but, despite being closer than CDG, it is not as frequently used by international airlines, and public-transport options aren't quite as straightforward.

TRAIN

Gare du Nord (www.gares-sncf.com; rue de Dunkerque, 10e; M Gare du Nord) Eurostar's (www.eurostar.com) London–Paris line runs from St Pancras International to Gare du Nord, taking 2¼ hours. Thalys (www.thalys.com) trains pull into Paris' Gare du Nord from Brussels, Amsterdam and Cologne.

Gare de Lyon (bd Diderot, 12e; M Gare de Lyon) Trains from Lyon, Provence, the Côte d'Azur, the French Alps, Italy, Spain and Switzerland.

Gare de l'Est (www.gares-sncf.com; place du 11 Novembre 1918, 10e; M Gare de l'Est) Trains from Luxembourg, southern Germany (Frankfurt, Munich, Stuttgart) and further east (including a weekly Moscow service). Regular and TGV Est trains to areas of France east of Paris (Champagne, Alsace and Lorraine).

Gare St-Lazare (www.gares-sncf.com; rue Intérieure, 8e; M St-Lazare) The terminus for trains from Normandy.

Gare Montparnasse (av du Maine & bd de Vaugirard, 15e; M Montparnasse Bienvenüe) Services from Brittany, the Loire Valley, Bordeaux, Toulouse, and Spain and Portugal. Some of these services will move to Gare d'Austerlitz by 2021, once refurbishment is complete.

Gare d'Austerlitz (bd de l'Hôpital, 13e; M Gare d'Austerlitz) Terminus for a handful of trains from the south, including services from Orléans, Limoges and Toulouse. High-speed trains to/from Barcelona and Madrid also use Austerlitz.

GETTING AROUND

BICYCLE

Paris is increasingly bike-friendly, with more cycling lanes and efforts from the city of Paris to reduce the number of cars on the roads. The **Vélib'** (01 76 49 12 34; www.velib-metropole.fr; day/week subscription for up to 5 people €5/15, standard bike hire up to 30/60min free/€1, electric bike €1/2) bike-share scheme changed operators in 2018; check the website for the latest information. When the handover is complete, it will put tens of thousands of bikes (30% of them electric) at 1400 stations throughout Paris.

BOAT

Batobus (www.batobus.com; adult/child 1-day pass €17/8, 2-day pass €19/10; 10am-9.30pm late Apr-Aug, shorter hours Sep-late Apr) runs glassed-in trimarans that dock every 20 to 25 minutes at nine small piers along the Seine, including Eiffel Tower, Musée d'Orsay, St-Germain des Prés, Notre Dame, Musée du Louvre and Champs-Élysées. Buy tickets online, at ferry stops or at tourist offices.

PUBLIC TRANSPORT

Paris' underground network consists of two separate but linked systems: the metro and the Réseau Express Régional (RER) suburban train line. The metro has 14 numbered lines; the RER has five main lines (but you'll probably only need to use A, B and C). When buying tickets consider how many zones your journey will cover; if you travel from Charles de Gaulle airport to Paris, for instance, buy a ticket for zones 1 to 5.

For information on the metro, RER and bus systems, visit www.ratp.fr. Metro maps are available for free at ticket windows, or download for free from the website.

The Mobilis and Paris Visite passes are valid on the metro, the RER, SNCF's suburban lines, buses, night buses, trams and the Montmartre funicular railway.

Mobilis Allows unlimited travel for one day and costs €7.50 (for two zones) to €17.80 (five zones).

Paris Visite Unlimited travel and other discounts. The 'Paris Centre' pass (zones 1 to 3) costs €12/26.65 for one/three days.

Where to Stay

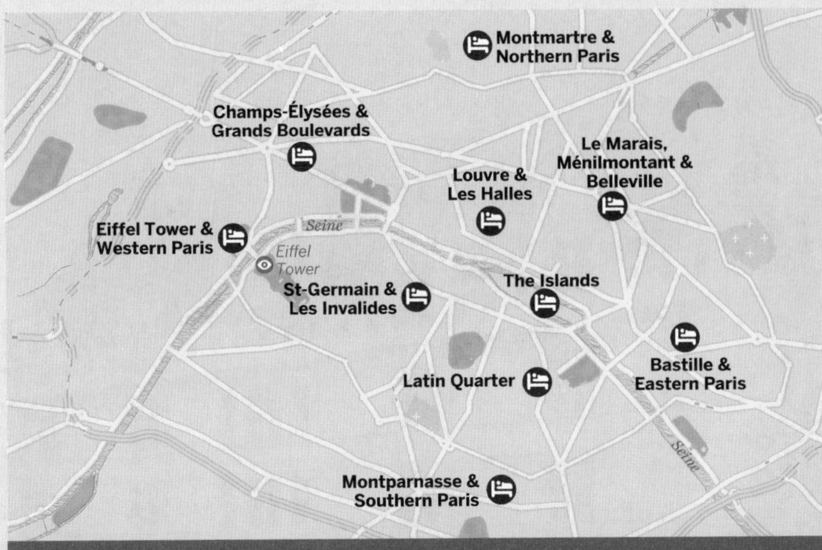

Neighbourhood	Atmosphere
Eiffel Tower & Western Paris	Close to Paris' iconic tower and museums. Upmarket area with quiet residential streets. Short on budget and midrange accommodation. Limited nightlife.
Champs-Élysées & Grands Boulevards	Luxury hotels, famous boutiques and department stores, gastronomic restaurants, great nightlife. Some areas pricey.
Louvre & Les Halles	Epicentral location, excellent transport links, major museums, shopping galore. Not many bargains. Noise can be an issue.
Montmartre & Northern Paris	Village atmosphere, views across Paris. Hilly streets; further out than some areas; some parts very touristy. Pigalle's red-light district, although well lit and safe, won't appeal to all travellers.
Le Marais, Ménilmontant & Belleville	Buzzing nightlife, hip shopping, fantastic eating options in all price ranges. Excellent museums. Lively gay and lesbian scene. Very central. Can be noisy in areas that have bars and clubs.
Bastille & Eastern Paris	Few tourists, allowing you to see the 'real' Paris up close. Excellent markets, loads of nightlife. Some areas slightly out of the way.
The Islands	Accommodation centred on the peaceful, romantic Île St-Louis. No metro station on the Île St-Louis. Limited self-catering shops.
Latin Quarter	Energetic student area, stacks of eating and drinking options, late-opening bookshops. Rooms hardest to find during conferences and seminars from March to June and in October.
St-Germain & Les Invalides	Stylish, central location, superb shopping, sophisticated dining, close to Jardin du Luxembourg. Limited budget accommodation.
Montparnasse & Southern Paris	Good value, few tourists, excellent links to both major airports. Some areas out of the way and/or not well served by metro.

Château d'Azay-le-Rideau (p86)

LOIRE VALLEY

ANTOINE BARTHELEMY/ANTOINEBARTHELEMYPHOTOGRAPHY/500PX ©

In This Chapter

Loire Valley at a Glance...

If it's French splendour, style and gastronomy you seek, the Loire Valley will exceed your expectations. The entire area is an enormous Unesco World Heritage Site, poised on the crucial frontier between northern and southern France and a short train or autoroute ride from Paris. Kings, queens, dukes and nobles came here to establish feudal castles and, later on, sumptuous pleasure palaces.

With crenellated towers, soaring cupolas and glittering banquet halls, the region's châteaux attest to more than a thousand years of architectural and artistic creativity. The area is also known for its outstanding wines (red, white, rosé and sparkling).

Two Days in the Loire Valley

Limber up with **Château de Cheverny** (p92) before heading to **Chambord** (p82) for a cafe lunch and to tour the extravagant château. Head to **Blois** (p90) for an early-evening **old-city** (p90) stroll, dinner and an after-dark **son et lumière** (p92) show. Second day, visit **Chenonceau** (p84), then continue to **Azay-le-Rideau** (p86) or **Villandry** (p88).

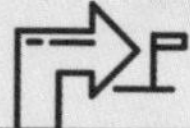

Four Days in the Loire Valley

Change the pace with some languid meandering around elegant Amboise and its royal **château** (p94) on day three. Buy a picnic lunch at its **Sunday food market** (p94) or dine in style at **L'Écluse** (p94). Devote the afternoon to the maker of the *Mona Lisa* at **Le Clos Lucé** (p93). On day four, rent some wheels and pedal your way along the river.

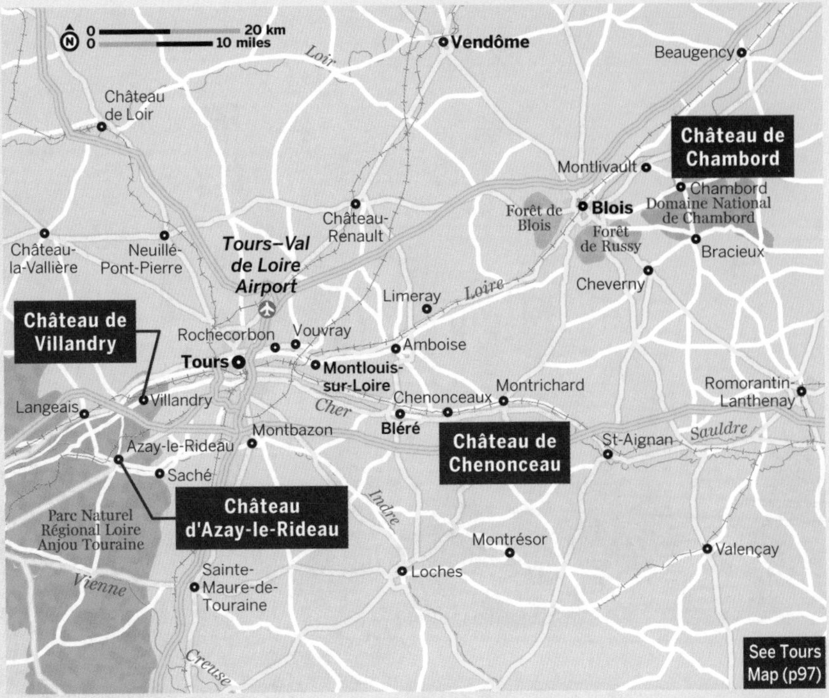

See Tours Map (p97)

Arriving in the Loire Valley

Tours–Val de Loire Airport Located 6km northeast of the town centre.

Tours Centre & St-Pierre-des-Corps Regular trains and a few TGVs use the city-centre train station, Tours-Centre; other TGV trains stop only at St-Pierre-des-Corps, 3km east and linked to Tours-Centre by frequent shuttle and TER trains.

Where to Stay

The Loire Valley has an enormous selection of places to stay. If you're on a budget, it's usually possible to find room in a rural *chambre d'hôte* (B&B) or a small hotel for as little as €65 a night for two, while travellers in the mood for luxury have options that range from 18th-century mansions to sumptuous suites in Renaissance châteaux.

Château de Chambord

One of the crowning achievements of French Renaissance architecture, Château de Chambord – with 426 rooms, 282 fireplaces and 77 staircases – is the Loire Valley's largest, grandest and most visited château.

Great For...

☑ Don't Miss

Summertime equestrian shows (adult/child €14.50/11; 45 minutes; April to September) with riders in medieval garb and birds of prey.

Begun in 1519 by François I (r 1515–47) as a weekend hunting lodge, Château de Chambord quickly grew into one of the most ambitious – and expensive – architectural projects ever attempted by a French monarch. In the end he stayed here for just 72 days during his entire 32-year reign.

Royal Quarters

Inside the main building, a film (subtitled in five languages) provides an excellent introduction to the château's history and architecture. On the ground floor you can visit 18th-century kitchens, while the 1st floor is where you'll find the most interesting (though lightly furnished) rooms, including the royal bedchambers. Rising through the centre of the structure, the world-famous double-helix staircase – very possibly designed by the king's chum Leonardo da

Royal bedchambers

TOMSICKOVA TATYANA/SHUTTERSTOCK ©

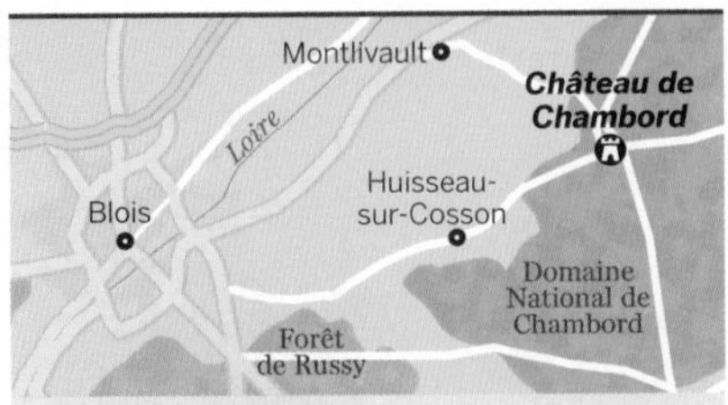

Need to Know

info 02 54 50 40 00, tour & show reservations 02 54 50 50 40; www.chambord.org; adult/child €13/free, parking distant/near €4/6; 9am-6pm Apr-Oct, to 5pm Nov-Mar

Take a Break

In the château cafe or drive to downtown Blois for lunch on the pretty terrace at Les Planches (p91).

★ Top Tip

DIY tour with audioguide (adult/child €5/3) or a Histopad tablet (€6.50) with a treasure hunt for kids.

Vinci – ascends to the great lantern tower and the rooftop, where you can marvel at a veritable skyline of cupolas, domes, turrets, chimneys and lightning rods and gaze out across the vast grounds.

First Modern Building

The quintessential French Renaissance château is a mix of classical components and decorative motifs (columns, tunnel vaults, round arches, domes etc) with the rich decoration of Flamboyant Gothic. It ultimately showcased wealth, ancestry and refinement. Defensive towers (a historical seigniorial symbol) were incorporated into a new decorative architecture, typified by its three-dimensional use of pilasters and arcaded loggias, terraces, balconies, exterior staircases, turrets and gabled chimneys. Heraldic symbols were sculpted on soft stone façades, above doorways and fireplaces, and across coffered ceilings.

Domaine National de Chambord

The 54-sq-km hunting reserve around the Château de Chambord – the largest walled park in Europe – is reserved for the exclusive use of very high-ranking French government officials. About 10 sq km of the park, north and northwest of the château, is open to the public, with trails for walkers, cyclists and horse riders.

Outdoor Action

Hire bikes, *rosalies* (pedal carts), *golfettes* (electric golf carts), rowboats and electric boats at a **rental kiosk** (02 54 50 40 00; hire bicycle 1/4hr €6/15, rowboat 1hr €12, golf cart 45min €25; 10am-6.30pm Apr-early Nov) near the *embarcadère* (dock) midway between the Château de Chambord and its entrance pavilion. From April to early November, carriage rides (adult/child €11/6) begin at the château's *écurie* (stables).

Château de Chenonceau

Spanning the languid Cher River atop a graceful arched bridge, Chenonceau is one of France's most elegant châteaux. Its formal gardens, glorious setting and stylised architecture are the embodiment of French romance.

Great For...

☑ Don't Miss

On the upper level of the gallery, the **Galerie Médicis**, a well-presented exhibition (in French and English) on the château's colourful history.

Powerful Women

This extraordinary complex is largely the work of several remarkable women, hence its nickname, Château des Dames. The initial phase of construction started in 1515 for Thomas Bohier, a court minister of Charles VIII's, although much of the work and design was actually overseen by his wife, Katherine.

The distinctive arches and the eastern formal garden were added by Diane de Poitiers, mistress of Henri II. Following Henri's death Catherine de Médicis, the king's scheming widow, forced Diane (her second cousin) to exchange Chenonceau for the rather less grand Château de Chaumont. Catherine completed the château's construction and added the yew-tree maze and the western rose garden. Louise of Lorraine's most singular contribution was her black-walled mourning room on the top

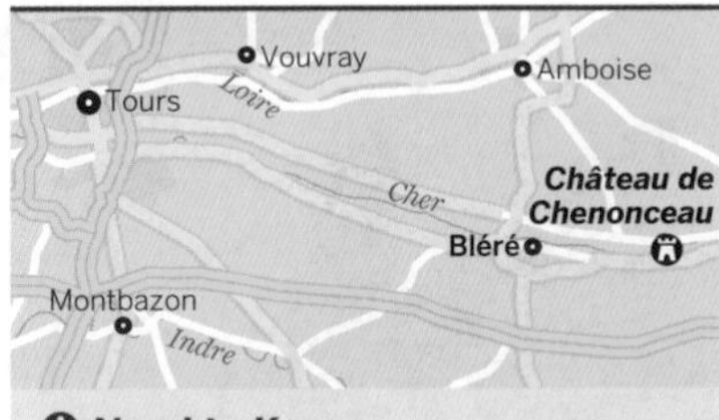

Need to Know

☎02 47 23 90 07; www.chenonceau.com; adult/child €14/11, with audioguide €18/14.50; ⌚9am-6.30pm or later Apr-Oct, to 5pm or 6pm Nov-Mar

Take a Break

Mid-March to mid-November, lunch in gastronomic French restaurant **L'Orangerie**, in the castle grounds.

★ Top Tip

Grab an audioguide, plus the kid's iPod version for seven to 12 year olds.

floor, to which she retreated when her husband, Henri III, was assassinated in 1589.

Chenonceau had an 18th-century heyday under the aristocratic Madame Dupin, who made the château a centre of fashionable society; guests included Voltaire and Rousseau. During the Revolution, at the age of 83, she was able to save the château from destruction at the hands of angry mobs thanks to quick thinking and some strategic concessions.

Grande Galerie

The château's pièce de résistance is the 60m-long, chequerboard-floored Grande Galerie over the Cher, scene of many an elegant party hosted by Catherine de Médicis and Madame Dupin. Used as a military hospital during WWI, it served from 1940 to 1942 as an escape route for *résistants,* Jews and other refugees fleeing from the German-occupied zone (north of the Cher) to the Vichy-controlled zone (south of the river). The upper level of the gallery, the Galerie Médicis, has a well-presented exhibition (in French and English) on the château's colourful history and the women who moulded it.

Artworks

Rare furnishings and a fabulous art collection that includes works by Tintoretto, Correggio, Rubens, Murillo, Van Dyck and Poussin decorate its other-worldly interior. Don't miss the portrait of *Les Trois Graces* (The Three Graces) by Van Loo, which hangs next to the Renaissance chimney in François I's bedroom.

How to Get There

The château is 33km east of Tours, 13km southeast of Amboise and 40km southwest of Blois. From the town of Chenonceaux (spelt with an x), just outside the château grounds, trains go to Tours (€7, 25 minutes, nine to 11 daily).

Salon de Biencourt

NAUGHTYNUT/SHUTTERSTOCK ©

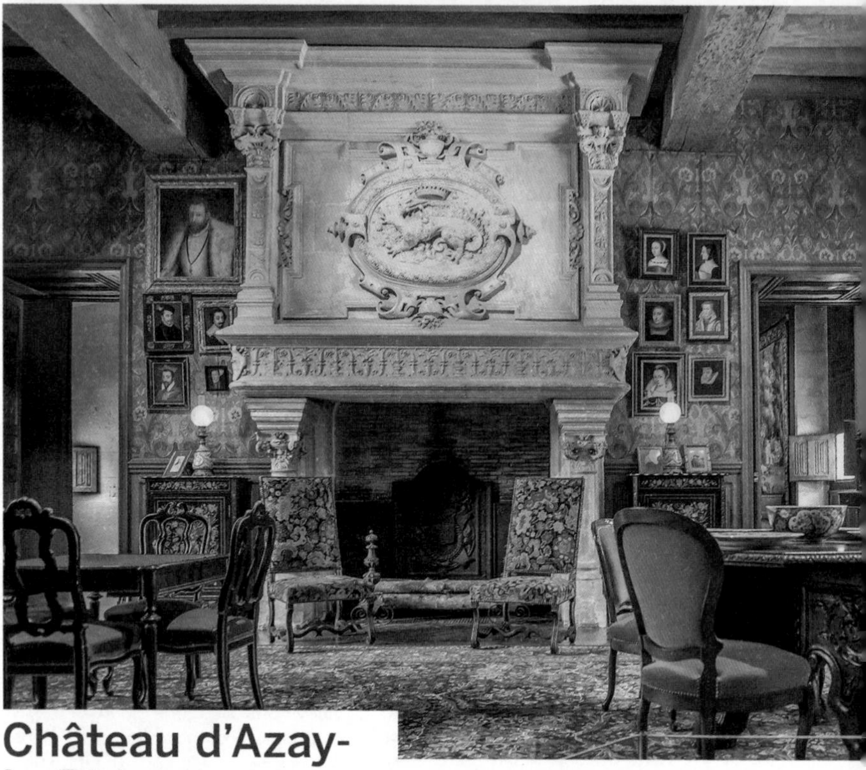

Château d'Azay-le-Rideau

Built in the early 1500s, romantic, moat-ringed Azay-le-Rideau is celebrated for its elegant turrets, perfectly proportioned windows, delicate stonework and steep slate roofs.

Great For...

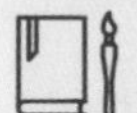

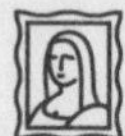

☑ Don't Miss

The **Jardin des Secrets** (April to September), featuring heritage vegetables and flowers.

The Diamond Palace

Built in the early 1500s on a natural island in the middle of the Indre River, Château d'Azay-le-Rideau is one of the Loire's loveliest castles: Honoré de Balzac called it a 'multifaceted diamond set in the River Indre'. The famous, Italian-style loggia staircase overlooking the central courtyard is decorated with the salamanders and ermines of François I and Queen Claude.

Water Mirror

Visit on a sunny day when the reflection of Azay's pearly white façade – adorned with decorative fortifications and turrets indicating the rank of the owners – shimmers like a mirage in the surrounding lily-

Need to Know

☎02 47 45 42 04; www.azay-le-rideau.fr; adult/child €10.50/free, audioguide €3; ⏲9.30am-11pm Jul & Aug, to 6pm Apr-Jun & Sep, 10am-5.15pm Oct-Mar

Take a Break

Gastronomic French on an idyllic terrace at **Auberge du XIIe Siècle**, 7km east in Saché.

★ Top Tip

Audioguides are available in five languages; one-hour guided tours in French are free.

pricked waters. This *miroir d'eau* was only created in the 1950s when one branch of the river was extended in order for the water to lick the château walls.

Château Interior

The interior decor of the château is mostly 19th century, created by the Marquis Charles de Biencourt (who bought the property after the Revolution) and his heirs. The Salon de Biencourt was given historically coherent furnishings – plucked from the extensive collection of the French government – and comprehensively restored to its 19th-century glory in 2016. The lovely English-style gardens were restored and partly replanted from 2015 to 2017.

Azay the Burnt

The fate of the old Gallo-Roman settlement of Azay has been inextricably linked to that of its château, ever since the first defensive edifice was razed in the Middle Ages. The bloodiest incident in its history occurred in 1418 when the crown prince (later Charles VII) was insulted by a Burgundian guard during a visit to Azay's fortified castle. Enraged, the future king had the town burned to the ground and executed 350 soldiers and officers. For a period the town became known as Azay-le-Brûlé (Azay the Burnt).

How to Get There

Azay-le-Rideau is 26km southwest of Tours. The D84 and D17, on either side of the Indre, are great for countryside cycling. The train station, 2.5km west of the château, is linked to Tours (€5.90, 26/41 minutes by train/bus, six to eight daily) and Chinon (€5.30, 20 minutes, six to 11 daily).

Château de Villandry

Villandry's six glorious landscaped gardens are among France's finest, with more than 6 hectares of cascading flowers, ornamental vines, manicured lime trees, razor-sharp box hedges and tinkling fountains.

Great For...

☑ Don't Miss

Gardening workshops during late September's two-day garden festival, **Journées du Potager**.

Gardens

The original gardens and château were built by Jean Le Breton, who served François I as finance minister and ambassador to Italy (and supervised the construction of Chambord). During his ambassadorial service, Le Breton became enamoured with the art of Italian Renaissance gardening, later creating his own ornamental masterpiece at newly constructed Villandry. The current gardens, tended by 10 full-time expert gardeners, were recreated starting in 1908.

Wandering the garden's pebbled walkways, you'll see the classical **Jardin d'Eau** (Water Garden), the hornbeam **Labyrinthe** (Maze) and the **Jardin d'Ornement** (Ornamental Garden),

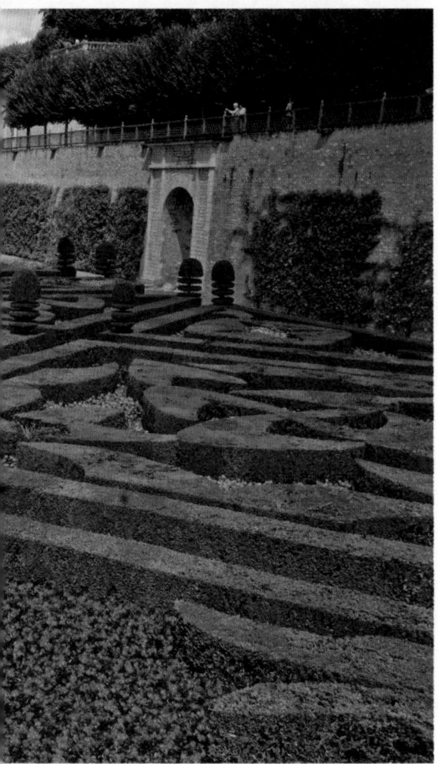

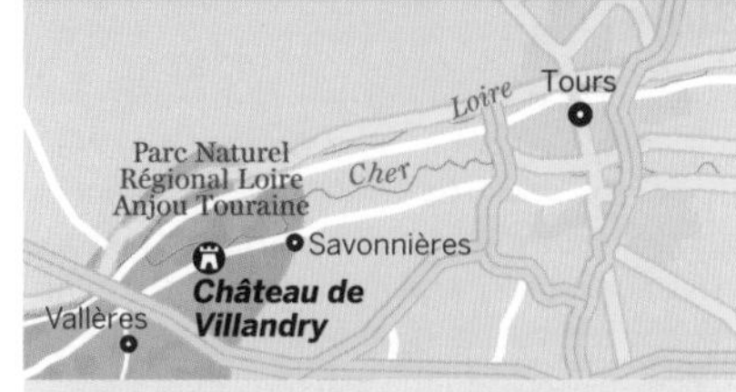

Need to Know

☎02 47 50 02 09; www.chateauvillandry.com; 3 rue Principale; chateau & gardens adult/child €11/7, gardens only €7/5, cheaper Dec-Feb, audioguide €4; ⏰9am-5pm or 6.30pm year-round, château interior closed mid-Nov–late Dec & early Jan-early Feb

Take a Break

There are several restaurants and a *boulangerie* (bakery) near Villandry's parking area.

★ Top Tip

Visit when the gardens – all of them organic – are blooming, between April and October.

which depicts various aspects of love (fickle, passionate, tender and tragic) using geometrically pruned hedges and coloured flowerbeds. The **Jardin du Soleil** (Sun Garden) is a looser array of gorgeous multicoloured and multiscented perennials. But for many the highlight is the 16th-century-style **Jardin des Simples** (Kitchen Garden), where cabbages, leeks and carrots are laid out to create nine geometrical, colour-coordinated squares.

Tickets are valid all day (get your hand stamped).

Inside the Château

After the gardens, the Renaissance château (built in the 1530s), surrounded by a watery moat, is a bit of a let-down. Nevertheless, highlights include the **Oriental Drawing Room**, with a gilded Moorish ceiling taken from a 15th-century palace near Toledo, and a gallery of Spanish and Flemish art. Best of all are the bird's-eye views across the gardens and the nearby Loire and Cher Rivers from the top of the 12th-century **donjon** (the only remnant of the original medieval château) and three **belvédères** (hillside panoramic viewpoints).

How to Get There

The château is 16km southwest of Tours and 11km northeast of Azay-le-Rideau. Trains link Savonnières, 4km northeast of Villandry, with Tours (€3.50, 13 minutes, two or three daily).

Blois

Towering above the northern bank of the Loire, Blois' royal château, one-time feudal seat of the powerful counts of Blois, offers a gripping introduction to some key periods in French history and architecture. Parts of the city still have a medieval vibe, and Blois makes an excellent base for visits to the châteaux, villages and towns of the central Loire Valley.

SIGHTS

Château Royal de Blois Château

(☎02 54 90 33 33; www.chateaudeblois.fr; place du Château; adult/child €12/6.50, audioguide €4; ⏰9am-6.30pm or 7pm Apr-Oct, 10am-5pm Nov-Mar) Seven French kings lived in Blois' royal château, whose four grand wings were built during four distinct periods in French architecture: Gothic (13th century), Flamboyant Gothic (1498–1501), early Renaissance (1515–20) and classical (1630s). You can easily spend a half-day immersing yourself in the château's dramatic and bloody history and its extraordinary architecture. In July and August there are free tours in English (at 10.30am, 1.15pm and 3pm).

Old City Historic Site

Blois' medieval and Renaissance old town is well worth a stroll. The façade of **Maison des Acrobates** (3bis place St-Louis) – one of Blois' few surviving 15th-century houses – is decorated with wooden sculptures of figures from medieval farces. The **Hôtel de Villebrême** (13 rue Pierre de Blois), another 15th-century townhouse, is nearby.

The Gothic-style **Cathédrale St-Louis** (place St-Louis; ⏰9am or 10am-6pm or 7pm), rebuilt after a terrible storm in 1678, has a western façade mixing late-Gothic and neoclassical elements. The church's stained glass, bearing enigmatic Latin inscriptions, was created by Dutch artist Jan Dibbets in 2000.

Lovely panoramas unfold across town from the peaceful **Jardins de l'Évêché** (the gardens behind the cathedral) and from the top of the **Escalier Denis Papin**, a grand staircase linking rue du Palais with the commercial precinct around rue Denis Papin.

From left: Château Royal de Blois interior; Bas-relief, entrance to Château Royal de Blois; Maison de la Magie; Cathédrale St-Louis

YURI TURKOV/SHUTTERSTOCK ©

SERGEY BERESTETSKY/SHUTTERSTOCK ©

Maison de la Magie Museum

(☎02 54 90 33 33; www.maisondelamagie.fr; 1 place du Château; adult/child €10/6.50; ⏰10am-12.30pm & 2-6.30pm Apr-Aug & mid-Oct–early Nov, 2-6.30pm daily plus 10am-12.30pm Sat & Sun 1st 2 weeks Sep; 👪) This museum of magic occupies the one-time home of watchmaker, inventor and conjurer Jean Eugène Robert-Houdin (1805–71), after whom the American magician Harry Houdini named himself. Dragons emerge roaring from the windows every half-hour, while inside the museum has exhibits on Houdin and the history of magic, displays of optical trickery and several daily magic shows.

SHOPPING

La Maison des Parapluies Fashion & Accessories

(☎02 54 46 99 92; www.lamaisondesparapluies.com; 2 rue des Fossés du Château; full-size umbrella €75-100, collapsible €55-70; ⏰2.30-7pm Mon, 9.30am-1pm & 2.30-7pm Tue-Sat) One of just a handful of artisanal umbrella makers in France, Nathalie Fraudeau uses skills learned in Normandy and six specialised machines to craft each *parapluie* (umbrella) and *ambrelle* (parasol). Visitors are welcome to drop by and watch her work. Special orders (including umbrellas with a customised photo printed on the dome) take a couple of days.

EATING

Les Planches Italian $

(☎02 54 55 08 00; 5 rue Grenier à Sel; mains €11.50-14.50; ⏰noon-1.30pm & 7-9pm Tue-Sat; 📶🖉) Hidden away on a tiny stone-paved square, Les Planches is a Blois favourite for its toasted bruschettas (open-face Italian sandwiches) and meal-size salads. Romantic, with a purple light on each table. It stays open later in summer.

Le Triboulet Grill $$

(☎02 54 74 11 23; www.letriboulet.com; 18 place du Château; menus €18.50-22.50, child's menu €10.80; ⏰noon-2pm & 7-9pm daily Jul & Aug, closed Sun dinner & Mon Sep-Jun, also closed Sun lunch mid-Sep–Easter) Succulent beef, mutton and *andouillette* (sausages made from pigs' intestines), grilled on an open wood

Château de Cheverny

Perhaps the Loire's most elegantly proportioned château, **Château de Cheverny** (☎02 54 79 96 29; www.chateau-cheverny.fr; av du Château; château & gardens adult/child €11.50/8.20; ⊙9.15am-6.30pm Apr-Sep, 10am-5pm Oct-Mar) represents the zenith of French classical architecture. Highlights downstairs include the formal dining room, with 34 painted wooden panels depicting the story of Don Quixote. The arms room is full of pikestaffs, claymores, crossbows and suits of armour – including one made to measure for a four-year-old duke.

The 18th-century **Orangerie** is now a tearoom (open April to mid-November). During low-season school holidays there's a cafe near the **kennels**, which house around 100 hunting dogs.

Fans of **Tintin** might find the Château de Cheverny's façade strangely familiar: Hérgé used it as a model for Moulinsart (Marlinspike) Hall, the ancestral home of Tintin's irascible sidekick, Captain Haddock. Devotees large and small may enjoy **Les Secrets de Moulinsart** (combo ticket incl château adult/child €16/12.10), whose interactive exhibits explore the world of Tintin.

Cheverny is 14km southeast of Blois and 18km southwest of Chambord.

Arms room display
YURI TURKOV/SHUTTERSTOCK ©

fire right in the dining room, keep connoisseurs coming back to this traditional French restaurant and its spacious terrace. Dishes are made with local products, such as mushrooms from the Sologne. Has a good selection of Touraine wines.

L'Orangerie du Château Gastronomy **$$$**
(☎02 54 78 05 36; www.orangerie-du-chateau.fr; 1 av du Dr Jean Laigret; menus €40-86; ⊙noon-1.45pm & 7-9.15pm Tue-Sat; P) This Michelin-starred restaurant serves *cuisine gastronomique inventive* inspired by both French tradition and culinary ideas brought from faraway lands. The excellent wine list comes on a tablet computer. For dessert try the house speciality, *soufflé chaud* (hot soufflé).

ENTERTAINMENT

Son et Lumière Live Performance
(Sound & Light Show; ☎02 54 90 33 33; Château Royal de Blois; adult/child €10.50/6.50; ⊙10pm or 10.30pm late Apr-late Sep) A sound-and-light show brings the château's history and architecture to life with dramatic lighting and narration; an all-new 360-degree *spectacle* was inaugurated in 2018.

INFORMATION

Tourist Office (☎02 54 90 41 41; www.blois-chambord.co.uk; 6 rue de la Voûte du Château; ⊙9am-7pm Apr-Sep, 10am-12.30pm & 2-5pm Mon-Sat, plus Sun school holidays, Oct-Mar) Has maps of the town and sells châteaux combo and concert tickets. A smartphone audioguide of Blois (in French and English) can be downloaded via the website. Sells walking-tour brochures (€2) in six languages.

GETTING THERE & AWAY

BUS

The tourist office has a brochure detailing public-transport options to nearby châteaux.

A *navette* (shuttle bus; €6) run by **Rémi** (☎02 54 58 55 44; www.remi-centrevaldeloire.fr) makes it possible to do a Blois–Chambord–Cheverny–Beauregard–Blois circuit on Wednesday, Saturday and Sunday from early April to 5 November.

From early April to August, this line runs daily during school-holiday periods and on public holidays.

TRAIN

Blois-Chambord train station (av Dr Jean Laigret) is 600m west (up the hill) from Blois' château.

Amboise €7.20, 20 minutes, 15 to 20 daily

Orléans €11.50, 25 to 56 minutes, 17 to 24 daily

Paris Gare d'Austerlitz €18 to €32.40, 1½ hours, five direct daily

Tours €11.20, 30 to 46 minutes, 16 to 22 daily

GETTING AROUND

Just outside the city centre, all-day parking costs €5 in green parking zones. For free parking, head to the train-station area, quai du Foix (on the riverfront towards Pont Mitterrand) or quai St-Jean (next to the Police Nationale).

Royal Connection (☎06 98 43 82 15; http://royal-connection.fr) Transport to Chambord or Cheverny costs €25 per person (minimum two people); a circuit to two or three sites costs €40 to €59 per person. Reservations can be made via Blois' tourist office.

Taxi Radio Blois (☎02 54 78 07 65) Based at the train station.

Amboise

Elegant Amboise, childhood home of Charles VIII and final resting place of the incomparable Leonardo da Vinci, is gorgeously situated on the southern bank of the Loire, guarded by a soaring château. With some seriously posh hotels, outstanding dining and one of France's most vivacious weekly markets (on Sunday morning), Amboise is a convivial base for exploring the Loire countryside and nearby châteaux by car or bicycle.

SIGHTS

As you walk up to Le Clos Lucé, keep an eye out for the **habitats troglodytiques** (cave houses) carved into the rock face overlooking rue Victor Hugo. Pedestrian-only **rue Nationale** is packed with attractive boutiques.

Le Clos Lucé Historic Building

(☎02 47 57 00 73; www.vinci-closluce.com; 2 rue du Clos Lucé; adult/child €15.50/11, mid-Nov–Feb €13.50/10.50; ⏲9am-7pm or 8pm Feb-Oct, 9am or 10am-6pm Nov-Jan, last entry 1hr before closing; 👪) It was at the invitation of François I that Leonardo da Vinci (1452–1519), aged 64, took up residence in this grand manor house, built in 1471. An admirer of the Italian Renaissance, the French monarch named Da Vinci 'first painter, engineer and king's architect', and the Italian spent his time here sketching, tinkering and dreaming up ingenious contraptions.

Château Gaillard Château

(☎02 47 30 33 29; www.chateau-gaillard-amboise.fr; 95-97 av Léonard de Vinci & 29 allée du Pont Moulin; adult/child €12/8; ⏲1-7pm Apr-early Nov) The most exciting Loire château to open to visitors in years, Gaillard is the earliest expression of the Italian Renaissance in France. Begun in 1496, the château was

Nature Reserve

The 54-sq-km **hunting reserve** around the Château de Chambord – the largest walled park in Europe – is a great place for wildlife spotting, especially during the deer mating season between mid-September and mid-October. Five observatories let you discreetly view the park's residents; set out at dawn or dusk to maximise your chances of spotting stags, boars, red deer and wild sheep. To visit parts of the reserve normally closed to the public, take a 1½-hour **Land Rover safari tour** (☎02 54 50 50 40; www.chambord.org; adult/child €18/12; ⏲up to 6 times a day summer, 1-3 times a day winter) conducted by French-speaking guides; most speak at least a bit of English. Call ahead to book.

Wine in the Loire Valley

Splendid scenery and densely packed vineyards make the Loire Valley an outstanding wine-touring destination, with a range of excellent reds, rosés, whites, dessert wines and crémants (sparkling wines). Equipped with *Sur la Route des Vins de Loire* (On the Loire Wine Route), a free map from the winegrowers association (www.vinsvaldeloire.fr), or the *Loire Valley Vineyards* booklet, available at area tourist offices and *maisons des vins* (wine visitor centres), you can put together a web of wonderful wine-tasting itineraries, drawing from over 320 wine cellars.

The predominant red is cabernet franc, though you'll also find cabernet sauvignon, pinot noir and others. Appellations (AOCs) include Anjou, Saumur-Champigny, Bourgueil and Chinon.

For whites, Vouvray's chenin blancs are excellent, and Sancerre and the appellation across the Loire River, Pouilly-Fumé, produce great sauvignon blancs. The bubbly appellation Crémant de Loire spans many communities, but you can easily find it around Montrichard (eg Château Monmousseau).

One of the most densely packed stretches for wine tasting along the Loire River itself is around Saumur. Towns with multiple tasting rooms (from west to east) include **St-Hilaire-St-Florent**, **Souzay Champigny** and **Parnay**. Just east of Tours, another hot spot includes **Rochecorbon**, **Vouvray** and **Montlouis-sur-Loire**.

inspired by the refined living that Charles VIII fell in love with during his Italian campaign. The harmonious, Renaissance-style gardens were laid out by master gardener Dom Pacello (1453–1534), an Italian Benedictine monk who brought the first orange trees to France.

Château Royal d'Amboise Château

(☎02 47 57 00 98; www.chateau-amboise.com; place Michel Debré; adult/child €11.70/7.80, incl audioguide €15.70/10.80; ⏰9am-5.45pm Dec-Feb, to btwn 6.30pm & 8pm Mar-Nov, last entry 1hr before closing) Perched atop a rocky escarpment above town, Amboise's castle was a favoured retreat for all of France's Valois and Bourbon kings. Only a few of the château's original structures survive, but you can still visit the furnished Logis (Lodge) – Gothic except for the top half of one wing, which is Renaissance – and the Flamboyant Gothic Chapelle St-Hubert (1493), where Leonardo da Vinci's presumed remains have been buried since 1863. The ramparts afford thrilling views of the town and river.

EATING

Sunday Food Market Market $

(quai du Général de Gaulle; ⏰8am-1pm Sun, small market 8am-1pm Fri) Voted France's *marché préféré* (favourite market) a few years back, this riverfront extravaganza, 400m southwest of the château, hosts 200 to 300 stalls selling both edibles and durables. Worth timing your visit around.

Le Patio Modern French $$

(☎02 47 79 00 00; 14 rue Nationale; menus lunch €19, dinner €32; ⏰noon-2pm & 7-9pm Thu-Mon, daily Jul & Aug; 📶) The friendly staff here serves creative, beautifully presented French cuisine that garners rave reviews. Specialities include *cromesquis d'escargots* (crunchy fried balls of Burgundy snails) and slow-cooked lamb shank. Has a superb wine list, a glass-roofed courtyard and a Facebook page.

L'Écluse French $$

(☎02 47 79 94 91; www.ecluse-amboise.fr; rue Racine; lunch menu €19, other menus €25-39; ⏰noon-1.30pm & 7-9pm Tue-Sat) On the banks of the bubbling L'Amasse (or La Masse) River next to an *écluse* (river lock), L'Écluse has been generating enthusiasm and glowing

GASPAR JANOS/SHUTTERSTOCK ©

Château Royal d'Amboise

reviews since the moment it opened in 2017. The sharply focused menu is made up of just three entrées, three mains and three desserts, expertly prepared with fresh seasonal products from a dozen Loire-area producers.

DRINKING & NIGHTLIFE

Le Shaker Bar

(02 47 23 24 26; 3 quai François Tissard, Île d'Or; 6pm-2am Tue, Wed, Thu & Sun, to 4am Fri & Sat) The big draw at this convivial bar on Amboise's mid-Loire island: supremely romantic views of the château. Serves beer (€3.50) and light meals, but the speciality is cocktails.

INFORMATION

Tourist Office (02 47 57 09 28; www.amboise-valdeloire.co.uk; quai du Général de Gaulle; 9am or 10am-6pm or 7pm Mon-Sat, 10am-1pm & 2-5pm Sun Apr-Oct, 10am-12.30pm & 2-5pm Mon-Sat Nov-Mar;) Very helpful. Has three free walking-tour brochures and sells cycling maps and discount combo tickets for area châteaux (also available online). You can leave your bag(s) for €2. Situated across the street from the riverfront.

Cut-Price Castle-Hopping

You can save money on visits to many of the region's châteaux – and avoid waiting in line – by buying a **Pass' Châteaux** multi-site discount ticket. For information, contact the tourist offices in Blois and at Chambord, Chaumont and Cheverny. Popular combinations include the following:

- Blois–Chambord–Cheverny €31
- Blois–Chenonceau–Chambord–Cheverny €44
- Blois–Chaumont–Chambord–Cheverny €46.50
- Blois–Chambord–Amboise–Clos Lucé €45.50

Picturesque Pedalling

Funded by 65 Blois-area municipalities, **Les Châteaux à Vélo** (www.chateauxavelo.co.uk) maintains 400km of marked bike routes to and around Blois, Chambord, Cheverny and Chaumont-sur-Loire. Get route maps, a useful smartphone app and the latest weather reports from the website, or pick up brochures at local tourist offices. **Detours de Loire** (02 54 56 07 73; www.detoursdeloire.com; 39 av Dr Jean Laigret; per half-day/day/week from €10/16/60; 9.30am or 10am-12.30pm & 2.30-6.30pm or 7pm Tue-Sat year-round, plus Mon Apr-Oct, plus 9.30am-12.30pm & 6-7pm Sun May-Sep), part of a valley-wide bike-rental network, rents bikes a block from Blois train station.

In Amboise, head to veteran bike shop **Cycles Richard** (02 47 57 01 79; 2 rue de Nazelles; day/week €14/60, electric bike per day €38; 9am-noon & 2.30-6.30pm Tue-Sat year-round), directly across the river from the town centre, or **Détours de Loire** (02 47 30 00 55; www.detoursdeloire.com; quai du Général de Gaulle; half-day/day/week €10/16/60; Apr-Sep), in an oval pavilion along the river (across from the tourist office).

Cycling, Château de Chambord (p82)
MICHAL SZYMANSKI/SHUTTERSTOCK ©

GETTING THERE & AWAY

BUS

Run by **Rémi** (02 47 31 14 00; www.remi-centrevaldeloire.fr; all destinations €2.40), bus line C links Amboise's Théâtre with Tours' Halte Routière (bus station; one hour, eight daily Monday to Saturday) and Chenonceau (22 minutes, one or two daily Monday to Saturday), from where trains go to Tours.

TRAIN

Amboise's **train station** (bd Gambetta) is 1.5km north of the château, on the opposite side of the Loire.

Blois €7.20, 20 minutes, 15 to 20 daily

Paris €18.50 to €60.50, two hours; a handful of direct trains go to Gare d'Austerlitz, other trains serve Gare Montparnasse

Tours €5.70, 13 to 23 minutes, 13 to 22 daily

Tours

Bustling Tours is a smart and vivacious city, with an impressive medieval quarter, fine museums, well-tended parks and a university of some 30,000 students. Combining the sophisticated style of Paris with the conservative sturdiness of central France, Tours makes an ideal staging post for exploring the castles of the Touraine.

SIGHTS

Musée du Compagnonnage Museum
(02 47 21 62 20; www.museecompagnonnage.fr; 8 rue Nationale & 1 square Prosper Merimée; adult/child €5.80/4; 9am-12.30pm & 2-6pm, closed Tue mid-Sep–mid-Jun) This extraordinary museum – an absolute gem! – spotlights France's renowned *compagnonnages*, guild organisations of skilled craftspeople who have created everything from medieval cathedrals to the Statue of Liberty. Dozens of professions – from carpentry to saddle-making to locksmithing – are celebrated here with items handcrafted from wood, wrought iron, bronze, stone, brick, clay and leather; standouts include exquisite wooden architectural models of elaborate towers and a miniature wrought-iron gate that took 14 years to make.

Musée des Beaux-Arts Gallery
(02 47 05 68 73; www.mba.tours.fr; 18 place François Sicard; adult/child €6/3; 9am-12.45pm & 2-6pm Wed-Mon) This superb

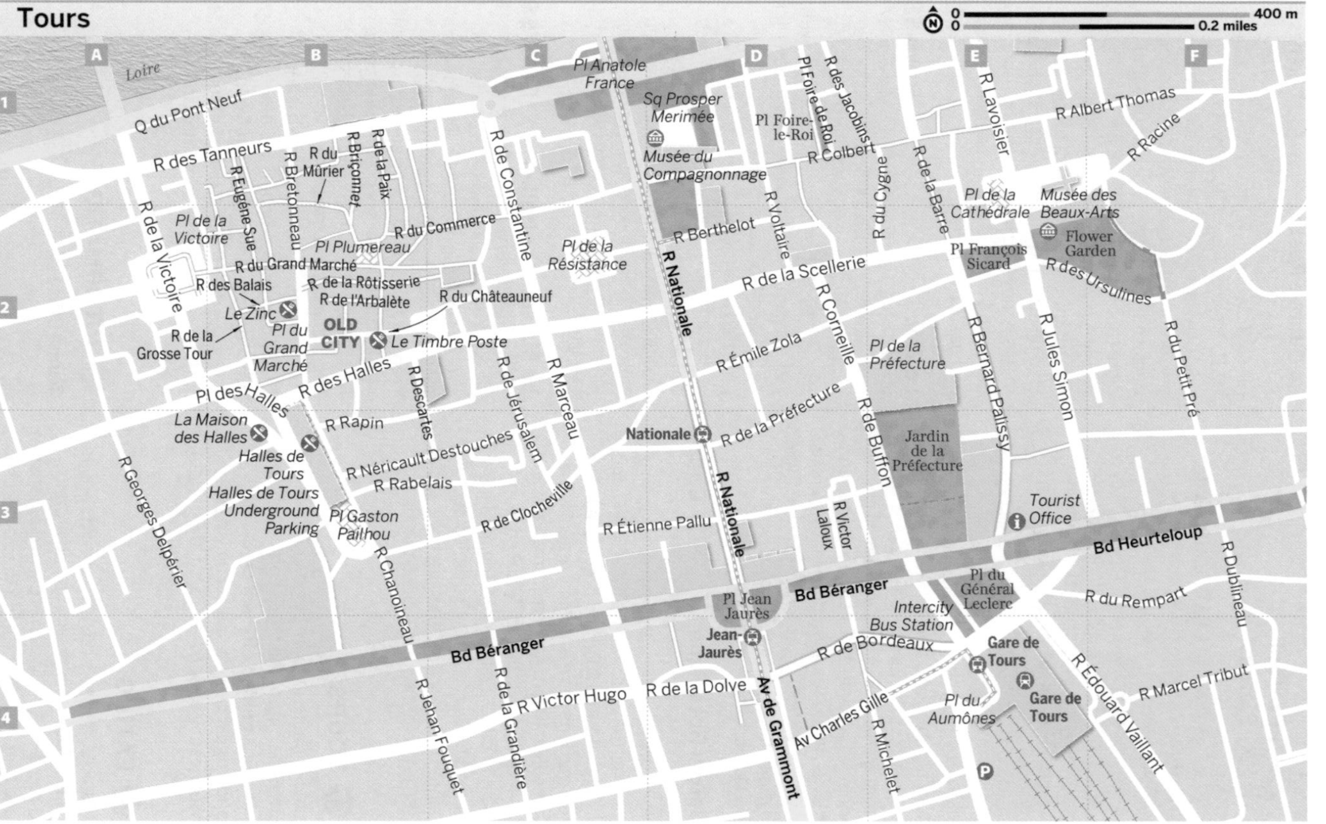
Tours
0
0
400 m
0.2 miles
A
B
C
D
E
F
1
2
3
4
Loire
Q du Pont Neuf
R des Tanneurs
R Eugène Sue
R Bretonneau
R du Mûrier
R Briçonnet
R de la Paix
Pl de la Victoire
R de la Victoire
R du Grand Marché
Pl Plumereau
R du Commerce
R des Balais
R de la Rôtisserie
R de l'Arbalète
R du Châteauneuf
Le Zinc
R de la Grosse Tour
Pl du Grand Marché
OLD CITY
Le Timbre Poste
Pl des Halles
R des Halles
La Maison des Halles
Halles de Tours
Halles de Tours Underground Parking
R Rapin
R Descartes
R Néricault Destouches
R Rabelais
Pl Gaston Pailhou
R Chanoineau
R Georges Delpérier
R de Constantine
R de Jérusalem
R Marceau
R de Clocheville
Pl Anatole France
Sq Prosper Merimée
Musée du Compagnonnage
Pl de la Résistance
R Berthelot
R Nationale
Nationale
R Étienne Pallu
Pl Foire-le-Roi
Pl Foire de Roi
R des Jacobins
R Colbert
R Voltaire
R de la Scellerie
R Émile Zola
R de la Préfecture
R Corneille
R de Buffon
R Victor Laloux
R du Cygne
R de la Barre
Pl de la Préfecture
Jardin de la Préfecture
R Lavoisier
Pl de la Cathédrale
Pl François Sicard
R Bernard Palissy
Musée des Beaux-Arts
Flower Garden
R des Ursulines
R Jules Simon
R Albert Thomas
R Racine
R du Petit Pré
Tourist Office
Bd Heurteloup
R Dublineau
Bd Béranger
Pl Jean Jaurès
Jean-Jaurès
Pl du Général Leclerc
Intercity Bus Station
R du Rempart
R de Bordeaux
Gare de Tours
R Édouard Vaillant
R Marcel Tribut
R Victor Hugo
R de la Dolve
Av de Grammont
Av Charles Gille
R Michelet
Pl du Aumônes
R Jehan Fouquet
R de la Grandière

Perfect Picnics

Tours' gastronomic heart is **Halles de Tours** (www.halles-de-tours.com; place Gaston Pailhou; ⏱7am-1pm & 3-7.30pm Tue-Sat, no midday closure Fri & Sat, 8am-1pm Sun;), whose 38 market stalls sell everything you could want for a picnic, including fine cheese, wine and prepared dishes.

fine-arts museum, in a gorgeous 18th-century archbishop's palace, features paintings, sculpture, furniture and *objets d'art* from the 14th to 20th centuries. Highlights include paintings by Delacroix, Degas and Monet, a rare Rembrandt miniature and a Rubens *Madonna and Child*. Outside there's a magnificent cedar of Lebanon planted in 1804 and a flowery garden.

Jardin Botanique Gardens

(☎02 47 21 62 67; www.tours.fr; 35 bd Tonnellé; ⏱7.45am-7.30pm Mar-May, Sep & Oct, to 9pm Jun-Aug, to 5.30pm Nov-Feb;) FREE Founded in 1843, Tours' delightful 5-hectare botanical gardens have a tropical greenhouse, a medicinal herb garden, a small zoo and children's playgrounds. Situated 2km west of place Jean Jaurès, the gardens are served by Fil Bleu bus 15 from place Jean Jaurès or bus 4 from the riverfront; get off at the Bretonneau or Tonnellé stops.

TOURS

Lots of château tours begin in Tours – for details, contact the tourist office, which also runs **guided city walks** (in July and August there's one in English every Wednesday at 6pm; adult/child €6/free).

EATING

Many of the city's best restaurants are in **Vieux Tours**, especially on and around place du Grand Marché (place du Monstre) and perpendicular rue du Grand Marché.

Le Timbre Poste Crêpes $

(☎02 47 64 84 14; www.letimbreposte.fr; 10 rue du Châteauneuf; lunch menu €11.90, crêpes €3-11; ⏱noon-1.45pm & 7-9.30pm Tue-Sat, closed holidays) Acclaimed by locals as one of Tours' best purveyors of savoury buckwheat galettes, sweet crêpes, and *cidre* (apple cider; €3.50/8 per glass/pitcher) from Normandy and Brittany, this restaurant also serves creative salads, including one in which chèvre (goat cheese) meets honey. The intimate dining room is decorated with old French postage stamps and postcards.

Le Zinc French $$

(☎02 47 20 29 00; lezinc37@gmail.com; 27 place du Grand Marché; menus €20.90-25.90; ⏱7.30-10.30pm Mon, noon-2pm & 7.30-10.30pm or 11pm Tue-Sat;) This intimate restaurant, with just a dozen tables, garners rave reviews for its outstanding traditional French cuisine, prepared *à l'ancienne* (in the old style, like your grandmother would have). Each dish – saltwater fish, duck breast, steak, rice pudding with caramel sauce – is prepared with exemplary finesse using market-fresh ingredients from the nearby Halles. Excellent value.

La Maison des Halles French $$

(☎02 47 39 96 90; www.maisondeshalles.com; 19 place des Halles; lunch menu €15.80, meat mains €20-26; ⏱noon-2pm & 7.30-10.30pm Tue-Thu, to 11pm Fri & Sat) Relaxed but refined, this French restaurant garners serves excellent steak and Touraine specialities, including *beuchelle à la tourangelle* (calf sweetbreads and kidneys combined with cream and mushrooms). The flagship dish is the 'All Black' *burger gastronomique*, made with ground Black Angus, black mayonnaise flavoured with truffles, black ketchup made with Noire de Crimée tomatoes and foie gras.

INFORMATION

Tourist Office (☎02 47 70 37 37; www.tours-tourisme.fr; 78-82 rue Bernard Palissy; ⏱8.30am-7pm Mon-Sat, 10am-12.30pm & 2.30-

VVOE/SHUTTERSTOCK ©

Amboise (p93)

5pm Sun Apr-Sep, 9am-12.30pm & 1.30-6pm Mon-Sat, 10am-1pm Sun Oct-Mar;) Abundant info in English on Tours, including for cultural events, and on the Loire Valley; sells slightly reduced-price château tickets.

GETTING THERE & AWAY

AIR

Tours–Val de Loire Airport (TUF; 02 47 49 37 00; www.tours.aeroport.fr; 40 rue de l'Aéroport), 6km northeast of the centre, is linked to Dublin and London Stansted by Ryanair.

BUS

Rémi (p96) operates buses to destinations around the Indre-et-Loire *département* from Tours' **intercity bus station** (Halte Routière; 02 47 05 30 49; 9 place du Général Leclerc; ticket counter 7am-7pm Mon-Fri, to 6.30pm Sat). Destinations include Amboise (one hour, seven daily Monday to Saturday), served by line C.

CAR

To park your car for more than two hours, use an underground garage; the one below the **Halles de Tours** (place Gaston Pailhou; per 1/24hr €1.80/12) also has some free spots at street level. **Avis** (02 47 20 53 27; www.avis.com) has an office at Tours' train station.

TRAIN

Tours is the Loire Valley's main rail hub. Regular trains and a few TGVs use the city-centre train station, **Tours-Centre** (place du Général Leclerc;); other TGV trains stop only at **St-Pierre-des-Corps**, 3km east and linked to Tours-Centre by frequent shuttle and TER trains. Bicycles can be taken aboard almost all trains.

Direct services from Tours-Centre include the following:

Amboise €5.70, 13 to 23 minutes, 13 to 22 daily

Azay-le-Rideau €5.90, 26/41 minutes by train/bus, six to eight daily

Blois €11.20, 30 to 46 minutes, 16 to 22 daily

Chenonceaux €7, 25 minutes, nine to 11 daily

Paris Gare d'Austerlitz €25.50, 2¼ hours, four Intercités trains daily

Paris Gare Montparnasse €52.50, 1¼ hours, four to seven TGVs daily

Étretat Cliffs (p116)

NORMANDY

In This Chapter

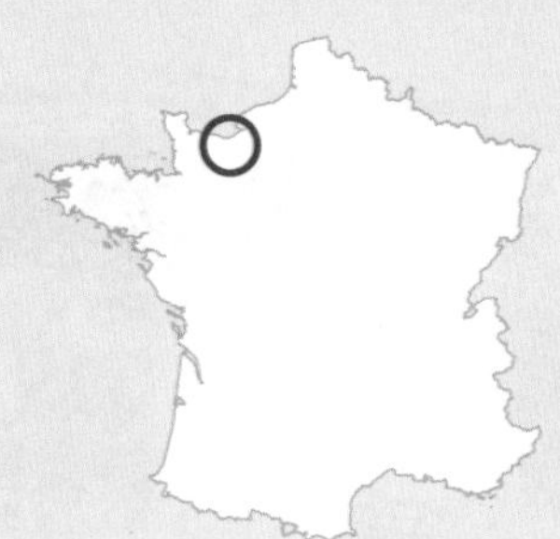

Normandy at a Glance...

From the Norman invasion of England in 1066 to the D-Day landings of 1944, Normandy has long played an outsized role in European history. This rich and often brutal past is brought vividly to life by the spectacular island monastery of Mont St-Michel; the Bayeux Tapestry, world-famous for its depictions of 11th-century life; and the war cemeteries and memorials along the D-Day beaches. Lower-profile charms include dramatic coastal landscapes, pebbly beaches, quiet pastoral villages and architectural gems, including Rouen's medieval old city. Camembert, apples, cider, cream-rich cuisine and the freshest fish and seafood provide further reasons to visit this accessible and beautiful region of France.

Two Days in Normandy

Gather picnic supplies – a round of Camembert and bottle of cider included – if Bayeux's **morning market** (p110) is on, then trip to majestic **Mont St-Michel** (p104) for the day. Day two, admire the epic **Bayeux Tapestry** (p109) and **Musée Mémorial** (p109), before heading to the **D-Day beaches** (p106) for sobering sights such as the American Cemetery and battery.

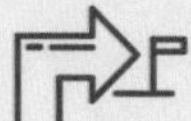

Four Days in Normandy

On day three, tour Caen's **château** (p113), established by William the Conqueror, and the emotive **Mémorial** (p113) before taking your pick of bistros and cafes. Fourth day, trip along to Étretat for spectacular **cliff views**, linger over a seaside lunch in **Honfleur** (p110) and spend the afternoon in Rouen (p111) admiring its awe-inspiring **abbey church** (p112) and **cathedral** (p112).

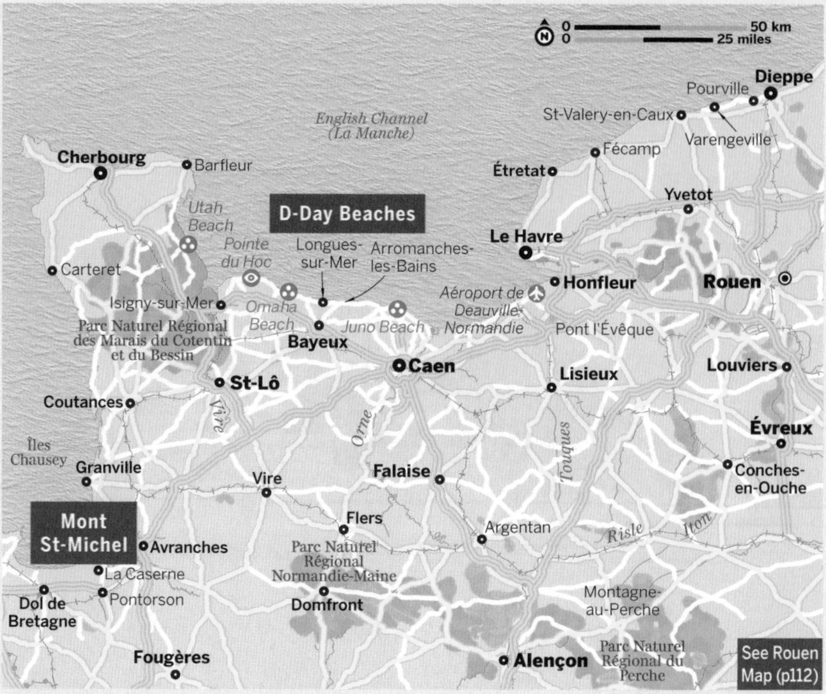

Arriving in Normandy

Boat Car ferries link Dieppe with the English port of Newhaven; Le Havre and Ouistreham (Caen) with Portsmouth; and Cherbourg with Poole and Portsmouth as well as the Irish ports of Dublin and Rosslare.

Train Rouen is just 70 minutes from Paris' Gare St-Lazare (€24.10, 1¼ hours, 25 daily Monday to Friday, 13 to 18 Saturday and Sunday). Most major towns are accessible by rail.

Where to Stay

Normandy has a wide range of accommodation options from inexpensive budget guesthouses with shared facilities to plush hotels with fine sea views. You'll find the widest variety in vibrant Rouen and atmospheric Caen but attractive and historic Bayeux, closer to both the D-Day beaches and Mont St-Michel, has many superb accommodation options.

Mont St-Michel

It's one of France's most iconic images: the slender spires, stout ramparts and rocky slopes of Mont St-Michel rising from the sea, or towering over slick sands laid bare by the tide. Despite large numbers of tourists, both the abbey and the labyrinth of alleys below still manage to transport visitors back to the Middle Ages.

Great For...

☑ Don't Miss

Nocturnes (night visits) with live chamber music, 7pm to midnight, Monday to Saturday from mid-July to August.

The Mont's star attraction is the stunning architectural ensemble high up on top: the abbey. Most areas can be visited without a guide, but it's well worth taking the 1¼-hour tour included in the ticket price.

History

Bishop Aubert of Avranches is said to have built a devotional chapel on the summit of the island in 708, following his vision of the Archangel Michael, whose gilded figure, perched on the vanquished dragon, crowns the tip of the abbey's spire. In 966, Richard I, Duke of Normandy, gave Mont St-Michel to the Benedictines, who turned it into a centre of learning and, in the 11th century, into something of an ecclesiastical fortress, with a military garrison at the disposal of both abbot and king.

Arches on granite pillars, La Merveille cloisters

MICHAEL WARWICK/SHUTTERSTOCK ©

In the 15th century, during the Hundred Years War, the English blockaded and besieged Mont St-Michel three times. The fortified abbey withstood these assaults and was the only place in western and northern France not to fall into English hands. After the Revolution, Mont St-Michel was turned into a prison. In 1966, the abbey was symbolically returned to the Benedictines as part of the celebrations marking its millennium.

Église Abbatiale

Built on the tip of the mountain cone, the transept of the **Église Abbatiale** (Abbey Church) rests on solid rock, while the nave, choir and transept arms are supported by the rooms below. This church is famous for its mix of architectural styles: the nave and south transept are solid Norman Romanesque, while the choir is Flamboyant Gothic.

Need to Know

02 33 89 80 00; www.abbaye-mont-saint-michel.fr/en; adult/child incl guided tour €10/free; 9am-7pm May-Aug, 9.30am-6pm Sep-Apr, last entry 1hr before closing

Take a Break

On main street Grand Rue, bistro classics and *galettes* (savoury buckwheat crêpes) at **Les Terrasses Poulard** (02 33 89 02 02; www.terrasses-poulard.fr; Grand Rue; menus €19-29; noon-2pm & 7-9pm).

★ Top Tip

Walk the eastern section of the ramparts from Tour du Nord (North Tower) to Porte du Roy for spectacular views.

La Merveille

The buildings on the northern side of the Mont are known as 'The Marvel'. The famous **cloître** (cloister) is surrounded by a double row of delicately carved arches resting on granite pillars. The early-13th-century, barrel-roofed **réfectoire** (dining hall) is illuminated by a wall of recessed windows – remarkable given that the sheer drop precluded the use of flying buttresses. The Gothic **Salle des Hôtes** (Guest Hall), dating from 1213, has two enormous fireplaces.

Other features to look out for include the **promenoir** (ambulatory) and the **Chapelle de Notre Dame sous Terre** (Underground Chapel of Our Lady), one of the abbey's oldest rooms, rediscovered in 1903.

Guided Tours

When the tide is out (the tourist office has tide tables), you can walk all the way around Mont St-Michel, a distance of about 1km, with a guide (doing so on your own is very risky). Straying too far from the Mont can be dangerous: you could get stuck in wet sand – from which Norman soldiers are depicted being rescued in one scene of the Bayeux Tapestry – or be overtaken either by the incoming tide or water gushing from the new dam's eight sluice gates.

Pointe du Hoc

PICS FACTORY/SHUTTERSTOCK ©

D-Day Beaches

Code-named 'Operation Overlord', the D-Day landings were the largest seaborne invasion in history. Early on 6 June 1944, landing craft hit the beaches of Normandy. Most of the Allied troops who arrived in France that day stormed ashore along 80km of beaches north of Bayeux, code-named Utah, Omaha, Gold, Juno and Sword.

Great For...

☑ Don't Miss

English-language tours of the Normandy American Cemetery.

Omaha Beach

D-Day's most brutal fighting took place on a 7km stretch of coastline northwest of Bayeux (known as 'Bloody Omaha' to US veterans). White marble crosses and Stars of David stretch off in seemingly endless rows at the **Normandy American Cemetery** (☎02 31 51 62 00; www.abmc.gov; Colleville-sur-Mer; ⏰9am-6pm mid-Apr–mid-Sep, to 5pm mid-Sep–mid-Apr) FREE, 17km northwest of Bayeux on a now-serene bluff. Featured in the opening scenes of Steven Spielberg's *Saving Private Ryan*, this is one of the largest American war cemeteries in Europe. Free 45-minute English-language **tours** depart daily at 2pm and, from mid-April to mid-September, at 11am. The **visitor centre** has an excellent multimedia presentation.

Normandy American Cemetery

PISAPHOTOGRAPHY/SHUTTERSTOCK ©

Pointe du Hoc

At 7.10am on 6 June 1944, 225 US Army Rangers under the command of Lieutenant Colonel James Earl Rudder scaled the 30m-high cliffs of Pointe du Hoc to disable five 155mm German artillery guns. After repelling fierce German counterattacks for two days, 81 of the rangers had been killed and 58 more had been wounded. Today the **memorial site** (www.abmc.gov; ⌚9am-6pm mid-Apr–mid-Sep, to 5pm rest of year) FREE looks much as it did right after the battle, pitted with huge bomb craters.

Juno Beach

A Cross of Lorraine marks the spot where General Charles de Gaulle came ashore after the landings. He was followed by Winston Churchill on 12 June and King George VI on 16 June. The **Juno Beach Centre** (www.junobeach.org; voie des Français Libres, Courseulles-sur-Mer; adult/child €7/5.50; ⌚9.30am-7pm Apr-Sep, 10am-6pm Oct & Mar, 10am-5pm Nov-Dec & Feb, closed Jan), has exhibits on Canada's role in the landings.

Need to Know

Information and reservations at Bayeux **tourist office** (☎02 31 51 28 28; www.bayeux-bessin-tourisme.com; Pont St-Jean; ⌚9am-7pm Mon-Sat, 10am-1pm & 2-6pm Sun Jul & Aug, shorter hours rest of year).

Take a Break

Lunch in Bayeux at **Alchimie** (☎02 14 08 03 97; 49 rue St-Jean; lunch menus €13-18).

★ Top Tip

Caen's Le Mémorial (p113) and Bayeux's Musée Mémorial (p109) provide a good overview of D-Day events.

Arromanches-les-Bains

To unload cargo, the Allies set up prefabricated marinas, code-named **Mulberry Harbours**. The remains of three dozen **caissons** can still be seen off Arromanches-les-Bains. The best view of Port Winston and **Gold Beach** is from the hill east of town, site of **Arromanches 360° Circular Cinema** (www.arromanches360.com; chemin du Calvaire; adult/child €6/5.50; ⌚closed 3 weeks in Jan & Mon mid-Nov–mid-Feb). On the beach, the **Musée du Débarquement** (www.musee-arromanches.fr; place du 6 Juin; adult/child €8/5.90; ⌚closed Jan) makes for an informative stop.

Longues-sur-Mer

Part of the Nazis' Atlantic Wall, the casemates and 150mm German guns near Longues-sur-Mer were designed to hit targets 20km away, including Gold Beach and Omaha Beach. Over seven decades later, the artillery pieces are still in their concrete emplacements. Contact the on-site **Longues tourist office** (☎02 31 21 46 87; www.bayeux-bessin-tourisme.com; Site de la Batterie; ⌚10am-1pm & 2-6pm, closed Nov-Mar) for tour details. The site itself is always open.

Bayeux

Two cross-Channel invasions, almost 900 years apart, gave Bayeux a front-row seat at defining moments in Western history. The dramatic story of the Norman invasion of England in 1066 is told in 58 vivid scenes by the world-famous and quite astonishing Bayeux Tapestry.

On 6 June 1944, 160,000 Allied troops, supported by almost 7000 naval vessels, stormed ashore along the coast just north of town. Bayeux was the first French town to be liberated (on the morning of 7 June 1944) and is one of the few places in Calvados to have survived WWII practically unscathed.

SIGHTS

A joint ticket for admission to the Musée d'Art et d'Histoire Baron Gérard and either the Bayeux Tapestry or the Musée Mémorial de la Bataille de Normandie is €12 (or €15 for all three).

Musée d'Art et d'Histoire Baron Gérard Museum

(MAHB; ☎02 31 92 14 21; www.bayeuxmuseum.com; 37 rue du Bienvenu; adult/child €7.50/5; ⊙9.30am-6.30pm May-Sep, 10am-12.30pm & 2-6pm Oct-Apr, closed 3 weeks in Jan) Make sure you drop by this museum – one of France's most gorgeously presented provincial museums – where exhibitions cover everything from Gallo-Roman archaeology through medieval art to paintings from the Renaissance and on to the 20th century, including a fine work by Gustave Caillebotte. Other highlights include impossibly fine local lace and Bayeux-made porcelain. The museum is housed in the former bishop's palace.

Cathédrale Notre Dame Cathedral

(rue du Bienvenu; ⊙8.30am-7pm) Most of Bayeux' spectacular Norman Gothic cathedral dates from the 13th century, though the crypt (take the stairs on the north side of the choir), the arches of the nave and the lower parts of the entrance towers are 11th-century Romanesque. The central tower was added in the 15th

Cathédrale Notre Dame, Bayeux

century; the copper dome dates from the 1860s. The crypt, with its colourful frescoes, is a highlight. Several plaques and stained-glass windows commemorate American and British sacrifices during the world wars.

Musée Mémorial de la Bataille de Normandie Museum

(Battle of Normandy Memorial Museum; ☎02 31 51 46 90; www.bayeuxmuseum.com; bd Fabien Ware; adult/child €7.50/5; ⏰9.30am-6.30pm May-Sep, 10am-12.30pm & 2-6pm Oct-Apr, closed 3 weeks in Jan) Using well-chosen photos, personal accounts, dioramas and wartime objects, this first-rate museum offers an excellent introduction to the Battle of Normandy. The 25-minute film is screened in both French and English. A selection of hardware – tanks and artillery pieces – is displayed outside.

Bayeux War Cemetery Cemetery

(bd Fabien Ware) The largest of the 18 Commonwealth military cemeteries in Normandy, this peaceful cemetery contains 4848 graves of soldiers from the UK and 10 other countries, including a few from Germany. Across the road is a memorial to 1807 Commonwealth soldiers whose remains were never found; the Latin inscription across the top reads: 'We, once conquered by William, have now liberated the Conqueror's native land'.

TOURS

Discovery Walks Bayeux Walking

(☎07 70 18 46 53, 07 83 02 70 27; 1 rue St-Jean; adult/child €25/free; ⏰9.30am & 5pm daily Apr-Sep) Guided 90-minute and two-hour walks around Bayeux, in English. Tours run daily at 9.30am (two hours) and 5pm (90 minutes) from April to September; there's a minimum of two adults. Outside these months you need to book a private tour (€15 per adult, minimum two). Prices are on a sliding scale: the larger the group, the cheaper it is per person.

Bayeux Tapestry

The world's most celebrated embroidery depicts the conquest of England by William the Conqueror in 1066 from an unashamedly Norman perspective. Commissioned by Bishop Odo of Bayeux, William's half-brother, for the opening of Bayeux' cathedral in 1077, the well-preserved **Bayeux Tapestry** (www.bayeuxmuseum.com; 15bis rue de Nesmond; adult/child incl audioguide €9.50/5; ⏰9.30am-12.30pm & 2-5.30pm Feb-Jun & Sep-Dec, 9am-7pm Mon-Sat, 9am-1pm & 2-6pm Sun Jul & Aug, closed Jan) tells the dramatic, bloody tale with verve and vividness as well as some astonishing artistry. What is particularly incredible is both its length (nearly 70m) and fine attention to detail.

In the centre of the canvas are 58 action-packed scenes of pageantry and mayhem, while religious allegories and illustrations of everyday 11th-century life, some of them bawdy, adorn the borders. The final showdown at the Battle of Hastings is depicted in graphic fashion, complete with severed limbs and decapitated heads (along the bottom of scene 52). Halley's Comet, which blazed across the sky in 1066, appears in scene 32.

A 16-minute film gives the historical, political and cultural context, plus there's a lucid and highly informative panel-by-panel audioguide, available in 14 languages, and a special audioguide for kids aged seven to 12 years (in French and English).

Tapestry detail depicting Edward the Confessor

Day Trip to Honfleur

Long a favourite with painters such as Monet, Normandy's most charming port town is a popular day-trip destination. Stop at the **tourist office** (☎02 31 89 23 30; www.ot-honfleur.fr; quai Lepaulmier; ⏰9.30am-12.30pm & 2-6pm Mon-Sat Sep-Jun, 9.30am-7pm Jul & Aug, also 10am-5pm Sun Easter-Sep; 📶) for a map or audioguide. Head north from the Lieutenance along quai des Passagers to **Jetée de l'Ouest** (Western Jetty), which forms the west side of the Avant Port, out to the broad mouth of the Seine. Possible stops include the **Jardin des Personnalités**, a park featuring local historical figures; the beach; and **Naturospace** (www.naturospace.com; bd Charles V; adult/child €9/7; ⏰10am-5pm Feb-Mar & Oct–mid-Nov, to 6.30pm Apr-Sep), a lush greenhouse filled with free-flying tropical butterflies and birds (500m northwest of the Lieutenance). Don't miss **Les Maisons Satie** (www.musees-honfleur.fr/maison-satie.html; 67 bd Charles V & 90 rue Haute; adult/child €6.20/free; ⏰10am-7pm Wed-Mon May-Sep, 11am-6pm Wed-Mon Oct-Apr), where each room conceals a surreal surprise.

Come lunch, **La Fleur de Sel** (www.lafleurdesel-honfleur.com; 17 rue Haute; menus €32-62; ⏰noon-1.30pm & 7.15-9pm Wed-Sun) offers roast meats and wild-caught seafood with inventive touches like ginger and kaffir-lime vinaigrettes and Camembert foams. For an inexpensive and casual meal, **La Cidrerie** (☎02 31 89 59 85; 26 place Hamelin; mains €8-12; ⏰noon-2.30pm & 7-9.30pm Thu-Mon) serves piping-hot *galettes* and fizzy Norman ciders.

EATING

Marché Market $

(place St-Jean & place St-Patrice; ⏰8am-12.30pm Wed & Sat) Stalls sell farm-fresh edibles at place St-Patrice (Saturday morning) and right in front of the tourist office (Wednesday morning).

La Reine Mathilde Pastries $

(☎02 31 92 00 59; 47 rue St-Martin; cakes from €2.50; ⏰9am-7.30pm Tue-Sun) With a vast acreage of glass in its windows and set with white-painted cast-iron chairs, this sumptuously decorated patisserie and *salon de thé* (tearoom), ideal for a sweet breakfast or a relaxing cup of afternoon tea, hasn't changed much since it was built in 1898. Size up the sweet offerings on display and tuck in.

La Rapière French $$

(☎02 31 21 05 45; www.larapiere.net; 53 rue St-Jean; lunch menus €16-21, dinner menus €36-49, mains €20-28; ⏰noon-1.30pm Tue & Thu-Sat, plus 7-8.15pm Tue-Sat, closed mid-Dec–early Feb) Housed in a late-1400s mansion composed of stone walls and big wooden beams, this atmospheric restaurant specialises in Normandy staples such as terrines, duck and veal with Camembert. The various fixed-price menus assure a splendid meal on any budget.

INFORMATION

Tourist Office (p107) Covers both Bayeux and the surrounding Bessin region as well as the D-Day beaches.

GETTING THERE & AWAY

BUS

Bus Verts (☎09 70 83 00 14; www.busverts.fr) Buses 70 and 74 (bus 75 in July and August) link Bayeux' train station and place St-Patrice with many of the villages, memorials and museums along Omaha, Gold and Juno D-Day beaches.

TRAIN

Bayeux' train station is 1km southeast of the cathedral. Direct services include the following:

Caen €6, 15 to 20 minutes, at least hourly

YURI TURKOV/SHUTTERSTOCK ©

Cathédrale Notre Dame (p112), Rouen

Pontorson (Mont St-Michel) €24, 1¾ hours, three daily

To get to Deauville, change at Lisieux. For Paris' Gare St-Lazare and Rouen, you may have to change at Caen.

GETTING AROUND

BICYCLE

Vélos (☎02 31 92 89 16; www.velosbayeux.com; 5 rue Larcher; adult bike per half-/full day from €7.50/10, child bike per half-/full day from €7.50/5; ⏰8am-8.30pm) Year-round bike rental from a fruit and veggie store a few paces from the tourist office.

CAR

There's free parking at Parking d'Ornano, at the southern end of rue Larcher.

TAXI

Taxi (☎02 31 92 92 40; www.bayeux-taxis.com) Can take you around Bayeux or out to the D-Day sites.

Rouen

With its soaring Gothic cathedral, beautifully restored medieval quarter, imposing ancient churches, excellent museums and vibrant cultural life, Rouen is one of Normandy's most engaging and historically rich destinations.

SIGHTS

The heart of the old city – in the area north of the Seine on the right bank – is rue du Gros Horloge, two blocks north of the city centre's main east–west thoroughfare, rue du Général Leclerc. The main shopping precinct is due north of the cathedral, on pedestrianised rue des Carmes and nearby streets.

Historial Jeanne d'Arc Museum

(☎02 35 52 48 00; www.historial-jeannedarc.fr; 7 rue St-Romain; adult/child €10.50/7.50; ⏰10am-6pm Tue-Sun) For an introduction to the great 15th-century heroine (who died in Rouen) and the events that earned her fame – and shortly thereafter condemnation – don't miss this excellent site. It's less of a museum,

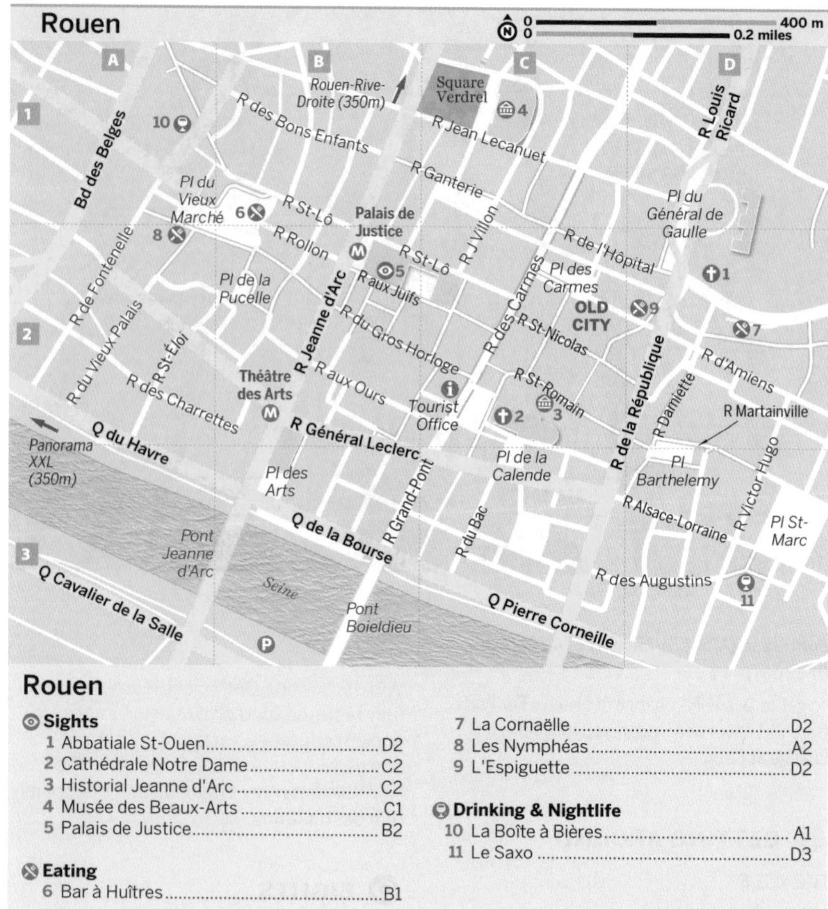

Rouen

Sights

1 Abbatiale St-Ouen D2
2 Cathédrale Notre Dame C2
3 Historial Jeanne d'Arc C2
4 Musée des Beaux-Arts C1
5 Palais de Justice B2

Eating

6 Bar à Huîtres B1
7 La Cornaëlle D2
8 Les Nymphéas A2
9 L'Espiguette D2

Drinking & Nightlife

10 La Boîte à Bières A1
11 Le Saxo D3

and more of a theatre-like experience, where you walk through medieval corridors and watch (and hear via headphones, in seven languages) the dramatic retelling of Joan's visions, her victories, the trial that sealed her fate, and the mythologising that followed in the years after her death.

Cathédrale Notre Dame Cathedral
(www.cathedrale-rouen.net; place de la Cathédrale; ⏲2-7pm Mon, 9am-7pm Tue-Sat, 8am-6pm Sun Apr-Oct, shorter hours Nov-Mar) Rouen's stunning Gothic cathedral, built between the late 12th and 16th centuries, was famously the subject of a series of canvases painted by Monet at various times of the day and year. The 75m-tall **Tour de Beurre** (Butter Tower) was financed by locals in return for being allowed to eat butter during Lent – or so the story goes. A free sound-and-light spectacular is projected on the façade every night from June (at 11pm) to late September (at 9.30pm).

Panorama XXL Gallery
(☎02 35 52 95 25; www.panoramaxxl.com; quai de Boisguilbert; adult/child €9.50/6.50; ⏲10am-7pm Tue-Sun May-Aug, to 6pm Tue-Sun Sep-Apr) In a

large, circular column on the waterfront, Panorama XXL is a massive 360-degree exhibition offering in-depth exploring of one astonishing landscape, created with photographs, drawings, digital images and recorded audio. Past years have featured the Great Barrier Reef, Amazonia, Ancient Rome and Rouen in 1431 – often with sunrise and sunset generating different moods, as well as storms. A 15m-high viewing platform in the middle of the room gives a fine vantage point over the scene.

Palais de Justice Architecture

(place Maréchal Foch & rue aux Juifs) The ornately Gothic Law Courts, little more than a shell at the end of WWII, have been restored to their early-16th-century glory. On rue Jeanne d'Arc, however, you can still see the very pock-marked façade, which shows the damage sustained during bombing raids in 1944. Around the corner on pedestrianised rue aux Juifs, you can peer in the spire- and gargoyle-adorned courtyard.

Musée des Beaux-Arts Gallery

(02 35 71 28 40; www.mbarouen.fr; esplanade Marcel Duchamp; 10am-6pm Wed-Mon) FREE Housed in a very grand structure flung up in 1870, Rouen's simply outstanding fine-arts museum features canvases by Rubens, Modigliani, Pissarro, Renoir, Sisley (lots) and, of course, several works by Monet, as well as a fine collection of Flemish oils. There's also one jaw-dropping painting by Caravaggio as well as a very serene cafe. Drop your bag in the lockers provided and follow the route through the galleries, which are arranged chronologically.

Captivating Caen

Founded by William the Conqueror in the 11th century, Caen has a magnificent **castle** (www.musee-de-normandie.caen.fr; 8am-10pm; P) FREE. Visitors can walk around the ramparts and tour the 12th-century **Église St-Georges** (Château de Caen).

For an insightful and vivid account of the Battle of Normandy, **Le Mémorial** (Memorial – A Museum for Peace; 02 31 06 06 44; www.memorial-caen.fr; esplanade Général Eisenhower; adult/child €19.80/17.50, family pass €51; 9am-7pm Apr-Sep, 9.30am-6pm Oct-Dec, 9am-6pm Feb-Mar, closed 3 weeks in Jan, shut most Mon in Nov & Dec) is unparalleled – it's one of Europe's premier WWII museums. It is situated 3km northwest of the city centre, reachable by bus 2 from place Courtonne.

There are at least six daily trains to/from Bayeux (€6, 15 to 20 minutes) and Rouen (from €28, 1¾ hours).

Caen Castle

EATING

L'Espiguette Bistro $

(02 35 71 66 27; 25 place St-Amand; weekday lunch menus €13, mains €17-24; noon-10pm Tue-Sat) This charmingly decorated eatery serves excellent bistro classics – think *osso buco* (veal casserole), filet of sole, beef tartare – with the day's offerings up on a chalkboard. It's quite popular with locals, so reserve ahead, even at lunchtime (the lunch *menu* is a great deal). Grab a seat at one of the outdoor tables on a warm day.

La Cornaëlle Crêperie $

(02 35 08 53 75; 174 rue Eau de Robec; crêpes €8-12; noon-3pm & 7-10pm Tue-Sat, noon-3pm Sun) Arched ceilings, pale stone walls and some low-playing blues set the scene for an enjoyable night nibbling on delicious *galettes* (savoury buckwheat crêpes), and sipping fizzy local cider. Finish off with a dessert crêpe (try the *poêlée Normande* with apples, caramel, cream and flambéed *calvados*).

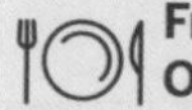

Fresh Oysters

Grab a seat at **Bar à Huîtres** (place du Vieux Marché; mains €10-16, oysters per half-dozen/dozen from €10/17; ⏲10am-2pm Tue-Sat) for uberfresh seafood. This casual but polished eatery is located inside Rouen's covered market. Specials change daily based on what's fresh, from giant shrimp to dorado and fillet of sole, but each is cooked up to perfection. Don't neglect the restaurant's namesake – the satisfying *huîtres* (oysters) with several different varieties on offer.

Les Nymphéas Gastronomy **$$$**

(☎09 74 56 46 19; www.lesnympheas-rouen.fr; 7 rue de la Pie; weekday lunch menus €27, other menus €40-77, mains €33-58; ⏲12.15-2pm Tue-Sun, 7-9pm Tue-Sat) With its formal tables arrayed under 16th-century beams, Les Nymphéas has long been a top address for fine dining in Rouen. Young chef Alexandre Dessaux serves up French cuisine that manages to be both traditional and creative. Reservations are a must on weekends. A vegan menu is available for either €30 or €39.

DRINKING & NIGHTLIFE

The bars and cafes around place du Vieux Marché and in the old town buzz from noon until the early hours. Rouen is also the centre of Normandy's gay life.

La Boîte à Bières Bar

(☎02 35 07 76 47; www.laboiteabieres.fr; 35 rue Cauchoise; ⏲5pm-2am Tue-Sat; 📶) This friendly, good-looking and half-timbered establishment has walls plastered with memorabilia. Affectionately known as BAB, it's often crowded, serving at least 16 beers on tap and another 230 in bottles, including local *bières artisanales* (microbrews).

Le Saxo Bar

(☎02 35 98 24 92; www.facebook.com/le.saxo.rouen; 11 place St-Marc; ⏲5pm-2am Mon-Sat) Le Saxo swings from jazz, to blues, rock, reggae and world music, with free concerts by local bands on Friday and Saturday from 10pm to 1.30am (except in July and August). It hosts jazz jam sessions every other Thursday from 9pm. Serves 13 beers on tap and 120 by the bottle.

INFORMATION

Tourist Office (☎02 32 08 32 40; www.rouentourisme.com; 25 place de la Cathédrale; ⏲9am-7pm Mon-Sat, 9.30am-12.30pm & 2-6pm Sun May-Sep, 9.30am-12.30pm & 1.30-6pm Mon-Sat Oct-Apr) Housed in a terrific 1500s Renaissance building facing the cathedral. Rouen's only exchange bureau is tucked away at the back.

GETTING THERE & AROUND

BICYCLE

Cy'clic (☎08 00 08 78 00; http://cyclic.rouen.fr; ⏲5am-1am), Rouen's version of Paris' Vélib', lets you rent a city bike from 24 locations. Credit-card registration for one/seven days costs €1/7, plus a deposit of €150. Use is free for the first 30 minutes; the second/third/fourth and subsequent half-hours cost €1/2/4 each.

TRAIN

The train station, **Rouen-Rive-Droite**, is 1.2km north of the cathedral. Direct services:

Caen €28, 1¾ hours, five or six daily

Le Havre €16, one hour, 16 to 20 daily Monday to Saturday, 10 Sunday

Paris' Gare St-Lazare €10 to €24.10, 1¼ to 1½ hours, 25 daily Monday to Friday, 13 to 18 Saturday and Sunday

Trouville & Deauville

The twin seaside towns of Trouville-sur-Mer (population 4800) and Deauville (population 3800), 15km southwest of Honfleur, are hugely popular with Parisians, who flock here year-round on weekends – and all week long from June to September and during Paris' school holidays.

Chic Deauville has been a playground of well-heeled Parisians ever since it was founded by Napoléon III's half-brother, the Duke of Morny, in 1861. Unpretentious Trouville is both a veteran beach resort, graced with impressive mansions from the late 1800s, and a working fishing port. Popular with middle-class French families, the town was frequented by painters and writers during the 19th century.

SIGHTS

In Deauville, the rich and beautiful strut their stuff along the beachside **Promenade des Planches**, a 643m-long boardwalk that's lined with a row of 1920s cabins. After swimming in the nearby 50m **Piscine Olympique** (Olympic swimming pool; ☎02 31 14 02 17; bd de la Mer, Deauville; weekday/weekend from €4/6; ⏱10am-2pm & 3.30-7pm Mon-Sat, 9am-4pm Sun, closed 2 weeks in Jan & 3 weeks in Jun), filled with seawater heated to 28°C, they – like you – can head to the beach, hundreds of metres wide at low tide.

Trouville has a waterfront casino, a wide beach and Promenade des Planches (boardwalk). At the latter, 583m long and outfitted with Bauhaus-style pavilions from the 1930s, you can swim in a freshwater swimming pool and windsurf; there's also a playground for kids.

Musée Villa Montabello — Museum

(☎02 31 88 16 26; 64 rue du Général Leclerc; adult/child €3/free, Sun free; ⏱2-5.30pm Wed-Mon Apr–mid-Nov, from 11am Sat, Sun & holidays) In a grand mansion dating to 1865, this municipal museum recounts Trouville's history and features works by Charles Mozin, Eugène Isabey and Charles Pecrus. It is situated 1km northeast of the tourist office, near the beach (and signed off the beach). The two towns and beach scenes of Trouville and Deauville play a starring role in the impressionist works in the small permanent collection.

The Cider Route

Normandy's signposted, 40km Route du Cidre, about 30km south of Deauville, wends its way through the **Pays d'Auge**, a rural area of orchards, pastures, hedgerows, half-timbered farmhouses and stud farms, through picturesque villages such as Cambremer and Beuvron-en-Auge. Signs reading 'Cru de Cambremer' indicate the way to 17 small-scale, traditional *producteurs* (producers) who are happy to show you their facilities and sell you their home-grown apple cider (about €3.50 a bottle), *calvados* (apple brandy) – affectionately known as *calva* – and *pommeau* (a mixture of apple juice and *calvados*).

Traditional Normandy cider takes about six months to make. Ripe apples are shaken off the trees or gathered from the ground between early October and early December. After being stored for two or three weeks, they are pressed, purified, slow-fermented, bottled and naturally carbonated, just like Champagne.

Normandy's AOC (Appellation d'Origine Contrôlée) cider is made with a blend of apple varieties and is known for being fruity, tangy and slightly bitter. You can enjoy it in crêperies and restaurants throughout Normandy.

EATING

In Trouville, there are lots of restaurants and buzzing brasseries along riverfront bd Fernand Moureaux. Inland, check out the small restaurants and cafes along and near rue d'Orléans and on pedestrianised rue des Bains. Deauville has a good selection of eateries scattered around town, with clusters around the tourist office and place Morny.

Les Vapeurs — Brasserie $$

(☎02 31 88 15 24; 160 bd Fernand Moureaux; mains €18-38; ⏱noon-11.30pm) Across from

Étretat Cliffs

The small and delightful village of Étretat's dramatic coastal scenery – it's framed by twin cliffs – made it a favourite of painters such as Camille Corot, Eugène Boudin, Gustave Courbet and Claude Monet.

The pebbly beach is separated from the town centre by a dyke. To the left as you face the sea, you can see the **Falaise d'Aval**, renowned for its beautiful arch – and the adjacent **Aiguille**, a needle of rock poking high up from the waves.

To the right as you face the sea towers the **Falaise d'Amont**, atop which a memorial marks the spot where two aviators were last seen before attempting to cross the Atlantic in 1927. The **tourist office** (☎02 35 27 05 21; www.etretat.net; place Maurice Guillard; ⊙9.30am-6.30pm mid-Jun–mid-Sep, 10am-noon & 2-6pm Mon-Sat mid-Sep–mid-Jun, Sun during school holidays) has a map of trails around town.

the fish market, Les Vapeurs has been going strong in Trouville since 1927. The huge menu is a showcase for seafood platters, oysters (from €15 for six), mussels in cream sauce, grilled haddock, lobster and classic brasserie fare (like steak tartare). It's served amid an old-time ambience, with black-and-white photos, a touch of neon and wicker chairs at the outdoor tables in front. There are dishes for the young ones too.

L'Essentiel Fusion **$$**
(☎02 31 87 22 11; 29 rue Mirabeau; lunch menus €27-32, dinner menus €69, mains €31-39; ⊙noon-2pm & 7.30-11pm Thu-Mon) One of Deauville's top dining rooms, L'Essentiel serves up an imaginative blend of French ingredients with Asian and Latin American accents. Start off with codfish croquettes with sweet potato aioli before moving on to scallops with broccoli yuzu, or wagyu flank steak with roasted turnips and smoked cashew juice.

ℹ INFORMATION

Deauville Tourist Office (☎02 31 14 40 00; www.indeauville.fr; quai de la Gare; ⊙10am-6pm Mon-Sat, 10am-1pm & 2-5pm Sun) Has a walking tour brochure with a Deauville map. The website has details on cultural events and horse races.

Trouville Tourist Office (☎02 31 14 60 70; www.trouvillesurmer.org; 32 bd Fernand Moureaux; ⊙10am-6pm Mon-Sat, to 1.30pm Sun Sep-Jun, 9.30am-7pm Mon-Sat, 10am-6pm Sun Jul & Aug) Has a free map of Trouville and sells map-brochures for two self-guided architectural tours (€4) of town and also two rural walks (€1).

ℹ GETTING THERE & AWAY

BUS

Deauville and Trouville's joint bus station is next to the Trouville-Deauville train station.

Bus Verts (p110) Bus 20 goes to Caen (€4.90, two hours, seven to 12 daily), Honfleur (€2.50, 30 minutes, four to seven daily) and Le Havre (€4.90, 1¼ hours, four to seven daily).

TRAIN

The Trouville-Deauville train station is in Deauville, right next to pont des Belges (the bridge to Trouville). Getting here usually requires a change at Lisieux (€8, 20 minutes, nine to 12 daily), though there are two or three direct trains a day to Paris' Gare St-Lazare (€35, two hours). Destinations that require a change of trains include Caen (€16, 1¼ to two hours, six to 11 daily) and Rouen (from €24, 1¼ to two hours, five to eight daily).

Le Havre

A Unesco World Heritage Site since 2005 and a regular port of call for cruise ships, Le Havre is a love letter to modernism, evoking, more than any other French city, France's postwar energy and optimism. All but obliterated in September 1944 by Allied bombing raids that killed 3000 civilians, the centre was completely rebuilt by the

Église St-Joseph

Belgian architect Auguste Perret – mentor to Le Corbusier – whose bright, airy modernist vision remains, miraculously, largely intact.

Attractions include a museum full of captivating impressionist paintings, a soaring modernist church with a mesmerising stained-glass tower, hilltop gardens with views over the city and a medieval church that rose again from the ashes of war.

> *Le Havre is a love letter to modernism...*

SIGHTS

Musée Malraux Gallery

(MuMa; ☎02 35 19 62 62; www.muma-lehavre.fr/en; 2 bd Clemenceau; adult/under 26yr €7/free; ⏰11am-6pm Tue-Fri, to 7pm Sat & Sun) Near the waterfront, this luminous and tranquil space houses a fabulous collection of vivid impressionist works – the finest in France outside Paris – by masters such as Monet (who grew up in Le Havre), Pissarro, Renoir and Sisley. You'll also find works by the Fauvist painter Raoul Dufy, born in Le Havre, and paintings by Eugène Boudin, a mentor of Monet and another Le Havre native.

Église St-Joseph Church

(bd François 1er; ⏰10am-6pm) Perret's masterful, 107m-high Église St-Joseph, visible from all over town, was built using bare concrete from 1951 to 1959. Some 13,000 panels of coloured glass make the soaring, sombre interior particularly striking when it's sunny. Stained-glass artist Margaret Huré created a cohesive masterpiece in her collaboration with Perret, and her use of shading and colour was thoughtfully conceived, evoking different moods depending on where the sun is in the sky – and the ensuing colours created by the illumination.

Jardins Suspendus Gardens

(rue du Fort; gardens free, greenhouses €2; ⏰10.30am-8pm Apr-Sep, to 5pm Oct-Mar) The Jardins Suspendus (Hanging Gardens) is an old hilltop fortress transformed into a beautiful set of gardens, whose greenhouses and outdoor spaces feature exquisite flowers, trees and grasses from five different continents, as fine views range over the harbour. It's a 30-minute uphill walk from the centre, or you can catch bus 1 along bd François I near the beach.

EATING

You'll find a concentration of restaurants along pedestrian-friendly rue Victor Hugo, one block north of Le Volcan. There's another cluster of restaurants in Quartier St-François, the area just south of the Bassin du Commerce – check out rue de Bretagne, rue Jean de la Fontaine and rue du Général Faidherbe.

Halles Centrales Market $

(rue Voltaire; 8.30am-7.30pm Mon-Sat, 9am-1pm Sun) The food stalls at Le Havre's main market include a patisserie, a *fromagerie* (cheese shop) and many tempting fruit stands; there's also a small supermarket here. You can find it a block west of Le Volcan.

La Taverne Paillette Brasserie $$

(02 35 41 31 50; www.taverne-paillette.com; 22 rue Georges Braque; lunch menus €15.50-31.20, mains €16-26; noon-midnight daily) Solid brasserie food is served up at this Le Havre institution whose origins, in a former incarnation, go back to the late 16th century. Think bowls overflowing with mussels, generous salads, gargantuan seafood platters and, in the Alsatian tradition, eight types of *choucroute* (sauerkraut). Diners leave contentedly well-fed and many are here for its famous beer too.

Bistrot des Halles Bistro $$

(02 35 22 50 52; 7 place des Halles Centrales; lunch menus €14, other menus €25, mains €15-25; noon-3pm & 7-11pm Mon-Sat, noon-3pm Sun) For a very French dining experience, this central and busy Lyon-style bistro is decked out with old-time enamel publicity plaques and old-style ambience. Specialities include steak, *magret de canard* (duck breast filet), *cassoulet* (rich bean, pork and duck stew) and large salads. Prices are reasonable and the bistro has a large fan base.

Jardins Suspendus (p117)

INFORMATION

Maison du Patrimoine (☎02 35 22 31 22; 181 rue de Paris; ⏰2-6pm Mon-Sat, 10am-1pm & 2-6pm Sun) The tourist office's city centre annexe has an exhibition on Perret's postwar reconstruction of the city.

Tourist Office (☎02 32 74 04 04; www.lehavretourisme.com; 186 bd Clemenceau; ⏰2-6pm Mon, 10am-12.30pm & 2-6pm Tue-Sat Nov-Mar, 9.30am-1pm & 2-7pm Apr-Nov) Has a map in English for a two-hour walking tour of Le Havre's architectural highlights and details on cultural events. Situated at the western edge of the city centre, one block south of the La Plage tram terminus.

GETTING THERE & AWAY

BOAT

Le Havre's car ferry terminal, situated 1km southeast of Le Volcan, is linked with the English port of Portsmouth via **Brittany Ferries** (www.brittany-ferries.co.uk). Ferries depart daily from late March to early November.

BUS

The bus station is next to the train station.

Bus Verts (p110) Heading south, bus 20 (four to six daily) goes to Honfleur (€4.90, 30 minutes) and Deauville and Trouville (€4.90, one hour).

Keolis (☎02 35 28 19 88; www.keolis-seine-maritime.com) For the Côte d'Albâtre, take scenic bus 24 (seven or more daily) to Étretat (€2, one hour) and Fécamp (€2, 1½ hours).

TRAIN

The train station, **Gare du Havre**, is 1.5km east of Le Volcan, at the eastern end of bd de Strasbourg. The tram stop out front is called 'Gares'. Trains go to these destinations:

Paris' Gare St-Lazare €30, 2¼ hours, 15 daily Monday to Friday, seven to nine Saturday and Sunday

Rouen €16, one hour, 16 to 20 daily Monday to Saturday, 10 Sunday

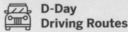

D-Day Driving Routes

Follow the D514 along the D-Day coast or signposted circuits around the battle sites – look for 'D-Day–Le Choc' signs in the American sectors, 'Overlord-L'Assaut' signs in the British and Canadian sectors. A free booklet called *The D-Day Landings and the Battle of Normandy*, available from tourist offices, has details on the eight major visitors' routes.

Gun emplacement, Omaha Beach (p106)
EDWARD HAYLAN/SHUTTERSTOCK ©

GETTING AROUND

Two tram lines run by LiA (www.transports-lia.fr) link the **train station** (Gare du Havre; www.voyages-sncf.com; cours de la République) with the city centre and the beach. A single ride costs €1.70; travelling all day is €3.80.

Location de Vélos (www.transports-lia.fr; per 2hr/half-day/full day €3/4/7) rents out bicycles (two hours/half-day/full day €3/4/7) at two sites, including the train station and a shop on 9 av René Coty, one block north of the Mairie du Havre.

St-Malo (p126)

BRITTANY

TATIANA POPOVA/SHUTTERSTOCK ©

In This Chapter

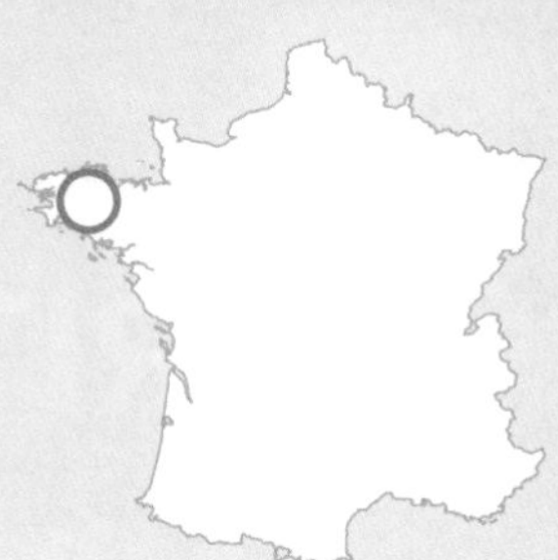

Brittany at a Glance...

Brittany is for explorers. The region (Breizh in Breton) has a wild coastline, medieval towns and thick forests. This is a land of prehistoric mysticism, proud tradition and culinary wealth, where fiercely independent locals celebrate Breton culture.

Brittany has world-famous sights, including stunning St-Malo, regal Dinard and charming Dinan. Unexpected gems, including the megaliths of Carnac, the rugged coastlines of Finistère, and its much-loved islands, reveal there's far more to Brittany than delicious crêpes and homemade cider. And wherever you go, keep an eye out for korrigans (fairies or spirits).

Two Days in Brittany

Spend day one in **St-Malo** (p126): explore its château and stroll the ramparts at sunset, drinking in views of town and ocean. On day two, rent wheels at Carnac-Plage and cycle between **prehistoric megaliths** (p124) around Carnac. Have a crêpe lunch in **Carnac town** (p132) and a late-afternoon dip (weather permitting!) in the Breton sea on Carnac's **Grande Plage** (p134). Round off the day with seafood in **Quiberon** (p134).

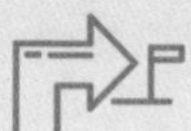

Four Days in Brittany

Day three, catch a ferry to **Belle Île** (p130) to admire geological wonders like the *aiguilles* (needles), kayak the bays and loll on marvellous stretches of sand like the **Plage des Grands Sables** (p131). On day four, spend time in labyrinthine **Vannes** (p133), rambling ramparts and finishing with a slap-up feast of Breton cuisine.

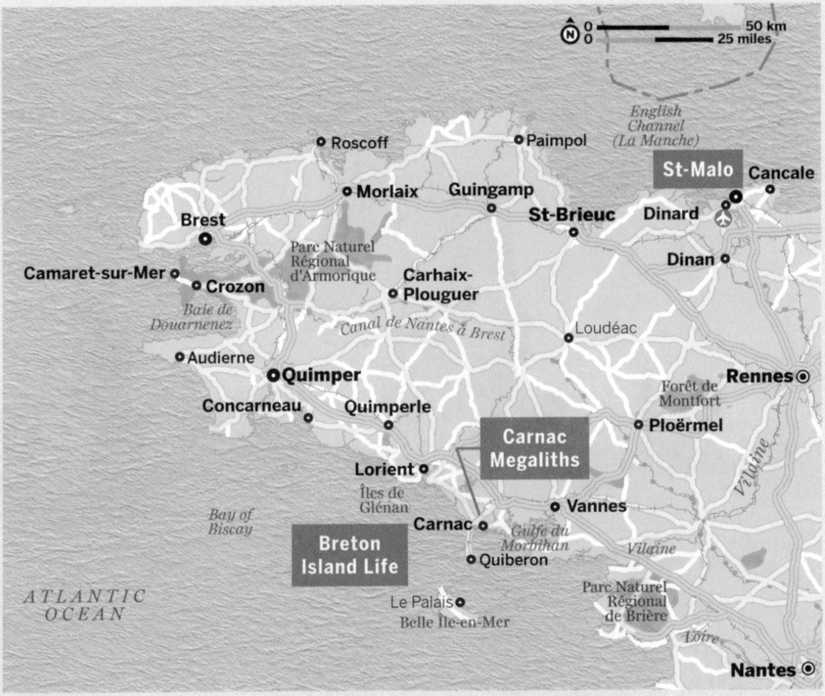

Arriving in Brittany

Gare Maritime du Naye Ferries between St-Malo and the Channel Islands, Portsmouth and Poole.

St-Malo train station Trains to/from Paris Montparnasse (€74, two hours 40 minutes, three direct TGVs daily) and Rennes (€15, one hour, roughly hourly).

Dinard–Pleurtuit–St-Malo Airport Ryanair flies to/from London Stansted, East Midlands. Aurigny Air flies from Guernsey. A taxi between Dinard and the airport costs €17 to €25.

BreizhGo (www.breizhgo.com) Handy transit website.

Where to Stay

Brittany offers a full range of sleeping options, from higher-end boutique B&Bs to simple ocean-side campgrounds. The region is a popular destination for international and domestic tourists alike, so it is essential to book ahead in summer, especially for Carnac, St-Malo and also Belle Île, which fills up completely in July and August. Some of the more rural establishments close in winter, and others, like those in Vannes, can stay busy year-round.

Carnac Megaliths

Predating Stonehenge by around 100 years, the Carnac (Garnag in Breton) area offers the world's greatest concentration of megalithic sites. There are no fewer than 3000 of these upright stones, erected between 5000 and 3500 BC. Hike, cycle and soak up some of the area's primordial energy.

Great For...

☑ Don't Miss

A superb primer on prehistory, including rare neolithic artefacts, at Carnac's Musée de Préhistoire (p132).

Two perplexing questions arise from Brittany's neolithic menhirs, dolmens, cromlechs, tumuli and cairns. Just how did the original constructors hew, then haul, these blocks (the heaviest weighs 300 tonnes), millennia before the wheel and the mechanical engine reached Brittany? And why? Theories abound, but common consensus is a spiritual impulse, the motivation for so much monument-building by humankind.

Just north of Carnac, a vast array of monoliths stand in several distinct alignments, all visible from the road, though fenced for controlled admission. The best way to appreciate their sheer size and numbers is to walk or bike between the **Ménec** and **Kerlescan** groups.

Kerlescan
Alignements de Kerlescan
Alignements du Ménec
Alignements de Kermario
Village du Menec
Maison des Mégalithes
Tumulus de Kercado
Carnac
Tumulus St-Michel

Need to Know

Between June and September, seven buses a day run between the Ménec and Kerlescan sites, as well as Carnac-Ville and Carnac-Plage.

Take a Break

Wolf down flambéed crêpes and *galettes* at Chez Marie (p132) in Carnac.

★ Top Tip

To cycle between megaliths, rent a bike (or tandem) from A Bicyclette (p133).

Maison des Mégalithes

Near the stones, the **Maison des Mégalithes** (www.menhirs-carnac.fr; rte des Alignements, D196; tour adult/child €9/5; 9.30am-7pm Jul & Aug, 9.30am-6pm Sep, Apr & Jun, 10am-1pm & 2-5pm Oct-Mar) explores the site's history and has a rooftop viewpoint. Due to erosion the sites are fenced off; certain areas are accessible only by guided tour. The Maison can organise one-hour guided visits, several times daily in French and weekly in English in summer. From March to October, selected parts are open for visitors to wander freely – ask the Maison for maps.

Menhir Fields

Opposite the Maison des Mégalithes, the largest menhir field – with 1099 stones – is the **Alignements du Ménec** (rte des Alignements), 1km north of Carnac-Ville. From here, the D196 heads northeast for about 1.5km to the equally impressive **Alignements de Kermario** (rte de Kerlescan), parts of which are open year-round. Climb the stone observation tower to see the alignment from above. The easternmost of the major groups is the **Alignements de Kerlescan** (rte de Kerlescan), a smaller grouping also accessible in winter.

Burial Mounds

The **Tumulus de Kercado** (rte de Kerlescan) lies just east of Kermario and 500m to the south of the D196. It's the massive burial mound of a neolithic chieftain dating from 3800 BC. Deposit your fee (€1) in an honour box at the entry gate. About 300m east of the Kercado turn-off along the D196 lies the parking area for the **Géant du Manio**. A 15-minute walk brings you to this vast rock, the highest menhir in the complex.

Tumulus St-Michel (chemin du Tumulus, Carnac-Ville), 400m northeast of the Carnac-Ville tourist office, and accessed off the D781 at the end of chemin du Tumulus, is a burial mound with a church on top. It dates back to at least 5000 BC and offers sweeping views.

St-Malo

The enthralling port town of St-Malo on Brittany's north coast has a dramatically changing landscape. With one of the world's greatest tidal ranges, this town is nature's finest theatre – and every tourist's summer haven.

Photo-op paradise, St-Malo is an ancient walled city where brewing storms under blackened skies see waves lash the top of the ramparts ringing its beautiful walled city. Hours later, blue sky merges with the deep cobalt sea as the tide recedes, exposing broad beaches and creating land bridges to granite outcrop islands. Stunning!

Construction of the city fortifications began in the 12th century. The town became a key port during the 17th and 18th centuries as a base for both merchant ships and government-sanctioned privateers (pirates, basically) against the threat of the English.

Intra-Muros

The tangle of streets within the walled city, known as Intra-Muros ('within the walls'), are a highlight of a visit to Brittany. Grand merchants' mansions and sea captains'

Great For...

☑ Don't Miss

Eye-popping views of the old city from the château's lookout tower.

houses line the narrow lanes, and open squares are tucked in its heart.

For the finest panoramas, stroll along the **jetty** that pokes out to sea off the southwestern tip of Intra-Muros from the end of which you'll get the wide angle view – or, to zoom in, clamber along the top of the **ramparts** which surround the town. Constructed at the end of the 17th century under military architect Vauban, and measuring 1.8km, the ramparts can be accessed at several points, including at all the main city gates.

The city's centrepiece, **Cathédrale St-Vincent** (place Jean de Châtillon; 9.30am-6pm), was constructed between the 12th and 18th centuries. During the ferocious fighting of August 1944 the cathedral was badly mauled; much of its original structure was reduced to rubble. The cathedral was rebuilt and reconsecrated in 1971.

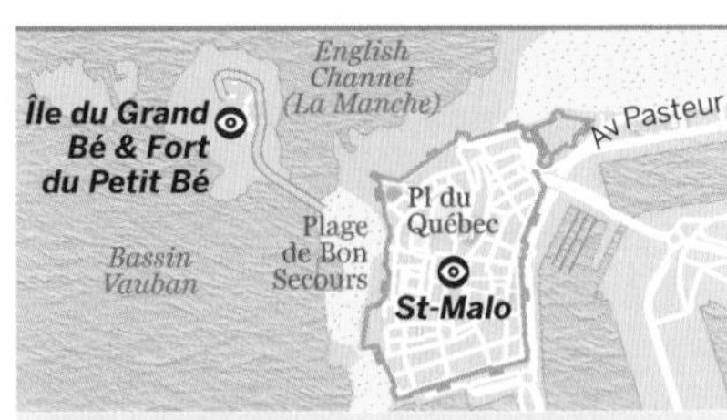

Need to Know

Tourist office (08 25 13 52 00; www.saint-malo-tourisme.com; esplanade St-Vincent; 9am-7.30pm Mon-Sat, 10am-7pm Sun Jul & Aug, shorter hours rest of year;)

Take a Break

Throw back a Breton beer at **L'Aviso** (12 rue Point du Jour; 6pm-3am Thu-Tue).

★ Top Tip

A combined ticket (€13/6 per adult/child) gives you access to St-Malo's four major monuments; buy it at any of the sights.

For the full low-down on the life and history of St-Malo, plus a hodgepodge of nautical exhibits, model boats and marine artefacts, head to the **Musée d'Histoire** (02 99 40 71 57; www.ville-saint-malo.fr/culture/les-musees; place Chateaubriand, Château de St-Malo; adult/child €6/3; 10am-12.30pm & 2-6pm Apr-Sep, 10am-noon & 2-6pm Tue-Sun Oct-Mar) inside Château de St-Malo, built by the dukes of Brittany in the 15th and 16th centuries.

Île du Grand Bé

At low tide, cross the beach to walk out via Porte des Bés to Île du Grand Bé, the rocky islet where the great St-Malo-born 18th-century writer Chateaubriand is buried. About 100m beyond the island is the privately owned, Vauban-built, 17th-century **Fort du Petit Bé**. The owner runs 30-minute guided tours in French; leaflets are available in English. Once the tide rushes in, the causeway remains impassable for about six hours; check tide times with the tourist office.

Belle Île (p130)

Breton Island Life

Brittany's south-coast islands are dotted with black sheep and crossed with craggy coastal paths. Some are barely sandy specks of land, others harbour communities of fisherfolk, farmers and artistic types. There's little to do but walk, cycle or picnic in perfect peace.

Great For...

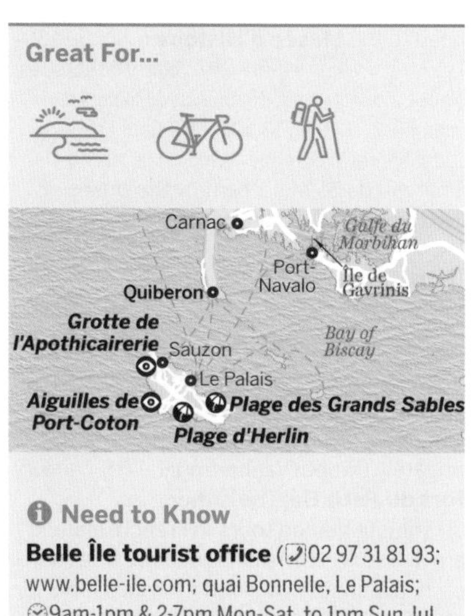

Need to Know

Belle Île tourist office (02 97 31 81 93; www.belle-ile.com; quai Bonnelle, Le Palais; 9am-1pm & 2-7pm Mon-Sat, to 1pm Sun Jul & Aug, shorter hours rest of year;)

★ Top Tip

Take a bicycle onto the ferry for €7.50, or rent one from Le Palais when you reach Belle Île.

TRAVELLIGHT/SHUTTERSTOCK ©

Belle Île

Belle Île (in full, Belle-Île-en-Mer, 'beautiful island in the sea') lives up to its name: rugged cliffs and rock stacks line the island's west coast while picturesque pastel ports nestle along the eastern side.

Accessed by ferries from Quiberon, the island's population swells tenfold in summer. Brittany's largest offshore island (20km by 9km) has two main settlements: the port of **Le Palais** on the east side of the island with a dramatic Vauban citadel, now a **history museum** (☎02 97 31 85 54; www.citadellevauban.com; Porte du Donjon, Le Palais; adult/child €8/5; ⌚9am-7pm Jul & Aug, shorter hours Sep-Dec & Feb-Jun); and smaller, even more charming **Sauzon** in the northeast.

The best way to appreciate the island's waterside charms is from the 95km coastal footpath. The fretted western coast has spectacular rock formations and caves, including **Grotte de l'Apothicairerie** where waves roll in from two sides; **Vives Eaux** (☎02 97 31 00 93; www.vives-eaux.fr; chemin de Port Puce, Sauzon; 3-hr tours adult from €34, 2-hr family tours from €27, rental per hr €11, per half-day €30; ⌚May-Oct) organises excellent guided kayaking tours.

Just off the western side of the island, the magnificent rock stacks of **Aiguilles de Port Coton** that resemble *aiguilles* (needles) are a must-see for photographers. The name Port Coton comes from the way the sea surges around the rocks, creating foam like cotton wool. These dramatic rock formations were depicted in a series of famous canvases by Claude Monet in 1886.

The island's northernmost point juts out at **Pointe des Poulains**. Flanked by craggy cliffs, this windswept headland is Belle Île's

Aiguilles de Port Coton

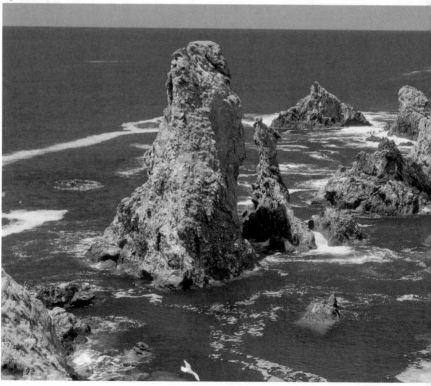

loftiest lookout, and was once the home of renowned actress Sarah Bernhardt. Her former fortress home is open to the public from April to October. There is a lighthouse here too, closer to the Pointe itself.

Beautiful Beaches

Belle Île is blessed with lovely beaches. The largest is 2km-long **Plage des Grands Sables**, spanning the calm waters of the island's eastern side. Sheltered **Plage d'Herlin**, on the south side, is best for kids.

☑ Don't Miss

Local *agneau de pré-salé*, tasty lamb with a distinct savoury flavour due to grazing on salty pastures. Pair with a crisp white wine.

Golfe du Morbihan

Around 40 islands peep out from the shallow waters of the Morbihan Gulf, which forms a breathtakingly beautiful inland sea that's easily accessible from Vannes. The bay's largest island is the 6km-long **Île aux Moines**. Nearby **Île d'Arz** is smaller (just 3km long and 1km wide) but it's the most scenic of the lot and features secluded sands and coastal walks. Tempted to stay? Both islands have a slew of B&Bs and eateries.

Lots of companies offer scenic cruises and ferry services to Île aux Moines and Île d'Arz and beyond. From April to September, check with **Navix** (02 97 46 60 00; www.navix.fr; Apr-Sep) and **La Compagnie du Golfe** (02 97 01 22 80; www.compagnie-du-golfe.fr; 7 allée Loïc Caradec, Vannes; cruise adult/child from €16.80/11.80; Apr-Sep). Year-round **Bateaux-Bus du Golfe** (02 97 44 44 40; www.ile-arz.fr; 7 allée Loïc Caradec; adult/child return €10.40/5.70; 6.30am-8pm) runs 10 to 14 boats per day between Vannes port or Conleau and Île d'Arz. **Izenah Croisières** (02 97 26 31 45; www.izenah-croisieres.com; adult/child return €5.20/2.90) runs boats from the port at Baden to Île aux Moines year-round.

Île de Gavrinis

One of the most special neolithic ruins along the Morbihan coast is the **Cairn de Gavrinis** (boat trip & tour adult/child €18/8; 9.30am-12.30pm & 1.30-6.30pm Apr-Sep), on the island of the same name. Dating from 4000 BC and measuring more than 50m in diameter, the beautifully situated tomb is well known for its profusion of intricate engravings. You access the site on a 15-minute boat trip from the harbour at Larmor-Baden (14km southeast of Auray), and it's important to reserve tickets in advance.

Take a Break

On Belle Île, enjoy a kettle of mussels at bistro **Le Verre à Pied** (02 97 31 29 65; 3 place de la République, Le Palais; mains €14-20; noon-2pm & 6-10pm Thu-Tue Feb-Dec) in central Le Palais. Finish with a slice of *far breton* (local flan) for dessert.

Carnac

Carnac is firmly on the map for its almost other-worldly collection of megalithic sites, but it's also blessed with enticing beaches and a pretty town centre.

Some 32km west of Vannes, Carnac comprises the old stone village Carnac-Ville and, 1.5km south, the seaside resort of Carnac-Plage, bordered by the 2km-long sandy beach, La Grande Plage.

SIGHTS

Musée de Préhistoire Museum

(☎02 97 52 22 04; www.museedecarnac.fr; 10 place de la Chapelle, Carnac-Ville; adult/child €6/3; ⏱10am-6.30pm Jul & Aug, 10am-12.30pm & 2-6pm Wed-Mon Apr-Jun & Sep, shorter hours Oct-Mar) The Musée de Préhistoire is chock full with the finds from the megalithic sites throughout the region, so it serves as a fantastic primer to the area and its prehistory. The museum chronicles life in and around Carnac from the Palaeolithic and neolithic eras to the Middle Ages. It's a must for admiring and understanding beautifully made neolithic axe heads, pottery, jewellery and other priceless and very rare artefacts.

EATING

Chez Marie Crêpes $

(☎02 97 52 07 93; 3 place de l'Église, Carnac-Ville; mains €6-13, menus €10-15; ⏱noon-2pm & 7-10pm Wed-Sun) Established in 1959, this Carnac institution churns out *galettes* (savoury buckwheat crêpes) and sweet crêpes in a charmingly traditional stone house opposite the church. Connoisseurs recommend its flambéed specialities, especially the Arzal *galette,* with scallops, apples and cider. There's a kids' menu (for under 10s) for €7.50, as well as a list of beers, ciders, wines and cocktails.

La Côte Gastronomy $$$

(☎02 97 52 02 80; www.restaurant-la-cote.com; impasse Parc Er Forn, Kermario; lunch menu €26, dinner menu 39-58; ⏱12.15-2.15pm Wed-Sun, 7.15-9.15pm Wed-Sat) Top recommendation on the Morbihan Coast goes to this Carnac restaurant run by Carnacois *maître-cuisinier* Pierre Michaud, who has

Carnac streetscape

won plaudits for his inventive cuisine that combines the very best Breton ingredients. The setting is another drawcard, with an elegant dining room and a soothing terrace overlooking a small fish pond. Find it in a quiet property close to the Alignements de Kermario.

 INFORMATION

Tourist Office (☎02 97 52 13 52; www.ot-carnac.fr; 74 av des Druides, Carnac-Plage; ⊙9.30am-7pm Mon-Sat, 3-7pm Sun Jul-Aug, 9.30-12.30pm & 2-6pm Mon-Sat, 3-6pm Sun Apr-Jun & Sep, shorter hours rest of year; 📶) This office in Carnac-Plage, next to the church, has an excellent map of nearby neolithic sites and a smartphone app.

 GETTING THERE & AROUND

BICYCLE

Hire bikes and cycle buggies from **A Bicyclette** (☎02 97 52 75 08; www.velocarnac.com; 93bis av des Druides, Carnac-Plage; bicycle per day from €10, buggy per hr from €8) down near the beach.

BUS

The main bus stops are in Carnac-Ville, outside the police station on rue St-Cornély, and in Carnac-Plage, beside the tourist office. **TIM** (☎08 00 88 10 87; www.tim-morlaix.com; ticket €2) runs a daily bus (line 1) to Auray (30 minutes), Vannes (80 minutes) and Quiberon (30 minutes).

TRAIN

The nearest useful train station is in Auray, 12km to the northeast. SNCF has an office in the tourist office where you can buy advance tickets.

Celtic Knees-Up

Celtic communities from Ireland, Scotland, Wales, Cornwall, the Isle of Man and Galicia in northwest Spain congregate with Bretons at the **Festival Interceltique de Lorient** (☎02 97 21 24 29; www.festival-interceltique.bzh; rue Pierre Guergadic, Lorient; ⊙early Aug) over 10 days in early August. Upwards of 600,000 people descend on the city of Lorient, about 30km northwest of Carnac, so book well ahead if you're planning to stay in town for the festival.

Celtic flags at festival parade
AFP/GETTY IMAGES ©

Vannes

Overlooking the Golfe du Morbihan, Vannes is one of the unmissable towns of Brittany. Spectacular fortifications encircle Vannes' meandering alleys and cobbled squares, and lead down to a sparkling marina lined with cafes and townhouses. The city still preserves much of its medieval atmosphere, but it's a vibrant place with a lively bar and restaurant scene year-round.

 SIGHTS

Within the walls, the old city is a delightful jumble of timber-framed houses and wonky merchants' mansions, especially around **place des Lices** and **place Henry IV**. Wandering at will is the order of the day, soaking up the atmosphere and seeing what you discover.

Ramparts Historic Site

Vannes' old town is surrounded by imposing ramparts and gates, which are in turn lined by a moat and, on the eastern edge, simply spectacular flower-filled gardens (p134). Tucked away behind rue des Vierges, stairs lead to the accessible section of the ramparts from which you can see the black-roofed **Vieux Lavoirs** (Old Laundry Houses) along the water. Or walk rue Francis Decker, on the wall's eastern exterior, to take it all in.

Jardins des Remparts Gardens

(rue Francis Decker; ⏰24hr) These beautifully manicured gardens lie just outside the walls of the town and are a gorgeous place to relax and take in some astonishing views.

La Cohue – Musée des Beaux-Arts Gallery

(☎02 97 01 63 00; place St-Pierre; adult/child €6.30/4.30, free Sun; ⏰1.30-6pm daily Jun-Sep, Tue-Sun Oct-May) Opposite the cathedral, the building called La Cohue has variously been a produce market, a law court and the seat of the Breton parliament. Today it's a well-curated museum of fine arts, displaying 19th-century paintings, sculptures and engravings, and rotating exhibitions of cutting-edge contemporary art.

The ticket price includes the **Musée d'Histoire et d'Archéologie** (☎02 97 01 63 00; 2 rue Noë; adult/child €6.30/4.30, free Sun; ⏰1.30-6pm Jun-Sep).

SHOPPING

In keeping with Vannes' artistic spirit, galleries such as **L'Echoppe St-Guénhaël** (☎02 97 47 92 37; 29 rue St-Guénhaël; ⏰10am-12.30pm & 2-7pm Mon-Sat) sell innovative (and often amusing) contemporary Breton art. If you have children with you then there's no way you'll get past colourful **Bilboquet** (www.bilboquet.com; 9 rue St-Guenhaël; ⏰10am-7pm Tue-Sun) – a classic old-fashioned toy shop – without buying a train, a kite or a doll.

EATING

Rue des Halles and its offshoots are lined with tempting eateries; classic and contemporary brasseries arc around the port. Book ahead in high season and on weekends. Market days are Wednesday and Saturday mornings.

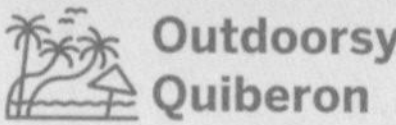

Outdoorsy Quiberon

Quiberon (Kiberen in Breton) sits right at the southern tip of a thin, 14km-long peninsula, flanked on the western side by the wave-lashed **Côte Sauvage** (Wild Coast). The setting is superb, with a heady mix of lovely rock-strewn beaches and dramatic, rugged inlets. It's wildly popular in summer and is also the departure point for ferries to Belle Île (p130).

Grande Plage is a long, family-friendly and attractive, sheltered sweep of sand. For active types, there are plenty of water sports; **Sillages** (☎06 81 26 75 08; www.kayak-sillages.com; 9 av de Groix, St-Pierre-Quiberon; adult/child from €20/16; ⏰daily by reservation) runs guided kayaking tours for all levels (beginners welcome). **Cycles Loisirs** (☎02 97 50 31 73; www.cyclesloisirs.free.fr; 32 rue Victor Golvan; touring/mountain bikes per day from €9.50/13, kids' bikes per day from €7), near the **tourist office** (☎02 97 50 07 84; www.quiberon.com; 14 rue de Verdun; ⏰9am-7pm Mon-Sat, 10am-1pm & 2-5pm Sun Aug, shorter hours rest of year; 📶), rents touring/mountain bikes. The highlight is touring the Route Côtière (D186A) along the Côte Sauvage, stopping off at various beaches.

Seafood features markedly on Quiberon menus. **Le Petit Hôtel du Grand Large** (☎02 97 30 91 61; www.lepetithoteldugrandlarge.fr/restaurant/; 11 quai St-Ivy, Portivy; lunch menu from €40, dinner menu €60-95) has earned a Michelin star.

Côte Sauvage

Dan Ewen Crêpes $

(☎02 97 42 44 34; 3 place Général de Gaulle; mains €3-10, menus €10-18; ⏰11.30am-2pm & 6.30-9pm Mon-Sat) A near-life-size statue of a smiling Breton lady bearing a tray greets you at the entrance of this popular stone and dark-wood crêperie. Generous fillings include frangipani, or flambéed options topped with *crème Chantilly*. You can wash it down with a *boule* (goblet) of local cider. To tempt in the young ones, a €6.90 kids' menu is at hand.

Restaurant de Roscanvec Gastronomy $$$

(☎02 97 47 15 96; www.roscanvec.com; 17 rue des Halles; lunch menu €25-30, dinner menu €55-70; ⏰12.15-2pm Tue-Sun, 7.45-9.15pm Tue-Sat Jul & Aug, closed Tue Sep-Jun) Hidden in the timber-frame houses of the old city, this stellar restaurant is overseen by one of Brittany's most talented names, Thierry Seychelles, whose cooking has been championed by most of the major culinary critics. Rightly so: his trademark six-course 'Hedonist Menu' (€70) combines seasonal French classics with global flavours, and the lunch *menu* is a gourmet steal.

DRINKING & NIGHTLIFE

Le Verre à L'Envers Bar

(6 place Général de Gaulle; ⏰4pm-1am Tue-Sat) A mature, in-the-know set favours this pearl of a place just beyond the ramparts. Snag a seat on the terrace to soak up the street atmosphere or snuggle up in its pocket-sized room. Knock back a wine by the glass or a beer, and graze on an excellent cheese or charcuterie platter. But the real queen of the drinks card is the mojito.

INFORMATION

Tourist Office (☎08 25 13 56 10, 02 97 47 24 34; www.tourisme-vannes.com; quai Eric Tabarly; ⏰9.30am-7pm Mon-Sat, 10am-6pm Sun Jul & Aug, 9.30am-12.30pm & 1.30-6pm Mon-Sat Sep-Jun; 📶) In a modern building on the marina.

Crêpe Capital

Crêpes and *galettes* are Brittany's traditional staple and are ubiquitous throughout the region. These large thin pancakes are made by spreading batter on a hot griddle. Crêpes are made with ordinary *froment* (wheat flour), while *galettes* are made using *sarrasin* or *blé noir* (buckwheat flour). The classic *galette* filling is *galette complète* (ham, egg and cheese), but there are plenty of more original combinations. Crêpes are often eaten as a sweet dessert or snack, slathered in jam or drowned in ice cream.

GETTING THERE & AROUND

BICYCLE

When we passed through, a new electric-bike system called Vélocéo was expected in Vannes.

BUS

The small bus station is opposite the train station. **TIM** (p133) has services throughout the region, including line 1 to Carnac (€2, 80 minutes) and on to Quiberon (€2, 1¾ hours, 8 daily), and line 9 to Rochefort-en-Terre (€2, 1¼ hours).

TRAIN

Vannes is on the train line running east to Quimper and west to Rennes, Nantes or Paris. Trains go to/from Paris Montparnasse (€48 to €85.60, 2½ hours, 10 direct daily), Rennes (€16 to €19.50, one to 1½ hours, 15 daily) and Nantes (€23.40, 1½ hours, five direct daily).

Vineyard, Montagne de Reims (p147)

CHAMPAGNE

MIKI STUDIO/SHUTTERSTOCK ©

In This Chapter

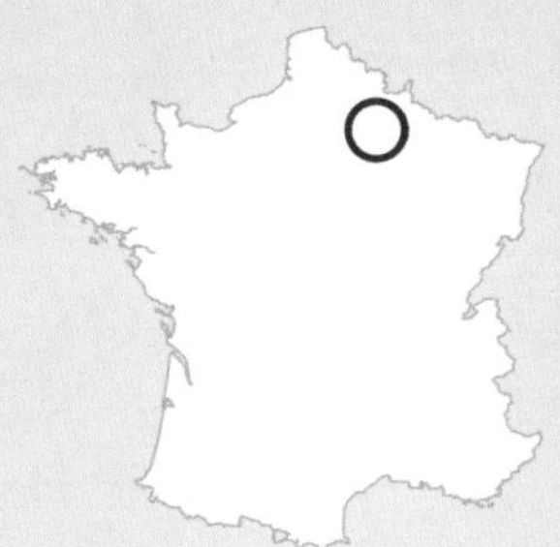

Champagne at a Glance...

Champagne arouses the senses: the eyes feast on vines parading up hillsides and processions of tiny, sparkling bubbles; the nose breathes in a heavenly bouquet; the ears rejoice at the clink of glasses and the barely audible fizz; and the palate tingles with every sip. Champagne cellar visits reveal the processes that transform the world's most pampered pinot noir, pinot meunier and chardonnay grapes into this Unesco World Heritage–listed region's most fabled wines.

The people of Champagne offer a warm welcome, both in the stylish cities and along the Champagne Routes, which wend their way through villages to family-run cellars and vineyards.

Two Days in Champagne

Begin in the heart of Champagne, **Épernay** (p152). Buy a picnic at the town's covered food market before touring your pick of world-famous **Champagne houses** (p140). Head out of town for a picnic lunch amid vines in **Hautvillers** (p144), first delightful stop on the picturesque Vallée de la Marne driving route. Day two, head to Reims to visit its **cathedral** (p147) and perhaps another Champagne house.

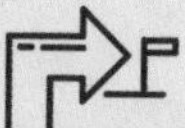

Four Days in Champagne

With four days, you can linger longer in the countryside. Spend two days slowly meandering along the **Côte des Blancs Champagne Route** (p145); overnight in an idyllically rural B&B in Avize or Le Mesnil-sur-Oger. Before setting out, book a tour in advance at the **Musée de la Vigne et du Vin** (p146).

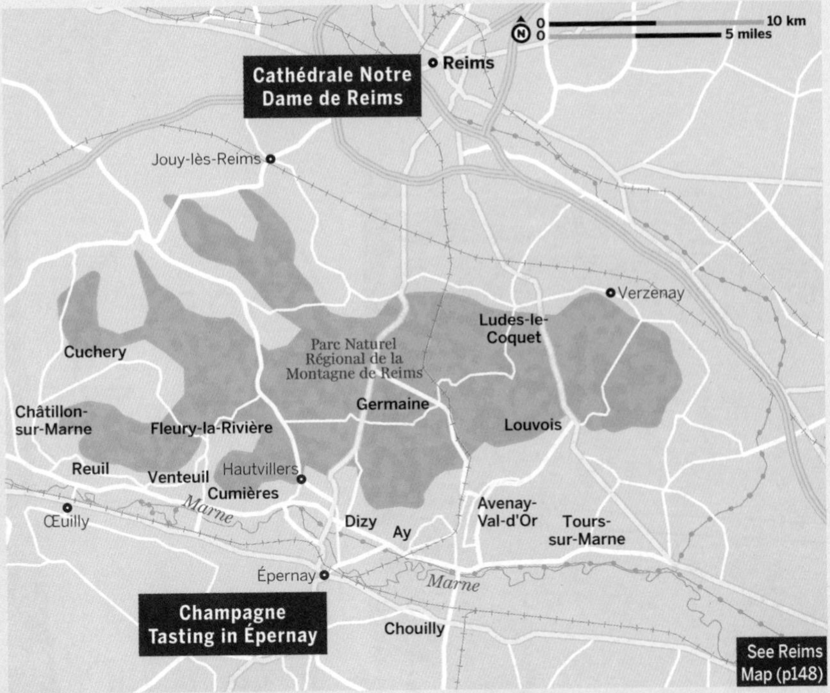

0 10 km
0 5 miles

Reims

Cathédrale Notre Dame de Reims

Jouy-lès-Reims

Verzenay

Ludes-le-Coquet

Cuchery

Parc Naturel Régional de la Montagne de Reims

Germaine

Châtillon-sur-Marne

Fleury-la-Rivière

Louvois

Reuil

Venteuil

Hautvillers

Cumières

Marne

Œuilly

Dizy

Ay

Avenay-Val-d'Or

Tours-sur-Marne

Épernay

Marne

Champagne Tasting in Épernay

Chouilly

See Reims Map (p148)

Arriving in Champagne

Reims train station Frequent services to Paris Gare de l'Est (€28 to €61, 46 minutes to one hour, 12 to 17 daily) and Épernay (€7.20, 30 minutes, 16 daily). Car-rental agencies are next to the station on bd Joffre.

Car The region makes a refreshing stop-over if you're driving from the Channel ports, Lille or Paris southeastwards towards Lyon or Provence.

Where to Stay

Reims and Épernay are appealing bases for driving tours along the Montagne de Reims, Vallée de la Marne and Côte des Blancs Champagne routes, with plentiful hotels and B&Bs. Troyes is a great choice for exploring the southern Côte des Bar route. Plan ahead and you can find charming digs in the heart of wine country – see local tourist offices and www.champagne-ardenne-tourism.co.uk.

Moët & Chandon

Champagne Tasting in Épernay

Prosperous Épernay, home to many of the world's most celebrated Champagne houses, is the finest spot on Earth for tasting bubbly – in a cinematic labyrinth of subterranean cellars.

Great For...

☑ Don't Miss

The stash of 400 Champagne varieties to pick from at wine bar C. Comme (p152).

Beneath the streets in 110km of subterranean cellars, more than 200 million bottles of Champagne are being aged. In 1950 one such cellar – owned by the irrepressible Mercier family – hosted a car rally!

Moët & Chandon

This prestigious **address** (☎03 26 51 20 20; www.moet.com; 20 av de Champagne; 1½hr tour with tasting €25-40, 10-17yr €10; ⏲tours 9.30-11.30am & 2-4.30pm) is the world's biggest producer of Champagne. It has frequent 90-minute tours that are among the region's most impressive, offering a peek at part of its 28km labyrinth of *caves* (cellars).

Champagne Georges Cartier

Hewn out of the chalk in the 18th century, the cellars and passageways at **Champagne Georges Cartier** (☎03 26 32 06 22;

De Castellane

DAAN KLOEG/SHUTTERSTOCK ©

www.georgescartier.com; 9 rue Jean Chandon-Moët; adult incl 6-glass tasting €15, cellar tour & 1-glass tasting €12.50, cellar tour & 6-glass tasting €23.50; ⏰10am-7pm Tue-Thu & Sun, 10am-8pm Fri & Sat) is incredibly atmospheric. Look out for graffiti dating to when they were used as bunkers during WWII. Tours include a tasting of one to six glasses.

Mercier

France's most popular brand, **Mercier** (☎03 26 51 22 22; www.champagnemercier.fr; 68-70 av de Champagne; adult incl 1/2/3 glasses €18/22/25, 12-17yr €8; ⏰tours 9.30-11.30am & 2-4.30pm, closed mid-Dec–mid-Feb) was founded in 1847 by Eugène Mercier, the virtual creator of cellar tours. The Mercier cellars were renovating when we passed through, and due to reopen in 2019.

Need to Know

Reserve cellar tours with *dégustation* (tasting) at Épernay's tourist office (p153).

Take a Break

Coffee and *Baba* (a cork-shaped, Champagne-flavoured pastry with vanilla cream) at Pâtisserie Vincent Dallet (p152).

★ Top Tip

Get walking, cycling and driving route maps at the tourist office (p153).

De Castellane

The 45-minute tours, in French and English, at **De Castellane** (☎03 26 51 19 11; www.castellane.com; 57 rue de Verdun; adult incl 1 glass €14, under 12yr free; ⏰tours 10-11am & 2-5pm, closed Christmas–mid-Mar) take in an informative bubbly museum. Climb 237 steps up the 1905-built tower for a fine panoramic view.

Atelier 1834: Champagne Boizel

This wonderfully intimate Champagne **house** (☎03 26 55 91 49; www.boizel.com; 46 av de Champagne; tours incl 2 Champagne tastings €22-40; ⏰10am-1pm & 2.30-5.30pm Mon-Fri, 10am-1pm & 2.30-6pm Sat) is run with passion by the Boizel family. These are very much working cellars but there are hidden treasures – several bottles (still drinkable, apparently) hail from 1834. *Dégustations* (tastings) take place upstairs.

Taste Like a Pro

Two-hour workshops at **Villa Bissinger** (☎03 26 55 78 78; www.villabissinger.com; 15 rue Jeanson, Ay), home to the International Institute for the Wines of Champagne, are educative and include a tasting of four Champagnes. Find it 3.5km northeast of Épernay in Ay. Reserve ahead.

Cathédrale Notre Dame de Reims

Lavishly encrusted with sculptures, Reims' resplendent Gothic cathedral has been inscribed on Unesco's list of World Heritage Sites since 1991. Swoon at its ornate tracery and centuries-old statues, then join a tour to scale the tower.

Great For...

☑ Don't Miss

One-hour tours to climb the tower's 250 steps; book at Palais du Tau.

Imagine the egos and extravagance of a French royal coronation. The focal point of such bejewelled pomposity was Reims' cathedral, begun in 1211 on a site occupied by churches since the 5th century. The cathedral was seriously damaged by artillery and fire during WWI, and was repaired during the interwar years, thanks, in part, to significant donations from the American Rockefeller family.

Gothic Façade

Nothing can prepare you for that first skyward glimpse of Reims' gargantuan Gothic cathedral, rising golden and imperious above the city. To get the most impressive first view, approach the cathedral from the west, along rue Libergier. Here your gaze will be drawn to the heavily restored architectural features of the façade, lavishly

L'Ange au Sourire (Smiling Angel)

IVAN VARYUKHIN/SHUTTERSTOCK ©

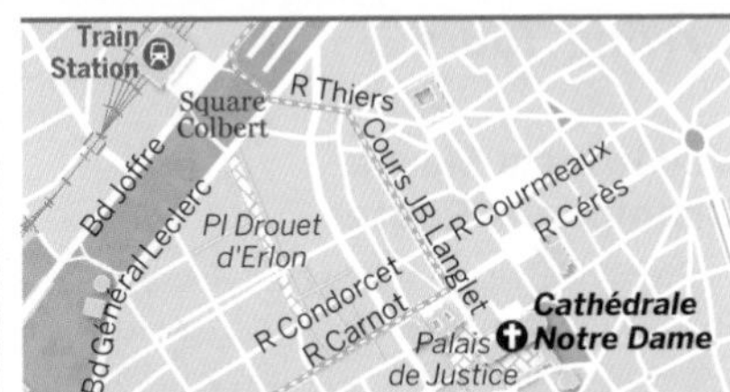

Need to Know

Map p148; ☎03 26 47 81 79; www.cathedrale-reims.fr; 2 place du Cardinal Luçon; tower adult/child €8/free, incl Palais du Tau €11/free; ⏰7.30am-7.30pm, tower tours 10am, 11am & 2-5pm Tue-Sat, 2-5pm Sun May-Aug, 10am, 11am & 2-4pm Sat, 2-4pm Sun Sep, Oct & mid-Mar–Apr

Take a Break

Enjoy a glass of bubbly at bijou Le Wine Bar by Le Vintage (p151).

★ Top Tip

Reims' tourist office (p151) rents audio-guides for self-paced cathedral tours.

encrusted with sculptures. Among them is the 13th-century *L'Ange au Sourire (Smiling Angel)*, presiding beneficently above the central portal. Look for Goliath's worn figure up on the west façade.

Royal Coronations

The single most famous event to take place in the cathedral was the coronation of Charles VII, with Joan of Arc at his side, on 17 July 1429. This is one of 25 coronations that took place here between 1223 and 1825.

Interior Treasures

The interior is a rainbow of stained-glass windows; the finest are the western façade's great rose window, the north transept's rose window and the vivid Chagall creations (1974) in the central axial chapel.

Other interior highlights include a flamboyant **Gothic organ case** topped with a figure of Christ, a 15th-century wooden astronomical **clock**, and a statue of **Joan of Arc** in full body armour (1901); there's a second statue of her outside on the square, to the right as you exit the cathedral.

Palais du Tau

When in town for their coronations, French princes stayed at **Palais du Tau** (www.palais-du-tau.fr; 2 place du Cardinal Luçon; adult/child €8/free, incl cathedral tower €11/free; ⏰9.30am-6.30pm Tue-Sun May–mid-Sep, 9.30am-12.30pm & 2-5.30pm Tue-Sun mid-Sep–Apr) – and threw banquets here afterwards. Today another Unesco World Heritage Site, the former archbishop's residence was redesigned in neoclassical style between 1671 and 1710. Its museum displays truly exceptional statuary, liturgical objects and tapestries from the cathedral, some in the impressive, Gothic-style **Salle de Tau** (Great Hall).

Driving Tours

Vallée de la Marne Champagne Route

A stronghold of pinot meunier vines, this 90km itinerary winds from Épernay to Dormans, heading more or less west along the hillsides north of the River Marne, then circles back to the east along the river's south bank. The GR14 long-distance walking trail and its variants (eg GR141) pass through the area.

Hautvillers

Perched above a sea of emerald vines and ablaze with forsythia and tulips in spring, Hautvillers, 6km north of Épernay, is where Dom Pierre Pérignon is popularly believed to have created Champagne. He is buried in the **Église Abbatiale** (rue de l'Abbaye; ⏲9am-6.30pm Mon-Fri, 10am-6.30pm Sat & Sun).

The village is one of Champagne's prettiest, with ubiquitous medieval-style wrought-iron signs providing pictorial clues to the activities taking place on the other side of the wall. On the main square, the **tourist office** (☎03 26 57 06 35; www.tourisme-hautvillers.com; place de la République; ⏲9.30am-1pm & 1.30-5.30pm Mon-Sat, 10am-4pm Sun, shorter hours winter) has maps detailing vineyard walks. It can also arrange Champagne tasting (€9) and half-day electric bike tours of the vineyards (€45).

For stylish Champagne tasting, hit **Au 36** (www.au36.net; 36 rue Dom Pérignon; ⏲10.30am-6pm Apr-Oct, 10.30am-4pm Fri-Tue Nov-Dec & Mar), a slinky wine boutique with a 'wall' of Champagne arranged by aroma and a laid-back tasting room.

Gorge on astonishing vineyard views a few hundred metres north of the centre along rte de Fismes (D386); south along rte de Cumières (a road leading to D1); and along the GR14 long-distance walking trail (red-and-white markings) and local vineyard footpaths (yellow markings).

Châtillon-sur-Marne

Some 20km west of Hautvillers, sloping picturesquely down a hillside braided with vines, this village's biggest claim to fame is as the

Traditional wrought-iron sign, Hautvillers

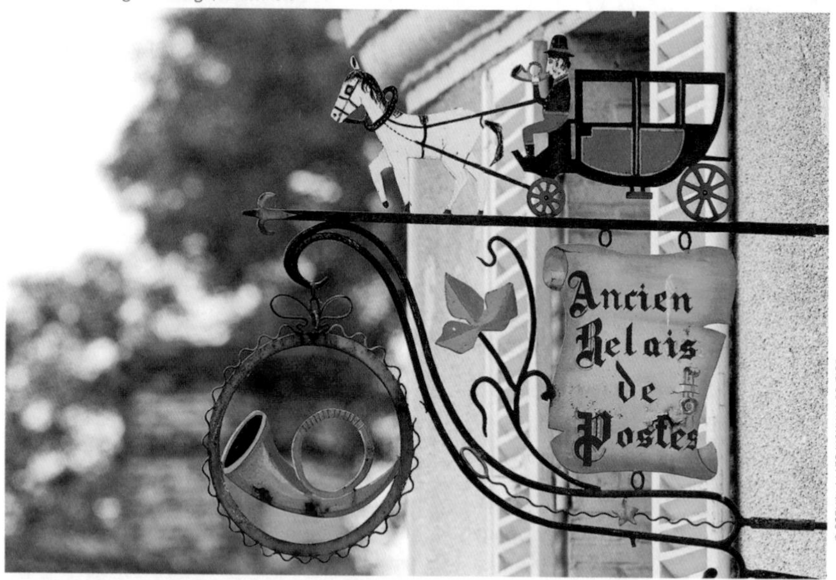

home town of Pope Urban II. A map panel on central place Urbain II details an 11km, four-hour vineyard walk. Its cellars also produce Champagnes worth lingering for. The **tourist office** (03 26 58 32 86; www.tourisme-chatillon-marne.fr; 4 rue de l'Eglise; 10am-1pm & 2.30-6.30pm Tue-Sun, 2.30-6.30pm Mon, shorter hours Oct-Mar) has plenty of info on the village and the surrounding region.

Cuchery

You're assured a warm, English-speaking welcome and a fascinating cellar tour at **Albert Levasseur** (03 26 58 11 38; www.champagne-levasseur.fr; 6 rue Sorbier, Cuchery; by appointment only) FREE, 7.5km north-east of Châtillon-sur-Marne. A friendly Franco-Irish couple turn grapes grown on 4.2 hectares into 35,000 to 40,000 bottles of Champagne each year. Phone or email ahead if possible. Find the hamlet of Cuchery 18km northwest of Épernay on the D24.

Œuilly

Blink and you'll miss dinky Œuilly, 6km southeast of Châtillon-sur-Marne, but that would be a shame. This cute grey-stone village, flower-draped in summer, is topped by a 13th-century **church** (place de la Mairie) and home to the **Écomusée d'Œuilly** (www.ecomusee-oeuilly.fr; cour des Maillets; adult/child €7/4; tours 10.30am & 2pm Wed-Mon) spotlighting winegrowing life of yore.

Côte des Blancs Champagne Route

This 100km route, planted almost exclusively with white chardonnay grapes (the name means 'hillside of the whites'), begins along Épernay's majestic av du Champagne and then heads south to Sézanne and beyond. The gently rolling landscape is at its most attractive in late summer and autumn.

Cramant

For views of the neatly tended vines and patchwork colours of the Champagne countryside, check out the view from the ridge above this village, whose northern entrance is adorned by a two-storey-high **champagne bottle**. Find it 9km southeast of Épernay on D10.

Champagne Varieties

Blanc de Blancs Champagne made using only chardonnay grapes. Fresh and elegant, with very small bubbles and a bouquet reminiscent of 'yellow fruits' such as pear and plum.

Blanc de Noirs A full-bodied, deep golden Champagne made solely with black grapes (despite the colour). Often rich and refined, with great complexity and a long finish.

Rosé Pink Champagne (mostly served as an aperitif), with a fresh character and summer fruit flavours. Made by adding a small percentage of red pinot noir to white Champagne.

Prestige Cuvée The crème de la crème of Champagne. Usually made with grapes from *grand cru* vineyards and priced and bottled accordingly.

Millésimé Vintage Champagne produced from a single crop during an exceptional year. Most Champagne is nonvintage.

Vineyard, Montagne de Reims (p147)

Avize

Right in the heart of Blancs des Blancs country and surrounded by rows of immaculately tended vines, Avize is lauded far and wide for its outstanding Champagnes. It's home to the **Avize Viti Campus** (Champagne High School of Winemaking; www.avizeviticampus.fr; rue d'Oger) and the renowned

Making Champagne

Champagne is made from the red pinot noir (38%), the black pinot meunier (35%) or the white chardonnay (27%) grape. Each vine is vigorously pruned and trained to produce a small quantity of high-quality grapes. Indeed, to maintain exclusivity (and price), the designated areas where grapes used for Champagne can be grown and the amount of wine produced each year are limited.

Making Champagne according to the *méthode champenoise* (traditional method) is a complex procedure. There are two fermentation processes, the first in casks and the second after the wine has been bottled and had sugar and yeast added. Bottles are then aged in cellars for two to five years, depending on the *cuvée* (vintage).

For two months in early spring the bottles are aged in cellars kept at 12°C and the wine turns effervescent. The sediment that forms in the bottle is removed by *remuage,* a painstakingly slow process in which each bottle, stored horizontally, is rotated slightly every day for weeks until the sludge works its way to the cork. Next comes *dégorgement:* the neck of the bottle is frozen, creating a blob of solidified Champagne and sediment, which is then removed.

Pressing grapes, Hautvillers
DAAN KLOEG/SHUTTERSTOCK ©

Sanger Cellars (☎03 26 57 79 79; www.sanger.fr; 33 rue du Rempart du Midi; tour incl 2-/4-/9-flute tasting €10/17.50/30, full-day masterclass €60; ⌚8am-noon & 2-5pm Mon-Fri), where tours take in both traditional equipment and the latest high-tech production facilities; they conclude with tasting and a shopping spree in the discounted *cave*. The entrance is on the D19; if the door is locked, push the intercom button.

Once the abbey church of a Benedictine convent, **Église St-Nicolas** (rue de l'Église, D10) mixes Romanesque, Flamboyant Gothic and Renaissance styles. From here, aptly named rue de la Montagne leads up the hill (towards Grauves), past an oversized Champagne bottle, to **Parc Vix** (D19), which affords panoramic vineyard views; a map sign details a 6.5km, two-hour walk through forest and field.

Oger

The tiny hamlet of Oger is known for its *grand cru* fields, prize-winning flower gardens and the **Musée du Mariage** (www.champagne-henry-devaugency.fr; 1 rue d'Avize, D10; adult/child €8/free; ⌚9.30am-noon & 2-6pm Tue-Sun). Featuring colourful and often gaudy objects associated with 19th-century marriage traditions, highlights include a tableau of newlyweds in their nuptial bed – but they're not alone, for they've been woken up early by family and friends bearing Champagne, chocolate and broad smiles. The collection was assembled by the parents of the owner of Champagne Henry de Vaugency (founded 1732), an eighth-generation Champagne grower. An explanatory sheet in English is available. Admission includes a Champagne tasting.

Le Mesnil-sur-Oger

This comely winegrowing village, 15km south of Épernay, is among the most famous in Champagne, with 100% of its chardonnay vines producing the superlative *grand cru* Champagnes. It's worth the pilgrimage alone for an insight into Champagne making and its history at the **Musée de la Vigne et du Vin** (☎03 26 57 50 15; www.champagne-launois.fr; 2 av Eugène Guillaume, cnr D10; adult incl 3 flutes €12; ⌚tours 10am & 3pm Mon-Fri, 10.30am Sat & Sun). This wine museum, assembled by a family that has been making Champagne since 1872, is so outstanding that it's worth planning your day around a two-hour tour. Highlights include a massive 16-tonne oak-beam grape press from 1630. Reservations can be made by phone or through its website; tours are available in French and English.

Montagne de Reims Champagne Route

Linking Reims with Épernay by skirting the Parc Natural Régional de la Montagne de Reims, a regional park covering the forested Reims Mountain plateau, this meandering, 70km route passes through vineyards planted mainly with pinot noir vines.

Verzenay

With vines spreading like a ribbed blanket over the hillsides and top-of-the-beanstalk views from its lighthouse, Verzenay makes an attractive stop on the Montagne de Reims Champagne Route. Its vines are planted mostly with pinot noir grapes – 100% *grand cru*.

For the region's best introduction to the art of growing grapes and the cycles of the seasons, head to its **Phare & Musée de Verzenay** (Verzenay Lighthouse; www.lepharedeverzenay.com; D26; lighthouse adult/child €3/2, museum €8/4, combined ticket €9/5; ⏲10am-5pm Tue-Fri, to 5.30pm Sat & Sun, closed Jan), on a hilltop at the eastern edge of the village. Exactly 101 spiral stairs lead to the top of the lighthouse, constructed as a publicity stunt in 1909, which rewards visitors with unsurpassed 360-degree views of vine, field and forest – and, if you're lucky, a tiny TGV zipping by in the distance.

The Sillery **sugar mill**, visible on the horizon, turns an astounding 16,000 tonnes of beets (a major regional crop) into 2600 tonnes of sugar each day. After brushing up on the seasonal processes involved in Champagne production in the **museum**, stop by the tasting room for a glass of fizz (there are 30 varieties to sample).

Étienne and Anne-Laure Lefevre (☎03 26 97 96 99; www.champagne-etienne-lefevre.com; 30 rue de Villers; ⏲10am-noon & 2-6pm Mon-Fri, to 5pm Sat) run group tours of their family-owned vineyards and cellars – ring ahead. There are no flashy videos or multimedia shows; the emphasis is firmly on the nitty-gritty of Champagne production.

Parc Natural Régional de la Montagne de Reims

The 500-sq-km Montagne de Reims Regional Park is best known for a botanical curiosity, 800 spectacularly contorted dwarf beech trees known as *faux de Verzy*. To get a good look at the trees, which have tortuously twisted trunks and branches that hang down like an umbrella, take the **Balade des Faux** forest walk from 'Les Faux' parking lot, 2km up D34 from Verzy (situated on D26).

Across D34, a 500m gravel path leads through the forest to a *point de vue* (panoramic viewpoint) – next to a concrete WWI bunker – atop 288m-high **Mont Sinaï**.

Reims

Endowed with handsome pedestrian boulevards, Roman remains, art deco cafes and a flourishing fine-dining scene, Reims was meticulously restored after WWI and again following WWII. Along with Épernay, it is the most important centre of Champagne production.

◎ SIGHTS

Basilique St-Rémi Basilica

(place du Chanoine Ladame; ⏲9am-7pm) This 121m-long former Benedictine abbey church, a Unesco World Heritage Site, mixes Romanesque elements from the mid-11th century (the worn but stunning nave and transept) with early Gothic features from the latter half of the 12th century (the choir, with a large triforium gallery and, way up top, tiny clerestory windows). Next door is the **Musée St-Rémi** (http://musees-reims.fr; 53 rue Simon; adult/child €5/free; ⏲10am-noon & 2-6pm Tue-Sun).

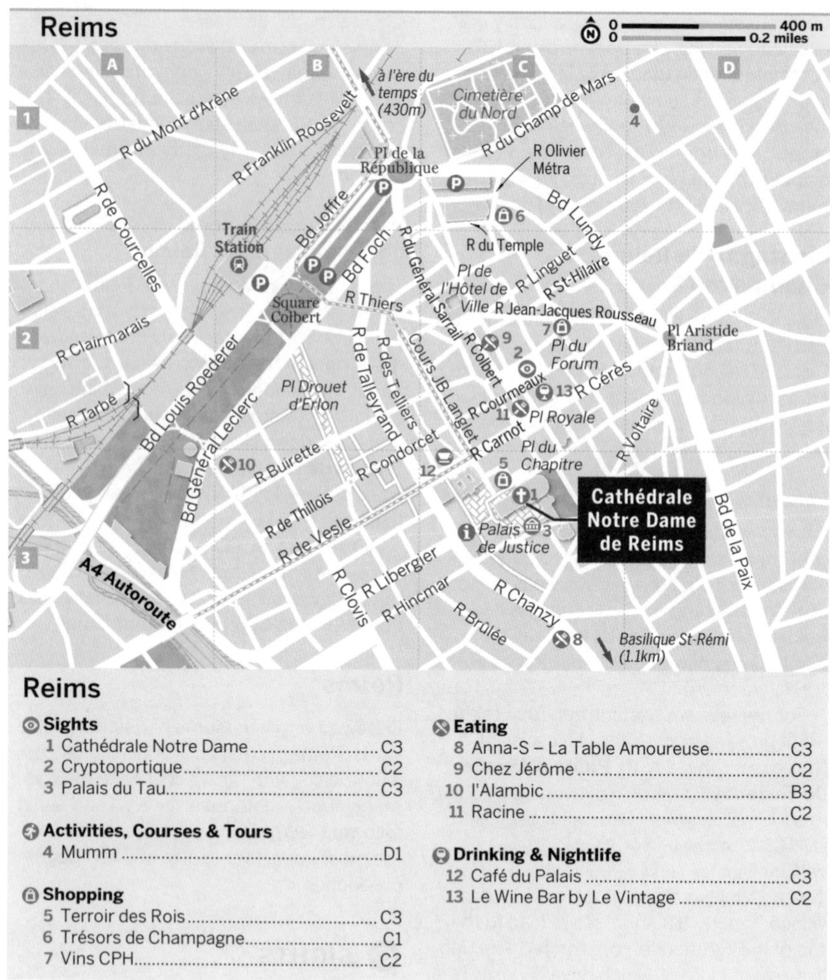

Cryptoportique Historic Site

(place du Forum; ⏲2-6pm May-Sep) FREE One of Reims' Roman standouts, the below-street-level Cryptoportique is thought to have been used for grain storage in the 3rd century AD.

TOURS

The musty *caves* (cellars) and dusty bottles of the 10 Reims-based Champagne houses (known as *maisons* – literally, 'houses') can be visited on guided tours with tasting sessions. Cellar temperatures are 10°C to 12°C (dress warmly).

Veuve Clicquot Ponsardin Wine

(☎03 26 89 53 90; www.veuveclicquot.com; 1 place des Droits de l'Homme; public tours & tastings €26-53, private tour & tasting €250; ⏲tours 9.30am, 10.30am, 12.30pm, 1.30pm, 2pm, 3.30pm & 4.30pm Tue-Sat Mar-Dec) One of the most impressive cellar tours in the region is offered by Veuve Clicquot, a venerable *maison* founded in 1772. Guides lead you deep into the cavernous, pyramid-shaped *crayères* (craters), used for chalk excavation in Gallo-Roman times. Now they harbour millions of bottles of Champagne, one of which (the yellow-label brut) you get to taste on the 1½-hour public tours.

Taittinger Wine

(03 26 85 45 35; https://cellars-booking.taittinger.fr; 9 place St-Niçaise; tours €19-55; tours 10am-4.30pm) The headquarters of Taittinger are a highly atmospheric place to come for a clear, straightforward presentation on how Champagne is actually made – there's no claptrap about 'the Champagne mystique' here. A spiral staircase twists down to the cellars occupying 4th-century *crayères*, Gallo-Roman chalk quarries; other bits were excavated by 13th-century Benedictine monks and became the cellars of St-Niçaise Abbey.

Mumm Wine

(03 26 49 59 70; www.mumm.com; 34 rue du Champ de Mars; tours incl tasting €20-39; tours 9.30am-1pm & 2-6pm daily, shorter hours & closed Sun Oct-Mar) Mumm (pronounced 'moom'), the only *maison* in central Reims, was founded in 1827 and is now the world's third-largest Champagne producer (almost eight million bottles a year). Engaging and edifying guided tours take you through cellars filled with 25 million bottles of fine bubbly and conclude with a tasting. Wheelchair accessible. Phone ahead if possible.

EATING

à l'ère du temps Crêpes $

(03 26 06 16 88; www.aleredutemps.com; 123 av de Laon; lunch menus €9.90, mains €7-14; noon-2pm & 7-9.30pm Tue-Sat) A short stroll north of place de la République brings you to this sweet and simple crêperie. It does a roaring trade in homemade crêpes, *galettes* (savoury buckwheat crêpes) and gourmet salads.

Champagne Shopping

Want to take a few bottles home? Shop like the locals at **Vins CPH** (www.vinscph.com; 3 place Léon Bourgeois; 9.30am-12.30pm & 2.30-7pm Tue-Sat), which sells 1000 vintages, including over 150 Champagnes. Strikingly illuminated by Champagne bottles, swish **Trésors de Champagne** (www.boutique-tresors-champagne.com; 2 rue Olivier Métra; 2-7pm Tue & Wed, 10.30am-12.30pm & 2-7pm Thu, 10.30am-12.30pm & 2-9.30pm Fri & Sat) plays host to 27 vintners and more than 200 Champagnes. There is a different selection available to taste each week. For bubbly and accompanying nibbles, head to **Terroir des Rois** (www.terroirdesrois.fr; 8 rue du Préau; 10am-7pm Tue-Sun) to stock up on Champagne, macarons, *biscuits roses* (pink ladyfinger sponge biscuits) and other regional treats.

Terroir des Rois, Reims
MARTIN BENNETT/ALAMY STOCK PHOTO ©

Chez Jérôme Bistro $

(03 26 24 36 73; 23 rue de Tambour; menus €15-20; 11am-6pm Tue-Fri, to 10.30pm Sat) So cosy it's like stepping into a friend's eccentric dining room, this bistro is run with passion by the inimitable one-man-band that is Jérôme – cook, waiter and chief bottle-washer. Made according to the chef's whim and what's available, the tasty, unfussy *menus* are prepared with seasonal, market-fresh ingredients. Everything, from the vintage lights to ceramics and furnishings, is for sale.

Day Trip to Troyes

An easy trip by car from Reims or Épernay, historic Troyes wings you back to the Middle Ages, with its warren of cobbled streets and half-timbered houses. Most of the big-hitter sights cluster in the city centre, which is shaped like a Champagne cork. The best place for aimless ambling is the area bounded by rue Général de Gaulle, the Hôtel de Ville, rue Général Saussier and rue de la Pierre.

All at once imposing and delicate with its filigree stonework, Troyes' **cathedral** (place St-Pierre; 9.30am-12.30pm & 2-6pm Mon-Sat, 2-6pm Sun Apr-Oct, to 5pm Nov-Mar) is a stellar example of *champenoise* Gothic architecture. The flamboyant west façade dates from the mid-1500s, while the 114m-long interior is illuminated by spectacular stained-glass windows (13th to 17th centuries).

South of here, housed in the Renaissance-style Hôtel de Mauroy, the **Maison de l'Outil et de la Pensée Ouvrière** (MOPO; http://mopo3.com; 7 rue de la Trinité; adult/child €7/3.50; 10am-6pm daily, closed Tue Oct-Mar) brings to life a world of manual skills made obsolete by the Industrial Revolution.

Lunch on market-driven specialities in the cobbled courtyard of **Le Valentino** (http://levalentino.com; 35 rue Paillot de Montabert; menus €28-58; noon-1.30pm & 7.30-9.30pm Tue-Sat), and finish with a glass of bubbly at chic **Chez Philippe** (www.bullesetdouceurs.com; 11 rue Champeaux; 5pm-1.30am Tue-Sat, 6-10pm Sun).

Half-timbered houses, Troyes

Anna-S – La Table Amoureuse French $$

(03 26 89 12 12; www.annas-latableamoureuse.com; 6 rue Gambetta; 3-course lunch €18.50, dinner menus €36-50; noon-1.30pm & 7-9pm Tue & Thu-Sat, noon-1.30pm Wed & Sun) So what if the decor is chintzy – there is a reason why this bistro is as busy as a beehive. Friendly service and a menu packed with well-done classics – Arctic char with Champagne jus, fillet of veal in rich, earthy morel sauce – hit the mark every time. The three-course lunch is a steal at €18.50.

l'Alambic French $$

(03 26 35 64 93; www.restaurant-lalambic.fr; 63bis rue de Chativesle; mains €14-25; noon-2pm & 7-9.30pm Tue-Fri, 7-9.30pm Sat & Mon;) Ideal for an intimate dinner, this vaulted cellar dishes up well-prepared French classics – along the lines of home-smoked trout with horseradish, cod fillet with Champagne-laced *choucroute* (sauerkraut), and pigeon served two ways with Reims mustard sauce. Save room for terrific desserts such as crème brûlée with chicory ice cream. The *plat du jour* is a snip at €11.

L'Assiette Champenoise Gastronomy $$$

(03 26 84 64 64; www.assiettechampenoise.com; 40 av Paul-Vaillant-Couturier, Tinqueux; menus €95-315; noon-2pm & 7.30-10pm Thu-Mon) Heralded far and wide as one of Champagne's finest tables and crowned with the holy grail of three Michelin stars, L'Assiette Champenoise is headed up by chef Arnaud Lallemen. Listed by ingredients, his intricate, creative dishes rely on outstanding produce and play up integral flavours – be it Breton scallops, or milk-fed lamb with preserved vegetables. One for special occasions.

Racine Japanese $$$

(03 26 35 16 95; www.racine.re; 8 rue Colbert; tasting menus €75-100; 12.15-2pm & 7.15-9pm Fri-Mon, 7.15-9pm Thu) With strong Japanese roots and a generous pinch of love for his adopted home, chef Kazuyuki Tanaka

Café du Palais

creates menus that sing with bright flavours and are delivered with finesse at slick, monochrome, Michelin-starred Racine. They're listed in the modern, ingredient-driven way, so turbot with squash and pistachio, pineapple with lemon and Champagne ice cream, and the like.

DRINKING & NIGHTLIFE

The liveliest bars, cafes and pubs huddle around place Drouet d'Erlon, rue Chanzy and place du Forum.

Café du Palais Cafe

(www.cafedupalais.fr; 14 place Myron-Herrick; 8.30am-8.30pm Tue-Fri, 9am-9.30pm Sat)
Run by the same family since 1930, this art deco cafe is *the* place to sip a glass of Champagne. Lit by a skylight is an extraordinary collection of bric-a-brac ranging from the inspired to the kitsch.

Le Wine Bar by Le Vintage Wine Bar

(http://winebar-reims.com; 16 place du Forum; 6pm-12.30am Tue-Thu, to 1.30am Fri & Sat)
This bijou wine bar is a convivial spot to chill over a glass of wine or Champagne (some 500 are offered) with a tasting plate of charcuterie and cheese. The friendly brothers who own the place are happy to give recommendations.

INFORMATION

The **tourist office** (03 26 77 45 00; www.reims-tourisme.com; 6 rue Rockefeller; 10am-5pm Mon-Sat, 10am-12.30pm & 1.30-5pm Sun;) has stacks of information on the Champagne region and Reims (plus free city maps), as well as some incredibly cool giant cork stools where you can perch while using the free wi-fi.

GETTING THERE & AROUND

Reims train station, 1km northwest of the cathedral, has services to/from Paris Gare de l'Est (€28 to €61, 46 minutes to one hour, 12 to 17 daily). Direct services also go to Épernay (€7.20, 30 minutes, 16 daily). The journey to Troyes (€36 to €64, 2½ to 3½ hours, 10 daily) involves at least one change.

Sparkling Nights

It may come as little surprise that the tipple of choice in Épernay is Champagne, and it's as readily available (and almost as reasonably priced) in the bars dotted about town as wine is elsewhere.

The downstairs cellar of wine bar **C. Comme** (☎03 26 32 09 55; www.c-comme.fr; 8 rue Gambetta; 2-/4-/6-glass Champagne tasting €13/26.60/37.50; ⏲10am-8pm Mon, Tue & Thu, 3-8pm Wed, 10am-midnight Fri & Sat) stashes away 400 different varieties of Champagne; sample them in the softly lit bar-bistro upstairs, accompanied by a tasting plate of regional cheese, charcuterie and *rillettes* (pork pâté). A few doors down, **La Fine Bulle** (17 rue Gambetta; ⏲boutique 10am-midnight, bar 6.30-11.30pm) is a smart Champagne bar, boutique and restaurant rolled into one. Each week there are five/six (€15/18) Champagnes available for tasting.

As of 2018, Reims has a new self-service bike-rental scheme courtesy of Gobee.bike. To locate a bike, visit http://gobeebike.fr and download the app, then scan your code to unlock. Rental costs €0.50 for 30 minutes.

Épernay

The self-proclaimed *capitale du Champagne* is the best place to tour cellars and sample bubbly, and it makes an excellent base for exploring the Champagne Routes.

SIGHTS

Avenue de Champagne Street

Épernay's handsome av de Champagne fizzes with *maisons de champagne* (Champagne houses). The avenue is lined with mansions and neoclassical villas, rebuilt after WWI. Peek through wrought-iron gates at Moët's private **Hôtel Chandon**, an early-19th-century pavilion-style residence set in landscaped gardens, which counts Wagner among its famous past guests. The haunted-looking **Château Perrier**, a red-brick mansion built in 1854 in neo–Louis XIII style, is aptly placed at number 13! It's set to open as a new Champagne museum in 2019.

The roundabout presents photo ops with its giant cork and bottle-top.

Dom Pérignon Statue

(av de Champagne) Everyone who visits Moët & Chandon invariably stops to strike a pose next to the statue of Dom Pérignon (c 1638–1715), after whom the *prestige cuvée* is named. The Benedictine monk played a pivotal role in making Champagne what it is – perfecting the process of using a second, in-the-bottle fermentation to make ho-hum wine sparkle.

EATING

Épernay's main eat street is rue Gambetta and adjacent place de la République. For picnic fixings, head to rue St-Thibault.

Pâtisserie Vincent Dallet Pastries $

(www.chocolat-vincentdallet.fr; 26 rue Général Leclerc; pastries €2-5, light meals €8-18; ⏲7.30am-7.45pm Tue-Sun) A sweet dream of a *chocolaterie*, patisserie and tearoom, with delectable pralines, macarons and pastries. A *champenoise* speciality is the *Baba*, vanilla cream topped by a cork-shaped pastry flavoured with Champagne. Or go straight for a *café gourmand*, coffee with a selection of mini desserts.

La Grillade Gourmande French $$

(☎03 26 55 44 22; www.lagrilladegourmande.com; 16 rue de Reims; lunch menus €21, dinner menus €33-59, mains €20-26; ⏱noon-1.45pm & 7.30-9.30pm Tue-Sat) This chic, red-walled, art-slung bistro is an inviting spot to try chargrilled meats and dishes rich in texture and flavour, such as crayfish pan-fried in Champagne and lamb cooked in rosemary and honey until meltingly tender. Diners spill out onto the covered terrace in the warm months. Both the presentation and service are flawless.

Le Théâtre French **$$**

(☎03 26 58 88 19; www.epernay-rest-letheatre.com; 8 place Mendès-France; menus €26-51; ⏱noon-2pm & 7.30-9pm Mon & Thu-Sat, noon-2pm Tue & Sun) Sidling up to Épernay's **theatre** (☎box office 03 26 51 15 99; http://theatrelesalmanazar.fr; place Mendès-France; tickets €9-35), Le Théâtre raises a curtain on a delightfully old-school brasserie with splashes of high-ceilinged art nouveau charm. The Belgian chef, Lieven Vercouteren, prides himself on using superb seasonal produce in *menus* that might begin, say, with pheasant terrine with juniper berries and move on to mains such as tender leg of lamb with seasonal vegetables.

La Cave à Champagne French **$$**

(☎03 26 55 50 70; www.la-cave-a-champagne.com; 16 rue Gambetta; menus €22-40; ⏱noon-2pm & 7-10pm Thu-Mon; 👪) 'The Champagne Cellar' is well regarded by locals for its humble *champenoise* cuisine (snail-and-pig's-trotter casserole, fillet of beef in pinot noir), served in a warm, traditional, bourgeois atmosphere. Pair these dishes with inexpensive regional Champagnes and wines.

INFORMATION

Tourist Office (☎03 26 53 33 00; www.ot-epernay.fr; 7 av de Champagne; ⏱9am-12.30pm & 1.30-7pm Mon-Sat, 10.30am-1pm & 2-4.30pm Sun mid-Apr–mid-Oct, 9.30am-12.30pm & 1.30-5.30pm Mon-Sat mid-Oct–mid-Apr; 📶) The team here hands out English brochures and maps with walking, cycling and driving tour options. Staff can also make cellar visit reservations. Free wi-fi.

Champagne Festival

Épernay's biggest summer bash is **La Champagne en Fête** (www.epernay.fr; ⏱late Jun), three days of pop-up Champagne bars, concerts, exhibitions, open-cellar visits, tastings, fireworks and more. The focal point is the av de Champagne.

Avenue de Champage street sign

STOCKNSHARES/GETTY IMAGES ©

GETTING THERE & AROUND

BICYCLE

The tourist office rents out bikes (city/children's/electric bicycles €20/11/30 per day). Pick up cycling maps and map-cards (€0.50) here.

CAR

Épernay is bang in the heart of Champagne country, making it a perfect base for a driving tour. It's situated on the D951 road 29km south of Reims. Car hire is available locally at **Europcar** (☎03 26 54 90 61; www.europcar.com; 20 rempart Perrier).

TRAIN

The **train station** (place Mendès-France) has direct services to Reims (€7.20, 27 minutes, 14 daily) and Paris Gare de l'Est (€24 to €69, 1¼ to 2¾ hours, seven daily).

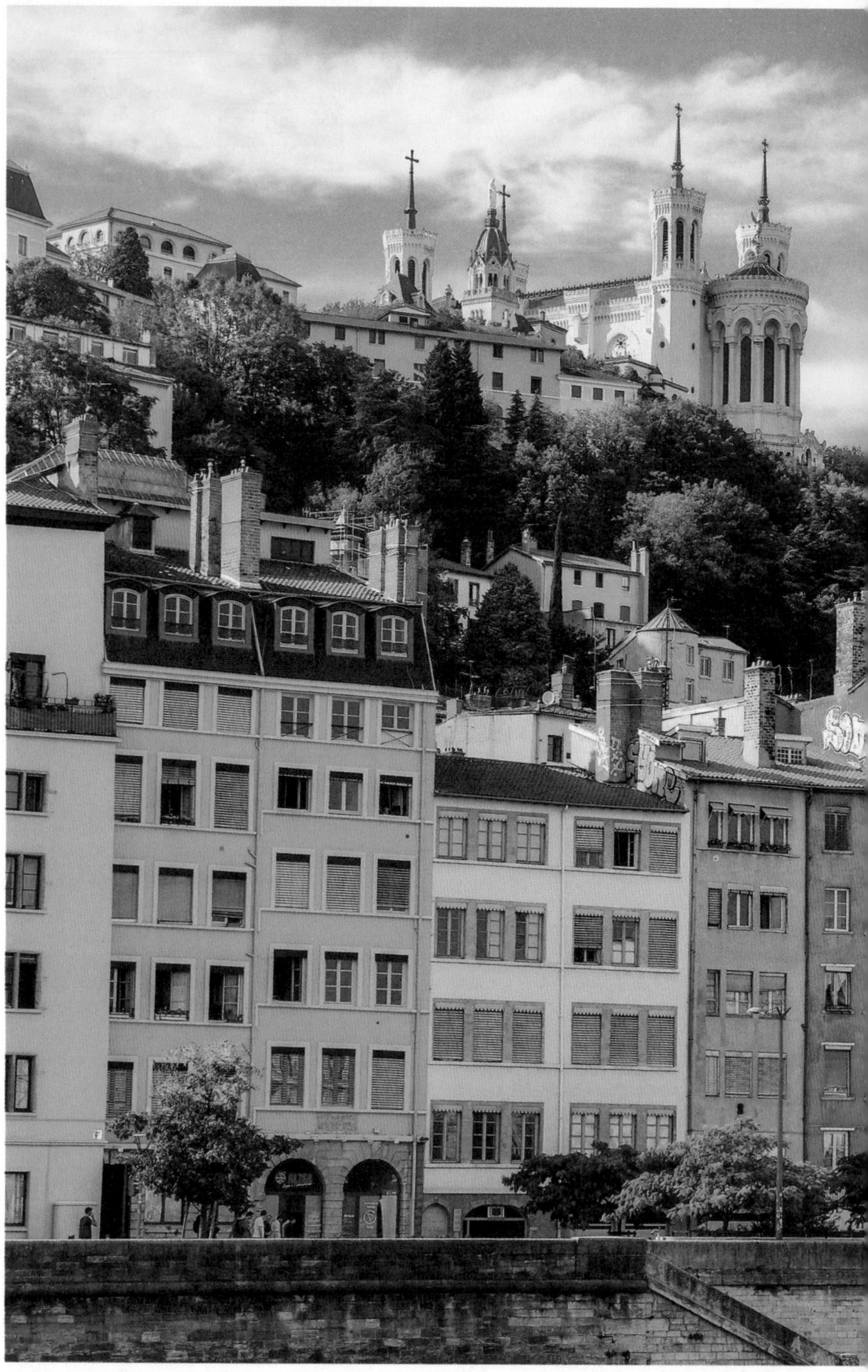

LYON

In This Chapter

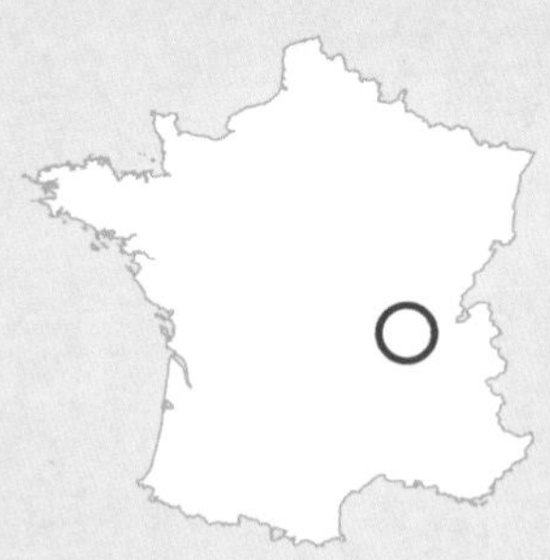

Lyon at a Glance...

Commanding a strategic spot at the confluence of the Rhône and the Saône Rivers, Lyon has been luring people ever since the Romans named it Lugdunum in 43 BC. Commercial, industrial and banking powerhouse for the past 500 years, Lyon is France's third-largest city, and offers today's urban explorers a wealth of enticing experiences.

Outstanding museums, a dynamic cultural life, busy clubbing and drinking scenes, a thriving university and fantastic shopping lend the city a distinctly sophisticated air, while adventurous gourmets can indulge their wildest gastronomic fantasies. Don't leave the city without sampling some Lyonnais specialities in a bouchon (small bistro) – the quintessential Lyon experience.

Lyon in Two Days

Enjoy a city overview and local insights on a **walking tour** (p165), then hit **Vieux Lyon** (p162) for lunch and an afternoon exploring its cobbled streets and *traboules* (secret passageways). Hike or ride the funicular up to **Fourvière** (p163) for a fabulous city panorama. Day two, head uphill to **Croix Rousse** (p169): get lost in its rabbit warren of *traboules*, visit the **food market** (p169) and discover its silk-weaving heritage.

Lyon in Four Days

Spend day three absorbing more of Lyon's rich history at its cache of museums: the **Musée des Beaux-Arts** (p164) followed by lunch on its terrace. In the afternoon catch a **puppet show** (p170) with Guignol, dine in a Lyonnais *bouchon* and enjoy after-dark **drinks** (p169) aboard the Rhône's *péniches* (barges). Day four, sail to the edgy La Confluence 'hood to visit the cutting-edge **Musée des Confluences** (p164).

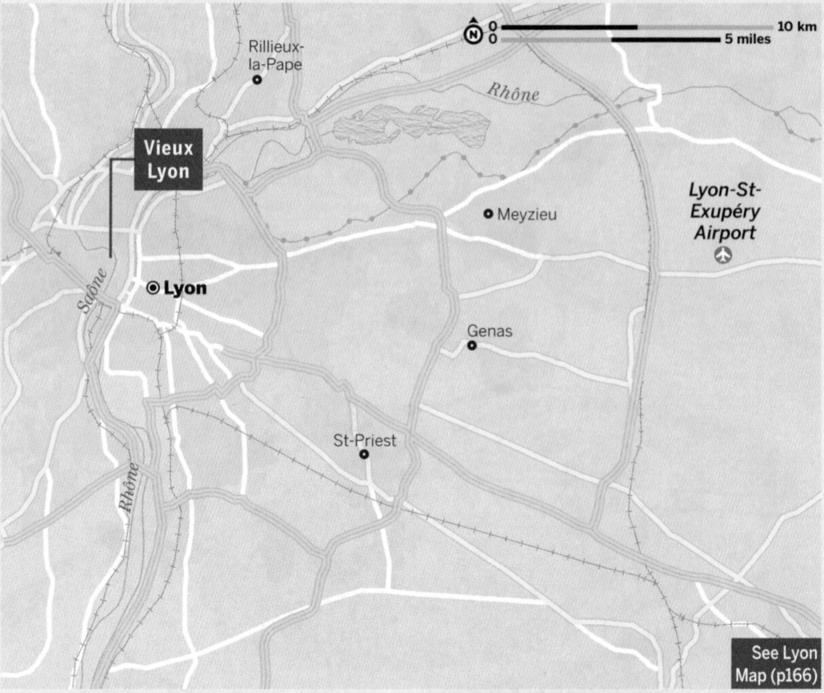

0 10 km
0 5 miles
Rillieux-la-Pape
Rhône
Vieux Lyon
Lyon-St-Exupéry Airport
Meyzieu
Saône
Lyon
Genas
St-Priest
Rhône
See Lyon Map (p166)

Arriving in Lyon

Lyon-St-Exupéry Airport Rhônexpress tramway links the airport with Part-Dieu train station in under 30 minutes. Trams depart every 15 minutes between 6am and 9pm, and half-hourly from 5am to 6am and 9pm to midnight. A taxi between the airport and city centre costs around €53 by day or €68 at night.

Part-Dieu & Perrache train stations Each have their own metro stop (single ticket €1.90).

Where to Stay

From B&Bs and apartments to business hotels and boutique ventures, Lyon has a wealth of accommodation to suit every taste and budget. If you have a car, ask ahead about parking availability at your lodgings, as car parks in Lyon are pricey. Lyon's tourist office runs a free reservation service (http://book.lyon-france.com/en/accommodation) and occasionally offers deals like free breakfasts or discounts on multinight stays.

Quenelles (feather-light flour, egg and cream dumplings

/SHUTTERSTOCK ©

Bouchon Dining

A bouchon might be a 'bottle stopper' or 'traffic jam' elsewhere in France, but in Lyon it's a small, friendly bistro that cooks up traditional cuisine using regional produce.

Great For...

☑ Don't Miss

The informal, post-dinner history tours run by gregarious owner at *bouchon* Le Musée (p168).

Bouchons originated in the first half of the 20th century when many large bourgeois families had to let go of their in-house cooks, who then set up their own restaurant businesses. The first of these *mères* (mothers) was Mère Guy, followed by Mère Filloux, Mère Brazier (under whom world-famous Lyonnais chef Paul Bocuse trained) and others.

Many of the best *bouchons* are certified by Les Authentiques Bouchons Lyonnais – look for a metal plaque outside depicting traditional puppet Gnafron with a glass of Beaujolais in hand.

What to Drink

Kick-start a memorable gastronomic experience with a *communard,* a blood-red aperitif of Beaujolais mixed with *crème de cassis* (blackcurrant liqueur), named

Chef preparing dish at Daniel et Denise *bouchon* (p168)

RIVER THOMPSON/LONELY PLANET ©

after the supporters of the Paris Commune killed in 1871. When ordering wine with your meal, ask for a pot – a classically Lyonnais 46cL glass bottle adorned with an elastic band to prevent wine drips – of local Brouilly, Beaujolais, Côtes du Rhône or Mâcon.

Traditional Dishes

Start with *tablier de sapeur* ('fireman's apron'; actually meaning breaded, fried tripe), *salade de cervelas* (salad of boiled pork sausage sometimes studded with pistachios or black truffle specks), or caviar de la Croix Rousse (lentils in creamy sauce). Hearty main dishes include *boudin blanc* (veal sausage), *boudin noir aux pommes* (blood sausage with apples), *quenelles* (feather-light flour, egg and cream dumplings) or *quenelles de brochet* (pike dumplings served in a creamy crayfish sauce). *Bouchon* aficionados can't get enough of *andouillette* (a seriously feisty sausage made from pigs' intestines), *gras double* (a type of tripe) and *pieds de mouton/veau/couchon* (sheep/calf/pig trotters).

Need to Know

Many of the best *bouchons* are shut weekends; advance reservations are recommended.

Take a Break

Mingle with local foodies over a *bouchon* lunch at Le Poêlon d'Or (p168).

Top Tip

Get your taste buds in gear with a morning stroll around food market, Les Halles de Lyon Paul Bocuse (p169).

Cheese & Dessert

For the cheese course, choose between a bowl of *fromage blanc* (a cross between cream cheese and natural yoghurt); *cervelle de canut* ('brains of the silk weaver'; *fromage blanc* mixed with chives and garlic), which originated in Croix Rousse and accompanied every meal for 19th-century weavers; or local St-Marcellin ripened to gooey perfection.

Desserts are grandma-style: think *tarte aux pommes* (apple tart), or the Lyonnais classic *tarte aux pralines,* a brilliant rose-coloured confection made with crème fraiche and crushed sugar-coated almonds.

Dining Etiquette

Little etiquette is required. Seldom do you get clean cutlery for each course, and mopping your plate with a chunk of bread is fine. In the most popular and traditional spots, you'll often find yourself sitting elbow-to-elbow with your fellow diners at a long row of tightly wedged tables.

Traboule in Vieux Lyon

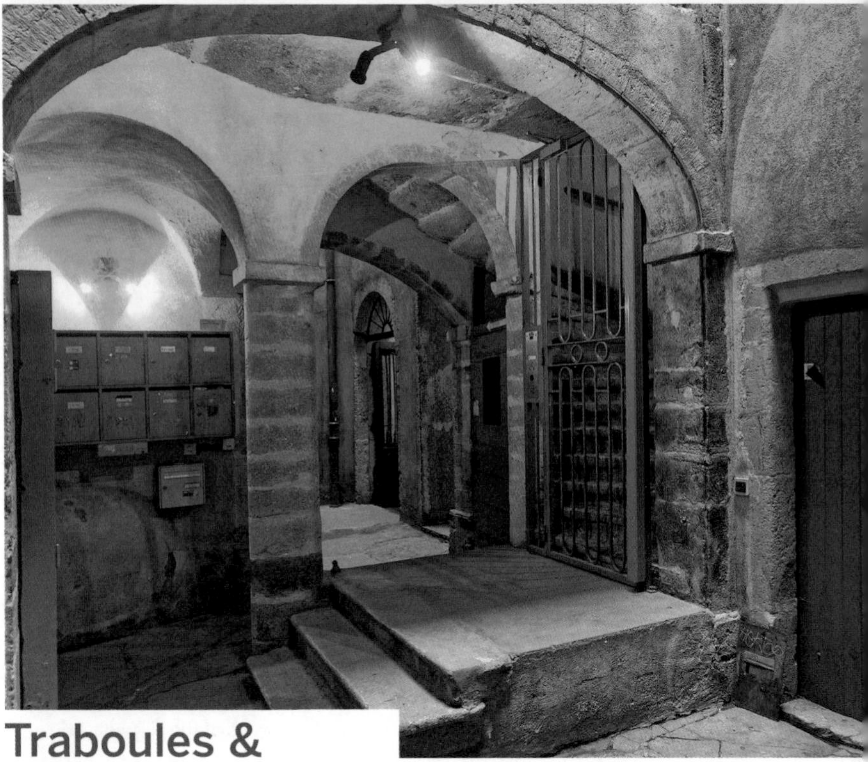

Traboules & Canuts

Deep within Vieux Lyon and Croix Rousse, a labyrinth of* traboules *(secret passages) snakes through apartment blocks, under streets and into courtyards – perfect for offbeat urban exploration.

Great For...

☑ Don't Miss

Four 14th- to 17th-century houses wrapped around a *traboule* and Italianate loggia at **Cour des Loges** (www.courdesloges.com; 2-8 rue du Bœuf, 5e; d €250-450, ste €430-580; ; Vieux Lyon).

Across the city 315 passages link 230 streets, with a combined length of 50km. Renaissance courtyards, spiral stone staircases, romantic loggias and interesting building façades painted a rainbow of muted hues pepper the route – only sections of which are open to visitors. Many are closed or unmarked, and exploring Lyon's *traboules* is as much about unearthing unmarked doorways as admiring unique architecture.

Traboules v Miraboules

Genuine *traboules* (derived from the Latin *trans ambulare*, meaning 'to pass through') cut from one street to another. Passages that fan out into a courtyard or cul-de-sac aren't *traboules* but *miraboules* (two of the finest examples are at 16 rue Bœuf and 8 rue Juiverie, both in Vieux Lyon).

Canut (silk weaver) weaving velvet

POOL BENAINOUS/TINACCI/GAMMA-RAPH/GETTY IMAGES ©

Vieux Lyon

Some of Vieux Lyon's *traboules* date from Roman times, but most were constructed by *canuts* (silk weavers) in the 19th century to transport silk in inclement weather. Resistance fighters found them handy during WWII.

Vieux Lyon's most celebrated *traboules* include those connecting 27 rue St-Jean with 6 rue des Trois Maries and 54 rue St-Jean with 27 rue du Bœuf (push the intercom button to buzz open the door).

Croix Rousse

Step into Croix Rousse's underworld at 9 place Colbert, crossing **Cour des Voraces** – built by silk weavers in 1840 on the *pentes* (slopes) of Croix Rousse with a monumental open-air, seven-storey

Need to Know

Lyon tourist office runs guided *traboule* tours (adult/child €12/7; advance reservation).

Take a Break

Linger over coffee and pastries, brunch or lunch at L'Instant (p169).

★ Top Tip

Download the free app **Traboules** (http://www.traboules-lyon.fr) and/or grab a free map at the tourist office.

staircase – to 14bis montée St-Sébastien, and eventually emerging at 29 rue Imbert Colomès. From further *traboules* zigzag down the *pentes* to place des Terreaux.

The City's Silk Weavers

Following the introduction of the mechanical Jacquard loom in 1805, Lyonnais *canuts* built tens of thousands of workshops in Croix Rousse, an independent hilltop quarter that only became part of Lyon in 1852. Their workshops sported huge windows to let in light and huge wood-beamed ceilings, more than 4m high, to accommodate the bulky machines. Weavers spent 14 to 20 hours a day hunched over their looms breathing in silk dust. Two-thirds were illiterate and everyone was paid a pittance; strikes in 1830–31 and 1834 resulted in the death of several hundred weavers.

No *traboule* evokes the fate of Lyonnais weavers more than Cour des Voraces, a place of refuge for hundreds of weavers during subsequent 19th-century worker revolts. Learn about their labour-intensive life and see manual looms in use at Croix Rousse's fascinating **Maison des Canuts** (☎04 78 28 62 04; www.maisondescanuts.com; 10-12 rue d'Ivry, 4e; adult/child €7.50/4.50; ⏰10am-6.30pm Mon-Sat, guided tours 11am & 3.30pm Mon & Sat mid-Mar–mid-Oct; Ⓜ Croix Rousse).

Basilique Notre Dame de Fourvière

GIMAS/SHUTTERSTOCK ©

Vieux Lyon

Lyon's old town, with its cobbled lanes and medieval and Renaissance architecture, is a Unesco World Heritage Site. Its atmospheric web of streets divides into three quarters: St-Paul (north), St-Jean (middle) and St-Georges (south).

Great For...

☑ Don't Miss

A traditional puppet show at one of Lyon's most famous puppet theatres, Théâtre Le Guignol de Lyon (p170).

Lovely old buildings line rue du Bœuf, rue St-Jean and rue des Trois Maries. Crane your neck upwards to see gargoyles and other cheeky stone characters carved on window ledges along rue Juiverie, home to Lyon's Jewish community in the Middle Ages.

Cathédrale St-Jean-Baptiste

Lyon's partly Romanesque **cathedral** (www.cathedrale-lyon.fr; place St-Jean, 5e; ⏰cathedral 8.15am-7.45pm Mon-Fri, 8am-7pm Sat & Sun; Ⓜ Vieux Lyon) was built between the late 11th and early 16th centuries. The portals of its Flamboyant Gothic façade, completed in 1480 (and recently renovated), are decorated with 280 square stone medallions. Inside, the highlight is the **astronomical clock** in the north transept.

Guignol, Lyon's iconic puppet

NEVSKII DMITRII/SHUTTERSTOCK ©

Need to Know

Shop in style: art galleries, antiquarian and secondhand bookshops fill Vieux Lyon's pedestrian streets.

Take a Break

Cool down with a lavender ice cream from **Terre Adélice** (www.terre-adelice.eu; 1 place de la Baleine, 5e; Ⓜ Vieux Lyon) or a neobistro lunch at Cinq Mains (p165).

★ Top Tip

The tourist office (p171) organises excellent tours through Vieux Lyon.

Musées Gadagne

Housed in a 16th-century mansion built for two Florentine bankers, this twin-themed **exhibition space** (www.gadagne.musees.lyon.fr; 1 place du Petit Collège, 5e; adult/child €8/free, both museums €9/free; ⌚11am-6.30pm Wed-Sun; Ⓜ Vieux Lyon) incorporates a local history museum, **Musée d'Histoire de Lyon**, chronicling the city's layout as its silk-weaving, cinema and transportation evolved, and an international puppet museum, **Musée des Marionettes du Monde**, paying homage to Lyon's iconic puppet, Guignol.

Le Petit Musée Fantastique de Guignol

The star of this tiny, two-room **museum** (www.le-petit-musee-fantastique-de-guignol.boutiquecardelli.fr; 6 rue St-Jean, 5e; adult/child €5/3; ⌚10.30am-12.30pm & 2-6.30pm Tue-Sun, 2-6pm Mon; Ⓜ Vieux Lyon) is Guignol, the Lyonnais puppet famous for its slapstick antics and political commentary. Ask staff to set up the English soundtrack on the cute, sensor-activated exhibits.

What's Nearby

From Vieux Lyon, tree-shaded footpaths wind steeply uphill to **Fourvière**. The least taxing way up is the funicular; catch it just up the escalators from the Vieux Lyon metro station.

Over two millennia ago, the Romans built the city of Lugdunum on these slopes, crowned today by 19th-century **Basilique Notre Dame de Fourvière** (www.fourviere.org; place de Fourvière, 5e; ⌚7am-7pm; Fourvière). From April to November, free 30-minute discovery visits take in the main features of the basilica and crypt. Nearby, the **Musée Gallo-Romain de Fourvière** (www.museegalloromain.grandlyon.com; 17 rue Cléberg, 5e; adult/child €4/free; ⌚11am-6pm Tue-Fri, from 10am Sat & Sun; Fourvière) hosts a wide-ranging collection of ancient artefacts found in the Rhône Valley as well as superb mosaics.

SIGHTS

A number of sights lie in the city centre, which occupies a long peninsula between the rivers known as Presqu'île. Rising to the north of the Presqu'île is the hillside Croix Rousse, which also harbours worthwhile museums and buildings. West across the Saône sits the medieval quarter of Vieux Lyon.

Musée des Beaux-Arts — Museum

(☎04 72 10 17 40; www.mba-lyon.fr; 20 place des Terreaux, 1er; adult/child €8/free; ⏰10am-6pm Wed, Thu & Sat-Mon, 10.30am-6pm Fri; Ⓜ Hôtel de Ville) This stunning and eminently manageable museum showcases France's finest collection of sculptures and paintings outside of Paris from antiquity onwards. Highlights include works by Rodin, Monet and Picasso. Pick up a free audioguide and be sure to stop for a drink or meal on the delightful stone terrace off its cafe-restaurant or take time out in the tranquil cloister garden.

Musée des Confluences — Museum

(☎04 28 38 12 12; www.museedesconfluences.fr; 86 quai Perrache, 6e; adult/child €9/free; ⏰11am-7pm Tue, Wed & Fri, to 10pm Thu, 10am-7pm Sat & Sun; 🚊T1) This eye-catching building, designed by the Viennese firm Coop Himmelb(l)au, is the crowning glory of Lyon's newest neighbourhood, the Confluence, at Presqu'île's southern tip. Lying at the confluence of the Rhône and Saône rivers, this ambitious science-and-humanities museum is housed in a futuristic steel-and-glass transparent crystal. Its distorted structure is one of the city's iconic landmarks.

Opéra de Lyon — Architecture

(www.opera-lyon.com; 1 place de la Comédie, 1er; Ⓜ Hôtel de Ville) Lyon's neoclassical 1831-built opera house was modernised in 1993 by renowned French architect Jean Nouvel, who added the striking semi-cylindrical glass-domed roof. On its northern side, boarders and bladers buzz around the fountains of **place Louis Pradel**, surveyed by the **Homme de la Liberté** (Man of Freedom) on roller skates, sculpted from scrap metal by Marseille-born César Baldaccini.

Opéra de Lyon

Centre d'Histoire de la Résistance et de la Déportation Museum

(☎04 78 72 23 11; www.chrd.lyon.fr; 14 av Berthelot, 7e; adult/child €8/free; ⏰10am-6pm Wed-Sun; Ⓜ Perrache, Jean Macé) The WWII headquarters of Gestapo commander Klaus Barbie evokes Lyon's role as the 'Capital of the Resistance' through moving multimedia exhibits. The museum includes sound recordings of deportees and Resistance fighters, plus a varied collection of everyday objects associated with the Resistance (including the parachute Jean Moulin used to re-enter France in 1942).

 TOURS

Walking Tours Walking

(☎04 72 77 69 69; www.visiterlyon.com/visites-guidees; adult/child from €12/8; ⏰by reservation) The tourist office organises a variety of excellent tours through Vieux Lyon and Croix Rousse with local English-speaking guides. Book in advance (online, by phone or in person at the tourist office).

Cyclopolitain Cycling

(☎04 78 30 35 90; www.visite-insolite-cyclopolitain.com; tours 2 people €40-70; ⏰noon-5.30pm Tue-Fri, 10am-5.30pm Sat; Ⓜ Bellecour) Tiny and/or tired feet can rest aboard a cycle-taxi tour. Choose from four different itineraries, each running either one or two hours.

Les Bateaux Lyonnais Boating

(Croisière Promenade; ☎04 78 42 96 81; www.lesbateauxlyonnais.com; 2 quai des Célestins, 2e; river excursions adult/child from €14/8; ⏰daily Apr-Oct; Ⓜ Bellecour, Vieux Lyon) From April to October, river excursions depart from Lyon City Boat's dock along the Saône. Advance bookings are essential for lunch and dinner **cruises** (Croisière Restaurant; ☎04 78 42 96 81; www.lyoncityboat.com; 16 quai Claude Bernard, 7e; 2½hr lunch/dinner cruise €50/59, 5½hr lunch cruise €69; ⏰Tue-Sun by reservation; Ⓜ Ampère, Guillotière, 🚋T1), which leave from a separate dock on the Rhône.

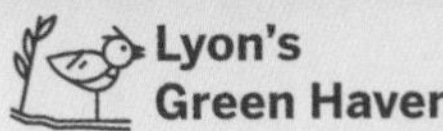

Lyon's Green Haven

If you're museumed out, head to **Parc de la Tête d'Or** (www.loisirs-parcdelatetedor.com; bd des Belges, 6e; ⏰6.30am-10.30pm mid-Apr–mid-Oct, to 8.30pm rest of year; 🚌C1, C5, Ⓜ Masséna), an idyll for nature lovers and families north of the centre. Spanning 117 hectares, France's largest urban park was landscaped in the 1860s. It's graced by a lake (rent a row boat), botanic gardens with greenhouses, rose gardens, a zoo and a tourist train. Take bus C1 (from Part-Dieu train station) or bus C5 (from place Bellecour and Hôtel de Ville) to the Parc Tête d'Or-Churchill stop.

Bridge over stream at Parc de la Tête d'Or
L F FILE/SHUTTERSTOCK ©

 EATING

 Vieux Lyon

Vieux Lyon has a surfeit of restaurants, most aimed at tourists.

Cinq Mains Neobistro $$

(☎04 37 57 30 52; www.facebook.com/cinqmains; 12 rue Monseigneur Lavarenne, 5e; menu lunch/dinner €19/33; ⏰noon-1.30pm & 7.30-9.30pm; Ⓜ Vieux Lyon) When young Lyonnais Grégory Cuilleron and his two friends opened this neobistro in early 2016, it was an instant hit. They're working wonders at this cool loft-like space with a mezzanine, serving up tantalising creations based on what they find at the market. A new generation of chefs and a new spin for Lyonnais cuisine.

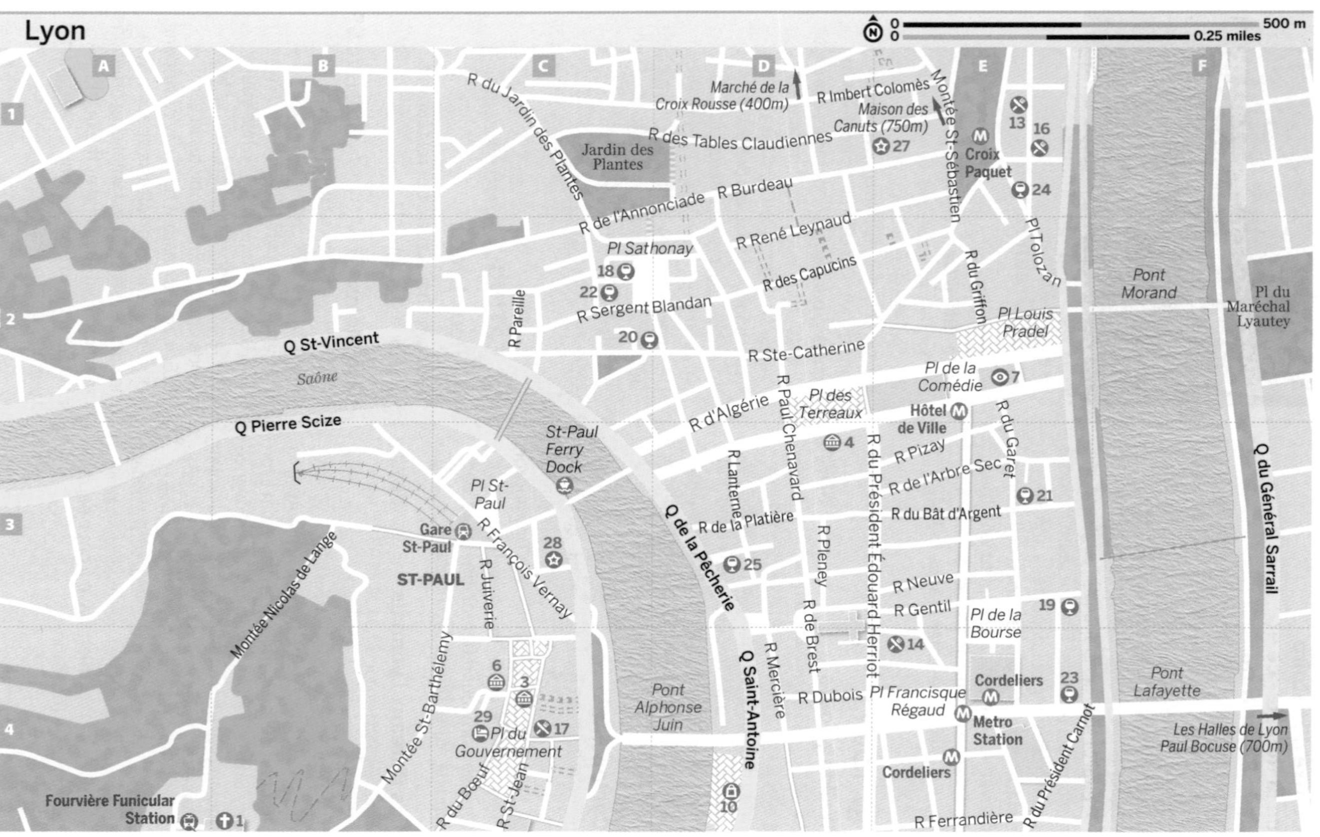
Lyon
0
0
500 m
0.25 miles
A
B
C
D
E
F
1
2
3
4
R du Jardin des Plantes
Jardin des Plantes
Marché de la Croix Rousse (400m)
R Imbert Colomès
Maison des Canuts (750m)
R des Tables Claudiennes
27
Montée St-Sébastien
Croix Paquet
13
16
24
R de l'Annonciade
R Burdeau
Pl Sathonay
R René Leynaud
R des Capucins
18
22
R Sergent Blandan
R Pareille
20
R du Griffon
Pl Tolozan
Pl Louis Pradel
Pont Morand
Pl du Maréchal Lyautey
Q St-Vincent
Saône
R Ste-Catherine
Pl de la Comédie
7
R d'Algérie
Pl des Terreaux
R Paul Chenavard
Hôtel de Ville
R du Garet
Q Pierre Scize
St-Paul Ferry Dock
4
R Lanterne
R du Président Édouard Herriot
R Pizay
R de l'Arbre Sec
21
Q du Général Sarrail
Pl St-Paul
R du Bât d'Argent
R de la Platière
Gare St-Paul
R François Vernay
Q de la Pêcherie
28
25
R Pleney
ST-PAUL
R Juiverie
Montée Nicolas de Lange
R Neuve
R Gentil
Pl de la Bourse
19
R de Brest
14
Montée St-Barthélemy
6
3
R Mercière
Q Saint-Antoine
Cordeliers
23
Pont Lafayette
Pont Alphonse Juin
R Dubois
Pl Francisque Régaud
Metro Station
29
Pl du Gouvernement
17
Les Halles de Lyon Paul Bocuse (700m)
Cordeliers
R du Président Carnot
Fourvière Funicular Station
1
R du Bœuf
R St-Jean
10
R Ferrandière

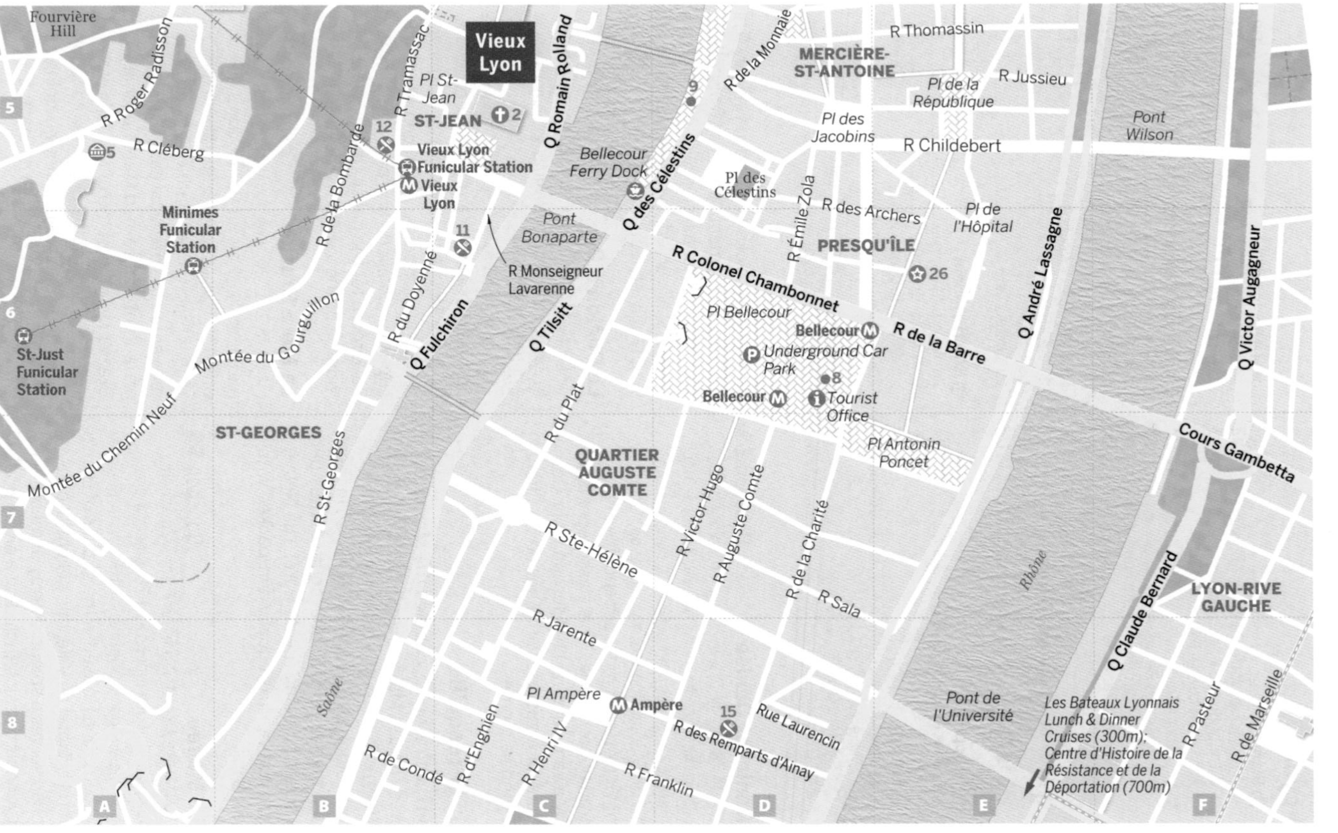

Fourvière Hill
Vieux Lyon
R Thomassin
MERCIÈRE-ST-ANTOINE
R Jussieu
Pl de la République
Pont Wilson
R de la Monnaie
9
Pl St-Jean
R Tramassac
R Roger Radisson
ST-JEAN
2
Q Romain Rolland
Pl des Jacobins
R Childebert
12
Vieux Lyon Funicular Station
Vieux Lyon
5
R Cléberg
Bellecour Ferry Dock
Q des Célestins
Pl des Célestins
R Émile Zola
R des Archers
Pl de l'Hôpital
Minimes Funicular Station
R de la Bombarde
Pont Bonaparte
11
R Monseigneur Lavarenne
PRESQU'ÎLE
26
Q André Lassagne
Q Victor Augagneur
R Colonel Chambonnet
Pl Bellecour
Bellecour
R de la Barre
Underground Car Park
8
Tourist Office
Pl Antonin Poncet
6
St-Just Funicular Station
Montée du Gourguillon
R du Doyenné
Q Fulchiron
Q Tilsitt
R du Plat
ST-GEORGES
Montée du Chemin Neuf
R St-Georges
QUARTIER AUGUSTE COMTE
Cours Gambetta
7
R Ste-Hélène
R Victor Hugo
R Auguste Comte
R de la Charité
R Sala
Rhône
LYON-RIVE GAUCHE
Q Claude Bernard
R Jarente
Pl Ampère
Ampère
15
Rue Laurencin
R des Remparts d'Ainay
Pont de l'Université
Les Bateaux Lyonnais Lunch & Dinner Cruises (300m); Centre d'Histoire de la Résistance et de la Déportation (700m)
R Pasteur
R de Marseille
8
Saône
R de Condé
R d'Enghien
R Henri IV
R Franklin
A
B
C
D
E
F

Lyon

Sights

1 Basilique Notre Dame de Fourvière B4
2 Cathédrale St-Jean-Baptiste C5
3 Le Petit Musée Fantastique de Guignol C4
4 Musée des Beaux-Arts D3
5 Musée Gallo-Romain de Fourvière A5
6 Musées Gadagne C4
7 Opéra de Lyon E2

Activities, Courses & Tours

8 Cyclopolitain D6
9 Les Bateaux Lyonnais D5

Shopping

10 Marché St-Antoine D4

Eating

11 Cinq Mains C6
12 Daniel et Denise B5
13 La Mère Brazier E1
14 Le Musée E4
15 Le Poêlon d'Or...D8
16 L'Ourson qui Boit E1
17 Terre Adélice...C4

Drinking & Nightlife

18 Dam's Pub C2
19 La Ruche E3
20 L'Antiquaire...C2
21 Le L Bar E3
22 Le Vin des Vivants C2
23 Le XS Bar... E4
24 L'Imperial E1
25 United Café D3

Entertainment

26 Fnac Billetterie E6
27 La Clef de Voûte.......................................E1
Opéra de Lyon.................................(see 7)
28 Théâtre Le Guignol de Lyon.....................C3

Sleeping

29 Cour des Loges C4

Daniel et Denise Bouchon **$$**
(04 78 42 24 62; www.danieletdenise.fr; 36 rue Tramassac, 5e; mains €17-29, 2-course lunch menu €21, dinner menus €33-51; noon-2pm & 7.30-9.30pm Tue-Sat; M Vieux Lyon) One of Vieux Lyon's most dependable and traditional eateries, this classic spot is run by award-winning chef Joseph Viola. Come here for elaborate variations on traditional Lyonnais themes.

Presqu'île

In the Presqu'Île, cobbled rue Mercière and rue des Marronniers – both in the 2e (metro Bellecour) – are chock-a-block with sidewalk terraces in summer. In the 1er, the tangle of streets south of the opera house, including rue du Garet, rue Neuve and rue Verdi, is equally jam-packed with eateries.

Le Musée Bouchon **$$**
(04 78 37 71 54; 2 rue des Forces, 2e; lunch mains €14, lunch menus €19-26, dinner menus €23-32; noon-1.30pm & 7.30-9.30pm Tue-Sat; M Cordeliers) Housed in the stables of Lyon's former Hôtel de Ville, this delightful *bouchon* serves a splendid array of meat-heavy Lyonnais classics, including a divine *poulet au vinaigre* (chicken cooked in vinegar). The daily changing *menu* features 10 appetisers and 10 main dishes, plus five scrumptious desserts, all served on cute china plates at long family-style tables.

Le Poêlon d'Or Bouchon **$$**
(04 78 37 65 60; www.lepoelondor-restaurant.fr; 29 rue des Remparts d'Ainay, 2e; lunch menus €18-20, dinner menus €27-33; noon-2pm & 7.30-10pm Mon-Fri; M Ampère-Victor Hugo) This upmarket *bouchon*, around the corner from the Musée des Tissus, is well known among local foodies, who recommend its superb *andouillette* and pike dumplings. Save room for the delicious chocolate mousse or the vanilla crème brûlée.

La Mère Brazier Gastronomy **$$$**
(04 78 23 17 20; www.lamerebrazier.fr; 12 rue Royale; lunch menus €57-70, dinner menus €125-160; noon-1pm & 8-9pm Mon-Fri Sep-Jul; M Croix Paquet) Chef Mathieu Vianney has reinvented the mythical early-20th-century restaurant that earned Mère Eugénie Brazier Lyon's first trio of Michelin stars in 1933 (a copy of the original guidebook takes pride of place). Vianney is doing admirable justice to Brazier's legacy, claiming

two Michelin stars himself for his assured cuisine accompanied by an impressive wine list.

 Croix Rousse

Croix Rousse is a great neighbourhood for foodies, with a range of affordable eateries with bags of character.

L'Instant Cafe $

(☎04 78 29 85 08; www.linstant-patisserie.fr; 3 place Marcel Bertone, 4e; pastries €2-3.50, weekend brunch €22; ⏲8am-7pm; 📶; Ⓜ Croix Rousse) A great place in Croix Rousse to start the day, this hybrid cafe-pastry shop overlooking lovely place Marcel Bertone packs a punch. Stop in for a tea or coffee coupled with one of the delightful in-house *tartes* (tarts; there's also brunch on weekends). The mellow setting and relaxed urban vibe add to the appeal. Ample outdoor seating on warm days.

L'Ourson qui Boit Fusion $$

(☎04 78 27 23 37; 23 rue Royale, 1er; lunch/dinner menu €20/32; ⏲noon-1.30pm & 7.30-9.30pm Mon, Tue & Thu-Sat; Ⓜ Croix Paquet) On the fringes of Croix Rousse, Japanese chef Akira Nishigaki puts his own splendid spin on French cuisine, with plenty of locally sourced fresh vegetables and light, clean flavours. The ever-changing *menu* of two daily appetisers and two main dishes is complemented by good wines, attentive service and scrumptious desserts. Well worth reserving ahead.

 DRINKING & NIGHTLIFE

Along quai Victor Augagneur on the Rhône's left bank, a string of *péniches* (barges with on-board bars) serve drinks from mid-afternoon onwards, with many of them rocking until the wee hours.

L'Antiquaire Cocktail Bar

(☎06 34 21 54 65; 20 rue Hippolyte Flandrin, 1er; ⏲5pm-1am Tue & Wed, to 3am Thu-Sat, 6.30pm-1am Sun & Mon; Ⓜ Hôtel de Ville) Old-time jazz, flickering candles and friendly suspenders-wearing barkeeps set the mood in this atmospheric speakeasy-style bar. The painstakingly prepared cocktails are first-rate (try a Penicillin made from scotch, ginger, honey, lemon and peat whisky) and are best sipped slowly at one of the dark wood and leather booths.

Le Vin des Vivants Wine Bar

(www.levindesvivants.fr; 6 place Fernand Rey, 1er; ⏲6.30-9pm Tue & Wed, to 11.30pm Thu-Sat; Ⓜ Hôtel de Ville) This relaxed stone-walled corner bar on a pretty backstreet square specialises in organic wines.

 Local Food Markets

Lyon's famed indoor food market **Les Halles de Lyon Paul Bocuse** (☎04 78 62 39 33; www.hallespaulbocuse.lyon.fr; 102 cours Lafayette, 3e; ⏲7am-10.30pm Tue-Sat, to 4.30pm Sun; Ⓜ Part-Dieu) has more than 60 stalls selling their renowned wares. Pick up a round of impossibly runny St Marcellin from legendary cheesemonger Mère Richard, and a knobbly Jésus de Lyon from pork butcher Collette Sibilia. Or enjoy a sit-down lunch of local produce at the stalls, lip-smacking *coquillages* (shellfish) included.

Lyon has two main outdoor food markets: the **Marché de la Croix Rousse** (bd de la Croix Rousse, 1er; ⏲6am-1pm Tue-Sun; Ⓜ Croix Rousse) and the **Marché St-Antoine** (quai St-Antoine, 1er; ⏲6am-1pm Tue-Sun; Ⓜ Bellecour, Cordeliers). Each has more than 100 vendors.

Sausages for sale at Lyonnais market
ELENA POMINOVA/SHUTTERSTOCK ©

Michelin Stars

Some 7km north of Lyon, triple-Michelin-starred **Restaurant Paul Bocuse** (☎04 72 42 90 90; www.bocuse.com; 40 quai de la Plage, Collonges au Mont d'Or; menus €175-275; ⏰noon-1.30pm & 8-9pm) was the flagship of the city's most decorated chef, Paul Bocuse. Although Bocuse is no longer around, his recipes continue to dazzle foodies, with the likes of escargots with parsley butter, thyme-roasted rack of lamb and Bocuse's signature *soupe aux truffes noires VGE* (truffle soup created for French president Valéry Giscard d'Estaing in 1975).

Restaurant Paul Bocuse
RICOCHET64/SHUTTERSTOCK ©

Dam's Pub Bar
(www.damspub.com; 4 place Sathonay, 1er; ⏰7am-1am; Ⓜ Hôtel de Ville) A staple of Lyon's easygoing pub scene, Dam's is a lively spot for a pint no matter the hour. It has good beers on tap (including the Belgian ale St Stefanus), televised sport, decent pub grub and a well-placed terrace overlooking place Sathonay.

ENTERTAINMENT

The leading what's-on guide with both print and online editions is *Le Petit Bulletin* (www.petit-bulletin.fr/lyon). Tickets are sold at **Fnac Billetterie** (www.fnacspectacles.com; 85 rue de la République, 2e; ⏰10am-7.30pm Mon-Sat; Ⓜ Bellecour).

Le Sucre Live Music
(www.le-sucre.eu; 50 quai Rambaud, 2e; ⏰8.30pm-midnight Wed & Thu, 6.30pm-1am Fri, to 5am Sat, 4-11pm Sun; 🚊T1) Down in the Confluence neighbourhood, Lyon's most innovative club hosts DJs, live shows and eclectic arts events on its super-cool roof terrace atop a 1930s sugar factory, La Sucrière.

La Clef de Voûte Jazz
(☎04 78 28 51 95; www.laclefdevoute.fr; 1 place Chardonnet; ⏰7pm-midnight Wed-Mon; Ⓜ Croix-Paquet) One of Lyon's most atmospheric music venues, La Clef de Voûte is set in a stone-walled, candelit cellar dating from the 18th century. Aside from an excellent line-up of live jazz, there's cheese and anti-pasti platters, and good wines by the glass. Concerts start at 8.30pm.

Théâtre Le Guignol de Lyon Puppet Theatre
(☎04 78 29 83 36; www.guignol-lyon.net; 2 rue Louis Carrand, 5e; adult/child €10/7.50; Ⓜ Vieux Lyon) One of Lyon's most famous puppet theatres, Théâtre Le Guignol de Lyon has a collection of about 300 puppets. As with many other puppet theatres, shows run just under an hour, and you'll be able to go backstage after the performance.

Hangar du Premier Film Cinema
(www.institut-lumiere.org; 25 rue du Premier Film, 8e; Ⓜ Monplaisir-Lumière) This former factory and birthplace of cinema now screens films of all genres and eras in their original languages. From approximately June to September, the big screen moves outside.

Opéra de Lyon Opera
(www.opera-lyon.com; place de la Comédie, 1er; Ⓜ Hôtel de Ville) Lyon's premier venue for opera, ballet and classical music.

INFORMATION

The excellent-value **Lyon City Card** (www.lyoncitycard.com; 1/2/3 days adult €25/35/45, child €17/24/31) offers free admission to every

Lyon museum, the roof of Basilique Notre Dame de Fourvière, guided city tours, Guignol puppet shows and river excursions (April to October), along with numerous other discounts. The card also includes unlimited citywide transport on buses, trams, the funicular and the metro.

Tourist Office (04 72 77 69 69; www.lyon-france.com; place Bellecour, 2e; 9am-6pm; ; Bellecour) In the centre of Presqu'île.

GETTING THERE & AWAY

AIR

Lyon-St-Exupéry Airport (www.lyonaeroports.com), located 25km east of the city, with 40 airlines (including many budget carriers) serves more than 120 direct destinations across Europe and beyond.

The **Rhônexpress tramway** (www.rhonexpress.fr; adult/youth/child €16.10/13.40/free) links the airport with the Part-Dieu train station in under 30 minutes.

BUS

International bus companies **Eurolines** (08 92 89 90 91; www.eurolines.fr; Gare de Perrache, 2e; 6.30am-9.15pm Mon-Sat, noon-4pm & 8.15-10pm Sun; Perrache) and **Linebús** (04 72 41 72 27; www.linebus.es; Gare de Perrache; 7am-9pm Mon-Sat, noon-4pm Sun; Perrache) offer service to Spain, Portugal, Italy and Germany from the Centre d'Échange building at the north end of the Perrache train complex.

TRAIN

Lyon has two main-line train stations: **Gare de la Part-Dieu** (place Charles Béraudier, 3e; Part-Dieu), 1.5km east of the Rhône, and **Gare de Perrache** (cours de Verdun Rambaud, 2e; Perrache). Some local trains stop at **Gare St-Paul** (www.ter.sncf.com/rhone-alpes; 11bis place St-Paul, 5e; Vieux Lyon) and **Gare Jean Macé** (www.ter.sncf.com/rhone-alpes; place Jean Macé, 7e; Jean Macé). There's also a TGV station at Lyon-St-Exupéry Airport. Buy tickets at the stations or at the **SNCF Boutique** (2 place Bellecour; 10am-6.45pm Tue-Fri, to 5.45pm Sat; Bellecour) downtown.

Destinations by direct TGV include the following:

Lille-Europe €90, three hours, at least eight daily

Marseille €52, 1¾ hours, every 30 to 60 minutes

Paris Charles de Gaulle Airport €88, two hours, at least 11 daily

Paris Gare de Lyon €75, two hours, every 30 to 60 minutes

GETTING AROUND

BICYCLE

Pick up a red-and-silver bike at one of the 300-odd bike stations throughout the city and drop it off at another with Lyon's **Vélo'v** (www.velov.grandlyon.com; 1st 30min free, next 30min €1, each subsequent 30min period €2) bike-rental scheme. Start by paying a one-time flat fee for a *carte courte durée* (short-duration card; €1.50 for 24 hours, €5 for seven days).

BOAT

Le Vaporetto (08 20 20 69 20; www.confluence.fr/notrenavettevaporetto; one-way adult/child €4/2; mid-Mar–Dec) operates *navettes* (passenger ferry boats) to Lyon's Confluence neighbourhood. Travel time is 30 minutes from the **St-Paul dock** (quai de Bondy, 5e; Hôtel de Ville, Vieux Lyon) and 20 minutes from the **Bellecour dock** (quai des Célestins, 2e; Bellecour, Vieux Lyon).

PUBLIC TRANSPORT

Buses, trams, a four-line metro and two funiculars linking Vieux Lyon to Fourvière and St-Just are operated by TCL (www.tcl.fr). Public transport runs from around 5am to midnight.

Tickets valid for all forms of public transport cost €1.90 (€16.90 for a *carnet* of 10) and are available from bus and tram drivers as well as machines. An all-day ticket costs €5.80. Time-stamp tickets on all forms of public transport.

Gordes (p178)

PROVENCE

FESUS ROBERT/SHUTTERSTOCK ©

In This Chapter

Provence at a Glance...

The pastoral landscapes of Provence are a French fantasy come true: fields of lavender, ancient olive groves and snowcapped mountains. For the quintessential Provençal countryside, the best place to begin is inland around the valleys and hills of the Luberon and Var. Further inland rises Provence's highest peak, Mont Ventoux, and beyond it, the snowy peaks of the Hautes-Alpes.

In Provence, food is an all-consuming passion. Dominated by the hallowed ingredients of Mediterranean cooking – olive oil, wine, tomatoes and garlic – the region's cuisine is a highlight, be it savouring a simple bowl of soupe au pistou or shopping for delicate courgette flowers and sweet Cavaillon melons at the markets.

Two Days in Provence

Spend day one in Avignon exploring the old town and the **Palais des Papes** (p186), restoring your energies with fruit tarts from **Maison Violette** (p187). When the afternoon light turns golden, visit **Pont St-Bénezet** (p186). After sundown, indulge yourself at **Restaurant L'Essentiel** (p187). On day two, make a day trip to the **Pont du Gard** (p184) for Roman history and memorable canoeing action on the River Gard.

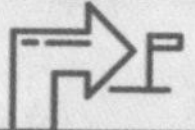

Four Days in Provence

Day three, motor an hour southeast to Aix-en-Provence for **market shopping** (p182) and lunch. For the afternoon, drive another hour north for a red-rock hike in **Roussillon** (p178) and sunset in **Gordes** (p178). Devote the fourth day to exploring starry **Moustiers Ste-Marie** (p190) and its impressive gastronomy.

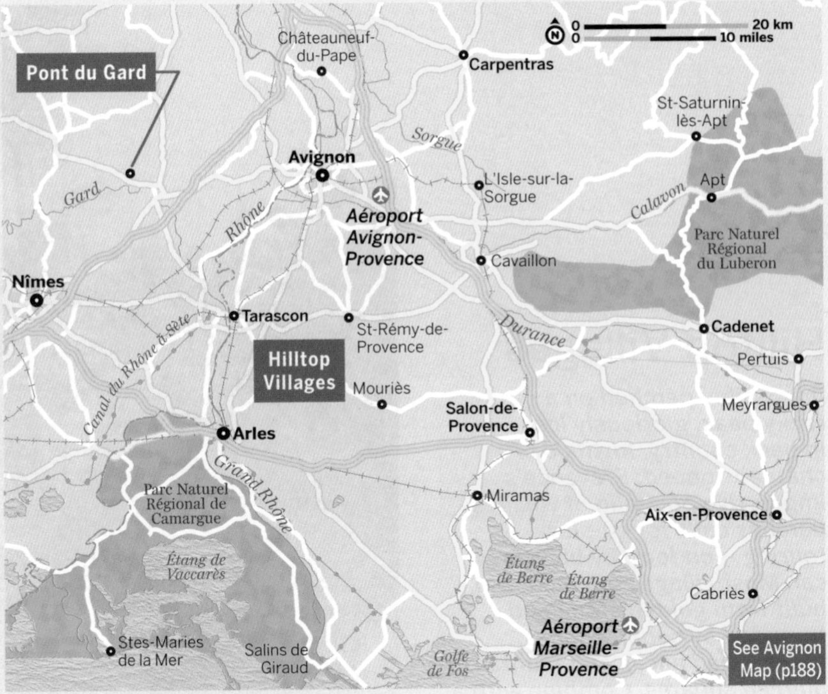

Arriving in Provence

Aéroport Marseille Provence (Marseille) Buses run to Marseille and Aix-en-Provence every 20 minutes. Direct trains reach destinations including Marseille, Arles and Avignon. Allow €50 for a taxi to Marseille.

Train stations Major cities, including Nice, Marseille and Avignon, are linked by fast TGVs. Avignon has a direct link to Paris and the Eurostar (you can reach the UK in under four hours).

Where to Stay

There's a huge variety of accommodation on offer: rural *mas* (farmhouses), smart B&Bs, designer hotels and everything in between. Finding a place to suit your budget might be the biggest challenge. It's wise to book well ahead everywhere in summer (online is easiest); prices are at their highest in July and August. Avignon is a good base for exploring the surrounding region.

Sentier des Ocres (p178)

Hilltop Villages

Impossibly perched on a rocky peak, gloriously lost in back country, fortified or château-topped: Provence's impressive portfolio of villages perchés calls for go-slow touring – on foot, by bicycle or car. Most villages are medieval, built from golden stone and threaded by cobbled lanes, flower-filled alleys and fountain-pierced squares. Combine with a long lazy lunch for a perfect day.

Great For...

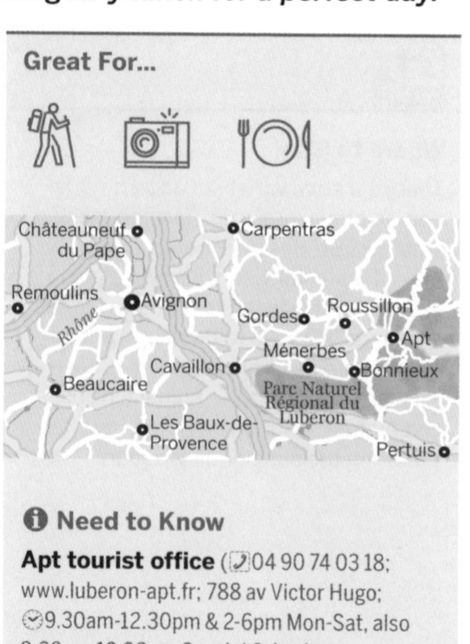

Need to Know

Apt tourist office (☎04 90 74 03 18; www.luberon-apt.fr; 788 av Victor Hugo; ⏰9.30am-12.30pm & 2-6pm Mon-Sat, also 9.30am-12.30pm Sun Jul & Aug)

★ Top Tip

Visit early in the morning or just before sunset for the best light and fewer crowds.

LOTTIE DAVIES/LONELY PLANET ©

Gordes

Arguably the scenic queen of the Luberon's hilltop villages, the tiered village of Gordes seems to teeter improbably on the edge of sheer rock faces, a jumble of terracotta rooftops, church towers and winding lanes. It's a living postcard – but unfortunatel y it's also seethingly popular in summer, so arrive early or late to avoid the worst crowds.

Follow the locals downhill along rue Baptistin Picca to the pocket-sized **Boulangerie de Mamie Jane** (☎04 90 72 09 34; rue Baptistin Picca; dishes €7-10; ⏲6.30am-1pm & 2-6pm Thu-Tue) for outstanding bread, pastries, cakes and biscuits, including lavender-perfumed goodies.

Les Baux-de-Provence

Clinging precariously to an ancient limestone *baou* (Provençal for 'rocky spur'), this fortified hilltop village is among France's most visited. Narrow cobbled streets wend up to the ruined castle of **Château des Baux** (☎04 90 54 55 56; www.chateau-baux-provence.com; adult/child Apr-Sep €10.50/8.50, Oct-Mar €8.50/6.50; ⏲9am-8pm Jul & Aug, to 7pm Apr-Jun & Sep, reduced hours Oct-Mar), dating to the 10th century. Medieval-themed entertainment abounds in summer.

Roussillon

Red by name, red by nature, dazzling Roussillon was once the centre of local ochre mining and is still unmistakably marked by its vivid crimson colour. Artists' workshops lace its streets and the **Sentier des Ocres**

Les Baux-de-Provence

(Ochre Trail; adult/child €2.50/free; 9.30am-5.30pm;) plunges visitors into a mini-desert landscape of chestnut groves, pines and sunset-coloured ochre formations. Information panels along the two circular trails (30 or 50 minutes) highlight flora to spot. Wear walking shoes, and don't wear white!

Châteauneuf-du-Pape

Châteauneuf-du-Pape is prized by wine lovers the world over. Three kilometres from the village, **Mont-Redon** (04 90 83 72 75; www.chateaumontredon.com; rte d'Orange, D88; 9am-7pm Apr-Sep, reduced hours Oct-Mar) is easy for wine-tasting drop-ins.

As the village's name hints, the hilltop **château** after which the wine is named was originally built as a summer residence for Avignon's popes. Wraparound views of the surrounding Rhône valley are epic, stretching all the way to Mont Ventoux.

☑ Don't Miss

Rows of summertime lavender in bloom at **Abbaye Notre-Dame de Sénanque** (www.abbayedesenanque.com; adult/child €7.50/3.50; 9-11.30am Mon-Sat Apr-Nov, shorter hours Dec-Mar), a peaceful Cistercian abbey 4km northwest of Gordes.

BORIS STROUJKO/SHUTTERSTOCK ©

Ménerbes

Hilltop Ménerbes gained fame as the home of expat British author Peter Mayle, whose books *A Year in Provence* and *Toujours Provence* recounted his tales of renovating a farmhouse just outside the village in the late 1980s. Opposite the 12th-century church, the **Maison de la Truffe et du Vin** (www.vin-truffe-luberon.com; place de l'Horloge; 10am-noon & 2.30-6pm daily Apr-Oct, Thu-Sat Nov-Mar) represents 60 local *domaines* (wine-growing estates). April to October, there is free wine-tasting and wine sales at great prices. Winter brings truffle workshops.

Bonnieux

Settled during the Roman era, bewitching Bonnieux still preserves its medieval character. It's intertwined with alleyways, cul-de-sacs and hidden staircases: from place de la Liberté, 86 steps lead to the 12th-century church. The **Musée de la Boulangerie** (04 90 75 88 34; 12 rue de la République; adult/student/child €3.50/1.50/free; 10am-12.30pm & 2.30-6pm Wed-Mon Apr-Oct), in an old 17th-century bakery building, explores the history of bread-making. Time your visit for the lively Friday market.

Take a Break

Allow 30 minutes from Bonnieux to vine-shaded **Le Sanglier Paresseux** (www.sanglierparesseux.com; Caseneuve; 2-/3-/4-course menus €32/39/59; 12.30-2.30pm & 7.30-9.30pm Wed-Sun May-Oct, plus Tue Jul & Aug, shorter hours Nov-Apr) in hilltop Caseneuve. Cuisine is inventive, unfussy and seasonal. Reserve ahead.

Market display of cheese, L'Isle-sur-la-Sorgue (p183)

Provençal Markets

Stalls groaning with fruit and veg, trays of cheese and saucisson sec (dry cured sausage) to sample, stallholders loudly plying their wares – markets are an essential element of Provençal life. Practically every village has at least one weekly market, packed with locals shopping and gossiping, and with dozens of stalls selling everything from locally farmed produce to spices, soaps and handmade crafts.

Great For...

Need to Know

Aix-en-Provence tourist office (04 42 16 11 61; www.aixenprovencetourism.com; 300 av Giuseppe Verdi, Les Allées; 8.30am-7pm Mon-Sat, 10am-1pm & 2-6pm Sun Apr-Sep, 8.30am-6pm Mon-Sat Oct-Mar;)

★ **Top Tip**

Take your own woven straw basket to blend in with the local crowd.

TEAL SUN/SHUTTERSTOCK ©

Aix-en-Provence

A pocket of left-bank Parisian chic deep in Provence, Aix (pronounced like the letter X) is all class: its leafy boulevards and public squares are lined with 17th- and 18th-century mansions, punctuated by gurgling moss-covered fountains. Haughty stone lions guard its grandest avenue, cafe-laced **cours Mirabeau**, where fashionable Aixois pose on polished pavement terraces sipping espresso.

At the city's **food market** (place Richelme; ⏲7am-noon) trestle tables are piled with marinated olives, goat's cheese, garlic, lavender, honey, peaches, melons, cherries and a bounty of other sun-kissed fruit, veg and seasonal foods. You can also buy hot and precooked food. Plane trees shade the atmospheric T-shaped square where Aixois catch up over *un café*.

Flower markets fill place des Prêcheurs (Sunday morning) and place de l'Hôtel de Ville (Tuesday, Thursday and Saturday mornings); and a **flea market** (place de Verdun; ⏲Tue, Thu & Sat mornings) promises quirky vintage items three mornings a week.

Carpentras

The **Friday morning market** in Carpentras is as Provençal as it gets. More than 350 food stalls fill rue d'Inguimbert, av Jean Jaurès and many side streets, bulging with bread, honey, cheese, olives, fruit and a rainbow of *berlingots*, Carpentras' striped, pillow-shaped hard-boiled sweets. In winter Carpentras' annual fair, the **Foire de la St-Siffrein** (www.foire-saint-siffrein-carpentras.com; ⏲Nov), has live music, food stalls and the first of the season's truffle harvest.

Markets aside, Carpentras is a rather run-of-the-mill agricultural town with a handful of historic sights including a **Roman arch** (behind the cathedral) and 14th-century **synagogue** (☎04 90 63 39 97; place Juiverie; ⏲10am-noon & 3-4.30pm Mon-Thu, 10-11.30am & 3-3.30pm Fri). For access, ring the doorbell on the half-hour.

Apt

The principal town in the Luberon, Apt, has a huge **Saturday-morning market** attracting locals and tourists alike. Look out for

☑ Don't Miss

Breads baked by Benoît Fradette at **Farinoman Fou** (www.farinomanfou.fr; 3 rue Mignet; bread €1.40-3; ⏲7am-7pm Tue-Sat), a phenomenal Aix bakery with constant queues.

✕ Take a Break

Lunch at Carpentras' hip brasserie **Chez Serge** (☎04 90 63 21 24; www.chez-serge.com; 90 rue Cottier; 2-/3-course dinner €29/39; ⏲noon-2pm & 7.30-10pm Jun-Sep, noon-1.30pm & 7.30-9.30pm Oct-May; 📶👪), washed down with local wine.

Aix-en-Provence

Apt's local speciality: *fruits confits* (candied fruits, also known as glacé or crystallised fruit). Made with real fruit, the water is removed and replaced with a sugar syrup to preserve these jewel-like treats.

Apt is also a hub for 1650-sq-km **Parc Naturel Régional du Luberon** (www.parcduluberon.fr), a regional nature park criss-crossed by hiking trails.

L'Isle-sur-la-Sorgue

A moat of flowing water encircles the 12th-century town of L'Isle-sur-la-Sorgue. This 'Venice of Provence' is home to several **antiques villages** (noon-6pm Fri, 10am-6pm Sat-Mon), with 300-plus high-end stalls. Sunday is the big market day, with antique vendors participating as well, while Thursday offers a smaller market through the village streets. For bargains, it's better to come mid-August or Easter for the antiques fairs.

The historic centre is contained within canals dotted by creaking **waterwheels** – the one by the tiny park at av des Quatre Otages is particularly photogenic. The ancient **fishermen's quarter** is a tangle of narrow passageways.

A **tourist-office** (04 90 38 04 78; www.oti-delasorgue.fr; place de la Liberté; 9am-12.30pm & 2.30-5.30pm Mon-Sat, 9.30am-12.30pm Sun) brochure details attractions, and there's an app you can download.

Cavaillon

Cavaillon is synonymous with sweet cantaloupe melons – best shopped for at the small town's early-morning Monday market, May to September, or during July's four-day **Fête du Melon**.

Pont du Gard

Southern France has some fine Roman sites, but nothing can top the Unesco World Heritage–listed Pont du Gard, a breathtaking three-tiered aqueduct 25km west of Avignon.

Great For...

☑ Don't Miss

With kids: fun, hands-on learning in the **Ludo** play area.

The extraordinary three-tiered Pont du Gard was once part of a 50km-long system of channels built around 19 BC to transport water from Uzès to Nîmes. The scale is huge: the bridge is 48.8m high, 275m long and graced with 52 precision-built arches; it was sturdy enough to carry up to 20,000 cu metres of water per day.

Engineering Marvel

Each block was carved by hand and transported from nearby quarries – no mean feat, considering the largest blocks weighed over 5 tonnes. The height of the bridge descends by 2.5cm across its length, providing just enough gradient to keep the water flowing – an amazing demonstration of the precision of Roman engineering. At the visitor centre on the

Need to Know

04 66 37 50 99; www.pontdugard.fr; adult/child €8.50/6, Pass Aqueduc incl guided visit of topmost tier €11.50/6; 9am-11pm Jul & Aug, to 10pm Jun & Sep, to 9pm May, to 8pm Apr & Oct, to 6pm Nov-Mar

Take a Break

Dine at outstanding restaurant **Le Tracteur** (www.lucietestud.com/le tracteur) in nearby Argilliers.

★ Top Tip

Evening is a good time to visit: admission is cheaper and the bridge is illuminated.

left, northern bank, there's an impressive, high-tech **museum**.

Mémoires de Garrigue

You can walk across the tiers for panoramic views over the Gard River, but the best perspective on the bridge is from downstream, along the 1.4km Mémoires de Garrigue walking trail.

Canoeing on the Gard

For a unique perspective on the Pont du Gard, you need to see it from the water. The best time is between April and June, as winter floods and summer droughts can sometimes make the river impassable.

Most local hire companies are based in Collias, 8km from the bridge (a journey of about two hours by kayak). Depending on the season and the height of the river, you can make a longer journey by being dropped upstream at Pont St-Nicholas (19km, about five hours) or Russan (32km, seven to eight hours); the latter option also includes a memorable trip through the Gorges du Gardon.

There's a minimum age of six. Life jackets are always provided, but you must be a competent swimmer.

Outdoor Activities

Canoë Collias (04 66 22 87 20; www.canoe-collias.com; 194 chemin de St-Privat, Collias; adult/child €23/12; 8am-8pm mid-Mar–late Oct) Rents one- to four-person boats.

Canoë Le Tourbillon (04 66 22 85 54; www.canoeletourbillon.com; 3 chemin du Gardon, Collias; adult/child from €23/17; 9am-7pm Apr-Sep) Offers canoe rental and equipment for via ferrata climbs on nearby Gardon massif (€15 for two hours).

Avignon

Attention, quiz fans: name the city where the pope lived during the early 14th century. Answered Rome? Bzzz: sorry, wrong answer. For 70-odd years of the early 1300s, the Provençal town of Avignon was the centre of the Roman Catholic world, and though its stint as the seat of papal power only lasted a few decades, it's been left with an impressive legacy of ecclesiastical architecture.

SIGHTS

Palais des Papes Palace

(Papal Palace; ☎tickets 04 32 74 32 74; www.palais-des-papes.com; place du Palais; adult/child €12/10, with Pont St-Bénezet €14.50/11.50; ⏲9am-8pm Jul, to 8.30pm Aug, shorter hours Sep-Jun) The largest Gothic palace ever built, the Palais des Papes was erected by Pope Clement V, who abandoned Rome in 1309 in the wake of violent disorder after his election. Its immense scale illustrates the medieval might of the Roman Catholic church.

Ringed by 3m-thick walls, its halls, chapels and antechambers are largely bare today, but tickets now include tablets revealing VR representations of how the building would have looked in all its papal pomp.

Pont St-Bénezet Bridge

(☎tickets 04 32 74 32 74; bd de la Ligne; adult/child 24hr ticket €5/4, with Palais des Papes €14.50/11.50; ⏲9am-8pm Jul, to 8.30pm Aug, shorter hours Sep-Jun) Legend says Pastor Bénezet had three visions urging him to build a bridge across the Rhône. Completed in 1185, the 900m-long bridge linked Avignon with Villeneuve-lès-Avignon. It was rebuilt several times before all but four of its 22 spans were washed away in the 1600s, leaving the far side marooned in the middle of the Rhône.

Musée du Petit Palais Museum

(☎04 90 86 44 58; www.petit-palais.org; place du Palais; adult/child €6/free; ⏲10am-1pm & 2-6pm Wed-Mon) The archbishops' palace during the 14th and 15th centuries now houses collections of primitive, pre-Rennaissance, 13th- to 16th-century Italian religious paintings by artists including Botticelli, Carpaccio and Giovanni di Paolo – the most famous is Botticelli's *La Vierge et l'Enfant* (1470).

Palais des Papes

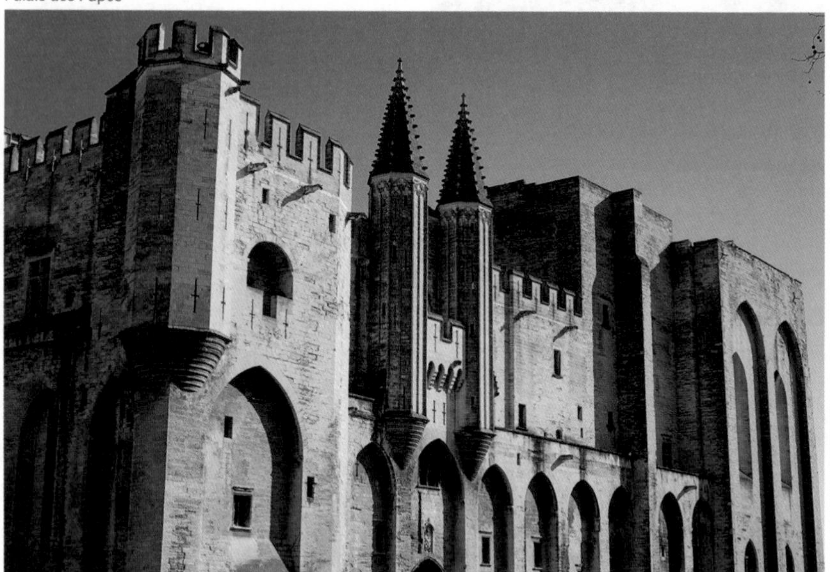

TOURS

Les Grands Bateaux de Provence Boating

(☎04 90 85 62 25; www.mireio.net; allées de l'Oulle; 1hr cruise €12) Runs hour-long boat cruises along the river, offering great views of the Palais des Papes and the Pont St-Bénezet. It also runs day-long boat tours to Arles, Châteauneuf-du-Pape and Tarascon, as well as dinner cruises.

EATING

Restaurants open seven days during the summer festival season in July, when reservations become essential. At other times of year many are closed at least two days a week.

Maison Violette Bakery $

(☎06 59 44 62 94; place des Corps Saints; ⏰7am-7.30pm Mon-Sat) We simply defy you not to walk into this bakery and not instantly be tempted by the stacks of baguettes, *ficelles* and *pains de campagnes* loaded up on the counter, not to mention the orderly ranks of eclairs, *millefeuilles,* fruit tarts and cookies lined up irresistibly behind the glass. Go on, a little bit of what you fancy does you good, *non*?

Restaurant L'Essentiel French $$

(☎04 90 85 87 12; www.restaurantlessentiel.com; 2 rue Petite Fusterie; menus €32-46; ⏰noon-2pm & 7-9.45pm Tue-Sat) In the top tier of Avignon's restaurants for many a year, this elegant restaurant remains (as its name suggests) as essential as ever. First there's the setting: a lovely, honey-stoned *hôtel particulier* (mansion) with a sweet courtyard garden. Then there's the food: rich, sophisticated French dining of the first order, replete with the requisite foams, veloutés and reductions.

Bar à Manger du Coin Caché Bistro $$

(☎04 32 76 27 16; 3 place des Chataignes; mains €12-15; ⏰noon-3pm & 7-10pm) This place is pure charm. On cobblestone place des Chataignes ('Chestnut Tree Square') it spills across to its ancient stone neighbour (Cloître St-Pierre). More bistro than bar, it cooks up seasonal dishes with a fusion twist. Kickstart the alfresco occasion with a sweet Vin de Noix de la St Jean, peachy Rinquinquin or other Provençal aperitif. No credit cards.

Culinary Know-How

Over 40 food stalls showcase seasonal Provençal ingredients at **Les Halles** (www.avignon-leshalles.com; place Pie; ⏰6am-1.30pm Tue-Fri, to 2pm Sat & Sun), Avignon's covered food market. Cooking demonstrations are held at 11am Saturday. Outside on place Pie, admire Patrick Blanc's marvellous vegetal wall.

Candied fruit, Avignon

Christian Etienne French $$$

(☎04 90 86 16 50; www.christian-etienne.fr; 10 rue de Mons; lunch/dinner menus from €35/75; ⏰noon-2pm & 7.30-10pm Tue-Sat) If it's the full-blown, fine-dining French experience you're after, then Monsieur Etienne's much-vaunted (and Michelin-starred) restaurant is the place to go. It's the real deal: truffles and foie gras galore, and the kind of multicourse menus that demand a second mortgage. It's a bit dated inside: sit on the lovely, leafy terrace for fine views of the medieval building.

Les 5 Sens Gastronomy $$$

(☎04 90 85 26 51; www.restaurantles5sens.com; 18 rue Joseph Vernet; menus lunch €22.50-29, dinner €39-56; ⏰noon-1.30pm & 7.30-11pm Fri-Tue) This gastronomic

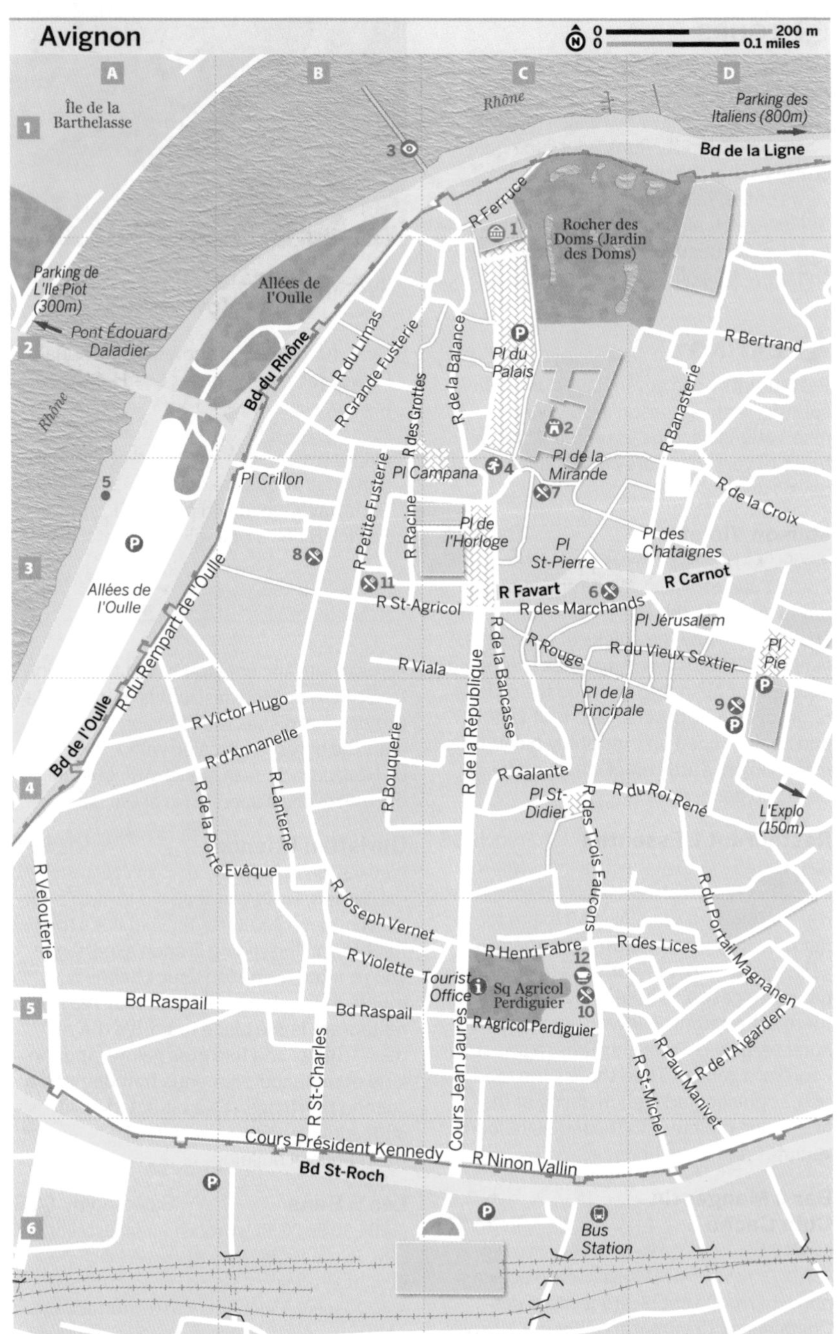
Avignon
0 200 m
0 0.1 miles
A
B
C
D
1
2
3
4
5
6
Île de la Barthelasse
Rhône
Parking des Italiens (800m)
Bd de la Ligne
R Ferruce
Rocher des Doms (Jardin des Doms)
Parking de L'Ile Piot (300m)
Allées de l'Oulle
Pont Édouard Daladier
Bd du Rhône
R du Limas
R Grande Fusterie
R des Grottes
R de la Balance
Pl du Palais
R Bertrand
R Banasterie
Pl de la Mirande
Pl Campana
Pl Crillon
R Petite Fusterie
R Racine
Pl de l'Horloge
Pl St-Pierre
Pl des Chataignes
R de la Croix
R Carnot
R Favart
R St-Agricol
R des Marchands
Pl Jérusalem
R du Rempart de l'Oulle
R Viala
R de la Bancasse
R Rouge
R du Vieux Sextier
Pl Pie
Pl de la Principale
R Victor Hugo
R d'Annanelle
R de la République
R Bouquerie
R Lanterne
R de la Porte Evêque
R Galante
Pl St-Didier
R des Trois Faucons
R du Roi René
L'Explo (150m)
Bd de l'Oulle
R Velouterie
R Joseph Vernet
R Henri Fabre
R des Lices
R du Portail Magnanen
R Violette
Tourist Office
Sq Agricol Perdiguier
R Agricol Perdiguier
Bd Raspail
R de l'Aigarden
R Paul Manivet
R St-Michel
R St-Charles
Cours Jean Jaurès
Cours Président Kennedy
R Ninon Vallin
Bd St-Roch
Bus Station

Avignon

Sights

1 Musée du Petit Palais C1
2 Palais des Papes C2
3 Pont St-Bénezet B1

Activities, Courses & Tours

4 Le Carré du Palais C3
5 Les Grands Bateaux de Provence A3

Eating

6 Bar à Manger du Coin Caché C3
7 Christian Etienne C3
8 Les 5 Sens B3
9 Les Halles D4
10 Maison Violette C5
11 Restaurant L'Essentiel B3

Drinking & Nightlife

12 Milk Shop C5

temple is a great option for a *très Français* fine-dining experience. Overseen by chef supremo Thierry Baucher, it's particularly known for its mix of Provençal and southwestern flavours – so expect contemporary spin on traditional dishes such as *cassoulet* (meat-and-bean stew), foie gras and *suprème de pintade* (guinea-fowl supreme).

DRINKING & NIGHTLIFE

L'Explo — Craft Beer

(2 rue des Teinturiers; 5pm-midnight Tue-Sat) It's a sunny evening and your inner beer nerd is in the market for a dry rye, hoppy IPA or boozy Belgian wheatbeer. Well you're in luck: this groovy little bar on happening rue des Teinturiers serves a big range of artisanal beers, many made locally.

Milk Shop — Cafe

(09 82 54 16 82; www.milkshop.fr; 26 place des Corps Saints; 7.45am-7pm Mon-Fri, 9.30am-7pm Sat;) Keen to mingle with Avignon students? Make a beeline for this *salon au lait* ('milk bar') where super-thick ice-cream shakes (€4.50) are slurped through extra-wide straws. Bagels (€5 to €7), cupcakes and other American snacks create a deliberate US vibe, while comfy armchairs and wi-fi encourage hanging out.

INFORMATION

Avignon Passion Free, 15-day pass offering cheaper admission to big-hitter museums and monuments. The first site visited is full price, but each subsequent site is discounted. Available at the tourist office and museums.

Tourist Office (04 32 74 32 74; www.avignon-tourisme.com; 41 cours Jean Jaurès; 9am-6pm Mon-Sat, 10am-5pm Sun Apr-Oct, shorter hours Nov-Mar) Offers guided walking tours and information on other tours and activities, including boat trips on the River Rhône and wine-tasting trips to nearby vineyards. Smartphone apps too.

Tourist Office Annexe (Gare Avignon TGV; Jun-Aug) During summer, Avignon has an information booth at the TGV station.

GETTING THERE & AWAY

AIR

Aéroport Avignon-Provence (AVN; 04 90 81 51 51; www.avignon.aeroport.fr; Caumont) In Caumont, 8km southeast of Avignon. Direct flights to London, Birmingham and Southampton in the UK.

BUS

Avignon **bus station** (bd St-Roch; information window 8am-7pm Mon-Fri, to 1pm Sat) is a major bus hub for the Vaucluse *département*.

Long-haul companies **Linebus** (04 90 85 30 48; www.linebus.com) and **Eurolines** (04 90 85 27 60; www.eurolines.com) have offices at the far end of bus platforms and serve places like Barcelona. TransVaucluse (www.vaucluse.fr) offers regional bus services in the Avignon area.

Aix-en-Provence €18, LER Line 23, 1¼ hours, six daily Monday to Saturday, two on Sunday

Carpentras €2.10, TransVaucluse Line 5, 45 minutes, 11 daily Monday to Saturday, six on Sunday

TRAIN

Avignon has two train stations: **Gare Avignon Centre** (42 bd St-Roch), on the southern edge of the walled town, and **Gare Avignon TGV** (Courtine), 4km southwest in Courtine.

Local shuttle trains link the two every 15 to 20 minutes (€1.60, six minutes, 6am to 11pm). Note that there is no luggage storage at the train station.

Eurostar (www.eurostar.com) services operate one to five times weekly between Avignon TGV and London St Pancras (from €78, 5¾ hours) en route to/from Marseille.

Aix-en-Provence €12.50 to €21, 25 minutes

Paris Gare du Lyon €45 to €90, 3½ hours

Marseille €12.50 to €19, 40 minutes

Nice €36 to €62, 3¼ hours

GETTING AROUND

BICYCLE

Provence Bike (☎04 90 27 92 61; www.provence-bike.com; 7 av St-Ruf; bicycles per day/week from €12/65, scooters €25/150; ⌚9am-6.30pm Mon-Sat, plus 10am-1pm Sun Jul) Rents city bikes, mountain bikes, scooters and motorcycles.

Vélopop (☎08 10 45 64 56; www.velopop.fr; per half-hour €0.50) Shared-bicycle service, with 17 stations around town. Membership per day/week is €1/5.

CAR & MOTORCYCLE

Find car-hire agencies at both train stations (reserve ahead, especially in July). Narrow, one-way streets and impossible parking make driving within the ramparts an absolute horror: park outside the walls.

The most convenient car park for the town centre is **Parking Palais des Papes** (place du Palais; per hr €2, 24hr €18.80; ⌚24hr), which fills quickly on busy summer days. There are 900 free spaces at **Parking de L'Ile Piot**, and 1150 at **Parking des Italiens**, both under surveillance and served by the free **TCRA shuttle bus** (Transports en Commun de la Région d'Avignon; ☎04 32 74 18 32; www.tcra.fr).

Moustiers Ste-Marie

Huddled at the base of soaring cliffs is the picturesque village of Moustiers Ste-Marie. Nicknamed 'Étoile de Provence' (Star of Provence) for the gold star crowning the village, Moustiers is a useful gateway to the Gorges du Verdon. In summer, it's clear that Moustiers' charms are no secret.

SIGHTS & ACTIVITIES

Chapelle Notre Dame de Beauvoir Church

High above the village, Moustiers' 14th-century church clings to a cliff ledge like an eagle's nest. A steep trail climbs beside a waterfall to the chapel, passing 14 Stations of the Cross en route. High above, a 227m-long chain bearing a shining gold star is stretched between the cliff walls – a tradition, legend has it, begun by the Knight of Blacas, in return for his safe return from the Crusades.

Musée de la Faïence Museum

(☎04 92 74 61 64; rue Seigneur de la Clue; adult/student/under 16yr €3/2/free; ⌚10am-12.30pm Jul & Aug, to 5pm or 6pm rest of year, closed Tue year-round) Moustiers' decorative faïence (glazed earthenware) once graced the dining tables of Europe's most aristocratic houses. Today each of Moustiers' 15 *ateliers* (workshops) has its own style, from representational to abstract. Antique masterpieces are housed in this little museum, adjacent to the town hall.

Des Guides pour l'Aventure Outdoors

(☎06 85 94 46 61; www.guidesaventure.com) Offers activities including canyoning (from €50 per half-day), rock climbing (€45 for three hours), rafting (€45 for 2½ hours) and 'floating' (€50 for three hours) – which is like rafting, except you have a buoyancy aid instead of a boat.

Moustiers Ste-Marie

 EATING

La Ferme Ste-Cécile Gastronomy $$

(☎04 92 74 64 18; www.ferme-ste-cecile.com; D952; 2-/3-course menu €30/39; ⏰noon-2pm & 7.30-10pm Tue-Sat, noon-2pm Sun) Just outside Moustiers, this wonderful *ferme auberge* (country inn) immerses you in the full Provençal dining experience, from the sun-splashed terrace and locally picked wines right through to the chef's meticulous Mediterranean cuisine. It's about 1.2km from Moustiers; look out for the signs as you drive towards Castellane.

La Bastide de Moustiers Gastronomy $$$

(☎04 92 70 47 47; www.bastide-moustiers.com; chemin de Quinson; menus €60-90; ⏰12.30-1.30pm & 7.30-9pm, closed Oct-Feb) A legendary table of Provence, founded by chef supremo Alain Ducasse. As you'd expect from this Michelin-starred, much-lauded restaurant, it's a temple to French cuisine – from the playful *amuses-bouches* to the rich, sauce-heavy mains and indulgent desserts. Much of the produce comes from the inn's own kitchen garden. Dress very smartly, and reserve well ahead.

INFORMATION

Tourist Office (☎04 92 74 67 84; www.moustiers.eu; passage du Cloître; ⏰9.30am-7pm Mon-Fri, 9.30am-12.30pm & 2-7pm Sat & Sun Jul & Aug, 10am-noon & 2-6pm Apr-Jun & Sep, closes around 5pm Oct-Mar; 📶) Tonnes of information on the various ways of exploring the Gorges du Verdon.

 GETTING THERE & AROUND

A car makes exploring the gorges much more fun, though if you're very fit, cycling is an option, too. LER bus 27 (www.info-ler.fr) travels from Marseille and Aix-en-Provence direct to Moustiers-Ste-Marie (€18.90). Moustiers is also served by the **Navette des Gorges du Verdon** (☎04 92 34 22 90; autocars.delaye@orange.fr).

NICE

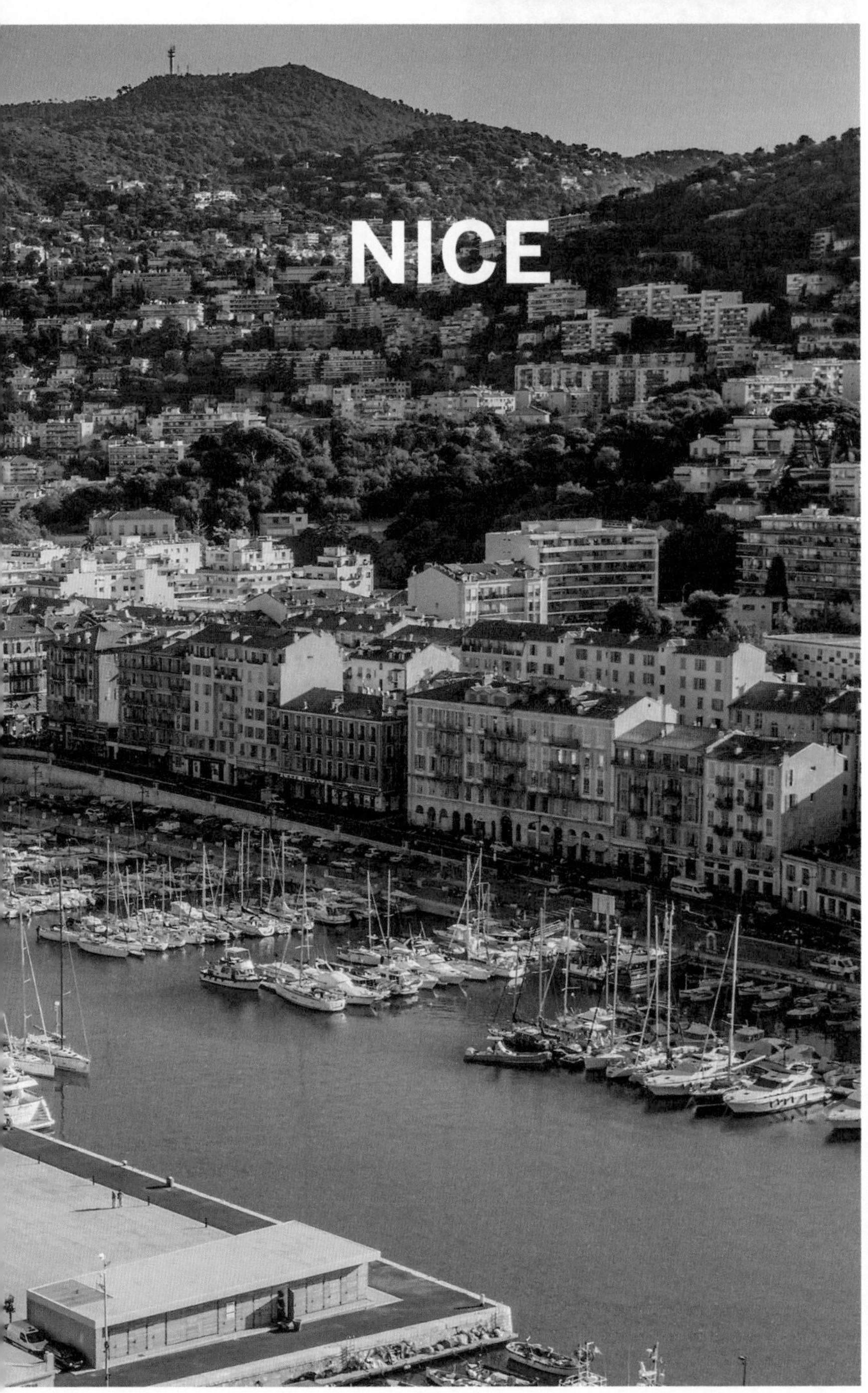

In This Chapter

Nice at a Glance...

Nice is an enticing mix of urban grit, old-world opulence, year-round sunshine and vibrant street life. The sea and the Mediterranean climate made Nice a tourist magnet as early as the 1700s; today it's the unofficial capital of the French Riviera (Côte d'Azur in French).

For any lover of French and Italian culture, Nice is the perfect hybrid: Italian influence is everywhere from pasta shops to tall-shuttered, ochre-hued buildings. The city is far from perfect – the traffic's horrendous and the beach is made entirely of pebbles – but there's no better place to soak up the Riviera vibe.

Two Days in Nice

Explore **Vieux Nice** (p196), take lunch at **Bar des Oiseaux** (p207) and end on a natural high at the **hilltop park** (p197). Walk, skate or swim along the **Promenade des Anglais** (p202), then dine at **La Rossettisserie** (p206). Day two, discover **Matisse and Chagall** (p203), then learn about belle époque Nice at **Musée Masséna** (p202). Finish with cheesy delights at **La Cave du Fromager** (p207).

Four Days in Nice

Day three, delve into avant-garde **Musée d'Art Moderne et d'Art Contemporain** (p202), lunch on pancakes at **Chez Pipo** (p206), and cruise to the villa-dotted coast near **Villefranche-sur-Mer** (p201). Day four, prowl stalls at **Marché de la Libération** (p205) and drop in for a chickpea beer at **Brasserie Artisanale de Nice** (p208). Come evening, see a show at **Opéra de Nice** (p208) or sip drinks on the outdoor bar terraces nearby.

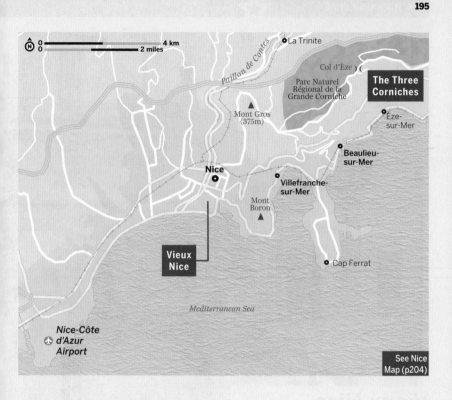

0 4 km
0 2 miles
La Trinite
Paillon de Contes
Col d'Èze
Parc Naturel Régional de la Grande Corniche
The Three Corniches
Mont Gros (375m)
Èze-sur-Mer
Beaulieu-sur-Mer
Nice
Villefranche-sur-Mer
Mont Boron
Vieux Nice
Cap Ferrat
Mediterranean Sea
Nice-Côte d'Azur Airport
See Nice Map (p204)

Arriving in Nice

Nice Côte d'Azur Airport Bus 98 runs to Vieux Nice (€6, 30 minutes), bus 99 to Nice-Ville train station (€6, 30 minutes) and tram 2 to the port (scheduled for completion in 2019, 20 to 25 minutes).

Nice Ville Train Station Tram 1 (€1.50) runs to Vieux Nice (10 minutes), Garibaldi (15 minutes) or Libération (five minutes).

Where to Stay

Accommodation in Nice is excellent and caters to all budgets, unlike many cities on the Côte d'Azur. The lion's share of hotels, hostels and other accommodation is located in the New Town. Hotels charge substantially more during the Monaco Grand Prix and get booked up quickly in July and August; book well in advance. **Nice Pebbles** (www.nicepebbles.com) offers dozens of rental apartments.

ROSTISLAV GLINSKY/SHUTTERSTOCK ©

Vieux Nice

Tucked into a pedestrian-friendly triangle is Nice's oldest neighbourhood. Vieux Nice's streets, overhung with 18th-century houses, are a joy to wander. Packed into these few blocks are enough markets, bars, bistros and boutiques for an entire vacation, and the beach is never more than five minutes away.

Great For...

☑ Don't Miss

A slice of *socca* on the raucous pavement terrace at **Chez René Socca** (2 rue Miralhéti; ⏲9am-9pm Tue-Sun, closed Nov).

Cours Saleya

No experience epitomises the Vieux Nice lifestyle like a trip to its morning market, overflowing with fruit, veggies, olives, cheeses and flowers from the surrounding Alpes-Maritimes region. Every morning, a massive **food market** (⏲6am-1.30pm Tue-Sun) fills much of the square, stalls laden with fruit and vegetables, olives marinated a dozen different ways, every herb and spice known under the Provençal sun – no market is a finer reflection of local Niçois life. An adjoining **flower market** (⏲6am-5.30pm Tue-Sat, 6.30am-1.30pm Sun) is worth a meander for its fragrant bucketfuls of blooms. Monday ushers in a **flea market** (Marché à la Brocante; ⏲7am-6pm Mon), selling furniture and trinkets of all kinds. Don't be afraid to bargain, as posted prices tend to run high.

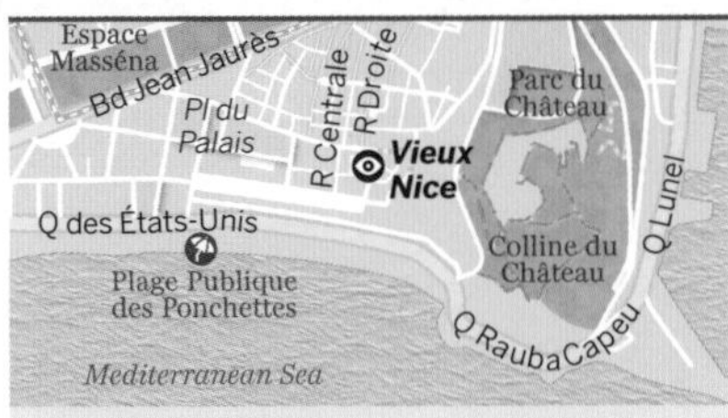

Need to Know

Themed walking tours in English can be booked at the Centre du Patrimoine (p203).

Take a Break

Queue for olive oil, violet or even beer-flavoured ice cream from Nice's king of the scoops, **Fenocchio** (www.fenocchio.fr; 2 place Rossetti; 1/2 scoops €2.50/4; 9am-midnight Mar-Nov).

★ Top Tip

Duck and dive your way through the old town to Nice's **fish market** (place St-François; 6am-1pm Tue-Sun).

Lofty Lookout

From Vieux Nice, staircases wind up to the **Colline du Château** (Castle Hill; 8.30am-8pm Apr-Sep, to 6pm Oct-Mar) FREE, or you can take the free **lift** (Ascenseur du Château; rue des Ponchettes; 9am-8pm Jun-Aug, to 7pm Apr, May & Sep, 10am-6pm Oct-Mar). Formerly a military outpost and today a city park, the hilltop affords panoramic vistas of the Promenade des Anglais from the **Tour Bellanda**. Stroll over to the **Cascade du Casteu** (an artificial 18th-century waterfall), or wander among the cypresses and ornate tombstones of the 18th-century **Cimetière du Château**.

Baroque Splendour

Baroque aficionados will adore architectural gems **Cathédrale Ste-Réparate** (04 93 92 01 35; place Rossetti; 2-6pm Mon, 9am-noon & 2-6pm Tue-Sun), honouring the city's patron saint; and exuberant **Chapelle de la Miséricorde** (cours Saleya; 2.30-5pm Tue Sep-Jun), a 1740 chapel renowned for its rich architecture. On a narrow lane sits **Palais Lascaris** (15 rue Droite; museum pass 24hr/7 days €10/20; 10am-6pm Wed-Mon late Jun–mid-Oct, from 11am mid-Oct–late Jun), a 17th-century mansion housing a frescoed orgy of Flemish tapestries and religious paintings, along with period musical instruments.

Cafe Culture

Lounging on a cafe terrace, watching the world go by over a glass of pastis (aniseed-flavoured aperitif) or post-beach cocktail, is a national pastime in Nice. No place in Vieux Nice offers better people-watching than the tables on the deck and terrace of **La Movida** (www.movidanice.com; 41 quai des États-Unis; 10am-2am). **Les Distilleries Idéales** (04 93 62 10 66; www.facebook.com/Idinice; 24 rue de la Préfecture; 9am-12.30am) has beers on tap, local wine by the glass, and a little balcony.

Panoramic view from Jardin Exotique d'Èze (p201)

The Three Corniches

This trio of corniches (coastal roads) hugs the cliffs between Nice and Monaco, each higher than the last, with dazzling views of the Med. For the grandest views, it's the Grande Corniche you want, but the Moyenne Corniche runs a close scenic second. The lowest of all, the Corniche Inférieure, allows access to a string of snazzy coastal resorts.

Great For...

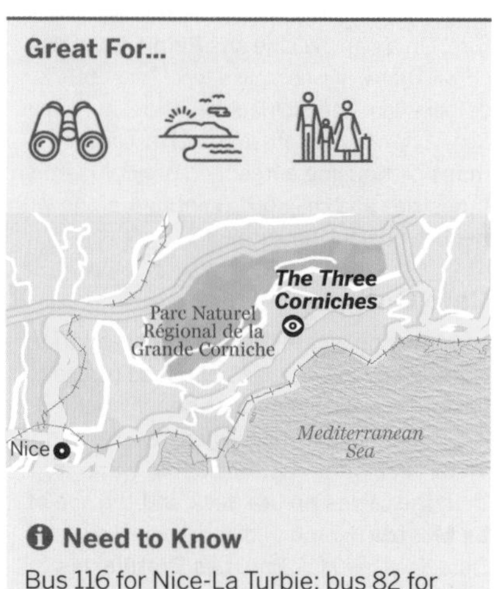

🛈 Need to Know

Bus 116 for Nice-La Turbie; bus 82 for Moyenne Corniche; trains and bus 100 for Corniche Inférieure (€1.50 per journey).

★ Top Tip

Time to linger? Explore walking paths along the rugged peninsula of Cap Ferrat.

Grande Corniche

Views from the spectacular cliff-hanging Grande Corniche are mesmerising. Alfred Hitchcock was sufficiently impressed by Napoléon's Grande Corniche to use it as a backdrop for his film *To Catch a Thief* (1956), starring Cary Grant and Grace Kelly. In a bitter stroke of fate, Kelly died in 1982 after crashing her car on this very same road.

Sitting 675m above the sea and just below Èze, **Fort de la Revère** is the perfect place to revel in 360-degree views. An orientation table helps you get your bearings. The fort was built in 1870 to protect Nice (it served as an allied prisoner of war camp during WWII). There are picnic tables under the trees for an alfresco lunch and dozens of trails in the surrounding **Parc Naturel Départemental de la Grande Corniche**, a protected area that stretches along the D2564 from Col d'Èze to La Turbie.

There are no villages of note along the Grande Corniche until you reach hilltop **La Turbie**, known for its monumental Roman triumphal monument called Trophée des Alpes, visible from all directions. This amazing monument was built by Emperor Augustus in 6 BC to celebrate his victory over the Celto-Ligurian Alpine tribes that had fought Roman sovereignty (the names of the 45 tribes are carved on the western side of the monument). The tower teeters on the highest point of the old Roman road, with dramatic views of Monaco.

Moyenne Corniche

Cut through rock in the 1920s, the Moyenne Corniche takes drivers from Nice past the Col de Villefranche (149m)

Villefranche-sur-Mer

to **Èze**, a rocky little village perched on an impossibly steep peak. A jewel in the Riviera crown, Èze is a medieval village with small higgledy-piggledy stone houses and winding lanes, galleries and shops, and mesmerising views of the coast.

Gorge on the best panorama from **Jardin Exotique d'Èze** (☎04 93 41 10 30; www.jardinexotique-eze.fr; rue du Château; adult/child €6/3.50; ⏱9am-7.30pm Jul-Sep, to 6.30pm Apr-Jun & Oct, to 4.30pm Nov-Mar), a cactus garden at the top of the village, next to old castle ruins. Take time to sit here or in the garden's Zen area to contemplate the stunning view.

☑ Don't Miss

In the old town of Villefranche-sur-Mer, don't miss eerie, arcaded **rue Obscure**, a historical monument a block in from the water.

HEMIS/ALAMY STOCK PHOTO ©

Corniche Inférieure

Skimming the villa-lined waterfront between Nice and Monaco, the lowest coastal road – the Corniche Inférieure – was built in the 1860s. It passes through a string of coastal resorts and is perfect for a dip in the sea.

Villefranche-sur-Mer is heaped above a picture-postcard harbour, its imposing **citadel** (Fort St-Elme; ☎04 93 76 33 27; place Emmanuel Philibert; ⏱10am-noon & 2-5.30pm Oct & Dec-May, 10am-noon & 3-6.30pm Jun-Sep, closed Sun morning & Nov) FREE overlooking the Cap Ferrat. Its 14th-century old town, with evocatively named streets broken by twisting staircases and glimpses of the sea, is a delight to amble. Villefranche was a favourite of Jean Cocteau (1889–1963), who sought solace here in 1924 after the death of his companion Raymond Radiguet and went on to decorate the interior of 14th-century **Chapelle St-Pierre** (€3; ⏱10am-noon & 3-7pm Wed-Mon Apr-Sep, 9.30am-12.30pm & 2-6pm Wed-Sun Oct-Mar) with a mirage of mystical frescoes.

In chic **St-Jean-Cap Ferrat** follow the crowds to **Villa Ephrussi de Rothschild** (☎04 93 01 33 09; www.villa-ephrussi.com/en; adult/child €14/11; ⏱10am-6pm Feb-Jun, Sep & Oct, to 7pm Jul & Aug, 2-6pm Mon-Fri, 10am-6pm Sat & Sun Nov-Jan), an over-the-top belle époque confection commissioned by Baroness Béatrice Ephrussi de Rothschild in 1912. The villa is filled with Fragonard paintings, Louis XVI furniture and Sèvres porcelain, and its nine exquisite themed gardens are stunning – sea views are supreme and fountains 'dance' to classical music every 20 minutes.

✕ Take a Break

Swoon over glittering sea views nursing a sundowner, or better yet, enjoying a first-class meal at restaurant-hotel **Château Eza** (☎04 93 41 12 24; www.chateaueza.com; rue de la Pise; lunch menus €52-62, tasting menus €120) in Èze.

SIGHTS

Promenade des Anglais — Architecture

(8, 52, 62) The most famous stretch of seafront in Nice – if not France – is this vast paved promenade, which gets its name from the English expat patrons who paid for it in 1822. It runs for the whole 4km sweep of the Baie des Anges with a dedicated lane for cyclists and skaters; if you fancy joining them, you can rent skates, scooters and bikes from **Roller Station** (04 93 62 99 05; www.roller-station.fr; 49 quai des États-Unis; skates, boards & scooters per hr/day €5/12, bicycles €5/15; 9am-8pm Jul & Aug, 10am-7pm May, Jun, Sep & Oct, to 6pm Nov-Apr).

Musée d'Art Moderne et d'Art Contemporain — Gallery

(MAMAC; 04 97 13 42 01; www.mamac-nice.org; place Yves Klein; museum pass 24hr/7 days €10/20; 10am-6pm Tue-Sun late-Jun–mid-Oct, from 11am rest of year; 1 to Garibaldi) European and American avant-garde works from the 1950s to the present are the focus of this sprawling multilevel museum. Highlights include many works by Christo and Nice's New Realists: Niki de Saint Phalle, César, Arman and Yves Klein. The building's rooftop also works as an exhibition space (with knockout panoramas of Nice to boot).

Musée Masséna — Museum

(04 93 91 19 10; 65 rue de France; museum pass 24hr/7 days €10/20; 10am-6pm Wed-Mon late-Jun–mid-Oct, from 11am rest of year; 8, 52, 62 to Congrès/Promenade) Originally built as a holiday home for Prince Victor d'Essling (the grandson of one of Napoléon's favourite generals, Maréchal Masséna), this lavish belle époque building is another of the city's iconic architectural landmarks. Built between 1898 and 1901 in grand neoclassical style with an Italianate twist, it's now a fascinating museum dedicated to the history of the Riviera – taking in everything from holidaying monarchs to expat Americans, the boom of tourism and the enduring importance of Carnival.

BEACHES

Be prepared for pebble beaches. Walking barefoot down the beach or lounging on nothing more than a towel are not as comfortable here as they would be in sandier circumstances.

Officially there are 25 named beaches strung out along the Baie des Anges. The Promenade des Anglais boasts more than a dozen named beaches between **Plage Carras** (near Côte d'Azur airport) and **Plage du Centenaire** (opposite Jardin Albert 1er, near Vieux Nice). Most are private, visibly fenced off with their own restaurants, bars, sun loungers and umbrellas for rent – figure about €20 to €25 per day for a beach umbrella and lounger.

Nudity is perfectly acceptable on Nice's beaches, and locals certainly aren't shy about letting it all hang out – but, of course, there's no obligation to bare all (or anything).

Plage Publique des Ponchettes — Beach

Right opposite Vieux Nice, this is generally the busiest beach of all, with oiled bodies either baking in the sun or punching a ball on the beach-volleyball court.

ACTIVITIES

Glisse Evasion — Water Sports

(06 10 27 03 91; www.glisse-evasion.com; 29 Promenade des Anglais; 8.30am-7pm May-Sep; 8, 52, 62 to Congrès/Promenade or Gambetta/Promenade) Based opposite the Hôtel Negresco, this water-sports operator has numerous methods of getting you out and about on the Med, including kayaking (€10 per hour), stand-up paddle boarding (€18 per hour), wakeboarding, waterskiing and floating around on rubber 'sofas'. Also offers paragliding (session €50).

Les Petits Farcis — Cooking

(www.petitsfarcis.com; 12 rue St-Joseph; course per person incl lunch €195; 9.30am-3pm, dates by arrangement) For over a decade, veteran food writer and cookbook author Rosa Jackson has offered these cooking courses, combining a visit to the Saleya market with a leisurely morning cooking in her Vieux Nice studio, then feasting on the Niçois delicacies you've just prepared. Classes are tailored to participants' interests and dietary restrictions; bookings of four or more receive a discount.

TOURS

Centre du Patrimoine Walking
(04 92 00 41 90; www.nice.fr/fr/culture/patrimoine; 14 rue Jules Gilly; tours adult/child €5/free; 9am-1pm & 2-5pm Mon-Thu, to 3.45pm Fri) The Centre du Patrimoine runs two-hour thematic walking tours. English-language tours must be booked two days in advance. The tourist office has a full listing.

Trans Côte d'Azur Boating
(www.trans-cote-azur.com; quai Lunel; Apr-Oct; 2 to Port Lympia) Trans Côte d'Azur runs one-hour boat cruises along the Baie des Anges and Rade de Villefranche (adult/child €18/13) from April to October. From late May to September it also sails to Île Ste-Marguerite (€40/31, one hour), St-Tropez (€65/51, 2½ hours), Monaco (€38.50/30, 45 minutes) and Cannes (€40/31, one hour).

SHOPPING

Shops abound in Nice, ranging from the boutiques of Vieux Nice to the New Town's designer fashion temples to the enormous Nice Étoile shopping mall. For vintage fashion and contemporary art, meander the hip Petit Marais near place Garibaldi. For gourmet gifts to take home, head for Vieux Nice, where you'll find olive oil, wine, candied fruits and much more.

Maison Auer Food
(04 93 85 77 98; www.maison-auer.com; 7 rue St-François de Paule; 9am-6pm Tue-Sat) With its gilded counters and mirrors, this opulent shop – run by the same family for five generations – looks more like a 19th-century boutique than a sweet shop, but this is

Giants of Art

The Côte d'Azur has ensnared many artists with the beauty of its light. The leafy Cimiez quarter, 2km north of the city centre, is home to museums dedicated to Matisse and Chagall, whose lives and works are strongly tied to Nice.

The **Musée Matisse** (04 93 81 08 08; www.musee-matisse-nice.org; 164 av des Arènes de Cimiez; museum pass 24hr/7 days €10/20; 10am-6pm Wed-Mon late Jun–mid-Oct, from 11am rest of year; 15, 17, 20 or 22 to Arènes/Musée Matisse) houses a fascinating assortment of works by Henri Matisse (1869–1954), including oil paintings, drawings, sculptures, tapestries and his famous paper cut-outs. Matisse was so smitten with Nice that he made it his home for 37 years; he is buried in the **Monastère Notre Dame de Cimiez** (place du Monastère; 8.30am-12.30pm & 2.30-6.30pm; 15, 17, 20 or 22 to Arènes/Musée Matisse) cemetery, across the park from the museum.

Marc Chagall (1887–1985) also fell in love with Nice. Chagall's dreamlike work is displayed at the **Musée National Marc Chagall** (04 93 53 87 20; www.musee-chagall.fr; 4 av Dr Ménard; adult/child €10/8; 10am-6pm Wed-Mon May-Oct, to 5pm Nov-Apr; 15 or 22 to Musée Chagall), which owns the largest public collection of the painter's work. The main hall displays 12 huge interpretations (1954–67) of stories from Genesis and Exodus.

Musée National Marc Chagall

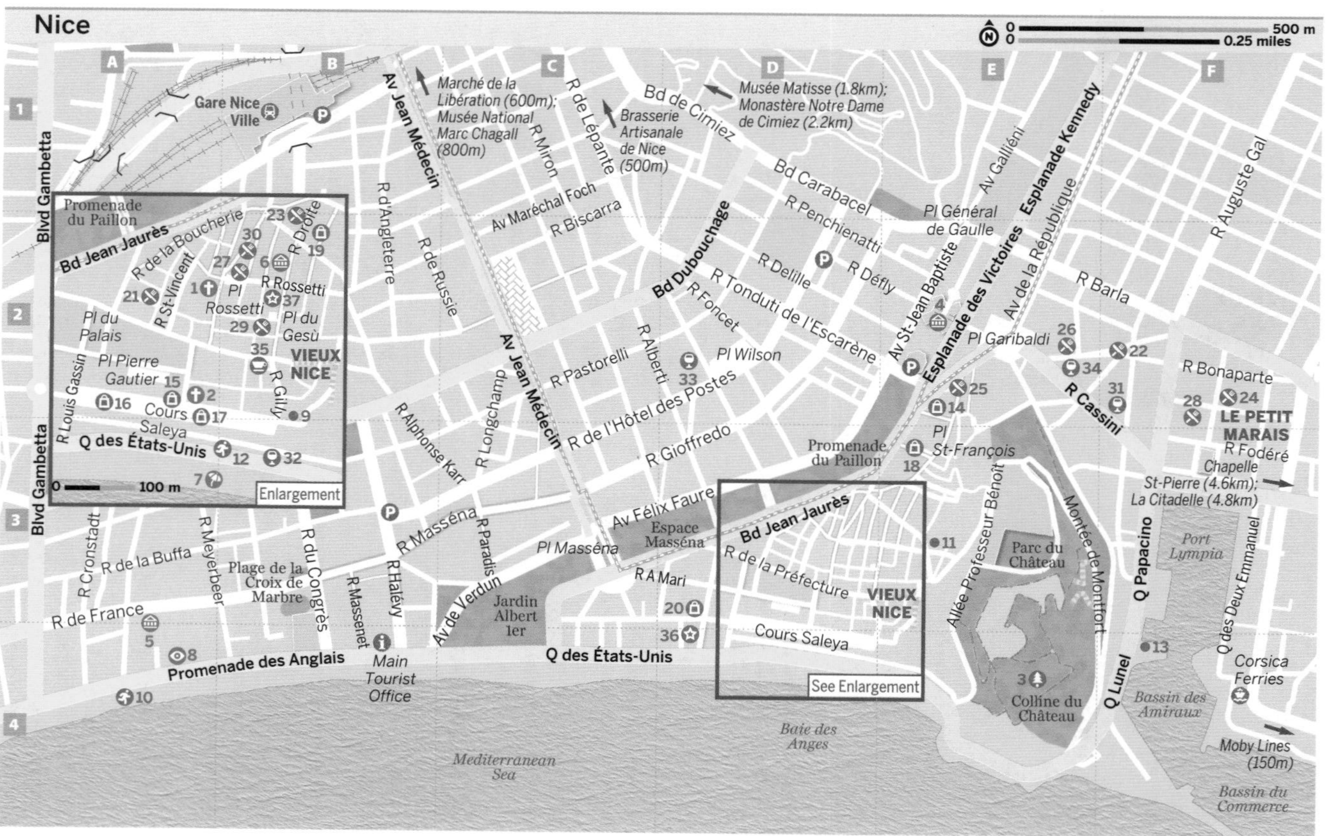
Nice
500 m
0.25 miles
Gare Nice Ville
Blvd Gambetta
Av Jean Médecin
Marché de la Libération (600m); Musée National Marc Chagall (800m)
R Miron
R de Lépante
Brasserie Artisanale de Nice (500m)
Bd de Cimiez
Musée Matisse (1.8km); Monastère Notre Dame de Cimiez (2.2km)
Bd Carabacel
Av Galliéni
Esplanade Kennedy
Av de la République
R Auguste Gal
Av Maréchal Foch
R Biscarra
R d'Angleterre
R de Russie
Bd Dubouchage
R Penchienatti
Pl Général de Gaulle
R Delille
R Défly
R Tonduti de l'Escarène
R Foncet
Av St-Jean Baptiste
Esplanade des Victoires
R Barla
Pl Garibaldi
R Bonaparte
LE PETIT MARAIS
R Fodéré
R Cassini
Chapelle St-Pierre (4.6km); La Citadelle (4.8km)
R Pastorelli
R Alberti
Pl Wilson
R de l'Hôtel des Postes
R Gioffredo
R Alphonse Karr
R Longchamp
Promenade du Paillon
Pl St-François
Av Félix Faure
Espace Masséna
Pl Masséna
R Masséna
R Paradis
Bd Jean Jaurès
R de la Préfecture
VIEUX NICE
Cours Saleya
See Enlargement
R A Mari
Jardin Albert 1er
Av de Verdun
R Cronstadt
R de la Buffa
R Meyerbeer
Plage de la Croix de Marbre
R du Congrès
R Massenet
R Halévy
R de France
Promenade des Anglais
Main Tourist Office
Q des États-Unis
Allée Professeur Bénoit
Parc du Château
Montée de Montfort
Colline du Château
Q Papacino
Q Lunel
Port Lympia
Q des Deux Emmanuel
Bassin des Amiraux
Corsica Ferries
Moby Lines (150m)
Bassin du Commerce
Baie des Anges
Mediterranean Sea
Promenade du Paillon
Bd Jean Jaurès
R de la Boucherie
R Droite
R St-Vincent
Pl Rossetti
R Rossetti
Pl du Gesù
Pl du Palais
Pl Pierre Gautier
R Louis Gassin
R Gilly
Cours Saleya
Q des États-Unis
100 m
Enlargement

Nice

Sights

Activities, Courses & Tours

Shopping

Eating

Drinking & Nightlife

Entertainment

where discerning Niçois have been buying their *fruits confits* (crystallised fruit) and *amandes chocolatées* (chocolate-covered almonds) since 1820.

Marché de la Libération Market
(place du Général de Gaulle; 6am-12.30pm Tue-Sun; 1 to Libération) After the Cours Saleya market, this is Nice's largest outdoor display of fresh fruit and veggies – and an authentically local experience. When it's in full swing, its dozens of stalls fill several city blocks along av Malausséna, place du Général de Gaulle, place de la Gare du Sud, rue Clément Roassal, rue Veillon and bd Joseph Garnier.

Cave de la Tour Wine
(04 93 80 03 31; www.cavedelatour.com; 3 rue de la Tour; 7am-8pm Tue-Sat, to 12.30pm Sun) Since 1947, locals have been trusting this atmospheric *cave* (wine cellar) to find the best wines from across the Alpes-Maritimes and Var. It's a ramshackle kind of place, with upturned wine barrels and blackboard signs, and a loyal clientele, including market traders and fishmongers getting their early-morning wine fix. Lots of wines are available by the glass.

Friperie Caprice Vintage
(09 83 48 05 43; www.facebook.com/CapriceVintageShop; 12 rue Droite; 2-7pm Mon, 11am-1.30pm & 2.30-7pm Tue-Sat) Nice's favourite vintage shop is a treasure trove of clothing, jewellery and accessories spanning much of the 20th century; what really sets it apart is the generous advice and assistance of amiable owner Madame Caprice, who knows every piece in the store.

EATING

Booking is advisable at most restaurants, particularly during the busy summer season. There are lots of restaurants on cours Saleya, but quality can be variable, so choose carefully.

Chez Palmyre French $
(04 93 85 72 32; 5 rue Droite; 3-course menu €18; noon-1.30pm & 7-9.30pm Mon, Tue, Thu & Fri) Look no further for authentic Niçois cooking than this packed, cramped, convivial

Niçois Street Food

Socca A savoury, griddle-fried pancake made from chickpea flour and olive oil. At the best places, there's always a line of people waiting for their *part* (serving), which will typically come served on a paper plate, sprinkled with black pepper.

Tourte aux blettes A kind of pie made with Swiss chard, raisins, pine nuts, apples, egg and cheese sandwiched between layers of dough and sprinkled with powdered sugar.

Pissaladière A scrumptious tart of caramelised onions spread over a bed of anchovy paste and topped with black Niçois olives.

Petits farcis Mixed vegetables (typically tomatoes, peppers, aubergines and/or zucchini) stuffed with ground meat, garlic, parsley and breadcrumbs.

Beignets Fritters made with everything from *fleurs de courgettes* (zucchini flowers) to sardines.

little space in the heart of the old town. The menu is very meat-heavy, with plenty of tripe, veal, pot-cooked chicken and the like, true to the traditional tastes of Provençal cuisine. It's a bargain, and understandably popular. Book well ahead, even for lunch.

Chez Pipo French $

(☎04 93 55 88 82; www.chezpipo.fr; 13 rue Bavastro; socca €2.90; ⏰11.30am-2.30pm & 5.30-10pm Wed-Sun; 🚋1 to Garibaldi, 2 to Port Lympia) Everyone says the best *socca* (chickpea-flour pancakes) can be found in the old town, but don't believe them – this place near Port Lympia has been in the biz since 1923 and, for our money, knocks *socca*-shaped spots off anywhere else in Nice.

La Rossettisserie French $

(☎04 93 76 18 80; www.larossettisserie.com; 8 rue Mascoïnat; mains €16.50-19.50; ⏰noon-2pm & 7-10pm Mon-Sat) Roast meat is the order of the day here: make your choice from beef, chicken, veal or lamb, and pair it with a choice of mashed or sautéed potatoes, ratatouille or salad. Simple and sumptuous, with cosy, rustic decor and a delightful vaulted cellar.

From left: *Beignets* (fritters) and sardines; Traditional Niçois restaurant menu; Chez Pipo; Vieux Nice street dining

TRAVELSTOCK44/ALAMY STOCK PHOTO ©

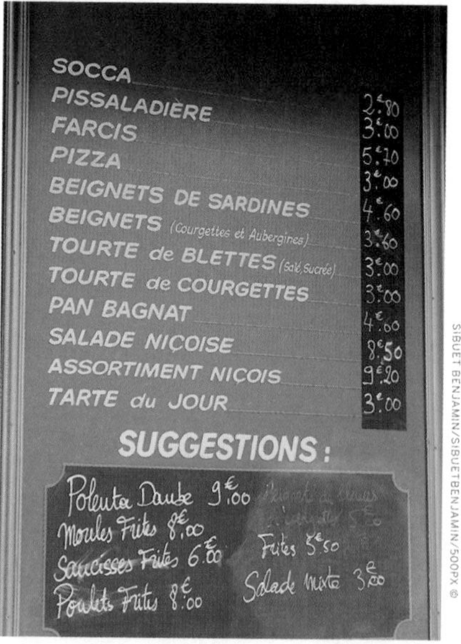

SIBUET BENJAMIN/SIBUETBENJAMIN/500PX ©

Bar des Oiseaux French $$

(04 93 80 27 33; 5 rue St-Vincent; 3-course lunch menu €20, dinner menus from €30; noon-1.45pm & 7.15-9.45pm Tue-Sat) Hidden down a narrow backstreet, this old-town classic has been in business since 1961, serving as a popular nightclub before reincarnating itself as a restaurant (some of its original saucy murals have survived the transition). Nowadays it's a lively bistro serving superb traditional French cuisine spiced up with modern twists. The weekday lunch special offers phenomenal value. Book ahead.

La Cave du Fromager French $$

(04 93 13 07 83; www.lacavedufromager.com; 29 rue Benoît Bunico; mains €18-23; 7-10pm Wed-Mon) *Fromage* is what fuels the convivial mood at this candlelit, brick- and stone-vaulted cellar bistro. The menu changes with the seasons but always revolves around cheese: roquefort-broccoli soup; baked camembert with hazelnuts, honey and *calvados* (apple-flavoured brandy); hearty old-fashioned *tartiflette* (the classic Savoyard casserole of potatoes, lardons, onions and melted Reblochon cheese...). The new owners exude youthful energy and speak excellent English.

Jan Gastronomy $$$

(04 97 19 32 23; www.restaurantjan.com; 12 rue Lascaris; 3-course lunch menus €55, dinner menus €98-118, incl wine pairings €137-164; 7-10pm Tue-Sat, noon-2pm Fri & Sat; 1 to Garibaldi, 2 to Port Lympia) For the full-blown fine-dining experience, make a pilgrimage to the Michelin-starred restaurant of South African chef Jan Hendrik van der Westhuizen. Dishes here are laced with Antipodean and New World flavours and crackle with artistic and culinary flair. There's nothing à la carte – Jan decides his *menus* on the day. It's high-end (dress smart) and sought after; reservations essential.

DRINKING & NIGHTLIFE

Cafe terraces on cours Saleya are lovely for an early-evening aperitif. Vieux Nice's bounty of pubs attracts a noisy, boisterous crowd; most bars have a happy hour from 6pm to 8pm.

TIM E WHITE/ALAMY STOCK PHOTO ©

AMANDA HALL/GETTY IMAGES ©

Monaco Glamour

Squeezed into just 200 hectares, Monaco might be the world's second-smallest country (only the Vatican is smaller), but what it lacks in size it makes up for in attitude. Day trip it from Nice, an easy 25-minute train journey (€4.10) along the coast.

Ogling at the legendary marble-and-gold **Casino de Monte Carlo** (☎98 06 21 21; www.casinomontecarlo.com; place du Casino; morning visit incl audioguide adult/child Oct-Apr €14/10, May-Sep €17/12, salons ordinaires gaming Oct-Apr €14, May-Sep €17; ⊙visits 9am-1pm, gaming 2pm-late) is essential. The building, open to visitors every morning, is Europe's most lavish example of belle époque architecture. To gamble, visit after 2pm (strictly over-18sonly).

Monaco's other must-see is the world-renowned **Musée Océanographique** (☎93 15 36 00; www.oceano.mc; av St-Martin; adult/child high season €16/12, low season €11/7; ⊙9.30am-8pm Jul & Aug, 10am-7pm Apr-Jun & Sep, to 6pm Oct-Mar), stuck dramatically to a cliff edge since 1910, featuring an aquarium with a 6m-deep lagoon where sharks and marine predators are separated from colourful tropical fishes by a coral reef.

Home to the world's largest succulent and cactus collection, **Jardin Exotique** (☎93 15 29 80; www.jardin-exotique.mc; 62 bd du Jardin Exotique; adult/child €7.20/3.80; ⊙9am-7pm mid-May–mid-Sep, to 6pm rest of year) offers dreamy views of the principality.

Casino de Monte Carlo
ANDRII LUTSYK/SHUTTERSTOCK ©

La Part des Anges Wine Bar
(☎04 93 62 69 80; www.lapartdesanges-nice.com; 17 rue Gubernatis; ⊙10am-8.30pm Mon-Thu, to midnight Fri & Sat; 🚌7, 9 to Pastorelli or Wilson) The focus at this classy wine shop–bar is organic wines – a few are sold by the glass, but the best selection is available by the bottle, served with homemade tapenades and charcuterie platters. The name means the 'Angel's Share', referring to the alcohol that evaporates as wines age. There are only a few tables, so arrive early or reserve ahead.

Beer District Craft Beer
(☎06 75 10 26 36; www.beerdistrict.fr; 13 rue Cassini; ⊙6pm-1am Tue-Sat; 🚊1 to Garibaldi, 2 to Port Lympia) One of Nice's coolest new nightspots, Beer District pours a regularly rotating line-up of 16 draught microbrews and 50 bottled beers from all over the world. The vibe is chilled and friendly, with free tastes cheerfully offered and little bowls of peanuts for snacking.

Brasserie Artisanale de Nice Brewery
(☎09 73 59 20 30; www.brasserie-nice.com; 14 av Villermont; 5-7pm Tue-Fri, 10am-noon & 4-7pm Sat; 🚊1 to Libération) Taste some of southern France's most interesting beers at this neighbourhood microbrewery, which opens to the public a few hours per week. Don't miss the flagship Zytha, a Niçois classic brewed with chickpeas, or the Blùna, made with bitter-orange peel and coriander.

✪ ENTERTAINMENT

Opéra de Nice Opera
(☎04 92 17 40 79; www.opera-nice.org; 4-6 rue St-François de Paule) The vintage 1885 grande dame hosts opera, ballet and orchestral concerts.

Shapko Live Music
(☎06 15 10 02 52; www.shapkobar.fr; 5 rue Rossetti; ⊙6pm-2.30am) Near the cathedral square, Shapko stages live music nightly in a variety of genres: blues, funk, jazz, R&B, soul, rock and more. Happy hour runs from 6pm to 9pm.

INFORMATION

Tourist Office (04 92 14 46 14; www.nicetourisme.com; 5 Promenade des Anglais; 9am-7pm daily Jun-Sep, to 6pm Mon-Sat Oct-May; ; 8, 52, 62 to Massenet) Nice's main tourist office on Promenade des Anglais provides a wealth of resources, including maps, brochures, information about attractions and help booking accommodation.

GETTING THERE & AWAY

AIR

Nice-Côte d'Azur Airport (08 20 42 33 33; www.nice.aeroport.fr; ; 98, 99, 2) is France's second-largest airport and has international flights to Europe, North Africa and the US, with regular and low-cost airlines. The airport has two terminals, linked by a free shuttle bus.

BOAT

Corsica Ferries (04 92 00 42 76; www.corsicaferries.com; quai du Commerce; 2 to Port Lympia) and **Moby Lines** (08 00 90 11 44; www.mobylines.fr; quai du Commerce; 2 to Port Lympia) offer regular ferry service from Nice to Corsica. Corsica Ferries also serves Golfo Aranci in Sardinia.

TRAIN

Nice has excellent train connections to pretty much everywhere on the coast, and many towns further afield too.

Marseille €36 to €42, 2¾ hours, hourly

Paris €86 to €142, 5¾ hours, hourly

GETTING AROUND

BUS

Buses and trams in Nice are run by **Lignes d'Azur** (08 10 06 10 06; www.lignesdazur.com). Tickets cost just €1.50 and include one connection, including intercity buses within the Alpes-Maritimes *département*. If you're using Nice's buses and trams a lot, consider purchasing a money-saving all-day ticket or multiday pass. Buses are particularly handy for getting to Cimiez. Between 9pm and 1am or 2am, night buses (numbered N1 through N5) run every 30 to 60 minutes.

BICYCLE

Vélo Bleu (04 93 72 06 06; www.velobleu.org) is Nice's shared-bicycle service, with 100-plus stations around the city – pick up your bike at one, return it at another. One-day/weeklong subscriptions cost €1.50/5, plus usage: free for the first 30 minutes, €1 the next 30, then €2 per hour thereafter. Some stations are equipped with terminals to register directly with a credit card; otherwise you'll need a mobile phone. It's worth downloading the handy Vélo Bleu app.

CAR & MOTORCYCLE

Traffic, a confusing one-way system, and pricey parking mean driving in Nice is a bad idea – it's better to explore the city first, then head back out to the airport and rent your car there instead.

Holiday Bikes (04 93 16 01 62; www.loca-bike.fr; 34 av Auber; 24hr rental 50cc/125cc scooter from €32/57; 9.30am-12.30pm & 2.30-6.30pm Mon-Sat year-round, plus 10am-noon & 5-6.30pm Sun Jun-Aug; 1 to Gare Thiers) rents scooters and motorcycles. It has another **office** (04 93 04 15 36; 6 rue Massenet; 9.30am-12.30pm & 2.30-6.30pm Mon-Sat year-round, plus 10am-noon & 5-6.30pm Sun Jun-Aug; 8, 52, 62 to Massenet) just off the Promenade des Anglais.

TRAM

Nice's sleek tram system (http://tramway.nice.fr) is great for getting across town, linking Nice-Ville train station with Vieux Nice and Le Port-Garibaldi to the southeast and Libération to the north. Trams run from 4.25am to 1.35am.

Nice's second tram line, scheduled for completion in 2019, will run east–west between the airport and the port.

Single-ride tickets cost €1.50; buy at any tram stop. Multiride tickets and passes are sold at the same machines, valid on both trams and buses. Validate all tickets in the machines on board.

BONBONS DU PIRATE
CAP CAMARAT

Vieux Port (p218)

ST-TROPEZ

RASTOS/SHUTTERSTOCK ©

In This Chapter

St-Tropez at a Glance...

Pouting screen siren Brigitte Bardot came to St-Tropez in the 1950s to star in Et Dieu Créa la Femme (And God Created Woman; 1956) and overnight transformed the peaceful fishing village into a sizzling jet-set favourite. Tropeziens have thrived on their sexy image ever since.

But St-Tropez has a serene side. Meander cobbled lanes in the old fishing quarter of La Ponche, sip pastis at a place des Lices cafe, watch old men play pétanque beneath plane trees, or walk in solitary splendour from beach to beach along the coastal path.

Two Days in St-Tropez

Explore St-Tropez, not missing its jam-packed market on **place des Lices** (p219), the **Musée de l'Annonciade** (p218) and the old fishing quarter of **La Ponche** (p218). Stroll along the **coastal path** (p219) and, come dusk, hobnob over an aperitif at the bewitching **Vieux Port** (p218). Make day two a beach day; reserve a table at **La Plage des Jumeaux** (p220) or one of Pampelonne's celebrity beach clubs.

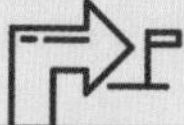

Four Days in St-Tropez

On the third day, head inland to the flowery hilltop village of **Ramatuelle** (p221), continuing to medieval **Gassin** (p221) for a 360-degree view of the St-Tropez peninsula and bay. Dine and dance the evening away back in St-Tropez. On your last day, take a boat trip with **Les Bateaux Verts** (p216) to Port Grimaud or Porquerolles.

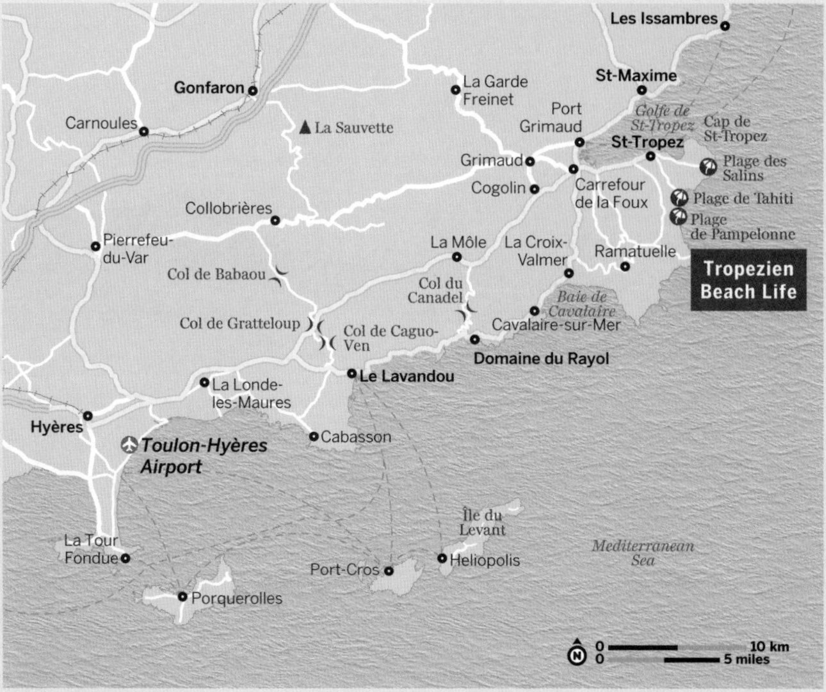

Arriving in St-Tropez

Aéroport Toulon-Hyères Bus shuttles run between the airport and St-Tropez (€15, 1½ hours); some require a transfer.

St-Raphäel train station Les Bateaux de St-Raphaël boats (www.bateauxdestraphael.com) run April to mid-October (€15, one hour) from the dock, 200m from the station; and VarLib buses (www.varlib.fr; €3, 1¼ hours to three hours depending on traffic) to St-Tropez.

Where to Stay

St-Tropez is home to celebrity-studded hangs, with prices to match – this is no shoestring destination, though campgrounds do sit southeast along Plage de Pampelonne. Most hotels close in winter; the tourist office lists what's open, and also has a list of B&Bs. If you're driving, double-check parking arrangements with your accommodation.

Plage de la Briande

MICHAEL MELFORD/GETTY IMAGES ©

Tropezien Beach Life

Few beaches are as sizzling or storied as those in St-Tropez. Don your hottest beachwear, grab your shades and get set to hobnob on some of Europe's finest golden sands.

Great For...

☑ **Don't Miss**

The Sentier du Littoral (p219) coastal path, snaking from beach to beach.

Plage de Pampelonne

The 5km-long, celebrity-studded Plage de Pampelonne sports a line-up of exclusive beach restaurants and clubs in summer. Find public entries (and parking for €5.50) at one of six access points: rte de Tahiti, chemin des Moulins, chemin de Tamaris, bd Patch, chemin des Barraques and rte de Bonne Terrasse.

Sémaphore de Camarat

Pampelonne stretches for 9km from Cap du Pinet to **Cap Camarat**, a rocky cape dominated by France's second-tallest lighthouse (nearly 130m), completed in 1832, electrified in 1946 and automated from 1977. Scale it for giddy views of St-Tropez and its peninsula. Guided tours run late June to September; book at Ramatuelle tourist office.

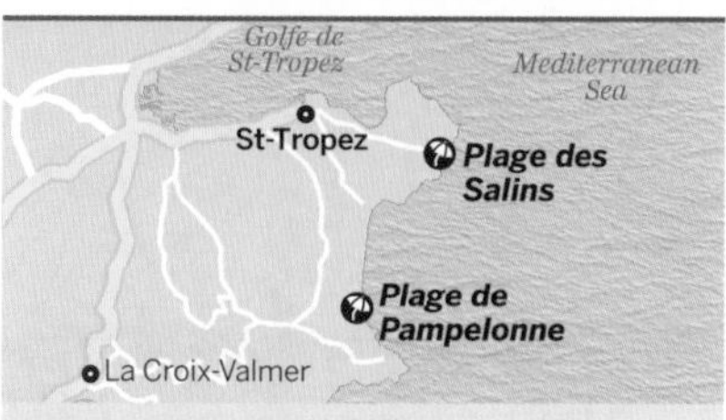

Need to Know

Ramatuelle tourist office (04 98 12 64 00; www.ramatuelle-tourisme.com; place de l'Ormeau; 9am-1pm & 2-6.30pm Mon-Sat, 10am-1pm & 2-6pm Sun)

Take a Break

Seafood at Pampelonne's top lunch address, La Plage des Jumeaux (p220).

★ Top Tip

Beach clubs generally open May to September; table and sun lounger (€15 to €20) reservations are essential.

Beach Clubs

St-Tropez' seaside scene is defined by its club-restaurants on the sand.

Le Club 55 (www.leclub55.fr; 43 bd Patch, Plage de Pampelonne; 10am-7pm Mar-Oct;) The longest-running beach club dates to the 1950s and was originally the crew canteen during the filming of *And God Created Woman*. Now it caters to celebs who do *not* want to be seen.

Nikki Beach (www.nikkibeach.com/sttropez; 1093 rte de l'Épi, Plage de Pampelonne; 11.30am-8pm Apr-Sep) Favoured by dance-on-the-bar celebs keen to be seen on Pampelonne.

Moorea Plage (www.mooreaplage.fr; chemin des Moulins, Plage de Tahiti; mains €24-35; 12.30-5pm Mar-Sep; P) Laid-back club-restaurant on Tahiti beach, ideal for conversation, backgammon and top steak.

Couleurs Jardin (www.restaurantcouleursjardin.com; 142 bd de Gigaro, La Croix-Valmer; mains €25-35; noon-2.30pm & 7.30-11pm Apr-Sep; P) Eclectic beachside space for dining or drinking. Loll beneath the trees or pick a table with nothing between you and the sea.

Shellona (C'est la Vie; www.shellonabeach.com; rte de l'Épi, Plage de Pampelonne; mains €41-47; Feb-Oct; P) More relaxed than some of its neighbours. A Greek restaurant and beach club where the sea's bright and the vibe's right.

Plage des Salins

Just east of St-Tropez, **Plage des Salins** (chemin des Salins) is a long, 600m-wide pine-fringed beach at the southern foot of Cap des Salins. At the northern end of the beach, on a rock jutting out to sea, is the tomb of Émile Olivier, who served as first minister to Napoléon III until his exile in 1870. It looks out towards **La Tête de Chien**, named after the dog who declined to eat the remains of St Torpes, who was beheaded for adopting Christianity.

Port Grimaud

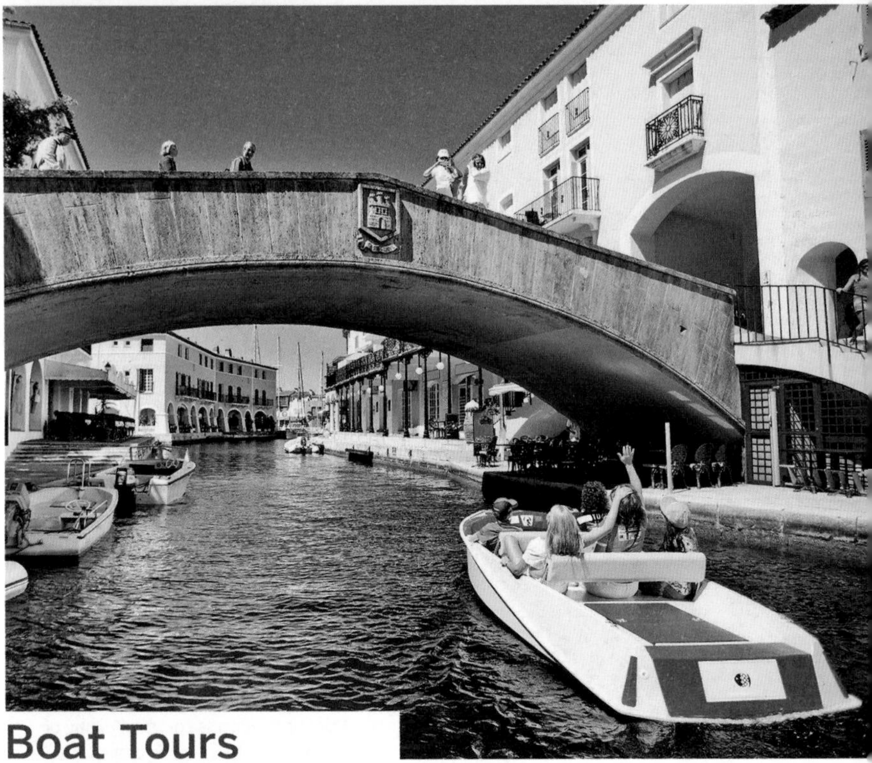

Boat Tours

In the height of summer when horrendous, four-hour traffic bottlenecks jam up the one road into St-Tropez, boat is by far the coolest, quickest and most serene means of navigating St-Tropez.

Great For...

☑ Don't Miss

Provençal-style seafood at Grimaud bistro **Fleur de Sel** (☎04 94 43 21 54; www.fleurdeselgrimaud.wixsite.com/fleur-de-sel-grimaud; 4 place du Cros; lunch menus €17, dinner menus €39-49; ⊙noon-2pm & 7-10pm Tue-Fri & Sun, noon-2pm Sat Apr-Oct), 7km inland.

April to September, St-Tropez operators including **Les Bateaux Verts** (☎04 94 49 29 39; www.bateauxverts.com; 7 quai Jean Jaurès) offer various boat trips from the port, including celebrity villa-spotting sailings around **Baie des Cannebiers** (adult/child from €11/6), dubbed 'Bay of Stars' after the celebrity villas dotting the coast.

Our tip: make a day of it and hit Port Grimaud for chic strolling and lunch or Porquerolles for walking, cycling and beach-lounging on an idyllic island.

Port Grimaud & Grimaud Village

Ferries cross between St-Tropez and **Port Grimaud** (adult/child €15/10, 20 minutes), the so-called 'Venice of Provence'. Built on the edge of the Golfe de St-Tropez on what was a mosquito-filled swamp in the 1960s, Port Grimaud is now a modern

Grimaud Village

S4SVISUALS/SHUTTERSTOCK ©

pleasure port. Inside the high wall that barricades the port from the busy N98, the yacht-laced waterways comprise 12km of quays and mooring space for thousands of luxury yachts. The **place du Marché** and **rue des Artisans** offer plenty of harbour-side dining.

Seven kilometres inland from the Golfe de St-Tropez lies the atmospheric medieval hilltop village of **Grimaud**, surrounded by vineyards, olives and the oak-and-beech clad foothills of the Massif des Maures. The **Château du Grimaud**, originally an 11th-century castle, is but a picturesque shell of its former glory. A **miniature train** (☎06 62 07 65 09; www.petit-train-de-grimaud.com; adult/child return €7.50/4; ⏰Apr-Oct; 👪) connects Port Grimaud and the inland village.

ℹ Need to Know

Grimaud Tourist Office (☎04 94 55 43 83; www.grimaud-provence.com; 679 rte Nationale; ⏰9am-12.30pm & 2-6pm Mon-Sat Sep-Jun, daily Jul & Aug, shorter hours rest of year)

Porquerolles Tourist Office (☎04 94 58 33 76; www.porquerolles.com; Carré du Port; ⏰9am-6.15pm Mon-Sat, to 1pm Sun Jul & Aug, shorter hours rest of year)

✕ Take a Break

Chill at a cafe terrace on Porquerolles' **place d'Armes**, local-life hub.

★ Top Tip

If possible, avoid Porquerolles in July and August when fire risk closes the island interior.

Île de Porquerolles

Count on two hours to sail to Porquerolles, a beautiful island that remains unspoilt despite up to 6000 day trippers per day in July and August. Two-thirds of its sandy white beaches, pine woods, maquis and eucalyptus are protected by the **Parc National de Port-Cros**, and a wide variety of indigenous and tropical flora thrive, including Requien's larkspur, which grows nowhere else in the world. April and May are the best months to spot some of the 114 bird species. Pottering along the island's rough unpaved trails on foot or by bicycle, breaking with a picnic lunch on the beach and a dip in crystal-clear turquoise water, is heavenly.

The northern coast is laced with beautiful sandy beaches. Cliffs line the island's more dangerous southern coast, where swimming and diving are restricted to **Calanque du Brégançonnet** and **Calanque de l'Oustaou de Diou**. Get info at the tourist office, where you can also pick up cycling and walking trail maps (€3). There's an abundance of places hiring bikes; head to **Le Cycle Porquerollais** (www.cycle-porquerollais.com; 1 rue de la Ferme; half-/full day from €13/16).

SIGHTS

Musée de l'Annonciade Gallery

(☎04 94 17 84 10; www.saint-tropez.fr/fr/culture/musee-de-lannonciade; place Grammont; adult/child €6/free; ⏰10am-6pm daily mid-Jun–Sep, Tue-Sun Oct–mid-Jun) In a gracefully converted 16th-century chapel, this small but famous museum showcases an impressive collection of modern art infused with that legendary Côte d'Azur light. Pointillist Paul Signac bought a house in St-Tropez in 1892 and introduced other artists to the area. The museum's collection includes his *St-Tropez, Le Quai* (1899) and *St-Tropez, Coucher de Soleil au Bois de Pins* (1896). Vuillard, Bonnard and Maurice Denis (the self-named 'Nabis' group) have a room to themselves.

Citadelle de St-Tropez Museum

(☎04 94 97 59 43; www.saint-tropez.fr/fr/culture/citadelle; 1 montée de la Citadelle; adult/child €3/free; ⏰10am-6.30pm Apr-Sep, to 5.30pm Oct-Mar; 👪) Built in 1602 to defend the coast against Spain, the citadel dominates the hillside overlooking St-Tropez to the east. The views are fantastic, as are the exotic peacocks wandering the grounds. Its dungeons are home to the excellent **Musée de l'Histoire Maritime**, an interactive museum that traces the history of humans at sea through fishing, trading, exploration, travel and the navy. The particular focus, of course, is Tropezien and Provençal seafarers.

Vieux Port Port

Yachts line the harbour (as their uniformed crews diligently scrub them) and visitors stroll the quays at the picturesque old port. In front of the sable-coloured townhouses, the **Bailli de Suffren statue** (quai Suffren) of a 17th-century naval hero, cast from a 19th-century cannon, peers out to sea. Duck beneath the archway, next to the tourist office, to uncover St-Tropez' daily morning fish market, on place aux Herbes.

La Ponche Historic Site

Shrug off the hustle of the port in St-Tropez' historic fishing quarter, La Ponche, northeast of the Vieux Port. From the southern

View from Citadelle de St-Tropez

end of quai Frédéric Mistral, place Garrezio sprawls east from 10th-century **Tour Suffren** to place de l'Hôtel de Ville. From here, rue Guichard leads southeast to iconic **Église de St-Tropez** (Église Notre Dame de l'Assomption; rue Commandant Guichard). Follow rue du Portail Neuf south to **Chapelle de la Miséricorde** (1-5 rue de la Miséricorde; ⏰10am-6pm).

Place des Lices Square

St-Tropez' legendary and very charming central square is studded with plane trees, cafes and *pétanque* (bowls) players. Simply sitting on a cafe terrace watching the world go by or jostling with the crowds at its twice-weekly **market** (place des Lices; ⏰8am-1pm Tue & Sat) extravaganza, jam-packed with everything from fruit and veg to antique mirrors and sandals, is an integral part of the St-Tropez experience.

Place des Lices has seen artists and intellectuals fraternising for decades here, most frequently in the famous Café des Arts, now simply called **Le Café** (☎04 94 97 44 69; www.lecafe.fr; Traverse des Lices; 2-course lunch menu €18, mains €22-29; ⏰8am-11pm) – and not to be confused with the newer, green-canopied Café des Arts on the corner of the square. Aspiring *pétanque* players can borrow a set from the bar.

ACTIVITIES

Sentier du Littoral Walking

A spectacular coastal path wends past rocky outcrops and hidden bays 35km south from St-Tropez, around the peninsula to the beach at Cavalaire-sur-Mer. In St-Tropez, the yellow-flagged path starts at **La Ponche**, immediately east of Tour du Portalet, and curves around Port des Pêcheurs, past the citadel. It then leads past the walled **Cimetière Marin** (Marine Cemetery; Pointe du Cimetière), **Plage des Graniers** and beyond.

The tourist office has maps with distances and walking times (eg Plage des Salins is 8.5km or around 2½ hours' walk).

Vieux Port Cafes

Cafes, restaurants, bistros and bars frame the Vieux Port quays. Jean-Paul Sartre wrote parts of *Les Chemins de la Liberté* (Roads to Freedom) at **Sénéquier** (☎04 94 97 20 20; www.senequier.com; quai Jean Jaurès; ⏰8am-1am; 📶), a portside cafe – in business since 1887 – which is hugely popular with boaties, bikers and tourists. Count €8 for a mere coffee. Friendly **Café de Paris** (☎04 94 97 00 56; www.cafedeparis.fr; 15 quai Suffren; ⏰8am-2am) is *the* place to sport your new strappy sandals at afternoon aperitifs. Or don your glad rags and order a cocktail at **Bar du Port** (☎04 94 97 00 54; www.barduport.com; 7 quai Suffren; ⏰7am-3am; 📶), a young and happening bar for beautiful people.

SHOPPING

St-Tropez is loaded with couture boutiques, gourmet food shops and art galleries.

Atelier Rondini Shoes

(☎04 94 97 19 55; www.rondini.fr; 18 rue Georges Clemenceau; ⏰10.30am-1pm & 3-6.30pm Tue-Sun) Colette brought a pair of sandals from Greece to Atelier Rondini (open since 1927) to be replicated. It's still making the iconic sandals today (from about €145).

K Jacques Shoes

(☎04 94 97 41 50; www.kjacques.com; 39bis rue Allard; ⏰10am-1pm & 2.30-8.30pm Mon-Sat, 10.30am-1pm & 3-8.30pm Sun) Hand-crafting sandals (from €240) since 1933 for such clients as Picasso and Brigitte Bardot. There's a **branch** (16 rue Seillon) nearby.

La Pause Douceur Food

(☎04 94 97 27 58; 11 rue Allard; ⏰9am-1pm & 2-8.30pm) Run by local Delphine and her mother, this irresistible little shop sells delicious homemade chocolates, biscuits and sweet treats. The praline chocolate is a favourite of chef and writer Nina Parker.

La Tarte Tropézienne

Don't leave town without sampling *tarte Tropézienne*, an orange-blossom-flavoured double sponge cake filled with thick cream, created by Polish baker A Mickla in 1955. Cafe-bakery **La Tarte Tropézienne** (04 94 97 94 25; www.latartetropezienne.fr; place des Lices; tarts/snacks from €5.50/3; 6.30am-10pm;) is the originator of this sugar-crusted, perfumed cake, along with decent breads and light meal options. There are smaller branches on rue Clemenceau and near the new port.

Tarte Tropézienne
EQROY/SHUTTERSTOCK ©

EATING

La Pesquière — Seafood $

(04 94 97 05 92; http://pesquiere.mazagran.free.fr; 1 rue des Remparts; menus adult/child €29/14; 9am-midnight late Mar-Oct) It's no surprise this old-fashioned place survives in restless, modish St-Tropez: since 1962 the one family has made an art of buying the day's freshest catch – whether that be dourade, red mullet, bass or prawns – and cooking it to simple perfection. Locals love it, as do visitors, and you feel you've had your money's worth.

Le Gorille — Cafe $

(04 94 97 03 93; www.legorille.com; 1 quai Suffren; sandwiches/mains €7/17; 7am-7pm) This portside hang-out gets its name from its previous owner – the short, muscular and apparently very hairy Henri Guérin! Stop for breakfast or a post-clubbing croque monsieur and fries. It's anything but pretentious.

Bistro Canaille — Fusion $$

(04 94 97 40 96; 28 rue des Remparts; plates €12-24; 7-11pm Tue-Sun Jun-Sep, Fri & Sat Mar-May & Oct-Dec) Probably the pick of the modern places to eat in town – creative, cosy and great value while still hitting the gourmet heights. It has the soul of a bistro, but specialises in fusion-style tapas dishes inspired by the owners' travels – like local dourade with olives and *yuzu* (a Japanese citrus fruit). More tempting combinations are chalked on the board.

La Plage des Jumeaux — International $$$

(04 94 58 21 80; www.plagedesjumeaux.com; rte de l'Épi, Plage de Pampelonne; mains €27-32; noon-5pm; P) The pick of Pampelonne's beach restaurants, Jumeaux serves beautiful seafood (including fabulous whole fish, ideal to share) and sun-busting salads on its dreamy white-and-turquoise-striped beach. Families are well catered for, with playground equipment, beach toys and a kids' menu.

Auberge des Maures — Provençal $$$

(04 94 97 01 50; www.aubergedesmaures.fr; 4 rue du Docteur Boutin; mains €35-45; 6.45pm-12.30am Apr-Oct) The town's oldest restaurant remains the locals' choice for always-good, copious portions of earthy Provençal cooking, like *daube* (braised beef stew), tapenade-stuffed lamb shoulder, lobster and *onglet* (skirt steak) grilled over the fire with eschallot sauce. Book a table (essential) in the leafy courtyard. The wine selection is pretty special, too.

DRINKING & NIGHTLIFE

Many places close in winter, but in summer it's party central seven days a week. To tap into the local gay scene, hit **Chez les Garçons** (04 94 49 42 67, 06 18 45 94 60; 21 rue du Cépoun; menus €32; 8-11pm May-Sep, Thu-Sun Mar, Apr & Oct) or **L'Esquinade** (04 94 79 83 42; 5 rue du Four; midnight-7am daily Jun-Sep, Thu-Sat Oct-May).

Les Caves du Roy Club
(www.lescavesduroy.com; Hôtel Byblos, av Paul Signac; ⏲10pm-6am Fri & Sat Apr-Oct, daily Jul & Aug) The star-studded bar at the infamous Hôtel Byblos remains the perennial champion of nightclubs in St-Tropez, if not the whole Riviera. Dress to impress if you hope to get in and mingle with starlets and race-car drivers.

White 1921 Bar
(☎04 94 45 50 50; www.white1921.com; place des Lices; ⏲8pm-late mid-May–mid-Oct) Blindingly white and appropriately expensive, White 1921 is owned by Louis Vuitton. It's a chic alfresco champagne lounge in a renovated townhouse on place des Lices. Can't make it home? Stay over in one of the swank rooms (from €345).

VIP Room Club
(☎01 58 36 46 00, 04 94 97 14 70; www.viproom.fr; residence du Nouveau Port; ⏲8pm-6am Jun-Sep) New York loft–style club at the Nouveau Port; around for aeons and still lures in the occasional VIP.

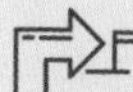

Ramatuelle & Gassin

Nine kilometres inland, into the lush St-Tropez peninsula, is the labyrinthine walled village of **Ramatuelle**. Its name originates from 'Rahmatu'llah', meaning 'Divine Gift' – a legacy of 10th-century Saracen rule. Jazz and theatre fill the tourist-packed streets during August's theatrical **Festival de Ramatuelle** (☎04 94 79 25 63; www.festivalderamatuelle.com; ⏲Jul-Aug) and **Jazz Fest** (☎04 94 79 10 29; www.jazzaramatuelle.com; ⏲Aug), and its tree-studded central square and old-world lanes make for an enchanting stroll.

Follow rte des Moulins de Paillas up over the hilltop for 2.5km towards Gassin, and you'll take in grand views and historic windmills. Medieval **Gassin**, atop a rocky promontory with a 16th-century church, offers a magnificent 360-degree panorama of the peninsula and St-Tropez bay.

ℹ INFORMATION

Tourist Office (☎08 92 68 48 28; www.sainttropeztourisme.com; quai Jean Jaurès; ⏲9.30am-1.30pm & 3-7.30pm Jul & Aug, 9.30am-12.30pm & 2-7pm Apr-Jun, Sep & Oct, to 6pm Mon-Sat Nov-Mar) Runs occasional walking tours April to October, and also has a **kiosk** (⏲9am-6pm Jul & Aug) in Parking du Port in July and August.

 GETTING THERE & AROUND

BICYCLE

Rolling Bikes (☎04 94 97 09 39; www.rolling-bikes.com; 50 av du Général Leclerc; per day bikes/scooters/motorcycles from €17/46/120; ⏲9am-12.30pm & 3-7pm Tue-Sat Sep-Jun, daily Jul & Aug) Do as the locals do and opt for two wheels.

BOAT

Trans Côte d'Azur (☎04 92 98 71 30; www.trans-cote-azur.co.uk; ⏲May-Oct) Ferries from Nice and Cannes.

CAR

During high season, those in the know avoid horrendous four-hour traffic bottlenecks on the one road into St-Tropez (and €40 parking, which is nonetheless hard to find) by parking in Port Grimaud or Ste-Maxime and taking a **Les Bateaux Verts** (p216) shuttle boat.

MARSEILLE

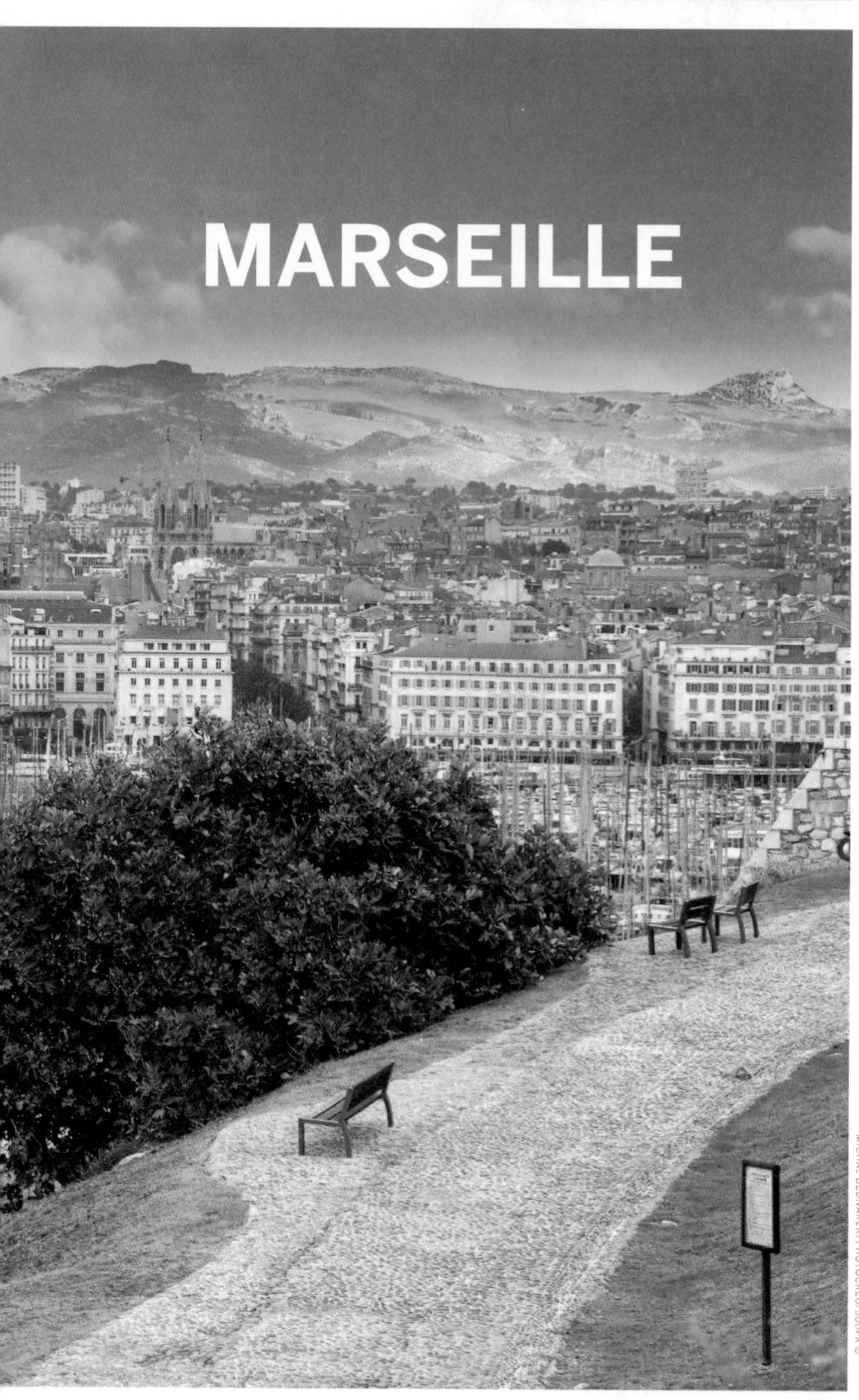

In This Chapter

Marseille at a Glance...

Lacking the glamour of Cannes or St-Tropez, this black sheep of the Provençal coastline has blossomed in cultural confidence. Marseille now has a brace of swanky museums and a fair claim to the mantle of France's second city.

Uphill from its vibrant Vieux Port (Old Port) is the ancient Le Panier neighbourhood. Also worth an explore is the stylish République quarter and Marseille's totemic cathedral. Allow yourself at least 48 hours to take in Marseille and the dramatic Les Calanques – the spectacular coastline that snakes southeast.

Two Days in Marseille

Climb to the soaring **basilica** (p230), snap photos from the **Jardin du Pharo** (p238), then sample real bouillabaisse at **Michel** (p236). Don't miss the **Musée Cantini** (p234) in the afternoon. Day two, breakfast quayside before taking a ferry to **Château d'If** (p231) and the **Îles du Frioul** (p231). Later, visit **MuCEM** (p230) before touring bars and boutiques in **Le Panier** (p228).

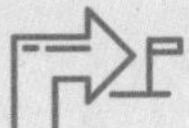

Four Days in Marseille

Day three, explore **La Cité Radieuse** (p231) and the **Vallon des Auffes** (p235), ideal for a seafood lunch. Bus 83 will carry you back to Opéra for bars, boutiques and restaurants. Day four, take the trip out to **La Friche La Belle de Mai** (p238), eating at its superb restaurant, then head to bohemian cours Julien for drinks at **Waaw** (p238) and dinner at intimate **L'Arôme** (p237).

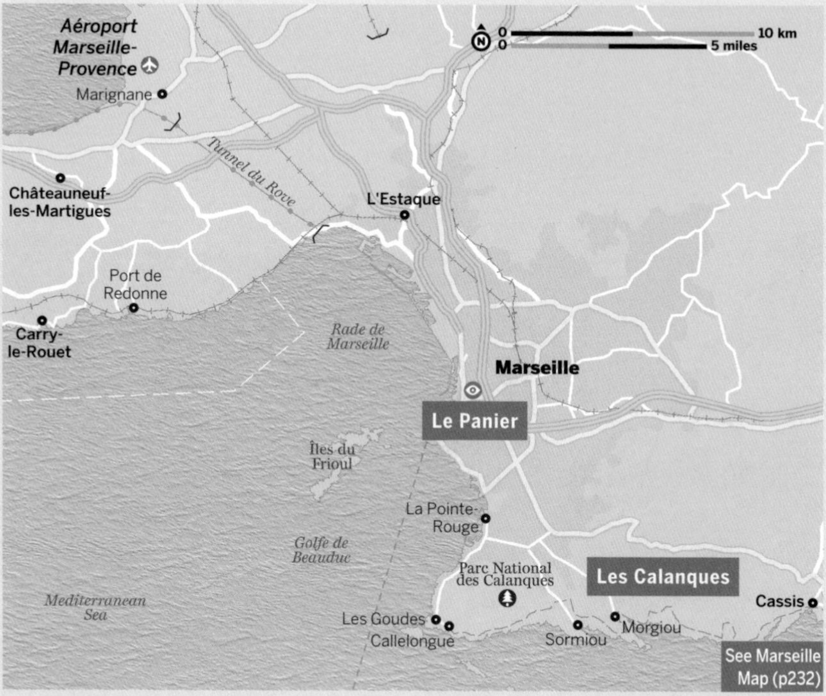

Aéroport Marseille-Provence
Marignane
Tunnel du Rove
Châteauneuf-les-Martigues
L'Estaque
Port de Redonne
Carry-le-Rouet
Rade de Marseille
Marseille
Le Panier
Îles du Frioul
La Pointe-Rouge
Golfe de Beauduc
Parc National des Calanques
Les Calanques
Mediterranean Sea
Les Goudes
Callelongue
Sormiou
Morgiou
Cassis
0 10 km
0 5 miles
See Marseille Map (p232)

Arriving in Marseille

Aéroport Marseille-Provence Flights to many European cities. Navette Marseille buses link the airport and Gare St-Charles (one-way/return €8.30/14, 30 minutes) every 15 to 20 minutes.

Gare St-Charles Regular and TGV trains serve Gare St-Charles, which is a junction for both of the city's metro lines. Tickets (one/10 trips €1.70/14) available from machines.

Where to Stay

There are modest hotels close to the train station, but the good local-transit system means that it's easy to reach the hotels scattered around the Vieux Port. Few hotels have their own parking facilities, but most central ones offer discounted rates at one of the city's car parks.

Calanque d'En-Vau

Les Calanques

A short distance from pulsing Marseille is the Parc National des Calanques, where sheer cliffs interrupt small idyllic beaches… it's easy to believe you're far from civilisation.

Great For...

☑ Don't Miss

Calanque de Morgiou's **Nautic Bar** (☎04 91 40 06 37; mains €18-27; ⏰noon-2.30pm & 7.30-9.30pm Apr-Oct) for seafood and dreamy sea views; reservations essential.

The Marseillais cherish Les Calanques, and come here to soak up the sun or take a long hike. The promontories have been protected since 1975 and shelter an extraordinary wealth of flora and fauna: 900 plant species, Bonelli's eagle, Europe's largest lizard (the 60cm eyed lizard) and its longest snake (the 2m Montpellier snake).

October to June, the best way to see the *calanques*, including the 500 sq km of the rugged **Massif des Calanques**, is to hike the many trails scented with aromatc maquis (scrub). Of the many *calanques* along the coastline, the most easily accessible are **Calanque de Sormiou** and **Calanque de Morgiou**; others require dedication and time to reach, either on foot or by **sea kayak** (www.destination-calanques.fr; half-/full day €35/55; ⏰Apr-Oct). Marseille's tourist office (p239) leads guided walks (ages eight and over).

Calanque de Morgiou

Rocky, pine-covered Cap Morgiou plunges to meet the Med at the eponymous Calanque de Morgiou – a pretty little port bobbing with fishing boats, and sheer rock faces spangled with thrill-seeking climbers.

The hair-raisingly steep, narrow road (3.5km) is open to motorists weekdays only from mid-April to May, and closed from June to September (when a one-hour distant car park is mandatory).

Thirty-seven metres below Morgiou's waters lies the entrance to the Grotte Cosquer, a miraculously preserved chamber daubed with 20,000-year-old Paleolithic art.

Calanque de Sormiou

The largest *calanque* hit headlines in 1991 when diver Henri Cosquer from Cassis swam through a 150m-long passage 36m underwater into a cave to find its interior adorned with wall paintings dating from around 20,000 BC. Now named Grotte Cosquer, the cave is a protected historical monument and closed to the public. Many more are believed to exist. Take bus 23 from Marseille's Rond-Point du Prado metro to the La Cayolle stop, from where it is a 3km walk.

Need to Know

Roads into each *calanque* are often closed to drivers, unless you have a reservation at one of the *calanque* restaurants.

Take a Break

Dine at seasonal **Le Château** (04 91 25 08 69; www.lechateausormiou.fr; mains €23-25; noon-2.30pm & 7.30-9.30pm Apr-Sep) in Calanque de Sormiou; reserve ahead.

★ Top Tip

Marseille's tourist office (p239) leads guided walks and has information about trail and road closures.

Hidden Coves

East of Calanque de Morgiou, the stone-sculptured coast brings you to three remote *calanques:* **En-Vau**, **Port-Pin** and **Port-Miou**. A steep three-hour marked trail leads from the car park (closed July to mid-September) on the **Col de la Gardiole** to En-Vau, with a pebbly beach and emerald waters encased by cliffs. The slippery and sheer descents into the *calanque* are very challenging. Its entrance is guarded by the **Doigt de Dieu** (God's Finger), a giant rock pinnacle.

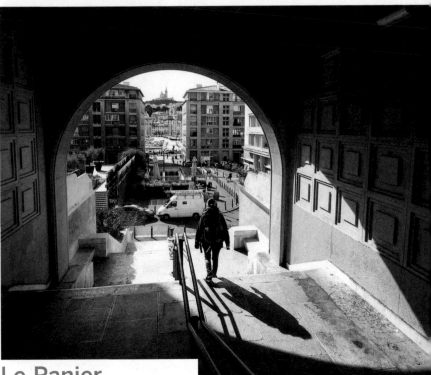

Le Panier

'The Basket' is Marseille's oldest quarter – site of the original Greek settlement and nicknamed for its steep streets and buildings. Its arty ambience, cool hidden squares and sun-baked cafes make it a delight to explore.

Great For...

☑ Don't Miss

Place de Lenche and rue des Pistoles, two pretty squares ideal for soaking up local boho charm.

Lapping up local life is a big draw of this artsy neighbourhood where narrow, sun-bleached streets give way to artist workshops and bijou squares. Main street Grande Rue follows the ancient road of the Greeks to place de Lenche, location of the original Greek *agora* (marketplace).

Rebuilt after destruction in WWII, its mishmash of lanes hide artisan shops, *ateliers* (workshops), and terraced houses strung with drying washing.

Art & Architecture

Located in the heart of the neighbourhood is **La Vieille Charité** (☎04 91 14 58 80; www.vieille-charite-marseille.com; 2 rue de la Charité; museums adult/child €6/3; ⏲10am-6pm Tue-Sun mid-Sep–mid-May, longer hours in summer; Ⓜ Joliette). This grand and gorgeous

Marseillais soap

AGE FOTOSTOCK /ALAMY STOCK PHOTO ©

almshouse was built by Pierre Puget (1620–94), an architect and sculptor born just a couple of streets away who rose to become Louis XIV's architect. With its neoclassical central chapel and elegant arcaded courtyard, it's a structure of great harmony and grace.

Entry is free, or pay to visit the **Musée d'Archéologie Méditerranéenne** (www.culture.marseille.fr; adult/child €6/free; 10am-7pm Tue-Sun mid-May–mid-Sep, to 6pm mid-Sep–mid-May), an archaeological museum exploring Mediterranean history.

A second museum, the **Musée d'Arts Africains, Océaniens et Amérindiens** (www.marseille.fr/node/630; adult/child €6/free; 10am-7pm Tue-Sun mid-May–mid-Sep, to 6pm mid-Sep–mid-May), makes quite an impression with its tribal masks, pottery, shrunken heads and other artefacts.

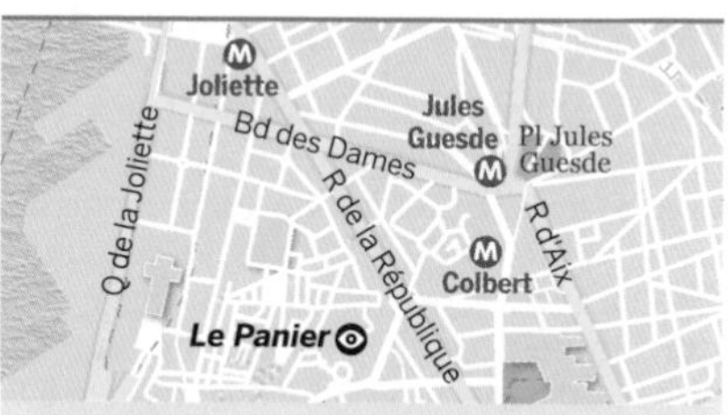

Need to Know

Ask at the tourist office (p239) about guided walks and rambles in Le Panier.

Take a Break

Chill with locals over a glass of pastis and charcuterie plates at Bar des 13 Coins (p236).

★ Top Tip

Savour multicultural Le Panier with spicy Moroccan tajines, *pastillas* and curries at Place Lorette (p237).

Marseillais Soap

Soapmaking in Marseille has been traced by some to the 14th century. Enter **La Grande Savonnerie** (www.lagrandesavonnerie.com; 36 Grande Rue; 9am-6pm Tue-Sun; M Vieux Port), an artisan soapmaker on Le Panier's fringe. Shop here for the genuine Marseillais article, made with olive oil and no added perfume, and shaped into cubes.

Another of Marseille's fine soap sellers is **72% Pétanque** (www.philippechailloux.com; 10 rue du Petit Puits; 10.30am-6.30pm; M Vieux Port or Joliette), known for its unusual perfumes like chocolate and aniseed.

Game for Boules

Pick up your very own travelling set of handmade *boules,* plus plenty of other souvenirs relating to France's iconic game at **Maison de la Boule** (04 88 44 39 44; www.museedelaboule.com; 4 place des 13 Cantons; 10am-7pm Mon-Sat, to 6pm Sun; 49, M Vieux Port). A little museum illustrates the history of the sport, including the curious figure of Fanny: tradition dictates if you lose a game 13-nil, you must kiss her bare bum cheeks.

SIGHTS

Greater Marseille is divided into 16 *arrondissements* (districts), which are indicated in addresses (eg 1er for the first *arrondissement* and so on). The city's main thoroughfare, La Canebière (from the Provençal word *canebe,* meaning 'hemp', after the city's traditional rope industry), in the 1st *arrondissement,* stretches eastwards from the Vieux Port towards the train station, a 10-minute walk or two metro stops from the water. North is Le Panier, Marseille's oldest quarter; south is the bohemian concourse of cours Julien; and southwest is the start of the coastal road.

Musée des Civilisations de l'Europe et de la Méditerranée — Museum

(MuCEM, Museum of European & Mediterranean Civilisations; ☎04 84 35 13 13; www.mucem.org; 7 promenade Robert Laffont; adult/child incl exhibitions €9.50/free; ⏰10am-8pm Wed-Mon Jul & Aug, 11am-7pm Wed-Mon May-Jun & Sep-Oct, 11am-6pm Wed-Mon Nov-Apr; 👪; Ⓜ Vieux Port|Joliette) The icon of modern Marseille, this stunning museum explores the history, culture and civilisation of the Mediterranean region through anthropological exhibits, rotating art exhibitions and film. The collection sits in a bold, contemporary building designed by architects Rudy Ricciotti and Roland Carta. It is linked by a vertigo-inducing footbridge to the 13th-century **Fort St-Jean** (Ⓜ Vieux Port), from which there are stupendous views of the Vieux Port and the surrounding sea. The fort grounds and their gardens are free to explore.

Basilique Notre Dame de la Garde — Basilica

(Montée de la Bonne Mère; ☎04 91 13 40 80; www.notredamedelagarde.com; rue Fort du Sanctuaire; ⏰7am-8pm Apr-Sep, to 7pm Oct-Mar; 🚌60) Occupying Marseille's highest point, La Garde (154m), this opulent 19th-century Romano-Byzantine basilica is Marseille's most-visited icon. Built on the foundations of a 16th-century fort, as an enlargement of a 13th-century chapel, the basilica is ornamented with coloured marble, superb Byzantine-style mosaics, and murals depicting ships sailing under the protection of La Bonne Mère ('The Good Mother'). The

Basilique Notre Dame de la Garde

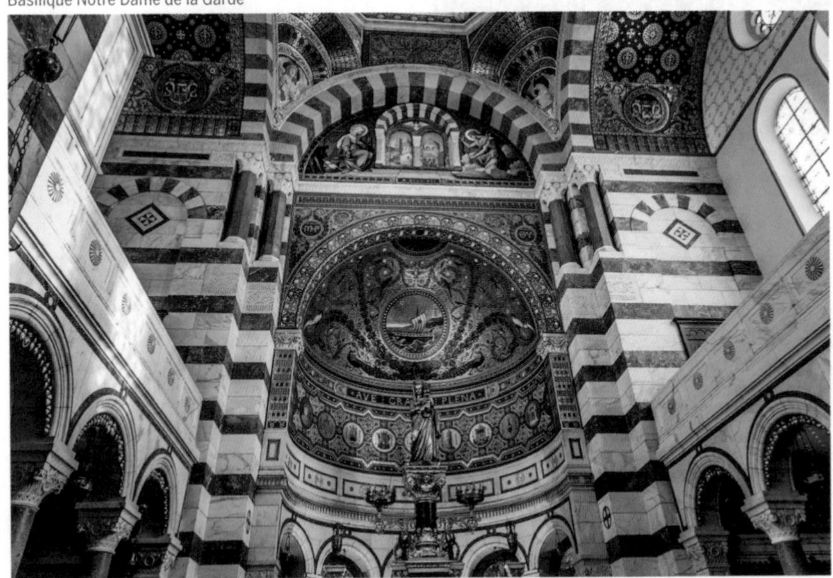

campanile supports a 9.7m-tall gilded statue of said Mother on a 12m-high pedestal, and the hilltop gives 360-degree panoramas of the city. The basilica is a steep 1km walk from the Vieux Port; alternatively, take bus 60, or the tourist train.

Vieux Port — Port

(Old Port; MVieux Port) Ships have docked for millennia at Marseille's birthplace, the vibrant Vieux Port. The main commercial docks were transferred to the Joliette area in the 1840s, but the old port remains a thriving harbour for fishing boats, pleasure yachts and tourist boats. Guarded by the forts St-Jean and **St-Nicolas** (1 bd Charles Livon; 83), both sides of the port are dotted with bars, brasseries and cafes, with more to be found around place Thiars and cours Honoré d'Estienne d'Orves, where the action continues until late.

For mobility-challenged (or exhausted) sightseers, there's also a **cross-port ferry** (one-way €0.50; 7.30am-8.30pm; MVieux Port).

Musée d'Histoire de Marseille — Museum

(History Museum of Marseille; 04 91 55 36 00; http://musee-histoire.marseille.fr; 2 rue Henri-Barbusse; adult/child €5/free; 10am-7pm Tue-Sun mid-May–mid-Sep, to 6pm mid-Sep–mid-May; MVieux Port) This intriguing 15,000-sq-metre museum traces the story of 'France's Oldest City' from prehistory (the paintings of the Cosquer Cave) to the present day, across 12 chronological exhibitions. The complex was built beside the remains of a Greek harbour uncovered during construction of the Bourse shopping centre. Highlights include the remains of a 3rd-century merchant vessel discovered in the Vieux Port in 1974: to preserve the soaked and decaying wood, it was freeze-dried where it now sits, behind glass.

La Cité Radieuse — Architecture

(Unité d'Habitation; 04 91 16 78 00; www.marseille-citeradieuse.org; 280 bd Michelet; 9am-6pm; 83 or 21, stop Le Corbusier) FREE Visionary modernist architect Le Corbusier

Island Fortress

Commanding access to Marseille's Vieux Port, photogenic **Château d'If** (06 03 06 25 26; www.if.monuments-nationaux.fr; Île d'If; adult/child €6/free; 10am-6pm Apr-Sep, to 5pm Tue-Sun Oct-Mar) was immortalised in Alexandre Dumas' 1844 classic *The Count of Monte Cristo*. Many political prisoners were incarcerated here, including the Revolutionary hero Mirabeau and the Communards of 1871. Other than the island itself there's not a great deal to see, but it's worth visiting just for the views of the Vieux Port. Frioul If Express runs boats (return €11, 20 minutes, up to ten daily) from Quai de la Fraternité.

Just west are the dyke-linked limestone islands of Ratonneau and Pomègues, known jointly as the the **Îles du Frioul**. Sea birds and rare plants thrive on these tiny outcrops, which measure around 200 hectares combined. The remains of old fortifications and quarantine stations add interest, and the islands offer excellent rambling.

Frioul If Express (04 96 11 03 50; www.frioul-if-express.com; 1 quai de la Fraternité) runs boats to Château d'If (return €11, 20 minutes, up to 10 daily) from quai de la Fraternité. It also serves the Îles du Frioul (one/two islands return €11/16, 35 minutes, up to 21 daily).

Château d'If

Marseille

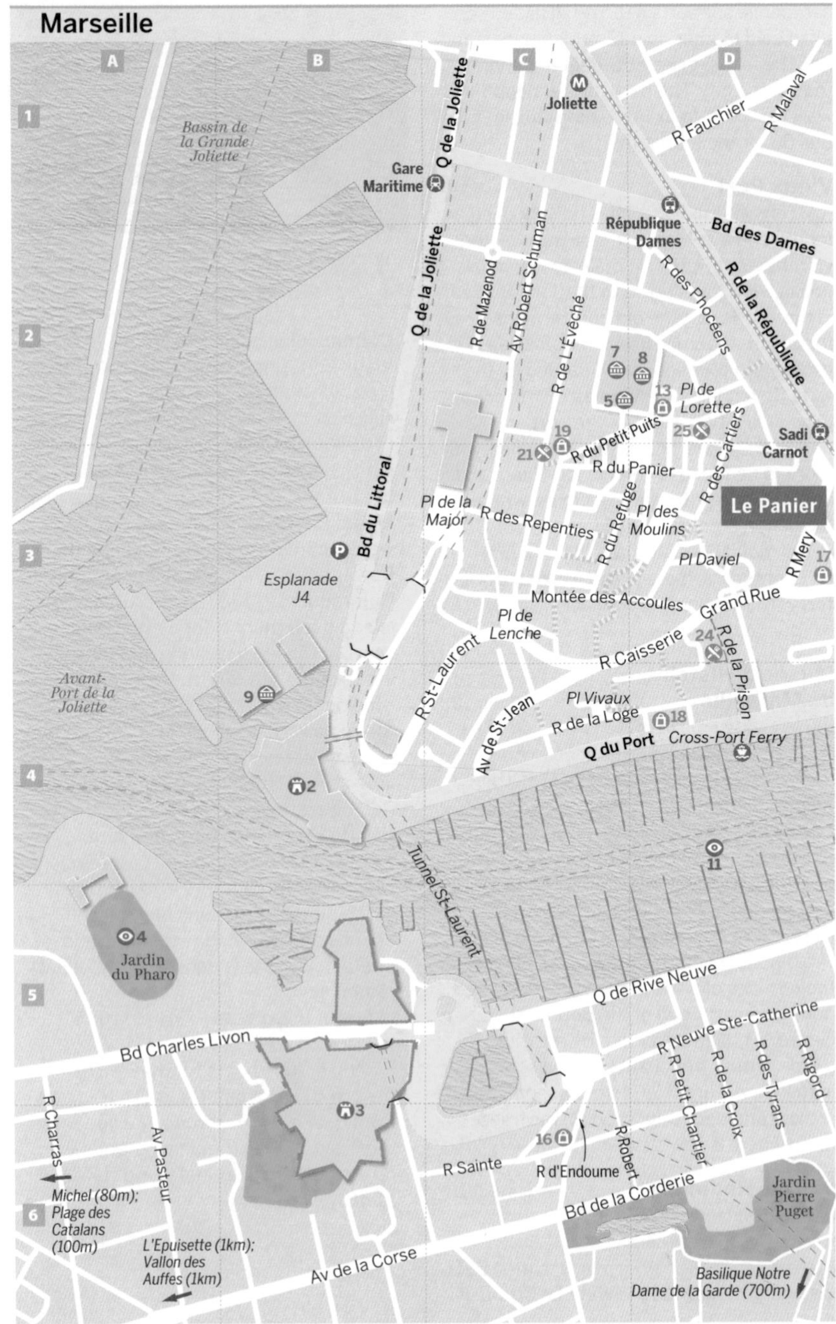

A
B
C
D
1
2
3
4
5
6
Bassin de la Grande Joliette
Q de la Joliette
Joliette
Gare Maritime
R Fauchier
R Malaval
République Dames
Bd des Dames
R des Phocéens
R de la République
Q de la Joliette
R de Mazenod
Av Robert Schuman
R de L'Évêché
7
8
5
13
Pl de Lorette
R des Cartiers
25
Sadi Carnot
19
21
R du Petit Puits
R du Panier
Bd du Littoral
Pl de la Major
R des Repenties
R du Refuge
Pl des Moulins
Le Panier
R Mery
17
Pl Daviel
Esplanade J4
Montée des Accoules
Grand Rue
Pl de Lenche
R St-Laurent
24
R Caisserie
R de la Prison
Avant-Port de la Joliette
9
Pl Vivaux
Av de St-Jean
R de la Loge
18
Q du Port
Cross-Port Ferry
2
11
Tunnel St-Laurent
4
Jardin du Pharo
Q de Rive Neuve
R Neuve Ste-Catherine
Bd Charles Livon
R Petit Chantier
R de la Croix
R des Tyrans
R Rigord
3
R Charras
Av Pasteur
16
R Robert
R Sainte
R d'Endoume
Bd de la Corderie
Jardin Pierre Puget
Michel (80m); Plage des Catalans (100m)
L'Epuisette (1km); Vallon des Auffes (1km)
Av de la Corse
Basilique Notre Dame de la Garde (700m)

0 500 m
0 0.25 miles
E
F
G
H
1
2
3
4
5
6
La Friche La Belle de Mai (1km)
Pl Victor Hugo
Gare St-Charles
Autoroute Nord
Bd Charles-Nédélec
Bd Maurice Bourdet
Bd Voltaire
R de la Joliette
Jules Guesde
Pl Jules Guesde
R Bernard du Bois
Pl des Marseillaises
St-Charles
R Flégier
R Ste-Barbe
R d'Aix
R des Petites Maries
Bd d'Athènes
Musée des Beaux Arts (900m)
Colbert
R des Dominicaines
R des Convalescents
Réformés Canebière
R Lafayette
Pl Sadi Carnot
R Puvis-de Chavannes
R Nationale
Pl de l'Hôtel des Postes
R Colbert
Pl des Capucins
Allées Léon Gambetta
Sq Léon Blum
THIERS
R du Petit St-Jean
Belsunce Alcazar
R du Tapis Vert
Cours Belsunce
Canebière Garibaldi
R Curiol
R Henri Barbusse
10
Jardins des Vestiges
Maison de la Région
R Sénac de Meilhan
R Henri Fiocca
14
Noailles
R de Bir Hakeim
R des Feuillants
R Coutelleine
Espace Infos RTM
Pl des Capucins
26
Q de la Fraternité
Tourist Office
R du Musée
20
R Pollack
R de l'Académie
Vieux Port
12
R Pavillon
R des Trois Mages
Pl du Général de Gaulle
Quai de la Fraternité
R Beauvau
R Vacon
R de Rome
R d'Aubagne
Vieux Port
29
23
R de Jeune Anacharsis
Cours Julien
R de Trois Rois
R Paradis
28
Frioul If Express
R Moustier
Cours Lieutaud
Q de Rive Neuve
R St-Saëns
R Molière
R St-Ferréol
15
1
Pl Thiars
R Corneille
30
R Francis Davso
R Estelle
Cours Honoré d'Estienne d'Orves
R Lulli
Notre Dame du Mont-Cours Julien
R Fort Notre Dame
R Breteuil
27
R Fortia
R Grignan
6
R de la Palud
Pl N-D du Mont
R Montgrand
R Armény
Bd L Salvator
R de la Paix
Estrangin-Préfecture
Pl de la Préfecture
R de Marengo
Cours Pierre Puget
Bd Notre Dame
R Roux de Brignoles
R Stanislas Torrents
R Paradis
R de Rome
R d'Italie
22

Marseille

Sights

1 Cours Julien ... H5
2 Fort St-Jean ... B4
3 Fort St-Nicolas ... B6
4 Jardin du Pharo ... A5
5 La Vieille Charité ... C2
6 Musée Cantini ... F5
7 Musée d'Archéologie Méditerranéenne .. C2
8 Musée d'Arts Africains, Océaniens & Amérindiens ... D2
9 Musée des Civilisations de l'Europe et de la Méditerranée ... B4
10 Musée d'Histoire de Marseille ... F3
11 Vieux Port ... D4

Activities, Courses & Tours

12 Croisières Marseille Calanques ... E4

Shopping

13 72% Pétanque ... D2
14 Centre Bourse Shopping Centre ... F3
15 Farmers' Market ... H5
16 Four des Navettes ... C6
17 La Grande Savonnerie ... D3
18 La Maison du Pastis ... D4
19 Maison de la Boule ... C3
20 Maison Empereur ... F4

Eating

21 Bar des 13 Coins ... C3
22 Café Populaire ... G6
23 L'Arôme ... H4
24 Le Café des Épices ... D3
Le Chalet du Pharo ... (see 4)
25 Place Lorette ... D2

Drinking & Nightlife

26 La Caravelle ... E4
27 La Part des Anges ... F5
28 Waaw ... H4

Entertainment

29 Espace Julien ... H4
30 Opéra Municipal de Marseille ... F5

redefined urban living in 1952 with the completion of this vertical 337-apartment tower, popularly known as La Cité Radieuse ('The Radiant City'). Its purpose was to increase residential density to allow for more green space. Today the apartments are joined by the Hôtel Le Corbusier, the high-end restaurant Le Ventre de l'Architecte and a rooftop terrace. English-language tours (10am Friday and Saturday; adult/child €10/5) can be booked through the tourist office (p239).

It's about 5km south of central Marseille, along av du Prado.

Musée Cantini — Gallery

(04 91 54 77 75; www.culture.marseille.fr; 19 rue Grignan; adult/child €6/free; 10am-7pm Tue-Sun mid-May–mid-Sep, to 6pm mid-Sep–mid-May; M Estrangin-Préfecture) Donated to the city by the sculptor Jules Cantini on his death in 1916, this 17th-century mansion-turned-museum conceals some superb art behind its wrought-iron gates. The core collection boasts fantastic examples of 17th- and 18th-century Provençal art, including André Derain's *Pinède à Cassis* (1907) and Raoul Dufy's *Paysage de l'Estaque* (1908). Another section is dedicated to work about Marseille, with pieces by Max Ernst, Joan Miró, André Masson and others.

Musée des Beaux-Arts — Museum

(04 91 14 59 30; www.marseille.fr/node/639; 7 rue Édouard Stephan; adult/child €6/free; 10am-7pm Tue-Sun mid-May–mid-Sep, to 6pm mid-Sep–mid-May; ; M Cinq Avenues-Longchamp, Longchamp) Set in the lavish, colonnaded Palais de Longchamp, Marseille's oldest museum owes its existence to an 1801 decree of pre-Napoléonic France's short-lived Consulate, which established 15 museums across the country. A treasure trove of 16th- to 19th-century Italian and Provençal painting and sculpture, it's set in parkland popular with local families seeking shade in Marseille's treeless centre. The spectacular fountains, constructed in the 1860s, in part disguise the water tower at which the Roquefavour Aqueduct terminates.

Cours Julien — Street

(www.coursjulien.marsnet.org; M Notre Dame du Mont-Cours Julien) Marseille's most vibrant bohemian quarter centres on Cours Julien, an elongated concrete square shaded by palm trees. It's lined with great bars, cafes and music venues, and its street-art-slathered side-streets are home to a wealth of bookshops, galleries, tattoo parlours and ethnic restaurants. Markets are held in the square on several days of the week: flowers on Wednesday and Saturday, antique books alternate Saturdays, and stamps or antique books on Sunday.

TOURS

Marseille Provence Greeters Walking

(www.marseilleprovencegreeters.com) A great idea: free walking tours led by locals, covering street art, history, food shops, football culture and lots more. Sign up in advance online and check whether your guide speaks English.

Raskas Kayak Kayaking

(☎04 91 73 27 16; www.raskas-kayak.com; impasse du Dr Bonfils, Auberge de Jeunesse Marseille; half-/full day €40/70) This well-established outfit is a great option for half- and full-day sea-kayaking excursions around the Vieux Port, offshore islands, Cap Croisette and Les Calanques, leaving either from Marseille or Cassis. Trips are season- and weather-dependent, and can be booked online.

Croisières Marseille Calanques Boating

(☎04 91 58 50 58; www.croisieres-marseille-calanques.com; 1 La Canebière, Vieux Port; MVieux Port) Runs 2¼-hour trips from the Vieux Port taking in six *calanques* (adult/child €23/18); 3¼-hour trips to Cassis passing 12 *calanques* (adult/child €29/22); and 1¾-hour trips around the Baie de Marseille (€10), including Château d'If (add €6).

SHOPPING

For chic shopping and large chains, stroll west of the Vieux Port to the 6th *arrondissement*, especially pedestrianised rue St-Ferréol. Major chains fill the **Centre Bourse shopping centre** (www.centre-bourse.com; 17 cours Belsunce; ⏰10am-7.30pm Mon-Sat) and line rue de la République.

Farmers Market Market

(www.coursjulien.marsnet.org; cours Julien; ⏰7am-1pm Wed; MNotre Dame du Mont) Every Wednesday morning the farmers market that runs along cours Julien squawks with life, colour and accordion music as traders flog mounds of organic vegetables, jars of homemade fruit jam, hand-collected quail

Beach Hopping

Mesmerising views of another Marseille unfold along **corniche Président John F Kennedy**, the coastal road that cruises south to the small, beach-volleyball-busy **Plage des Catalans** (3 rue des Catalans; ⏰8.30am-6.30pm; 🚌81, 82) and the boat-filled fishing cove of **Vallon des Auffes** (🚌83).

Further south, the vast **Prado beaches** are marked by Jules Cantini's 1903 marble replica of Michelangelo's *David*. The beaches, all gold sand, were created using backfill from the excavations for Marseille's metro.

Promenade Georges Pompidou continues south to **Cap Croisette**, from where the beautiful **Parc National des Calanques** (☎04 20 10 50 00; www.calanques-parcnational.fr; 141 av du Prado, Bâtiment A) can be reached on foot.

To head down the coast, take bus 83 from the Vieux Port. At av du Prado switch to bus 19 to continue further.

Plage des Catalans
OLRAT/SHUTTERSTOCK ©

Signature Dish: Bouillabaisse

Originally cooked by fisherfolk from the scraps of their catch, bouillabaisse is Marseille's signature dish. True bouillabaisse includes at least four kinds of fish. Don't trust tourist traps that promise cheap bouillabaisse; the real deal costs at least €50 per person. It's served in two parts: the *soupe de poisson* (broth), rich with tomato, saffron and fennel; and the cooked fish, de-boned tableside. On the side are croutons, *rouille* (a bread-thickened garlic-chilli mayonnaise) and grated cheese, usually gruyère. Spread *rouille* on the crouton, top with cheese, and float it in the soup.

Swanky **L'Epuisette** (04 91 52 17 82; www.l-epuisette.com; 158 rue du Vallon des Auffes; lunch/bouillabaisse menu €75/98; noon-1.30pm & 7.30-9.30pm Tue-Sat; 83) has a Michelin star and serves what may be Marseille's top bouillabaisse. Meanwhile, deceptively shabby-looking **Michel** (Brasserie Catalans; 04 91 52 30 63; www.restaurant-michel-13.fr; 6 rue des Catalans; bouillabaisse €75; noon-1.30pm & 8-9.30pm; 83) has been preparing some of Marseille's most authentic bouillabaisse since 1946.

eggs and bouquets of fragrant herbs. Once your shopping bags are brimming, head to a nearby cafe and settle down to watch the mostly boho crowd haggle with the stallholders.

Maison Empereur Homewares
(04 91 54 02 29; www.empereur.fr; 4 rue des Récolettes; 9am-7pm Mon-Sat; 3, 2) If you only have time to visit one store in Marseille, make it this one. Run by the same family since 1827, France's oldest hardware store remains a one-stop shop for beautifully made homeware items including Opinel cutlery, Savon de Marseille soaps, wooden toy sailing boats and ceramic shaving bowls.

Four des Navettes Food
(04 91 33 32 12; www.fourdesnavettes.com; 136 rue Sainte; 7am-8pm Mon-Sat, 9am-1pm & 3-7.30pm Sun; M Vieux Port) Opened in 1781, this is the oldest bakery in Marseille; it's been passed down between three families, and still uses the original 18th-century oven. It is *the* address to pick up Marseille's signature biscuits, the orange-perfumed *navettes de Marseille,* as well as *calissons* (Provençal almond biscuits), nougat and other delights.

La Maison du Pastis Drinks
(04 91 90 86 77; www.lamaisondupastis.com; 108 quai du Port; 10am-7pm Mon-Sat, to 5pm Sun; M Vieux Port) A bit touristy, perhaps, but if you're keen to sample some of 75 different varieties of Provence's favourite aperitif – the aniseed-flavoured firewater known as pastis – then this is the place to do it. La Maison also offers the chance to try absinthe, the notorious spirit known as *la fée verte* (the green fairy) for its supposedly hallucinogenic properties.

EATING

Café Populaire Bistro $$
(04 91 02 53 96; 110 rue Paradis; mains €19-24; noon-2pm & 8-10.30pm Mon-Fri, 8-10.30pm Sat, noon-3pm Sun; M Estrangin-Préfecture) Vintage furniture, latticed blinds, old books and antique soda bottles lend a retro air to this style-conscious, 1950s-styled jazz *comptoir* (counter) – a restaurant in all but name. The crowd is chic, and smiling chefs in the open kitchen churn out international dishes like *tagliata* (steak strips with rocket and parmesan) and black cod with miso and *yuzu* (a Japanese citrus fruit).

Bar des 13 Coins Brasserie $
(04 91 91 56 49; 45 rue Ste-Françoise; mains €13-16; 9am-11pm; M Vieux Port) Night and day, this corner bar is a classic Le Panier hang-out whether you're old, young, hip or in need of a hip replacement. It's on a

quiet backstreet with tables on the square, and serves bistro standards like entrecôte, bruschetta and charcuterie plates – but it's the chilled vibe you come for, best tasted over an evening pastis.

Place Lorette Moroccan $$
(☎09 81 35 66 75; 3 place de Lorette; mains €14-16; ⏱11am-6pm Thu-Sat, to 4pm Sun; ⓂColbert) Tucked away on a quiet square in the middle of polyglot Le Panier, this Moroccan restaurant serves up a fantastic lunch in an arched and art-strewn stone dining room – lamb and chicken tagines, semolina bread and crunchy *pastillas* (sweetly spiced chicken pastries), all washed down with fresh orange juice and mint tea. The Sunday brunch (€24) is a sharing feast.

L'Arôme Modern French $$
(☎04 91 42 88 80; 9 rue de Trois Rois; menus €23-28; ⏱7.30-11pm Mon-Sat; ⓂNotre Dame du Mont) Reserve ahead to snag a table at this fabulous little restaurant just off cours Julien. From the service – relaxed, competent, friendly without being overfamiliar – to the street art on the walls and the memorable food, it's a complete winner. Well-credentialled chef-owner Romain achieves sophisticated simplicity in dishes such as roast duckling served with polenta and a pecorino *beignet* (doughnut).

Le Café des Épices Modern French $$
(☎04 28 31 70 26; www.lecafedesepices-by-acdg.com; 4 rue du Lacydon; lunch/dinner menus €25/35; ⏱noon-2pm & 7.30-10pm Tue-Sat; 🚌55, ⓂVieux Port) One of Marseille's best chefs, Arnaud de Grammont, works thoughtfully with great produce and inventive flavours: think gurnard in chickpea broth with dried tomatoes and radish, or blonde d'Aquitaine beef with polenta and glazed carrots. Presentation is impeccable, the decor playful, and the outdoor terrace between giant potted olive trees is superb in good weather.

DRINKING & NIGHTLIFE

Near the Vieux Port, head to place Thiars and cours Honoré d'Estienne d'Orves for cafes that bask in the sun by day and buzz into the night.

Bouillabaisse

OXANA MEDVEDEVA/MYLT3EMPKL/500PX ©

Best View

Only Marseillais and those in the know are privy to **Le Chalet du Pharo** (☎04 91 52 80 11; www.le-chalet-du-pharo.com; 58 bd Charles Livon, Jardin du Pharo; menus €39-47; ⊙noon-3pm & 7.30-11pm Mon-Sat, noon-3pm Sun; MVieux Port) with a very big view, secreted in the **Jardin du Pharo** (58 bd Charles Livon; ⊙8am-9pm; 🚌81, 82, 83). Its hillside terrace, shaded by pines and parasols, stares across the water to Fort St-Jean, MuCEM and the Villa Méditerranée beyond. Grilled fish and meat dominate the menu. Online reservations are essential. No credit cards accepted.

Le Chalet du Pharo

ZYANKARLO/SHUTTERSTOCK ©

Waaw Bar

(☎04 91 42 16 33; www.waaw.fr; 17 rue Pastoret; ⊙4pm-midnight Wed & Sat, from 6pm Tue, Thu & Fri; MNotre Dame du Mont) Marseille's creative chameleon and the heart of the cours Julien scene, Waaw ('What an Amazing World') has everything you could possibly want for a night out. Whether that's a cold cocktail, a late-night dancehall DJ set or an innovative dinner made from local market produce, the city's unofficial cultural headquarters offers music, film, festivals and much more.

La Caravelle Bar

(☎04 91 90 36 64; www.lacaravelle-marseille.com; 34 quai du Port; ⊙7am-2am; 📶; MVieux Port) On the 1st floor of the Hotel Bellevue, this lovely little bar is styled with rich wood and leather, with a zinc bar and yellowing murals that hint of its 1920s pedigree. If it's sunny, snag a coveted spot on the portside terrace, and sip a pastis as you watch the throng below. On Friday there's live jazz from 9pm.

La Part des Anges Wine Bar

(☎04 91 33 55 70; www.lapartdesanges.com; 33 rue Sainte; ⊙9am-2am Mon-Sat, 9am-1pm & 6pm-2am Sun; MVieux Port) This fabulously convivial wine bar is named after the alcohol that evaporates through a barrel during wine or whisky fermentation: the 'angels' share'. Take your pick of dozens of wines by the glass, listed by region on a blackboard behind the bar, or buy a bottle to take away. Steak, pasta and other wine-friendly ballast is available.

ENTERTAINMENT

Cultural events are covered in *L'Hebdo* (€1.20), available around town, or at www.marseillebynight.com and www.journalventilo.fr.

La Friche La Belle de Mai Cultural Centre

(☎04 95 04 95 04; www.lafriche.org; 41 rue Jobin; ⊙ticket kiosk 11am-6pm Mon, to 7pm Tue-Sat, from 12.30pm Sun; 🚌49, 52) This 45,000-sq-metre former tobacco factory is now a vibrant arts centre with a theatre, cinema, bar, bookshop, artists' workshops, multimedia displays, skateboard ramps, electro- and world-music parties and much more. The on-site restaurant, **Les Grandes Tables** (☎04 95 04 95 85; www.lesgrandestables.com; mains €16; ⊙noon-2pm daily plus 8-10pm Thu-Sat), is a great bet for interesting, locally sourced food. Check the program online.

Opéra Municipal de Marseille Opera

(☎04 91 55 11 10; http://opera.marseille.fr; 2 rue Molière; ⊙box office 10am-5.30pm Tue-Sat; MVieux Port) Built in the 1920s on the site of its 18th-century predecessor, this 1800-seat neoclassical theatre has seen the French premieres of many notable operas, and hosted some of its most famous performers. The season runs from September to June.

Espace Julien Live Music

(☎04 91 24 34 10; www.espace-julien.com; 39 cours Julien; Ⓜ Notre Dame du Mont-Cours Julien) Rock, *opérock*, alternative theatre, reggae, hip hop, Afro groove and other cutting-edge entertainment all appear on the bill at this mainstay of the cours Julien scene. See the website for the program and to buy tickets.

INFORMATION

Maison de la Région (☎04 91 57 50 57; www.regionpaca.fr; 27 place Jules Guesde; ⏰11am-6pm Mon-Sat; Ⓜ Noailles) Info on Provence and the Côte d'Azur.

Marseille City Pass (www.resamarseille.com; 24/48/72hr €26/33/41) Admission to city museums and public transport, plus a guided city tour and a Château d'If boat trip. It's not necessary for children under 12, as many attractions are greatly reduced or free. Buy online or at the tourist office.

Tourist Office (☎08 26 50 05 00, box office 04 91 13 89 16; www.marseille-tourisme.com; 11 La Canebière; ⏰9am-6pm; Ⓜ Vieux Port) Guided city tours (by foot, bus, electric tourist train or boat) and trips to Les Calanques.

GETTING THERE & AWAY

AIR

Aéroport Marseille-Provence (Aéroport Marseille-Marignane; MRS; Map p175; ☎08 20 81 14 14; www.marseille.aeroport.fr) is located 25km northwest of Marseille in Marignane. There are regular year-round flights to nearly all major French cities, plus major hubs in the UK, Germany, Belgium, Italy and Spain.

BOAT

Gare Maritime de la Major (Marseille Fos; www.marseille-port.fr; quai de la Joliette; Ⓜ Joliette), the passenger ferry terminal, is located just south of place de la Joliette.

TRAIN

Eurostar (www.eurostar.com) offers between two and 10 weekly services between Marseille and London (from €213, seven hours) via Lille or Paris.

Regular and TGV trains serve **Gare St-Charles** (☎04 91 08 16 40; www.rtm.fr; rue Jacques Bory; Ⓜ Gare St-Charles SNCF), which is a junction for both metro lines. The **left-luggage office** (Consignes Automatiques; ⏰8.15am-9pm) is next to platform A. Sample fares:

Avignon €22, 1¼ hours, hourly

Nice €38, 2½ hours, up to six per day

Paris Gare de Lyon from €76, 3½ hours, at least hourly

GETTING AROUND

BICYCLE

With the **Le Vélo** (☎English helpline 01 30 79 29 13; www.levelo-mpm.fr) bike-share scheme, you can pick up and drop off bikes from 100-plus stations across the city and along the coastal road to the beaches. Subscribe online first (per week/year €1/5); bikes cost €1 per hour.

CAR

Trust us, you'll regret bringing a car into Marseille – car parks and on-street parking are very expensive, and the traffic can be horrendous. Central car parks include **Parking Bourse** (rue Reine Elisabeth; ⏰24hr; Ⓜ Vieux Port) and **Parking Indigo** (22 place du Général de Gaulle; ⏰24hr; Ⓜ Vieux Port), off La Canebière. Expect to pay at least €2 per hour or €30 per 24 hours.

PUBLIC TRANSPORT

Marseille has two metro lines, two tram lines and an extensive bus network. Bus, metro or tram tickets (one/10 trips €1.70/14) are available from machines in the metro, at tram stops and on buses. Most buses start in front of the **Espace Infos RTM** (www.rtm.fr; 6 rue des Fabres; Ⓜ Vieux Port), where you can obtain tickets.

St-Émilion (p254)

BORDEAUX

FREEPROD33/SHUTTERSTOCK ©

In This Chapter

Bordeaux at a Glance...

Bordeaux is among France's most vibrant and dynamic cities. This is a wine capital hemmed in by green, sun-drenched vineyards. Paired with the city's exceptional dining scene – a sassy mix of traditional kitchens, experimental neobistros and more – there is no tastier marriage.

The world's largest urban World Heritage Site cradles half the city (18 sq km) in its Unesco-listed treasure chest: palaces, tree-shaded boulevards and hôtels particuliers (mansions). Strolling, jogging or cycling along the river's edge is part of the lifestyle, and a high-spirited student population bolsters the undercurrent of creativity rippling through the city.

Two Days in Bordeaux

Begin at the **cathedral** (p248), admire bird's-eye views from Tour Pey Berland, then hit **Musée des Beaux-Arts** (p251). Lunch at **Le Bouchon Bordelais** (p253) then saunter to **Basilique St-Seurin** (p251) before dallying in **Jardin Public** (p251). Day two, stroll Esplanade des Quinconces, pausing to admire the showstopping wine stash at **L'Intendant** (p252). Lunch on oysters at **La Boîte à Huîtres** (p253) and enjoy a few hours in **La Cité du Vin** (p248).

Four Days in Bordeaux

Unless it's Monday, hit **Marché des Capucins** (p252) before driving or taking the train to medieval **St-Émilion** (p254) for a wine-fuelled afternoon. Back in Bordeaux in the evening, feast farmhouse-style at **La Tupina** (p253). On day four, take a day trip to the **Dune du Pilat** (p246); pack your beach gear and cycling legs. Finish by dancing at a chic nightspot like **Le Bal à Papa** (p247).

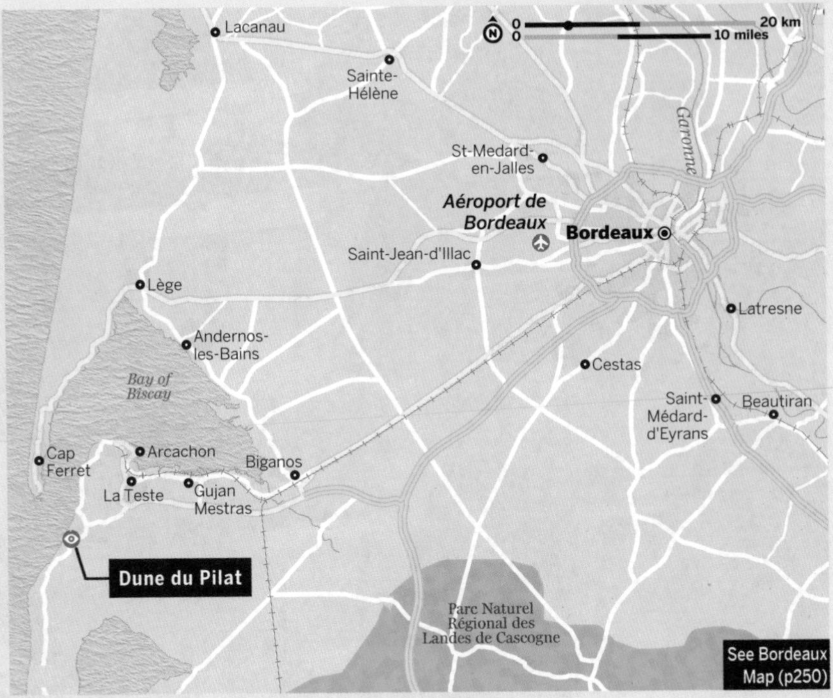

See Bordeaux Map (p250)

Arriving in Bordeaux

Aéroport de Bordeaux Buses to the city centre and train station (€1.60 or €8) every 10 minutes between 6am and 11pm. Expect to pay €50 for a taxi to the centre.

Gare St-Jean From the train station, bus line 1 to place de la Victoire or tram line C north along the river to public transport hub Esplanade des Quinconces (€1.60).

Where to Stay

Accommodation options are plentiful across all categories, with several delightful options sitting splendidly in the town centre around the cathedral. Book ahead in season (spring to early autumn). There are comprehensive accommodation listings at the tourist office, and Bordeaux Apartments (https://bordeauxapartments.fr) offers stylish, self-catering apartments in the centre.

Bordeaux Wine Trail

Bordeaux's exceptional array of vintages is the city's crowning glory, for visitors and the Bordelais themselves. Dozens of wine bars offer tastings, but for a guided dégustation with a sommelier, take a wine-tasting tour.

Vineyards cover an enviable 120,000 hectares on both sides of the River Garonne, prompting the eternal debate over which bank – Rive Gauche (Left Bank) or Rive Droite (Right Bank) – is best. The vines are tended by 6300 *vignerons* (winemakers) who produce up to 5.7 million hectolitres of red, white, rosé and sparkling wines each year. Every second, 21 bottles of Bordeaux wine are sold around the world.

The entire Bordeaux region is divided into 65 appellations (production areas). Each geographic subregion produces at least two or three different appellations – some produce up to a dozen. Unusually for a winegrowing region, almost all Bordeaux wines have earned the right to include the abbreviation AOC (Appellation d'Origine Contrôlée) stamp of quality on their labels.

Great For...

☑ Don't Miss

A glass of wine on the rooftop terrace of luxurious 18th-century **Le Grand Hôtel** (https://bordeaux.intercontinental.com; 2-5 place de la Comédie; d from €290).

JUSTIN FOULKES/LONELY PLANET ©

Need to Know

Browse one of France's grandest wine shops, L'Intendant (p252).

Take a Break

Dine at La Grande Maison (p254) and pore over its sensational wine list.

Top Tip

Taste Bordeaux wines by the glass at the grandiose Bar à Vin (p255).

Tours & Tastings

Both the tourist office (p255) and the excellent wine-information desk, **Espace Information Routes du Vin** (www.bordeauxwinetrip.fr; 134-150 quai de Bacalan, La Cité du Vin; ⌚10am-7pm Apr-Aug, shorter hours rest of year) inside La Cité du Vin, have reams of information on tastings, wine tours and cruises. Whet your palate with the **Bacchus Wine Tour** (three hours, €69) on foot around the city, or the half-day **Urban Wine Tour** (€42), which includes tastings in town and an out-of-town château. In autumn, it is possible to join in the grape harvest.

Serious students of the grape can enrol at highly regarded wine school **École du Vin de Bordeaux** (Bordeaux Wine School; ☎05 56 00 22 85; www.bordeaux.com; 3 cours du 30 Juillet; introductory workshops €32), inside the Maison du Vin de Bordeaux (Bordeaux House of Wine).

Château & Cellars

Guided visits of **Château Les Carmes Haut Brion** (☎07 77 38 10 64; www.les-carmes-haut-brion.com; 20 rue des Carmes; 1½ hr guided visit with tasting €30; ⌚9.30am-12.30pm & 2-6pm Mon-Sat), 4km southwest of the cathedral, include a tour of the 19th-century gardens and Philippe Starck cellar, and end with wine tasting. Advance reservations online or by telephone are essential. The château is in Pessac.

Wine Festival

The **Fête du Vin Nouveau et de la Brocante** is a two-day street festival in October, thrown to celebrate the first post-harvest wine. The *vin nouveau* (new wine) is solemnly blessed in church before the real party breaks out on rue Notre Dame and surrounding streets: think drinking, dancing, street food and dozens of stalls selling antiques and secondhand jumble.

Cooking Courses

There are a couple of courses open to tourists and, this being Bordeaux, most involve food and wine. Themed classes at **Le Saint James** (☎05 57 97 06 00; www.saintjames-bouliac.com; 3 place Camille Hostein, Bouliac; per person €75-155) last three to 3½ hours and cost €75 to €155 per person.

Dune du Pilat

Europe's largest sand dune has to be climbed – and gleefully romped down at speed. The coastal panorama is a stunner and nearby beaches have some of the Atlantic coast's best surf. It's an essential day trip from Bordeaux.

Great For...

☑ Don't Miss

The pine-scented cycle path linking Dune du Pilat with Arcachon, 8km south.

Sometimes referred to as the Dune de Pyla because of its location 4km from the bijou seaside town of Pyla-sur-Mer, this gargantuan sand dune stretches from the mouth of the Bassin d'Arcachon southwards for 2.7km. The dune is growing eastwards 1.5m a year – it has swallowed trees, a road junction and even a hotel, so local lore claims.

The view from the top – approximately 115m above sea level – is magnificent. To the west you see the sandy shoals at the mouth of the **Bassin d'Arcachon**, including Cap Ferret and the **Banc d'Arguin** bird reserve where up to 6000 couples of Sandwich terns nest each spring. Dense dark-green forests of maritime pines, oaks, ferns and strawberry trees (whose wood is traditionally used to build oyster-farmer shacks) stretch from the base of the dune eastwards almost as far as the eye can see.

Need to Know

Local **bus line 1** (€1) links Arcachon train station with the Dune du Pilat.

Take a Break

Picnic on the sand, or see and be seen over lunch at glam **La Co(o)rniche** (05 56 22 72 11; www.lacoorniche-pyla.com; 46 av Louis Gaume; 2-/3-course lunch menu €58/63, seafood platters €40-85).

★ Top Tip

Take care when swimming: powerful currents swirl out to sea from deceptively tranquil little bays.

Walking & Cycling

Cycling is the most invigorating way to get to/from the dune, although there is one hill on the final approach. The helpful **Espace Accueil** (05 56 22 12 85; www.ladunedupilat.com; Dune du Pilat; 9.30am-5pm Apr-Oct) distributes free cycling maps and has information on the flora, fauna and fragility of this protected natural site. It also organises free guided dune walks.

Dune Climb

Between Easter and early to mid-November, a wooden staircase – between 150 and 160 steps depending on the year – is erected on one side of the dune to help tourists scramble to its sandy top. Otherwise, clamber exhaustedly up the steep sand mountain – and exercise your inner child by flying down at an exhilarating sprint if you dare. Bare foot is preferable, although the sand can be perishing cold in winter and as hot as burning coals in the height of summer.

Be warned that it can be desperately windy atop the dune: swirling, whip-lashing sand can be particularly unpleasant for younger children.

Snack bars and touristy restaurants abound next to the Dune du Pilat car park – although on warm, sunny days with no wind, you might prefer to picnic on the sand.

Starry Nights

Want to drink and dance beneath the stars on hot summer nights? Laid-back Pyla-sur-Mer, a patchwork of colonial-style summer houses and pine trees, has something of a speakeasy party scene. Bars and clubs can almost be counted on one hand, but they have a designer vibe and attract a fashionable set. Bar-club hybrid **Le Bal à Papa** (05 56 22 73 70; www.lebalapapa.fr; 242 bd de l'Océan; 10pm-2am Thu-Sun) is *the* spot to drink cocktails and dance away summer nights to a wicked mix of 1980s hits.

SIGHTS

La Cité du Vin — Museum

(☎05 56 16 20 20; www.laciteduvin.com; 134-150 quai de Bacalan, 1 Esplanade de Pontac; adult/child €20/free; ⏲10am-7pm Apr-Aug, shorter hours rest of year) The complex world of wine is explored in depth at ground-breaking La Cité du Vin, a stunning piece of contemporary architecture resembling a wine decanter on the banks of the River Garonne. The curvaceous gold building glitters in the sun and its 3000 sq metres of exhibits are equally sensory and sensational. Digital guides lead visitors around 20 themed sections covering everything from vine cultivation, grape varieties and wine production to the ancient wine trade, 21st-century wine trends and celebrated personalities.

Tours end with a glass of wine – or grape juice for the kids – in panoramic **Le Belvédère**, with monumental 30m-long bar and chandelier made out of recycled wine bottles, on the 8th floor. Temporary art exhibitions, cultural events and brilliant, themed one-hour tasting workshops (€15 to €25) are also worth watching out for. To get here, take tram B (direction Bassins à Flots) from Esplanade des Quinconnes, or walk 2.5km north along the river.

Miroir d'Eau — Fountain

(Water Mirror; place de la Bourse; ⏲10am-10pm summer) FREE A fountain of sorts, the Miroir d'Eau is the world's largest reflecting pool. Covering an area of 3450 sq metres of black granite on the quayside opposite the imposing Palais de la Bourse, the 'water mirror' provides hours of entertainment on warm sunny days when the reflections in its thin slick of water – drained and refilled every half-hour – are stunning. Every 23 minutes a dense fog-like vapour is ejected for three minutes to add to the fun (and photo opportunities).

Cathédrale St-André — Cathedral

(☎05 56 44 67 29; www.cathedrale-bordeaux.fr; place Jean Moulin; ⏲2-7pm Mon, 10am-noon & 2-6pm Tue-Sun) FREE The Cathédrale St-André, a Unesco World Heritage Site prior to the city's classification, lords it over the city. The cathedral's oldest section dates from 1096; most of what you see today was built in the 13th and 14th centuries. Enjoy exceptional masonry carvings in the

From left: Jardin Public (p251); Cathédrale St-André; Place de la Comédie

PATRICE COPPEE/GETTY IMAGES ©

MARCOCIANNAREL/SHUTTERSTOCK ©

north portal. Even more imposing than the cathedral itself is the gargoyled, 50m-high Gothic belfry, **Tour Pey Berland** (☎05 56 81 26 25; www.pey-berland.fr; place Pey-Berland; adult/child €6/free; ⊙10am-1.15pm & 2-6pm Tue-Sun Jun-Sep, 10am-12.30pm & 2-5.30pm Tue-Sun Oct-May), erected between 1440 and 1466.

Musée d'Aquitaine — Museum

(☎05 56 01 51 00; www.musee-aquitaine-bordeaux.fr; 20 cours Pasteur; adult/child €5/free; ⊙11am-6pm Tue-Sun) Gallo-Roman statues and relics dating back 25,000 years are among the highlights at this bright and spacious, well-curated history and civilisations museum. Grab a bilingual floor plan at the entrance and borrow an English-language catalogue to better appreciate the exhibits that span prehistory through to 18th-century Atlantic trade and slavery, world cultures and the emergence of Bordeaux as a world port in the 19th century. Temporary exhibitions cost extra.

Musée du Vin et du Négoce — Museum

(☎05 56 90 19 13; www.museeduvinbordeaux.com; 41 rue Borie; adult/child incl tasting €10/free; ⊙10am-6pm) This small Wine and Trade Museum, hidden in one of the city's oldest buildings – an Irish merchant's house dating to 1720 in the ancient trading district of Chartrons – offers a fascinating insight into the historic origins of Bordeaux's wine trade and the importance of the *négociant* (merchant trader) in the 18th and 19th centuries. The vaulted cellars, 33m long, display dozens of artefacts, including hand-crafted stave oak barrels and every size of wine bottle from an Avion to a Melchior.

Discount Pass

Consider investing in the **Bordeaux Métropole City Pass** (www.bordeauxcitypass.com; 24/48/72 hours €29/39/46), covering admission to 20 museums and monuments. It also includes a free guided tour and unlimited use of public buses, trams and boats. You can buy it online or at the tourist office (p255).

YINGHUI LIU/SHUTTERSTOCK ©

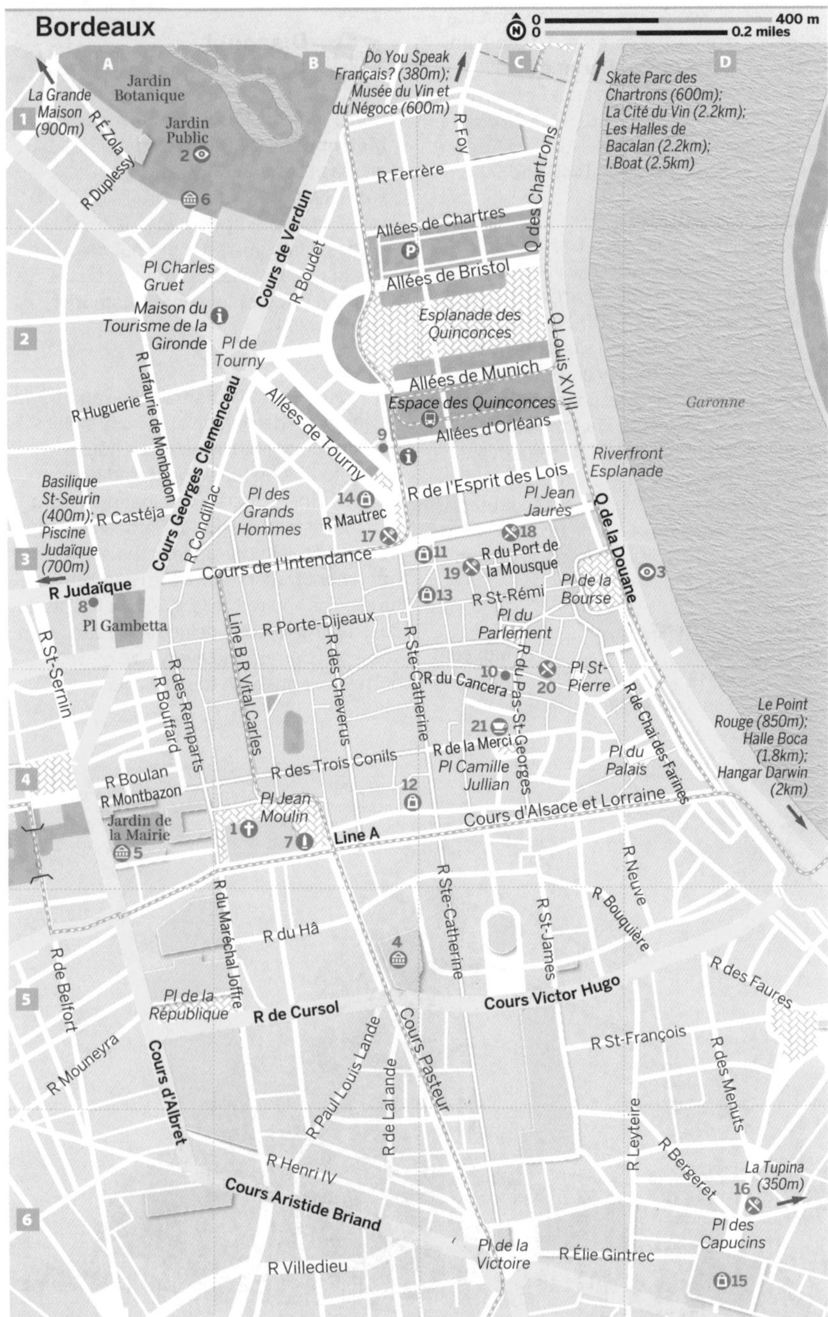
Bordeaux
0 400 m
0 0.2 miles
La Grande Maison (900m)
Jardin Botanique
Jardin Public
Do You Speak Français? (380m); Musée du Vin et du Négoce (600m)
Skate Parc des Chartrons (600m); La Cité du Vin (2.2km); Les Halles de Bacalan (2.2km); I.Boat (2.5km)
R É Zola
R Duplessy
R Foy
R Ferrère
Q des Chartrons
Cours de Verdun
Allées de Chartres
Allées de Bristol
R Boudet
Pl Charles Gruet
Maison du Tourisme de la Gironde
Pl de Tourny
Esplanade des Quinconces
Q Louis XVIII
Allées de Munich
Espace des Quinconces
Allées d'Orléans
Garonne
R Lafaurie de Monbadon
R Huguerie
Cours Georges Clemenceau
Allées de Tourny
Riverfront Esplanade
Basilique St-Seurin (400m); Piscine Judaïque (700m)
R Castéja
R Condillac
Pl des Grands Hommes
R Mautrec
R de l'Esprit des Lois
Pl Jean Jaurès
Q de la Douane
Cours de l'Intendance
R du Port de la Mousque
Pl de la Bourse
R Judaïque
Pl Gambetta
R St-Rémi
Pl du Parlement
Line B R Vital Carles
R Porte-Dijeaux
R des Cheverus
R Ste-Catherine
R du Cancera
R du Pas-St-Georges
Pl St-Pierre
R St-Sernin
R des Remparts
R Bouffard
R de Chai des Farines
Le Point Rouge (850m); Halle Boca (1.8km); Hangar Darwin (2km)
R de la Merci
Pl Camille Jullian
Pl du Palais
R Boulan
R Montbazon
R des Trois Conils
Pl Jean Moulin
Jardin de la Mairie
Cours d'Alsace et Lorraine
Line A
R Neuve
R du Maréchal Joffre
R Ste-Catherine
R St-James
R Bouquière
R du Hâ
R de Belfort
R des Faures
Pl de la République
R de Cursol
Cours Victor Hugo
Cours Pasteur
R St-François
R Mouneyra
Cours d'Albret
R Paul Louis Lande
R de Lalande
R des Menuts
R Leyteire
R Bergeret
La Tupina (350m)
R Henri IV
Cours Aristide Briand
Pl des Capucins
Pl de la Victoire
R Élie Gintrec
R Villedieu

Bordeaux

Sights
1 Cathédrale St-André ... B4
2 Jardin Public ... A1
3 Miroir d'Eau ... D3
4 Musée d'Aquitaine ... B5
5 Musée des Beaux Arts ... A4
6 Musée d'Histoire Naturelle ... A1
7 Tour Pey Berland ... B4

Activities, Courses & Tours
8 Café Baillardran ... A3
9 École du Vin de Bordeaux ... B3
10 Rustic Vines ... C4

Shopping
11 Au Comptoir Bordelaise ... C3
12 Blue Madone ... B4
13 Galerie Bordelaise ... C3
14 L'Intendant ... B3
15 Marché des Capucins ... D6

Eating
16 Au Bistrot ... D6
17 Brasserie Le Bordeaux ... B3
18 La Boîte à Huîtres ... C3
19 Le Bouchon Bordelais ... C3
20 Le Petit Commerce ... C4

Drinking & Nightlife
Bar à Vin ... (see 9)
Night Beach ... (see 17)
21 Utopia ... C4

Basilique St-Seurin Church

(05 56 48 22 08; www.saintseurin.info; place des Martyrs et de la Résistance; 8.30am-7.45pm Tue-Sat, 9am-8.15pm Sun) FREE It was around this vast Romanesque complex that the *quartier* of St-Seurin grew in the 11th century. As early as the 5th century, a church dedicated to St-Étienne has stood on this site where Gallo-Romans once buried their dead in a vast necropolis here. The church became a key stop for medieval pilgrims following the Camino de Santiago de Compostela (Way of St-James to Spain), and building work continued well into the 18th century.

Musée des Beaux-Arts Gallery

(05 56 10 20 56; www.musba-bordeaux.fr; 20 cours d'Albret; adult/child €5/free; 11am-6pm Wed-Mon) The evolution of Occidental art from the Renaissance to the mid-20th century is on view at Bordeaux's Museum of Fine Arts, which occupies two wings of the 1770s-built Hôtel de Ville, either side of elegant city park Jardin de la Mairie. The museum was established in 1801; highlights include 17th-century Flemish, Dutch and Italian paintings, and the last work painted by one of Bordeaux's earliest (and most celebrated) female artists, Rosa Bonheur (1822–99), who infamously wore trousers when she worked.

Jardin Public Gardens

(cours de Verdun) Landscaping is artistic as well as informative at the Jardin Public. Established in 1755 and laid out in the English style a century later, the grounds incorporate duck ponds, the meticulously catalogued **Jardin Botanique** dating from 1629, and the city's **Musée d'Histoire Naturelle** (5 place Bardineau). At the time of research it was closed for renovation work; it's slated to open again in late 2018.

TOURS

The tourist office (p255) has information on river cruises, including a 1½-hour cruise on the *Aquitania* riverboat (adult/child €15/2) and more elaborate, lunch or dinner cruises (adult/child €55/35). Innovative **Bordeaux Be Boat** (05 47 74 41 25; www.bordeauxbeboat.fr) offers half-day or day cruises to wineries and other riverside sites inaccessible to larger boats.

SHOPPING

Europe's longest pedestrian shopping street, rue Ste-Catherine, links place de la Victoire and place de la Comédie; the 19th-century shopping arcade **Galerie Bordelaise** (rue de la Porte Dijeaux & rue Ste-Catherine; hours vary) is nearby. Luxury fashion boutiques lace the Triangle d'Or ('Golden

Active Bordeaux

Rustic Vines (☎06 42 73 75 33, 06 89 12 13 35; http://rusticvinestours.com; 26 rue de la Devise; ⌚9am-1pm) Guided bike tours in and around the city.

Piscine Judaïque (☎05 56 51 48 31; 164 rue Judaïque; adult/child €4.95/3.55; ⌚hours vary Tue-Sun, to 9.30pm Thu) Swim in an art deco pool from 1936.

Skate Parc des Chartrons (quai des Chartrons; ⌚9am-10pm) Join other riders at this riverside skate park.

Hangar Darwin (☎09 53 01 86 22; www.hangardarwin.org; 87 quai des Queyries; €5; ⌚4-9pm Tue, Thu & Fri, 2-7pm Wed, Sat & Sun, 2-7pm Tue-Sun during school holidays; 🚊Maréchal Niel, 🚊Place Stalingrad) Edgy skateboarding venue in an old hangar.

Triangle') formed by cours Georges Clemenceau, cours de l'Intendance and allées de Tourny. Trendy independent boutiques and design shops are concentrated on rue St-James in the St-Pierre quarter and rue Notre-Dame in Chartrons.

Blue Madone — Vintage

(☎05 57 30 25 13; www.facebook.com/blue.madone.mode.vintage.creation; 59 rue du Loup; ⌚11am-7pm Tue-Sat) Vintage designer fashion for men and women is the mainstay of Mathilde Milande's exquisitely arranged boutique, peppered from head to toe with an enchanting medley of retro lampshades, furniture and plants. Part of the space ensnares the in situ *ateliers* (workshops) of seven local designers specialising in jewellery, floral art, painted textiles, leatherwork, fashion and upholstery. Watch them at work.

L'Intendant — Wine

(www.intendant.com; 2 allées de Tourny; ⌚10am-7.30pm Mon-Sat) Welcome to what must be the grandest wine shop in the whole of France. A magnificent central staircase spiralling up five floors is surrounded by cylindrical shelves holding 15,000 bottles of regional wine at this highly respected *caviste* (wine cellar). Bottle prices range from €7 to thousands of euros. Watch for tastings most Saturdays.

Do You Speak Français? — Concept Store

(☎06 24 99 64 12; www.facebook.com/doyouspeakfrancais; 93 rue Notre Dame; ⌚11am-7pm Tue-Sat) Gaëlle and Maxime are the creative duo behind this inspiring concept store stocking fashionable tote bags, T-shirts, fashion accessories and homewares. The boutique is easy to spot – look for the wrought-iron balcony painted candy-floss-pink above the ground-floor shop front.

Marché des Capucins — Market

(http://marchedescapucins.com; place des Capucins; ⌚6am-1pm Tue-Sun) A classic Bordeaux experience is a Saturday morning spent slurping oysters and white wine from a seafood stand in the city's legendary covered food market. Stalls overflowing with fruit, veg, cheese, meats, fish, bread and all sorts fill the space to bursting.

Au Comptoir Bordelais — Food & Drinks

(www.lecomptoirbordelais.com; 1 rue Piliers de Tutelle; ⌚9am-7.30pm) Rev up taste buds in this gourmet boutique selling local and regional food and drink specialities. Be tempted by local cheese, *canalés* (sand-castle-shaped cakes from Bordeaux), *bouchons de Bordeaux* (cork-shaped pastries filled with almonds), *raisins au Sauternes* (chocolate-enrobed raisins soaked in Sauternes wine), salted caramels, chocolate sardines, olive oils, sauces and condiments, craft beers, wine... The list is endless.

EATING

Les Halles de Bacalan — Food Hall $

(☎05 56 80 63 65; www.facebook.com/hallesdebacalan; 149 quai de Bacalan; ⌚8am-2.30pm & 5.30-8.30pm Tue & Wed, to 10pm Thu & Fri, 8am-2am Sat, 8am-5pm Sun) At home in a waterfront hangar opposite La Cité du Vin, this gleaming state-of-the-art market hall is a fantastic spot to grab a quick gourmet bite. Some 20 upmarket stalls cooking up everything from fish, burgers and meat to oysters, poultry, Italian products and cheese serve a daily menu. Seating is at bar stools or outside overlooking the wet docks.

Halle Boca International $

(http://halleboca.com; quai de la Palatade) As part of the ambitious Euratlantique development project that continues apace until 2020, derelict abattoirs on the riverfront have been transformed into this state-of-the-art food mall with covered market, gourmet food boutiques, cafes and bars. Boca, should you be wondering, is an abbreviation of Bordeaux ('BO') and 'Commerces & Alimentation' (CA) or 'Business & Food'.

Brasserie Le Bordeaux Cafe $$

(☎05 57 30 43 46; https://bordeaux.intercontinental.com; 2-5 place de la Comédie; 2-/3-course lunch menu from €29/39, mains €27; ⏰7am-10.30pm) To dine à la Gordon Ramsay without breaking the bank, reserve a table at his elegant belle époque brasserie with an interesting, Anglo-Franco hybrid cuisine – local Arcachon oysters, fish and chips, Gascon pork pie with piccalilli, braised beef chuck, hand-cut tartare – and a parasol-shaded pavement terrace overlooking people-busy place de la Comédie. Weekend brunch (€68) is a local hot date.

Le Bouchon Bordelais French $$

(☎05 56 44 33 00; www.bouchon-bordelais.com; 2 rue Courbin; 2-/3-course lunch menu from €23/39, 7-course dinner menu €55, mains €21) Seasonal market produce and a generous pinch of creativity form the backbone of this *bistrot coloré* (colourful bistro), tucked down a backstreet lane between place de la Bourse and place de la Comédie. With its exposed stone walls and terracotta floor tiles, interior decor is 100% traditional and quaint – the menu not.

Au Bistrot French $$

(☎06 63 54 21 14; www.facebook.com/aubistrotbordeaux; 61 place des Capucins; mains €18-24; ⏰noon-2.30pm & 7-11pm Wed-Sun) There's nothing flashy or fancy about this hardcore French bistro, an ode to traditional market cuisine with charismatic François front of house and talented French-Thai chef Jacques In'On in the kitchen. Marinated herrings, lentil salad topped with a poached egg, half a roast pigeon or a feisty *andouillette* (tripe sausage) roasted in the oven – 80% of produce is local or from the surrounding Aquitaine region.

La Boîte à Huîtres Seafood $$

(☎05 56 81 64 97; 36 cours du Chapeau Rouge; 12 oysters €16-32; ⏰noon-2pm & 6-11pm Tue-Sat, 10am-2pm Sun) The Oyster Box is the best place in Bordeaux to munch on fresh Arcachon oysters. Traditionally they're served with sausage but you can have them in a number of different forms, including with that other southwest delicacy, foie gras. They'll also pack them up so you can take them away for a riverfront picnic.

La Tupina French $$$

(☎05 56 91 56 37; www.latupina.com; 6 rue Porte de la Monnaie; lunch menu €18, dinner menus €44-52, mains €20-32; ⏰noon-2pm & 7-11pm Tue-Sun) Filled with the aroma of soup simmering inside a *tupina* ('kettle' in Basque) over an open fire, this iconic bistro is feted for its seasonal southwestern French fare: calf kidneys with fries cooked

Signature Cakes

Learn how to make *canelés,* the city's most famous cakes, at **Café Baillardran** (☎09 67 79 42 74; www.baillardran.com; 36 place Gambetta; ⏰8.30am-9pm Mon-Sat, 9am-7pm Sun). This Saturday-morning cookery class (two hours, €76 including tasting) shows the art behind these sandcastle-shaped cakes. Baked in a copper mould, they have a moist centre and caramelised crust, and are flavoured with a dash of vanilla and rum. Café Baillardran is also a pleasant spot for a *café gourmand* (€5.70), aka a coffee with a sweet treat on the side.

Day Trip to St-Émilion

The medieval village of St-Émilion, 47km east of Bordeaux, perches above vineyards renowned for producing full-bodied, deeply coloured red wines. Named after a miracle-working Benedictine monk who lived in a cave here between AD 750 and 767, it soon became a stop on pilgrimage routes, and the village and its vineyards are now Unesco-listed.

Reserve a 40-minute tasting at **Maison du Vin de St-Émilion** (☎05 57 55 50 55; www.maisonduvinsaintemilion.com; place Pierre Meyrat; ⊙9.30am-6.30pm May-Oct, 9.30am-12.30pm & 2-6pm Nov-Apr), or a formal wine-tasting course (in French and English; €25 per person, 1½ hours). In-the-know foodies adore **La Terrasse Rouge** (☎05 57 24 47 05; www.laterrasserouge.com; 1 Château La Dominique; 3-course menu €39, mains €16-22; ⊙noon-3pm & 7-10.30pm Jun-Sep, noon-3pm & 7-10.30pm Fri & Sat, noon-3pm Sun-Thu Oct-May) for its extraordinary wine list and locally sourced seasonal produce; advance reservations essential.

The **tourist office** (☎05 57 55 28 28; www.saint-emilion-tourisme.com; place des Créneaux; ⊙9.30am-7.30pm Jul & Aug, shorter hours rest of year) has maps of the village and surrounding vineyards, as well as walking and cycling trails. It also rents bicycles (€15/18 per half-/full day). From Bordeaux, direct trains run daily to/from St-Émilion (€9.50, 35 minutes).

in goose fat, milk-fed lamb, tripe and goose wings. Dining is farmhouse-style, in a maze of elegant rooms decorated with vintage photographs, antique furniture and silver tableware.

La Grande Maison Gastronomy **$$$**
(☎05 35 38 16 16; https://lagrandemaison-bordeaux.com; 10 rue Labottière; 3-course lunch menu €75, 4-/6-course dinner menu €175/195, mains €90-110; ⊙noon-1.30pm & 7-9.30pm Tue-Sat) Bordeaux winemaker Bernard Magrez is the creative clout behind this luxurious, five-star hotel restaurant, overseen by twin Michelin-starred chef Pierre Gagnaire. As one would expect of a château, dining is refined and traditional in a fireplace-clad dining room. Cuisine is firmly routed in the local *terroir* (land) and the wine list is sensational (but then Monsieur Magrez does own four Bordeaux Grands Crus).

DRINKING & NIGHTLIFE

Utopia Cafe, Bar
(☎05 56 79 39 25; www.cinemas-utopia.org; 3 place Camille Jullian; ⊙10am-1am summer, to 10.30pm winter) At home in an old church, this much-venerated art address is a local institution – its sunny terrace alone is fabulous. Art-house cinema, mellow cafe, hot lunch spot and bar rolled into one, it is one of the top addresses in the city to mingle over a drink, *tartine* (open sandwich; €7), salad (€13), or hot or cold organic veg soup (€6.50) with locals any time of day.

Le Point Rouge Cocktail Bar
(☎05 56 94 94 40; www.pointrouge-bdx.com; 1 quai de Paludate; ⊙6pm-2am Mon-Sat) A black steel door marked with a small, red doorbell (aka 'le point rouge', or 'the red dot') heralds the entrance to this trendy speakeasy, a theatrical scarlet affair hidden in the basement of a once-grandiose riverfront *hôtel particulier* (mansion). The encyclopedia of a cocktail list traces the history of cocktails in some 100 different elaborate creations. Ring the bell to enter.

Night Beach Bar

(https://bordeaux.intercontinental.com; 2-5 place de la Comédie, 7th fl, Grand Hôtel de Bordeaux; ⌚7pm-1am late May-late Sep) There is no finer, more elegant or romantic rooftop bar in Bordeaux than this achingly hip, drinking-and-hobnobbing joint on the 7th floor of historic Grand Hôtel de Bordeaux. Views of the city, River Garonne and vineyards beyond are a panoramic 360° degrees. French-chic seating is sofa style beneath parasols and DJ sets play at weekends.

Bar à Vin Wine Bar

(☎05 56 00 43 47; http://baravin.bordeaux.com; 3 cours du 30 Juillet; ⌚11am-10pm Mon-Sat) The decor – herringbone parquet, grandiose stained-glass depicting the godly Bacchus and sky-high ceiling – matches the reverent air that fills this wine bar inside the hallowed halls of the Maison du Vin de Bordeaux. Dozens of Bordeaux wines are served by the glass (€3.50 to €8) which, paired with a cheese or charcuterie platter, transport foodies straight to heaven. Gracious sommeliers know their *vin*.

I.Boat Club

(☎05 56 10 48 37; www.iboat.eu; quai Armand Lalande, Bassins à Flot 1; ⌚7.30pm-6am) Hip hop, rock, indie pop, psyche blues rock, punk and hardcore are among the varied sounds that blast out of this fun nightclub and concert venue, afloat a decommissioned ferry moored in the increasingly trendy, industrial Bassins à Flot district in the north of the city. Live music starts at 7pm, with DJ sets kicking in on the club dance floor from 11.30pm.

INFORMATION

Maison du Tourisme de la Gironde (☎05 56 52 61 40; www.gironde-tourisme.fr; 9 rue Fondaudège; ⌚9am-6pm Mon-Fri, 10am-1pm & 2-6.30pm Sat) Information on the surrounding Gironde *département*.

Tourist Office (☎05 56 00 66 00; www.bordeaux-tourisme.com; 12 cours du 30 Juillet; ⌚9am-6.30pm Mon-Sat, to 5pm Sun) Runs an excellent range of city and regional tours; reserve in advance online or in situ. It also rents pocket modems to hook you up with wi-fi. There's a small but helpful **branch** (☎05 56 00 66 00; rue Charles Domercq, Espace Modalis, Parvis Sud; ⌚9.30am-12.30pm & 2-6pm Mon-Fri) at the train station.

GETTING THERE & AWAY

AIR

Aéroport de Bordeaux (Bordeaux Airport; ☎information 05 56 34 50 50; www.bordeaux.aeroport.fr; Mérignac), also known as Bordeaux-Mérignac, is 10km west of the city centre. Domestic and increasing numbers of international flights to/from many western European and North African destinations use one of three neighbouring terminals here.

TRAIN

Bordeaux is one of France's major rail-transit points and just six hours from London by Eurostar (www.eurostar.com), with a change of train in Paris.

Paris Gare Montparnasse €69, 3¼ hours, at least 16 daily

GETTING AROUND

BICYCLE

Public bike-sharing scheme **V³** (www.vcub.fr), run by local public-transport company TBM, has 1800 banana-yellow bicycles available for use at bike stations all over the city. Pay €1.60 to access a bike for 24 hours, plus €2 per hour after the first 30 minutes (free) is up; you'll need to initially register online or with your credit card at a V³ station.

PUBLIC TRANSPORT

Urban buses and trams are run by TBM (www.infotbm.com) between 5am and 1am. Get timetable information and tickets from its **Espace des Quinconces** (☎05 57 57 88 88; www.infotbm.com; Esplanade des Quinconces; ⌚7am-7pm Mon-Fri, 9am-7pm Sat) information office, the main bus and tram hub. Single tickets (€1.60) are sold on board buses, and from machines at tram stops (stamp your ticket onboard).

FRENCH ALPS

In This Chapter

French Alps at a Glance...

High up in the French Alps, it's enthralling to imagine the forces that shaped these colossal peaks. The African and Eurasian tectonic plates collided some 35 million years ago, forcing the land skyward into a 1000km chain of saw-edged mountains. Rumbling across seven European countries, the Alps reach their height in France, at Mont Blanc (4810m).

Routes into the Alps' other-worldly realms are many: aboard cable cars that fly to knee-trembling heights, or in the company of mountain guides who set out into wintry oblivion. Winter or summer, this forbidding terrain commands respect: welcome to one of Europe's most epic landscapes.

Two Days in the French Alps

Acclimatise on day one with some gentle skiing (winter) or hiking (summer) in **Chamonix** (p266). Join the après-ski crowd in **Bar'd Up** (p267) before tucking into some cheesy **Savoyard specialities** (p264). On day two, hit the heady heights of the **Aiguille du Midi** (p260) and beyond into Italy with the cable-car ride of a lifetime. Cap it off with a gourmet feast at **Le Cap Horn** (p267).

Four Days in the French Alps

Devote day three to more of the exceptional ski slopes or hiking trails of **Chamonix** (p266); **Lac Blanc** (p269) is a summertime essential, while experienced skiers can hire a guide and tackle the challenging **Vallée Blanche** (p263). On day four, trip along to **Annecy** (p270) to see the glorious old town, stroll lakeside and savour a Michelin-starred dinner at **La Ciboulette** (p271).

Parc Naturel Régional du Haut-Jura
Lake Geneva (Lac Léman)
Col de la Faucille
Gex
Thonon-les-Bains
SWITZERLAND
Aiguille du Midi (3842m)
Oyonnax
Aéroport de Genève
Bourg-en-Bresse
Geneva
Annemasse
Les Gets
Martigny
Nantua
Bonneville
Col des Montets
Cluses
Allonzier-la-Caille
Mont Dolent (3819m)
Ambérieu-en-Bugey
Sallanches
Chamonix
Punta Helbronner (3462m)
Rhône
Annecy
Menthon-St-Bernard
Mont Blanc (4810m)
Sévrier
Talloires
Flumet
Mer de Glace
La Grande Rochère (3326m)
FRANCE
ITALY
Ugine
Colle del Piccolo San Bernardo
Parc Régional du Massif des Bauges
Albertville
Bourg St-Maurice
Bourgoin-Jallieu
Chambéry
Val d'Isère
Tignes
Parc National de la Vanoise
St-Martin de Belleville
0 20 km
0 10 miles

See Chamonix Map (p268)

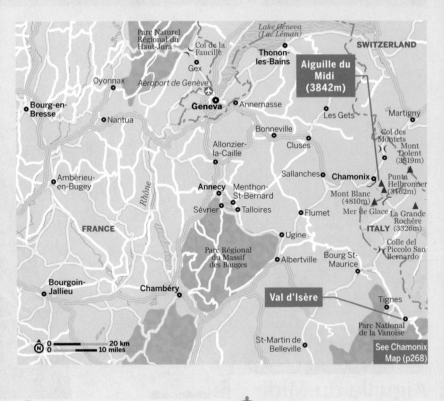

Arriving in the French Alps

Geneva (Cointrin) Airport In neighbouring Switzerland; has lots of cheap flights across Europe. Grenoble, Chambéry and Lyon are other major points of entry by air.

Chamonix & Annecy train stations Both are just footsteps from the town centre.

Tunnel du Mont Blanc (www.atmb.com) An 11.5km road link between Chamonix and Courmayeur in Italy's Val d'Aosta.

Where to Stay

From the humblest *gîtes* (self-catering accommodation) to the grandest slope-side pleasure palaces, the French Alps offer every stratum of accommodation. Demand skyrockets in ski resorts during school holidays and the Tour de France, so advance planning is essential. Ski resort tourist offices tend to have an adjoining accommodation desk. In the mountains, many places close for a while in spring and autumn.

Aiguille du Midi

The great rocky fang of the Aiguille du Midi (3842m), rising from the Mont Blanc massif, is one of Chamonix' most distinctive features. Soar high by cable car to marvel at the heavenly panorama at the top.

Great For...

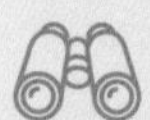

☑ **Don't Miss**

Standing on glass-floored **Step into the Void** (and hoping your knees don't tremble).

Téléphérique de l'Aiguille du Midi

If you can handle the altitude, the 360-degree views of the French, Swiss and Italian Alps from the summit are (quite literally) breathtaking. During most of the year, you can float in a cable car from downtown Chamonix, over forests and beyond the tree line, up to the Aiguille du Midi on the vertiginous **Téléphérique de l'Aiguille du Midi** (www.compagniedumontblanc.co.uk; place de l'Aiguille du Midi; adult/child return to Aiguille du Midi €61.50/52.30, to Plan de l'Aiguille €32.50/27.60; 1st ascent btwn 6.30am & 8.10am, last btwn 4pm & 5.30pm, mid-Dec–early Nov) – a series of two cable cars and a gondola.

In summer (especially mid-July to mid-August) there are massive lines (we're talking two-hour waits) so you may need

Need to Know

It's worth reserving ahead, particularly in high summer or during sky season. Check weather and buy tickets online at www.compagniedumontblanc.co.uk.

Take a Break

Savoyard classics like *boîte chaude*, a 'hot box' of baked cheese with potatoes and smoked ham, are served at Le Panier des 4 Saisons (p267), a short walk from the cable car's lower station.

★ Top Tip

Dress warmly: temperatures range from -10°C (summer) to -25°C (winter).

to obtain a boarding card (marked with the number of your departing and returning cable cars) along with your ticket. Essential items to include in your daypack: sunglasses, sun hat, sunscreen, warm clothes, sturdy shoes, snacks and water.

Step into the Void

Halfway up, **Plan de l'Aiguille** (2317m) is a terrific place to start hikes or to paraglide. Count on paying around €220 per adult to fly in tandem with other colourful paragliders in the sky wheeling down from heady heights. Up top at a breathtaking 3842m, you can gorge on the mountain panorama in literally every direction – including 1000m straight down – thanks to the glass-floored **Step into the Void**, a transparent viewing platform.

Télécabine Panoramique Mont Blanc

From the Aiguille du Midi, between late May and late September, you can continue for a further 50 minutes of mind-blowing Alpine scenery – think glaciers and spurs, seracs and shimmering ice fields – in the smaller bubbles of the **Télécabine Panoramique Mont Blanc** (www.montblancnaturalresort.com; Aiguille du Midi; adult/child return from Chamonix €89/75.70) to Pointe Helbronner (3466m) on the France–Italy border.

Skyway Monte Bianco

The spectacular, international cable car **Skyway Monte Bianco** (www.montebianco.com; Pointe Helbronner; single/return €37/49) continues 4km from Pointe Helbronner to Courmayeur in the Val d'Aosta, on the Italian side of Mont Blanc (Monte Bianco in Italian). The cars rotate a full 360 degrees, affording peerless views of Mont Blanc, the Matterhorn and Gran Paradiso.

La Vallée Blanche

Winter Skiing

Thrilling descents, glorious off-piste terrain and unbeatable Mont Blanc views – skiing in Chamonix is so fantastic that skiers don't even mind accessing the slopes using lots of land transport to and from the lifts.

Great For...

☑ Don't Miss

A world-famous *croûte aux fromages* at **Crèmerie du Glacier** (☎04 50 54 07 52; www.lacremerieduglacier.fr; 766 chemin de la Glacière; lunch menus €17-22, fondues €15-20; ⏲noon-2pm & 7-9pm mid-Dec–mid-May & late Jun–mid-Sep, closed Wed in winter).

Mountains loom large almost everywhere you look in Chamonix. Rediscovered as a tourist destination by Brits William Windham and Richard Pococke in 1741, Chamonix hosted the first-ever Winter Olympics in 1924. It has since become a wintertime playground of epic proportions, more than satisfying the most demanding skiers as well as the après-ski revellers who pack themselves into its boot-stompin' bars.

Ski Areas

Best for beginners are **Le Tour & Vallorcine**, **Les Planards**, **Les Chosalets**, **Les Houches** and **La Vormaine**. For speed and challenge, it has to be **Brévent-Flégère** (1030m to 2525m), above Chamonix, and **Les Grands Montets** (1235m to 3300m), accessible from the attractive village of Argentière, 9km north of the town. Boarders

Mont Blanc

STEPHENMEESE/GETTY IMAGES ©

seeking big air zip across to the kickers and rails at **Les Grands Montets** snow park and the natural halfpipe in Le Tour.

La Vallée Blanche

This jaw-dropping 2800m descent is probably Europe's most famous off-piste experience. Beginning at the Aiguille du Midi, the 20km route darts over the crevasse-riddled Mer de Glace glacier and returns to Chamonix through the forest. Skiers must be confident on red pistes and in good physical shape. The route can only be tackled with a *guide de haute montagne* (specially trained mountain guide).

Guided Adventures

Chamonix' most prestigious guides association, the **Compagnie des Guides de Chamonix** (☎04 50 53 00 88; www.chamonix-guides.com; 190 place de l'Église, Maison de la Montagne; ⊙8.30am-noon & 2.30-7.30pm mid-Dec–late Apr & mid-Jun–mid-Sep, closed Sun & Mon rest of year), which is nearly 200 years old, offers an impressive roll-call of outdoor activities, both winter and summer. High-mountain snowshoe walks, ice-climbing expeditions and heliskiing are all possible in winter, while summer brings the opportunity for trekking, canyoning and via ferrata trips.

Other recommended companies, offering extreme skiing expeditions, glacier trekking and other adventures, include **Association Internationale des Guides du Mont Blanc** (☎04 50 53 27 05; www.guides-du-montblanc.com; 9 passage de la Varlope) and **Chamonix Experience.** (☎04 50 93 23 14; www.chamex.com; 610 rte Blanche; ⊙9am-noon & 3-7pm Dec-early May, Jun-Sep)

Need to Know

Complete Mont Blanc low-down, trail information, weather and guides at Maison de la Montagne.

Take a Break

Lunch in a 250-year-old farmhouse at **Les Vieilles Luges** (http://lesvieillesluges.com; menus €20-35; ⊙noon-2pm Dec-Apr; ☎) in Les Houches. Cash only.

★ Top Tip

Chamonix' ski season runs from mid-December to mid-April. Buy lift passes at www.compagniedumontblanc.co.uk.

Lift Passes

Chamonix Le Pass (1/2/6 days €51.50/100/258.50) Most Chamonix ski domains, around 118km of pistes.

Mont Blanc Multipass (1/2/6 days €63/77/126) In summer, access to all lifts.

Mont Blanc Unlimited Pass (1/2/6 days €63.50/125/306) For serious skiers, access to the Chamonix Valley, Courmayeur in Italy, Verbier in Switzerland, and more.

View details of all passes and purchase online: www.montblancnaturalresort.com.

Val d'Isère town centre

Val d'Isère

Off-piste skiing and easy pistes, Michelin-starred gastronomy and farmhouse cooking, peaceful hikes and unbridled nightlife...all are gathered in twinkly Val d'Isère. Simultaneously chic and traditional, this mountain resort is a true crowd-pleaser.

Great For...

☑ Don't Miss

Farmhouse cheese and Savoyard sausage at **La Fermette de Claudine** (www.lafermettedeclaudine.com; Val Village; 🕗7am-8pm mid-Dec–Apr, Jul & Aug).

Hiking & Cycling

During Val d'Isère's summer season, from late June to the first weekend in September, hikers and cyclists flock. There are numerous hiking trails that wend from Val d'Isère into nearby **Parc National de la Vanoise** (☎04 79 62 30 54; www.vanoise-parc-national.fr). For more of a challenge, you can play (safely) among the cliffs at La Daille's two **via ferrata** fixed-cable routes.

Mountain biking is big in Val (it's forbidden within the national park) and there's an assortment of downhill trails for all levels. Five lifts are open to downhill cyclists as well as hikers (€10 per day).

Summer Skiing

Espace Killy (www.espacekilly.com; adult 1-/6-day pass €57/285, child 1-/6-day pass €46/228) is one of only two places in France that still

Hiking, Parc National de la Vanoise

JACQUES PIERRE/HEMIS.FR/GETTY IMAGES ©

has summer skiing, between early June and mid-July. Here it's on the Grande Motte and Pissaillas glaciers, near Tignes and Val d'Isère, respectively. A day's lift pass costs a knock-down €28.

Winter Sports

Val d'Isère and Tignes form Espace Killy, a giant for its scale – altitudes between 1550m and 3456m, 300km of pistes – and the length of its season (late November until very early May). The many ski schools include well-regarded **Top Ski** (☎04 79 06 14 80, 07 82 85 88 89; www.topski.fr; Immeuble Les Andes, av Olympique, Val Village; ⏰8.30am-7.30pm Dec-Apr) and **ESF** (☎La Daille 04 79 06 99 99, Val Village 04 79 06 02 34; www.esfvaldisere.com; place des Dolomites, Val Village; ⏰9.30am-12.30pm & 2.30-5pm Dec-Apr).

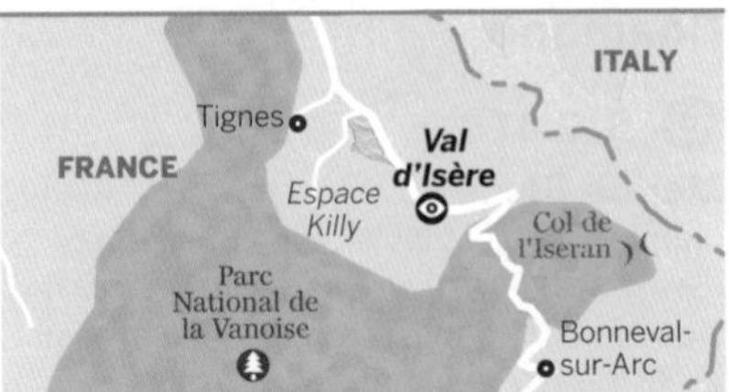

Need to Know

The state-of-the-art **tourist office** (www.valdisere.com; place Jacques Mouflier, Val Village; ⏰8.30am-7.30pm Sun-Fri, to 9pm Sat Dec-Apr & Jun-Aug; 📶) has activities info.

Take a Break

Dine at **L'Edelweiss** (www.restaurant-edelweiss-valdisere.com; Piste Mangard, Le Fornet; 2-/3-course menus €25/30), halfway up Le Fornet's Mangard blue run.

★ Top Tip

The **Village des Enfants** (www.village-des-enfants.fr; Rond Point des Pistes, Val Village; child 3-13yr 1/5 half-days €32/135) offers a nursery and activities for kids as young as six months.

Fine Dining

Even if you aren't staying at chic **Hôtel-Restaurant Avancher** (www.avancher.com/restaurant-and-bar; rte du Prariond), it's worth booking a table to enjoy its classy bistro meals. Book ahead for a spot at **L'Atelier d'Edmond** (www.atelier-edmond.com; rue du Fornet, Le Fornet; menus €115-175), where local ingredients are imaginatively transformed.

Après-Ski

Winter is party time across the French Alps. Most legendary is **La Folie Douce** (www.lafoliedouce.com; La Daille; ⏰9am-5pm mid-Dec–mid-Apr), where DJs and live bands fuel a party at the top of the La Daille cable car...from 2.30pm. Down in town, **Le Petit Danois** (www.lepetitdanois.com; rue du Coin; ⏰9.30am-1.30am Dec-Apr) gets busy late with DJs and live music. The sophisticate's choice is **La Cave...sur le Comptoir** (av Olympique; ⏰4.30pm-1am Dec-Apr), serving top-notch wine and cheese plates.

Chamonix

SIGHTS

Mer de Glace Glacier

France's largest glacier, the 200m-deep 'Sea of Ice', flows 7km down the northern side of Mont Blanc, scarred with crevasses formed by the immense pressure of its 90m-per-year movement. The **Train du Montenvers** (☎04 50 53 22 75; www.montblancnaturalresort.com; 35 place de la Mer de Glace; adult/child return €32.50/27.60; ⏲10am-4.30pm late Dec–mid-Mar, to 5pm mid-Mar–Apr), a picturesque, 5km-long cog railway opened in 1909, links Gare du Montenvers with Montenvers (1913m), from where a cable car descends to the glacier and, 420 stairs later, the **Grotte de Glace** FREE. Also worth a visit is the **Glaciorium**, an exhibition on the formation (and future) of glaciers.

Le Brévent Viewpoint

The highest peak on the western side of the Chamonix Valley, Le Brévent (2525m) has tremendous views of the Mont Blanc massif, myriad hiking trails through a nature reserve, ledges to paraglide from and some vertiginous black runs.

Reach it by linking the **Télécabine de Planpraz** (☎04 50 53 22 75; www.compagniedumontblanc.co.uk; 29 rte Henriette d'Angeville; adult/child return €32.50/27.60; ⏲from 8.50am Dec-Apr, Jun-Sep & late Oct-Nov), 400m west of the tourist office, with the **Téléphérique du Brévent** (www.compagniedumontblanc.co.uk; from Planpraz return adult/child €14.50/12.30; ⏲mid-Dec–mid-Apr & mid-Jun–mid-Sep). Plenty of family-friendly trails begin at **Planpraz** (2000m), and the Liaison cable car connects to the adjacent ski fields of La Flégère.

Musée Alpin Museum

(☎04 50 53 25 93; www.facebook.com/museealpinchamonixcc; 89 av Michel Croz; adult/child €5.90/free; ⏲2-6pm Wed-Mon Sep, late Dec-May, 10am-noon & 2-7pm Wed-Mon Jul, Aug & school holidays) This diverting two-level museum allows you to wander through Chamonix history, from butter moulds and farming tools of yore to the dawn of the 18th-century tourism boom. There's mountain

Chamonix

history galore, including the early days of the high mountain guides and fascinating stories of the first female alpinists, as well as 19th-century oil paintings of the valley's timeless landscape.

ACTIVITIES

In summer, hikers can take their pick of 350km of spectacular marked trails, many easy to get to by cable car (running mid-June to September). The challenging **Grand Balcon Nord** (⏲Jun-Oct) is up around 2000m, while the three-hour **Petit Balcon Sud** (from Argentière to Servoz) is slightly above the valley's villages at 1250m.

Cycling

Lower-altitude trails, such as the **Petit Balcon Sud** (1250m) running from Argentière to Servoz, are perfect for biking. Most outdoor-activity specialists arrange guided mountain-biking expeditions. Talk to well-established bike and board shop Zero G (p269) about gear hire and trail advice.

Mountaineering & High-Alpine Tours

Local guide companies offer exhilarating climbs for those with the necessary skill, experience and stamina. Options include **rock-climbing classes** (from €44 for a two-hour lesson to €620 for an intensive granite-climbing weekend workshop) or the incomparable **Mont Blanc ascent** (from €840 to €1650). Contact the Compagnie des Guides de Chamonix (p263).

EATING

Pizzeria des Moulins Pizza $

(☎06 47 07 75 10, 06 68 70 99 82; www.facebook.com/pizzeriadesmoulins; 107 rue des Moulins; mains from €15; ⏲noon-2.30pm & 6.30-11pm) Cham's best pizzas, piled with buffalo mozzarella, forest mushrooms and Savoyard ham, puff up in the oven of this little gourmet joint. Reservations are essential for dining in, but you can always get takeaway if (or rather, when) it's packed with ravenous diners.

Chamonix Nightlife

From après-ski (or hike) drinks around 4pm to bars that buzz until the early hours, Chamonix nightlife rocks. For après-ski G&T, head to low-key **La Jonction** (☎06 34 02 96 88; www.facebook.com/jonctioncoffee; 75 av Ravanel le Rouge; ⏲8am-8pm; 📶) and mingle with fellow snow-heads. Anglophone dive **Bar'd Up** (123 rue des Moulins; ⏲3pm-late) is the friendliest, grungiest place in Cham, on **rue des Moulins**, a great street for a bar crawl. A 10-minute walk northeast and you'll find Canadian-run **MBC** (Micro Brasserie de Chamonix; ☎04 50 53 61 59; www.mbchx.com; 350 rte du Bouchet; ⏲4pm-2am Mon-Fri, 10am-2am Sat & Sun), which pours its own locally made blonde, stout, pale ale and German-style wheat beer.

Le Panier des 4 Saisons French $$

(☎04 50 53 98 77; www.restaurant-panierdes4saisons.com; 262 rue du Docteur Paccard; menus €30-34, mains €20-32; ⏲7-10pm mid-Dec–May & Jul-Oct) Brimming with chatter and bonhomie, this semiformal, wood-panelled establishment serves substantial, Italian-influenced dishes such as deer served with polenta gnocchi and vegetable and ricotta tart, along with Savoyard classics like *boîte chaude* (a 'hot box' of baked cheese with potatoes and smoked ham).

Le Cap Horn French, Seafood $$$

(☎04 50 21 80 80; www.caphorn-chamonix.com; 74 rue des Moulins; lunch/dinner menus from €23/42; ⏲noon-3pm & 7-10.30pm; 🌶👪) Housed in a candelit, two-storey chalet

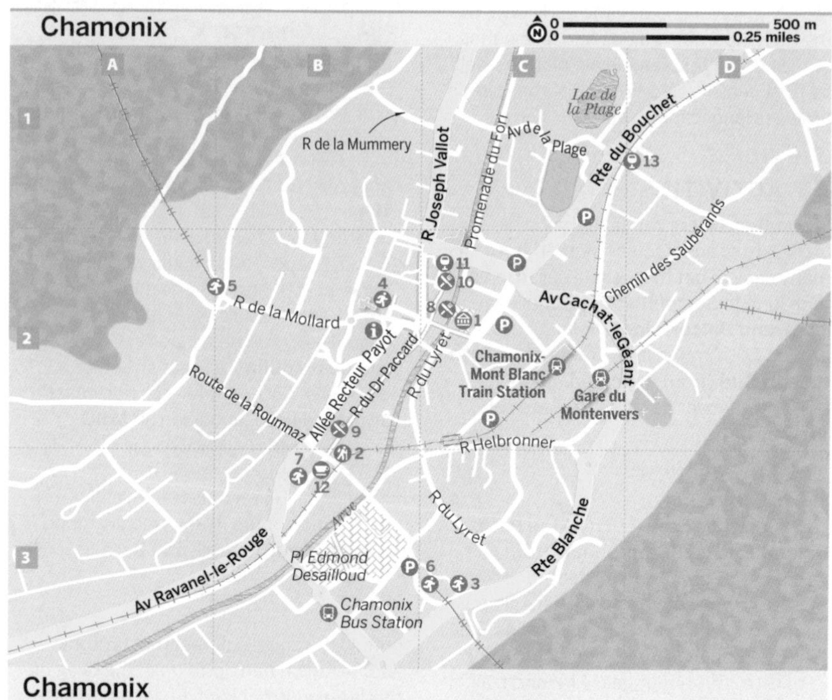

Chamonix

Sights
1 Musée Alpin C2

Activities, Courses & Tours
2 Association Internationale des Guides du Mont Blanc B3
3 Chamonix Experience C3
4 Compagnie des Guides de Chamonix B2
5 Télécabine de Planpraz B2
6 Téléphérique de l'Aiguille du Midi C3
7 Zero G B3

Eating
8 Le Cap Horn C2
9 Le Panier des 4 Saisons B2
10 Pizzeria des Moulins C2

Drinking & Nightlife
11 Bar'd Up C2
12 La Jonction B3
13 MBC D1

decorated with model sailing boats – joint homage to the Alps and Cape Horn – this highly praised restaurant, opened in 2012, serves French and Asian dishes such as pan-seared duck breast with honey and soy sauce, an ample sushi menu, and a marvellous range of seafood like red tuna *taquitos* (rolled tacos) and fish stew. Reserve for dinner Friday and Saturday in winter and summer.

INFORMATION

PGHM (☎04 50 53 16 89; www.pghm-chamonix.com; 69 rue de la Mollard) Mountain-rescue service for the Mont Blanc area.

Tourist Office (☎04 50 53 00 24; www.chamonix.com; 85 place du Triangle de l'Amitié; ⏰9am-7pm mid-Jun–mid-Sep & mid-Dec–Apr, 9am-12.30pm & 2-6pm rest of year, closed Sun Oct & Nov; 📶) Information on accommodation, day trips, conditions up on the mountain and cultural events.

 GETTING THERE & AWAY

BUS

It's worth dropping by the **bus station** (☎04 50 53 01 15; 234 av Courmayeur, Chamonix Sud; ⏰ticket office 8am-noon & 1.15-6.30pm in winter, shorter hours rest of year) for timetables and reservations or you can book tickets online on Ouibus (www.ouibus.com). Direct services reach Annecy (from €10, 1½ hours, six daily) and Lyon Perrache (from €26, 3½ to 4½ hours, at least one daily). International routes include Geneva (Switzerland) and Courmayeur (Italy).

CAR

Chamonix is linked to Courmayeur in Italy's Val d'Aosta by the 11.5km-long **Tunnel du Mont Blanc** (www.atmb.com; toll one way/return €44.40/55.40). The valley's only car-hire company is **Europcar** (☎04 50 53 63 40; www.europcar.com; 36 place de la Gare; ⏰8.30am-noon & 2-6pm Mon-Sat).

TRAIN

The scenic, narrow-gauge **Mont Blanc Express** (www.mont-blanc-express.com) glides from the Swiss town of Martigny to Chamonix, taking in Argentière and Vallorcine en route.

For destinations around France, including Lyon, Annecy and Paris, you'll need to change trains at St-Gervais-Les-Bains-Le-Fayet first (€11.40, 45 minutes, hourly).

 **Hiking to Lac Blanc**

Surrounded by the razor peaks of the Aiguilles Rouges, the jewel-like glacial **Lac Blanc** is usually accessible to hikers from June through October. Two gentle hours from **Télésiège de l'Index** (www.compagniedumontblanc.co.uk; adult/child return from Les Praz €29/24.70; ⏰Dec-Apr & Jun-Sep) leads along the western valley to the glacial lake (2352m). Experienced trekkers can take the 1050 vertical-metre hike from Argentière (3½ hours one way). Reserve a place at the **Refuge du Lac Blanc** (☎06 02 05 08 82; www.refugedulacblanc.fr; Les Houches; dm incl half board adult/child €56/50; ⏰mid-Jun–Sep), a wooden chalet famed for its top-of-Europe Mont Blanc views.

GETTING AROUND

BICYCLE

You can hire cross-country, mountain and downhill bikes from friendly, well-established **Zero G** (☎04 50 53 01 01; www.zerogchamonix.com; 90 av Ravanel-le-Rouge; ⏰9am-12.30pm & 3.30-7pm), which also rents out snowboard gear.

BUS

Public buses run by **Chamonix Bus** (www.chamonix-bus.com) serve all the towns, villages, ski lifts and attractions in the Chamonix Valley, from Argentière (Col des Montets in summer) in the northeast, to Servoz and Les Houches in the southwest. All buses are free with a Carte d'Hôte (Guest Card), except the wintertime Chamo' Nuit night buses linking Chamonix with Argentière and Les Houches (last departures from Chamonix 11.30pm or midnight; €2).

CAR

Parking in Chamonix involves either paid parking in the centre or free park-and-ride in the outskirts. There are numerous open-air and covered car parks in town (usually free for less than an hour, and around €12.50 for 24 hours). There are also several offering free parking on Chamonix' outskirts, five of them towards Argentière, linked to the city centre by a free shuttle bus.

TAXI

For a taxi, try **Alp Taxi** (☎06 81 78 79 51) or **Arve Taxi** (☎06 07 19 70 36), or head to the taxi rank

MNY-JHEE / SHUTTERSTOCK ©

Annecy

in front of the train station. Booked taxi transfers to/from Geneva Airport cost in the region of €160 to €200.

Annecy

Nestled by the northwestern shore of its namesake lake, Annecy is the jewel of the Haute-Savoie. Made great by the medieval Counts of Geneva and augmented by the Dukes of Savoy, Annecy still has numerous 16th- and 17th-century buildings, now awash in shades of peach and rose and housing restaurants, bakeries and boutiques. Canals trickle through town, earning Annecy its reputation as an 'Alpine Venice'.

SIGHTS & ACTIVITIES

When the sun's out, the beaches fringing the lake beckon. Some are patrolled in July and August, including **Plage d'Albigny** (av du Petit Port) FREE and **Plage des Marquisats** (rue des Marquisats) FREE, when they can become very crowded.

Château d'Annecy Castle

(☎04 50 33 87 34; www.musees.agglo-annecy.fr; place du Château; adult/child €5.50/3; ⏱10am-noon & 2-5pm Wed-Mon Oct-May, 10.30am-6pm daily Jun-Sep) Commanding views across the ochre rooftops of the Vieille Ville (Old Town) to the Massif des Bauges, the Château d'Annecy is at once imposing and elegant, a marriage between medieval defensive and decorative architectural styles. Residence of the counts of Geneva during the 13th and 14th centuries, a military barracks in the 1940s, and classified as a historical monument in the 1950s, today it's filled with regional art, from medieval sculpture and Savoyard furniture to Alpine landscape painting and contemporary art.

Palais de l'Isle Museum

(☎04 56 49 40 37; www.musees.agglo-annecy.fr; 3 passage de l'Île; adult/child €3.80/2; ⏱10.30am-6pm daily Jul-Sep, 10am-noon & 2-5pm Wed-Mon Oct-Jun) Sitting on a triangular islet surrounded by the Canal du Thiou, the Palais de l'Isle has been a lordly residence, a courthouse, a mint and a prison according to records dating back to the

14th century. Chambers within this stocky stone building now house permanent exhibits on local history, from medieval coins to the industrial 19th century, plus occasional temporary art exhibits.

Takamaka Outdoors
(☎04 50 45 60 61; https://annecy.takamaka.fr; 23 rue du Faubourg Ste-Claire; ⊙9am-noon & 2-6pm Mon-Fri, 10am-5pm Sat & Sun) Offers a wide range of outdoor adventures with licensed guides, including tandem paragliding (€95), rafting (€42 to €62), rock climbing (€49) and waterskiing (€42).

Roul' ma Poule Cycling
(☎04 50 27 86 83; www.annecy-location-velo.com; 4 rue des Marquisats; ⊙10am-6pm) This family bike shop rents rollerblades (€15/22 per half-day/24 hours), bicycles (€15/24), tandems (€33/52) and kids' trailers (€15/24), and is a great source for day-trip recommendations.

 EATING

Food Market Market $
(cnr rues Ste-Claire & de la République; ⊙7am-1pm Sun, Tue & Fri) This open-air food market reels you in with the scent of garlic-fried frogs' legs and Savoyard cheeses. Honey, gingerbread and *saucisson sec* (dried regional sausage) will tempt self-caterers, plus there's grab-and-go food such as steaming sausages and tureens of *choucroute garnie* (dressed cabbage stew).

Le Denti Seafood, French $$
(☎04 50 64 21 17; 25bis av de Loverchy; lunch menus €24, dinner menus €33-48; ⊙noon-1pm Thu-Mon, 7.30-9pm Mon & Thu-Sat) A few blocks south of the old town, this unassuming restaurant follows the seasons, drawing inspiration from local market produce. The menu's carefully assembled (if light on choice), and excels at seafood, like pollack on confit of sweet peppers or Mediterranean *denti* (after which the restaurant is named). Nonpescatarians also dine well on rotating specials (mustard-lashed pork cheek when we last visited).

La Ciboulette Gastronomy $$$
(☎04 50 45 74 57; www.laciboulette-annecy.com; Cour du Pré Carré, 10 rue Vaugelas; menus €39-130; ⊙noon-1pm & 7.30-8.45pm Tue-Sat) With 30 years in business and a Michelin star, there's no mistaking La Ciboulette's *haute cuisine* credentials. Chef Georges Paccard prepares seasonally driven combinations like turbot with Provence asparagus and nut-crumbed veal with mushroom and potato ravioli. A voluminous wine menu, best perused in the flowery courtyard, rounds out an elegant package.

DRINKING & NIGHTLIFE

Beer O'Clock Bar
(☎04 50 65 83 78; www.facebook.com/beeroclock74; 18 rue du Faubourg Ste-Claire; ⊙5pm-1am Tue-Sat, to 11pm Sun; 📶) This laid-back, high-tech establishment serves beer like petrol stations sell gasoline: you only pay for what you pump. After buying credit on a computerised magnetic card, you can drink as much or as little of the 12 brews on offer as you like – a fantastic way to compare and savour lots of microbrews side-by-side.

INFORMATION

Tourist Office (☎04 50 45 00 33; www.lac-annecy.com; 1 rue Jean Jaurès, courtyard of Centre Bonlieu; ⊙9am-12.30pm & 1.45-6pm Mon-Sat year-round, plus Sun mid-May–mid-Sep, 9am-12.30pm Sun Apr & early Oct & Dec) Has free maps and brochures, and details on cultural activities all around the lake. Can also help with finding accommodation.

GETTING THERE & AWAY

Services from Annecy's train station include:

Chamonix €24.90, 2½ hours, six daily, all via St-Gervais-Les-Bains-Le-Fayet

Lyon Part-Dieu €26.50, two hours, eight direct, more via Chambéry

Paris Gare de Lyon €76 to €110, 3¾ hours, two to five direct, more via Lyon or Chambéry

Basilique du Sacré-Cœur (p57), Paris

In Focus

Station F start-up campus, Paris

France Today

Having confronted terrorism and the rise of the far right in Europe, 'France is back', as the country's young and dynamic president has asserted more than once with dazzling confidence. And indeed, as French cities reinvent themselves to meet future challenges and urban strategists prepare for a greener future, this ancient country of Gallic pride and tradition has every reason to hold its head high.

Back on the World Stage

Presidential elections in 2017 placed the country squarely on an upward path to renewal and regeneration. All the traditional parties were eliminated in the first round of voting, paving the way for savvy 39-year-old Emmanuel Macron – a former investment banker – to win the second round of voting and form a centrist government with his freshly formed, pro-EU movement En Marche. Not only did Macron's overwhelming victory mark a dramatic break from political tradition in France, it also delivered a resounding blow to the country's far-right hopes of gaining power.

Macron's agenda was to reboot the economy, reduce taxes for businesses and make the country's notoriously rigid labour laws more flexible. On the world stage, he earned a reputation for being an eloquent global statesman and staunch champion of a unified Europe.

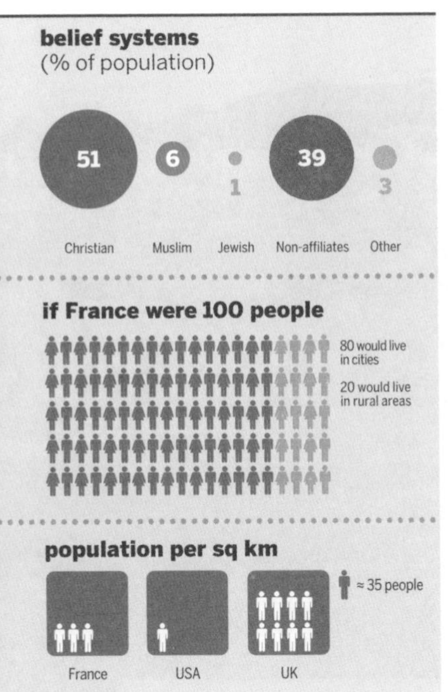

Start-Up Nation

President Macron is a digital native and innovator, and desires the same for France. Macron tweets and shares videos on Facebook in English and French, and speaks English at ease in public. In 2017 he unveiled the world's largest start-up campus in Paris, Station F, conceived and backed by French billionaire businessman Xavier Niel, where 3000 international entrepreneurs beaver away on ground-breaking new tech ideas and businesses, supported by 30 high-tech incubators and accelerators. The unique start-up ecosystem proves Macron's determination to lure world talent – be it in science, tech or banking – to France. A similar digital ecosystem, French Tech Totem, is due to open in Lyon in 2019.

A Greener France

France's commitment to limiting global warming has been made very clear to the world. Following the withdrawal of the US from the Paris climate-change agreement in June 2017, Macron openly invited American scientists and researchers to France to continue their vital climate research. During a subsequent official visit to the US in April 2018, the French president urged the US to reconsider its withdrawal, warning Congress 'There is no Planet B'.

National measures include banning single-use plastic bags, reducing supermarket food waste and prohibiting the sale of all petrol and diesel cars by 2040. In the capital, €150 million is being invested in environmentally friendly cycling infrastructure.

Urban Renaissance

In Lyon, the multimillion-euro Confluence project continues apace on the slip of land where the Rhône meets the Saône. Phase Two, overseen by Swiss architects Herzog and de Meuron (of Tate Modern and Beijing Olympic Stadium fame), is now introducing high-tech residential buildings and landscaped leisure spaces into the environmentally sustainable mix. Ultimately, 50km of riverbanks along the Saône will sport pedestrian walkways, cycling lanes, picnic areas and parks peppered with artworks for public recreational use.

In Bordeaux, an equally ambitious urban-renewal project is under way at Euratlantique, a sizzling new business and residential district. Riverbanks will likewise be greened up, with bags of space for urban walkers and cyclists to experience their city at a grassroots level.

Nothing can trump the gargantuan Grand Paris (Greater Paris) redevelopment project, designed to link the outer suburbs with each other as well as downtown through a new, decentralised metro system. Current completion date is 2030.

Carnac Megaliths (p124), Brittany

History

France is a living history book; even its tiniest villages are littered with reminders of the past. France's beginnings saw the mass migration of the nomadic Celts, subjugation by the Romans, their civilising influence, and the rise of a local nobility. Christianity brought a degree of unity, but nowhere else would such a strongly independent church continue to coexist under a powerful central authority. This is the essence of France's story.

c 7000 BC

Neolithic people turn their hands to monumental menhirs and dolmen during the New Stone Age, creating a fine collection in Brittany.

1500–500 BC

Celtic Gauls move into the region and establish trading links with the Greeks, whose colonies included Massilia (Marseille) on the coast.

55–52 BC

Julius Caesar launches an invasion of Britain; the Gauls defeat them near present-day Clermont-Ferrand, but the Romans prevail.

Stained-glass window depicting Joan of Arc, Cathédrale Notre Dame (p112), Rouen

Roman Gaul

What is now France was settled by several different groups of people in the Iron Age, but the largest and most organised were the Celtic Gauls. Within a few centuries Rome had imposed its government, roads, trade, culture and even language.

Centuries of conflict between the Gauls and the Romans ended in 52 BC when Julius Caesar's legions crushed a revolt by many Gallic tribes led by Celtic Arverni tribe chief Vercingétorix at Gergovia, near present-day Clermont-Ferrand. Gallic resistance collapsed and the Romans reigned supreme.

The stone architecture left by the occupiers was impressive, climaxing with the mighty Pont du Gard aqueduct. Sophisticated urban centres with markets and baths of hot and cold running water began to emerge. The Romans planted vineyards, notably in Burgundy and Bordeaux; introduced techniques to process wine; and introduced the newfangled faith of Christianity.

c AD 455–70
France remains under Roman rule until the 5th century, when the Franks and the Alemanii invade from the east.

987
Merovingian and Carolingian rule ends with the crowning of Hugh Capet; a dynasty that will rule for eight centuries is born.

1066
William the Conqueror and Norman forces occupy England, making Normandy and Plantagenet-ruled England formidable rivals of France.

★ Best Historical Sights

Bayeux Tapestry (p109)
D-Day Beaches (p106)
Carnac (p124)
Mont St-Michel (p104)
Château de Chambord (p82)
Château de Versailles (p46)

Château de Chambord (p82), Loire Valley

Royal Battles

When the Roman Empire collapsed, power passed to the Frankish dynasties. The dominant house to emerge was that of the Carolingians, reaching its apogee under Charlemagne, who extended the boundaries of the kingdom and was crowned Holy Roman Emperor (Emperor of the West) in AD 800. Around the same time, Scandinavian Vikings (also called Norsemen, thus Normans) raided France's western coast, settling in the lower Seine Valley and later forming the duchy of Normandy. By the time Hugh Capet ascended the throne in 987, the king's domain was a humble parcel of land around Paris and Orléans.

The tale of how William the Conqueror and his forces mounted a successful invasion of England from their base in Normandy in 1066 is told on the Bayeux Tapestry. In 1152 Eleanor of Aquitaine wed Henry of Anjou, bringing a further third of France under the control of the English crown. The subsequent rivalry between France and England for control of Aquitaine and the vast English territories in France lasted three centuries.

In 1337 hostilities degenerated into the Hundred Years War, fought on and off until the middle of the 15th century. There were heavy defeats for the French but, luckily, 17-year-old Jeanne d'Arc (Joan of Arc) came along with the outlandish tale that she had a divine mission to expel the English from France and bring about the coronation of French Charles VII in Reims.

Renaissance to Revolution

During the reign of François I (r 1515–47), the Renaissance arrived from Italy, and prompted a great flowering of culture, art and architecture across France. Lavish royal châteaux were built along the Loire Valley, showcasing the might and majesty of the French monarchy. The pomp and profligacy of the ruling elite didn't go down well with everyone.

By the late 1780s, the indecisive Louis XVI and his dominating consort, Marie Antoinette, had managed to alienate virtually every segment of society. Following a series of social and economic crises, and incensed by the corruption and bourgeois extravagance

1152
Eleanor of Aquitaine weds Henry of Anjou, bringing a further third of France under English control and sparking a long-lasting rivalry.

1337
Incessant struggles between the Capetians and England's King Edward III degenerate into the Hundred Years War (until 1453).

1530s
Reformation sweeps through France, pitting Catholics against Protestants, leading to the Wars of Religion (1562–98).

of the aristocracy, a Parisian mob took to the streets in 1789, storming the prison at Bastille and kick-starting the French Revolution.

Inspired by the lofty ideals of *liberté, fraternité, égalité* (freedom, brotherhood, equality), the Revolutionaries initially found favour with the French people. France was declared a constitutional monarchy, but order broke down when the hard-line Jacobins seized power. The monarchy was abolished and the nation was declared a republic on 21 September 1792. Three months later Louis XVI was publicly guillotined on Paris' place de la Concorde. Marie Antoinette suffered the same fate a few months later.

Chaos ensued. Violent retribution broke out across France. During the Reign of Terror (September 1793 to July 1794), churches were closed, religious monuments were desecrated, riots were suppressed and thousands of aristocrats were imprisoned or beheaded. The high ideals of the Revolution had turned to vicious bloodshed, and the nation was rapidly descending into anarchy. France desperately needed someone to re-establish order, give it new direction and rebuild its shattered sense of self. Enter a dashing (if diminutive) young Corsican general called Napoléon Bonaparte.

The Virgin Warrior

Many stories surround the origins of France's patron saint Jeanne d'Arc (Joan of Arc). Revelations delivered by the Archangel Michael prompted Jeanne to raise a siege against the city of Orléans and see the future Charles VII crowned king of France. Following a six-week interrogation, Jeanne d'Arc was sent by Charles VII to Tours, where she was equipped with intendants, a horse, a sword and her own standard featuring God sitting in judgement on a cloud. Jeanne d'Arc went on to defeat the English at Jargeau, Beaugency and Patay.

Battles between the English and the French waged until 1453, by which time the virginal warrior responsible for turning the war had been sold to the English, convicted of witchcraft and burned at the stake in Rouen (p111). She was canonised in 1920.

Napoléon & Empire

Napoléon's military prowess turned him into a powerful political force. In 1804 he was crowned emperor at Paris' Notre Dame Cathedral, and he subsequently led the French armies to conquer much of Europe. But his ill-fated campaign to invade Russia ended in disaster; in 1812 his troops captured Moscow, only to be killed off by the Russian winter. Two years later, Allied armies entered Paris and exiled Napoléon to Elba. In 1815 Napoléon escaped, re-entering Paris and reclaiming the throne. But his reign ended just three weeks later when his forces were defeated at Waterloo in Belgium. Napoléon was exiled again, this time to St Helena in the South Atlantic, where he died in 1821. His body was later reburied under Hôtel des Invalides in Paris.

1643
The Sun King Louis XIV, all of five years old, assumes the throne. In 1682 he moves his court to Versailles.

1789
The French Revolution begins when a mob arms itself with weapons and storms the prison at Bastille.

1851
Louis Napoléon proclaims himself Emperor Napoléon III of the Second Empire (1852–70), a period of significant economic growth.

Off with Their Heads!

Prior to the Revolution, public executions in France depended on rank: the nobility were generally beheaded with a sword or axe while commoners were usually hanged (particularly unlucky prisoners were also drawn and quartered). In the 1790s a group of French physicians and engineers set about designing a clinical new execution machine involving a razor-sharp weighted blade, guaranteed to behead people with a minimum of fuss or mess. Named after one of its inventors, physician Ignace Guillotin, the machine was first used on 25 April 1792.

During the Reign of Terror, at least 17,000 met their death beneath the machine's plunging blade. The last was in 1977, behind closed doors – by this time, the contraption could slice off a head in 2/100 of a second.

France was dogged by a string of ineffectual rulers until Napoléon's nephew, Louis Napoléon Bonaparte, came to power. He was initially elected president, but declared himself Emperor (Napoléon III) in 1851.

While the so-called Second Empire ran roughshod over many of the ideals set down during the Revolution, it proved to be a prosperous time. France enjoyed significant economic growth and Paris was transformed by urban planner Baron Haussmann, who created the famous 12 boulevards radiating from the Arc de Triomphe. But like his uncle, Napoléon III's ambition was his undoing. A series of costly conflicts, including the Crimean War (1854–56), culminated in humiliating defeat by the Prussian forces in 1870. France was once again declared a republic – for the third time in less than a century.

The Belle Époque

Though it ushered in the glittering belle époque (beautiful age), there was little else attractive about the start of the Third Republic. Another war with the Prussians resulted in a huge war bill and the surrender of Alsace and Lorraine. But the belle époque was an era of unprecedented innovation. Architects built a host of exciting new buildings and transformed many French cities. Engineers laid the tracks of France's first railways and tunnelled out Paris' metro system. Designers experimented with new styles and materials, while young artists invented a host of new 'isms' (including impressionism, which took its title from one of Claude Monet's seminal early paintings, *Impression, Soleil Levant*).

The era culminated in a lavish World's Fair in Paris in 1889, an event that summed up the excitement and dynamism of the age, and inspired the construction of one of France's most iconic landmarks – the Eiffel Tower.

The Great War

The joie de vivre of the belle époque wasn't to last. Within months of the outbreak of WWI in 1914, the fields of northern France had been transformed into a sea of trenches and shell craters; by the time the armistice was signed in November 1918, some 1.3 million French soldiers had been killed.

1905
The emotions aroused by the Dreyfus Affair and Catholic Church interference lead to the promulgation of *laïcité* (secularism).

1918
The armistice ending WWI sees the return of lost territories (Alsace and Lorraine). More than a million French soldiers are killed.

1939
Nazi Germany occupies France, dividing it into a zone under direct occupation and a puppet state led by General Pétain.

Desperate to forget the ravages of the war, Paris sparkled as the centre of the avant-garde in the 1920s and '30s. The liberal atmosphere (not to mention the cheap booze and saucy nightlife) attracted a stream of foreign artists and writers to the city, and helped establish Paris' enduring reputation for creativity and experimentation.

World War II

The interwar party was short-lived. Two days after Germany invaded Poland in 1939, France joined Britain in declaring war on Germany. Within a year, Hitler's blitzkrieg had swept across Europe, and France was forced into a humiliating capitulation in June the same year. Following the seaborne retreat of the British Expeditionary Force at Dunkirk, France – like much of Europe – found itself under Nazi occupation. The Germans divided France into two zones: the west and north (including Paris), which was under direct German rule; and a puppet state in the south based around the spa town of Vichy. The anti-Semitic Vichy regime proved very helpful to the Nazis in rounding up Jews and other so-called undesirables for deportation to the death camps.

While many people either collaborated with the Germans or passively waited out the occupation, the underground movement known as the Résistance, or Maquis, whose active members never amounted to more than about 5% of the French population, engaged in such activities as sabotaging railways, collecting intelligence for the Allies, helping Allied airmen who had been shot down, and publishing anti-German leaflets.

After four years of occupation, on 6 June 1944 Allied forces returned to French soil during the D-Day landings. Over 100,000 Allied troops stormed the Normandy coastline and, after several months of fighting, liberated Paris on 25 August. But the cost of the war was devastating for France: many cities had been razed to the ground and millions of French people had lost their lives.

Poverty to Prosperity

Soon after liberation most banks, insurance companies, car manufacturers and energy-producing companies fell under government control. By 1947 rationing remained in effect and France had to turn to the USA for loans as part of the Marshall Plan to rebuild Europe. Slowly, under the government of French war hero Charles de Gaulle, the economy began to recover and France began to rebuild its shattered infrastructure. The debilitating Algerian War of Independence (1954–62) and the subsequent loss of French colonies seriously weakened de Gaulle's government, however, and following widespread student protests in 1968 and a general strike by 10 million workers, de Gaulle was forced to resign from office in 1969. He died the following year.

Subsequent French presidents Georges Pompidou (in power 1969–74) and Valéry Giscard d'Estaing (1974–81) were instrumental in the increasing political and economic integration of Europe, a process that had begun with the formation of the EEC (European

1944
Normandy and Brittany are the first to be liberated by Allied troops after the D-Day landings, followed by Paris.

1949
France signs the pact uniting North America and Western Europe in a mutual defence alliance (NATO); Council of Europe is born.

1968
Anti-authoritarian student protests ('May 1968') escalate into a countrywide protest that brings down Charles de Gaulle.

★ Best History Museums

MuCEM, Marseille (p230)

Le Mémorial – Un Musée pour la Paix, Caen (p113)

Musée d'Art et d'Histoire Baron Gérard, Bayeux (p108)

Centre d'Histoire de la Résistance et de la Déportation, Lyon (p165)

View over MuCEM (p230) to Cathédrale de la Major, Marseille

Economic Community) in 1957, and continued under François Mitterrand with the enlarged EU (European Union) in 1991. During Mitterrand's time in office, France abolished the death penalty, legalised homosexuality, gave workers five weeks' annual holiday and guaranteed the right to retire at 60.

In 1995 Mitterrand was succeeded by the maverick Jacques Chirac, who was re-elected in 2002. Chirac's attempts at reform led to widespread strikes and social unrest, while his opposition to the Iraq war alienated the US administration (and famously led to the rebranding of French fries as Freedom fries).

Presidential Changes

Presidential elections in 2007 ushered out old-school Chirac (in his 70s with two terms under his belt) and brought in dynamic, ambitious and media-savvy Nicolas Sarkozy. However, his first few months in office were dominated by personal affairs as he divorced his wife Cecilia and wed Italian multimillionaire singer Carla Bruni a few months later. The 2008 global banking crisis saw the government inject €10.5 billion into France's six major banks. Unemployment hit the 10% mark in 2010 and in regional elections the same year, Sarkozy's party lost badly.

Sarkozy ran for a second term in office, but lost against left-wing candidate François Hollande (b 1954) of the Socialist party. Parliamentary elections a month later sealed Hollande's grip on power: the Socialists won a comfortable majority in France's 577-seat National Assembly, paving the way for Hollande to govern France during Europe's biggest economic crisis in decades.

His term got off to a rocky start. France officially entered recession, the country's credit rating was downgraded and unemployment reached 11.1% – the highest in 15 years. Rising anger at Hollande's failure to get the country's economy back on track saw his popularity plunge fast and furiously.

1994
The 50km-long Channel Tunnel linking France with Britain opens after seven years of hard graft by 10,000 workers.

2002
The French franc, first minted in 1360, is swapped for the euro, the official currency for another 14 EU member-states.

2004
France bans the wearing of crucifixes, the Islamic headscarf and other overtly religious symbols in state schools.

Recent Events

On 7 January 2015, the Paris offices of newspaper *Charlie Hebdo* were attacked in response to satirical images it had published of the prophet Muhammad. Eleven staff and one police officer were killed and a further 22 people injured. On 13 November 2015 terrorist attacks occurred in Paris and St-Denis, in which 130 people lost their lives and 368 were injured. More was to follow. In Nice on 14 July 2016, while thousands of people were gathered on Promenade des Anglais to celebrate Bastille Day, a lorry ploughed through the crowd. Hundreds were injured and 86 killed. France declared a state of emergency, and November 2017 brought a new anti-terrorism law giving authorities rights to search private homes, restrict free movement of individuals and close mosques if necessary.

In 2017 Hollande's popularity hovered at a record all-time low. As the country geared up for presidential elections, all eyes were on the increasingly powerful Front National (FN; National Front), known for its fervent anti-immigrant stance. The far right was clearly a force to be reckoned with, though the 2017 presidential elections saw the FN's Marine Le Pen convincingly defeated by 39-year-old centrist Emmanuel Macron.

Birth of the Bikini

Almost called *atome* (atom) rather than bikini, after its pinprick size, the scanty little two-piece bathing suit was the 1946 creation of Cannes fashion designer Jacques Heim and automotive engineer Louis Réard. It made its first appearance poolside in Paris at the Piscine Molitor.

Top-and-bottom swimsuits had existed for centuries, but it was the French duo who made them briefer than brief and plumped for the name 'bikini' – after Bikini, an atoll in the Marshall Islands chosen by the USA in the same year as the testing ground for atomic bombs.

Once wrapped top and bottom around the curvaceous 1950s star Brigitte Bardot on St-Tropez' Plage de Pampelonne, there was no looking back. The bikini was here to stay.

2013
Same-sex marriage is legalised in France. By the end of the year, 7000 gay couples have tied the knot.

2015
Deadly terrorist attacks occur at multiple locations, including satirical newspaper *Charlie Hebdo* and Paris concert hall Le Bataclan.

2017
Emmanuel Macron becomes France's youngest-ever president. Paris wins its bid to host the Summer Olympics and Paralympics in 2024.

The Neoclassical Arc du Carrousel at the Musée du Louvre (p40), Paris

Architecture

From prehistoric megaliths in Brittany to Vauban's star-shaped citadels built to defend France's 17th-century frontiers, French architecture has always been of grand-projet proportions. Paris' skyline shimmers with Roman arenas, Gothic cathedrals, postmodernist cubes and futuristic skyscrapers, while provincial France cooks up the whole gamut of mainstream architectural styles.

Roman to Gothic

The Romans left behind a colossal architectural legacy in Provence and on the French Riviera. To build the Pont du Gard, each stone block was carved by hand and transported from nearby quarries – an incredible undertaking, considering the largest weighed over 5 tonnes.

Several centuries later, architects adopted elements from Gallo-Roman buildings to create *roman* (Romanesque) masterpieces such as the exquisitely haunting Basilique St-Rémi in Reims, Caen's twinset of famous Romanesque abbeys and Provence's lavender-framed Abbaye Notre-Dame de Sénanque. In Normandy the nave and south transept of the abbey-church on Mont St-Michel are beautiful examples of Norman Romanesque.

Northern France's extraordinary wealth in the 12th century lured the finest architects, engineers and artisans, who created impressive Gothic structures with ribbed vaults carved with great precision, pointed arches, slender verticals and stained-glass windows – Rouen cathedral is a lovely example. Avignon's pontifical palace is Gothic architecture on a gargantuan scale.

Art Nouveau

Art nouveau (1850–1910) combined iron, brick, glass and ceramics in ways never before seen. See for yourself in Paris with Hector Guimard's noodle-like metro entrances or the fine art nouveau interiors in the Musée d'Orsay.

Renaisssance

The Renaissance, which began in Italy in the early 15th century, set out to realise a 'rebirth' of classical Greek and Roman culture. It impacted France at the end of that century when Charles VIII began a series of invasions of Italy, returning with new ideas.

To trace the shift from late Gothic to Renaissance, travel along the Loire Valley. During the very early Renaissance period, châteaux were used for the first time as pleasure palaces rather than defensive fortresses. Many edifices built during the 15th century to early 16th century in the Loire Valley – including Château d'Azay-le-Rideau and Château de Villandry – were built as summer or hunting residences for royal financiers, chamberlains and courtiers. Red-patterned brickwork – such as that on the Louis XII wing of Château Royal de Blois – adorned the façade of most châteaux dating from Louis XII's reign (1498–1515).

Neoclassicism

Neoclassicism peaked under Napoléon III, who used it extensively for monumental architecture intended to embody the grandeur of imperial France and its capital: the Arc de Triomphe, the Arc du Carrousel at the Louvre, the Assemblée Nationale building and the Palais Garnier.

It was during this period that urban planner Baron Haussmann, between 1850 and 1870 as Prefect of the Seine, completely redrew Paris' street plan, radically demolishing the city's maze of narrow, cramped medieval streets and replacing them with wide boulevards, sweeping parks and attractive *passages couverts* (covered passages).

The true showcase of this era is Casino de Monte Carlo in Monaco, created by French architect Charles Garnier (1825–98) in 1878.

Contemporary

For centuries French political leaders sought to immortalise themselves through the erection of huge public edifices (aka *grands projets*) in Paris. Georges Pompidou commissioned the once reviled, now much-loved Centre Pompidou (1977) in which the architects – in order to keep the exhibition halls as uncluttered as possible – put the building's insides out. Under François Mitterrand, IM Pei's glass pyramid at the hitherto sacrosanct and untouchable Louvre appeared.

France's arguably most talented architect, Jean Nouvel was the creative talent behind Paris' Institut du Monde Arabe (1987), one of the most beautiful and successful of France's contemporary buildings. He also designed the Philharmonie de Paris, an experimental concert hall for the city's symphonic orchestra, and is the architect behind the current €600 million renovation of Gare d'Austerlitz, slated to finish in 2021.

Claude Monet's home, Giverny, Normandy (p101)

BEKETOFF/SHUTTERSTOCK ©

Arts & Literature

Painting, literature, music: France's vast artistic heritage is the essence of French art de vivre (art of living). Music is embedded in the French soul, from rap and dance to electronica, while French painting continues to break new ground with provocative street art, and French writers Voltaire, Victor Hugo, Marcel Proust and Simone de Beauvoir walk the world hall of fame.

Painting France

Classical to Romantic

According to Voltaire, French painting proper began with Baroque painter Nicolas Poussin (1594–1665), known for his classical mythological and biblical scenes bathed in golden light. Wind forward a couple of centuries and modern still life emerged with Jean-Baptiste Chardin (1699–1779). A century later, neoclassical artist Jacques Louis David (1748–1825) wooed the public with vast history paintings; some are in the Louvre.

While Romantics such as Eugène Delacroix (1798–1863) revamped the subject picture, the Barbizon School effected a parallel transformation of landscape painting. Jean-François Millet (1814–75), son of a Normandy farmer, took many of his subjects from peasant life, and reproductions of his *L'Angélus* (The Angelus; 1857) – the best-known painting in France after the *Mona Lisa* – are strung above mantelpieces all over rural France. The original hangs in Paris' Musée d'Orsay.

The Impressionists

It was in a flower-filled garden in a Normandy village that Claude Monet (1840–1926) expounded impressionism, a term of derision taken from the title of his experimental painting *Impression, Soleil Levant* (Impression, Sunrise; 1874).

An arthritis-ravaged Renoir painted out his last impressionist days in a villa on the French Riviera, a part of France that inspired dozens of artists. In St-Tropez pointillism took off with Georges Seurat (1859–91), the first to apply paint in small dots or uniform brush strokes of unmixed colour. His pupil Paul Signac (1863–1935) is best known for pointillist works.

Street Art

Street art is big, thanks in part to the pioneering work of Blek Le Rat (http://bleklerat.free.fr) in the 1980s. The Parisian artist, born as Xavier Prou, began by spraying tiny rats in hidden corners of the streets of Paris, went on to develop stencil graffiti as a recognised form, and notably inspired British street artist Banksy. Other blockbuster names include Gregos (b 1972), whose 3D clay faces protrude out of walls all over France; Jérôme Mesnager (b 1961), known for his stencilled white figures; and Monsieur Chat (aka Thoma Vuille), who leaves cartoon cats with huge Cheshire-cat grins all over the place.

Matisse, Picasso & Klein

Twentieth-century French painting is characterised by a bewildering diversity of styles, including cubism, and Fauvism, named after the slur of a critic who compared the exhibitors at the 1906 autumn Salon in Paris with *fauves* (wild animals) because of their radical use of intensely bright colours. Spanish cubist Pablo Picasso (1881–1973) and Fauvist Henri Matisse (1869–1954) both chose southern France to set up studios.

With the close of WWII, Paris' role as artistic world capital ended. The focus shifted back to southern France in the 1960s with new realists such as Arman (1928–2005) and Yves Klein (1928–62), both from Nice. In 1960 Klein famously produced *Anthropométrie de l'Époque Bleue,* a series of imprints made by naked women (covered from head to toe in blue paint) rolling around on a white canvas, in front of an orchestra of violins and an audience in evening dress.

Urban Angst

Later in the 20th century, artists turned to the minutiae of everyday urban life to express social and political angst. Conceptual artist Daniel Buren (b 1938) reduced his painting to a signature series of vertical 8.7cm-wide stripes that is applied to any surface imaginable – white marble columns in the courtyard of Paris' Palais Royal included. The artist (who in 1967, as part of the radical group BMPT, signed a manifesto declaring he was not a painter) was the *enfant terrible* of French art in the 1980s. Partner-in-crime Michel Parmentier (1938–2000) insisted on monochrome painting – blue in 1966, grey in 1967 and red in 1968.

Conceptual Art

Paris-born conceptual artist Sophie Calle (b 1953) brazenly exposes her private life in public with eye-catching installations such as *Prenez Soin de Vous* (Take Care of Yourself; 2007), a compelling and addictive work of art in book form exposing the reactions of 107 women to an email Calle received from her French lover, dumping her. Her *Rachel, Monique* (2010) evoked the death and lingering memory of her mother in the form of a photographic exhibition first shown in Paris, later as a live reading performance at the Festival d'Avignon, and subsequently in a chapel in New York. In 2015 *Suite Vénitienne* was published, a beautiful hard-back

★ Best Art Museums

Musée du Louvre (p40), Paris

Musée d'Orsay (p62), Paris

Musée National Picasso (p61), Paris

Musée de l'Annonciade (p218), St-Tropez

Musée Matisse (p203), Nice

Musée d'Orsay (p62), Paris

MARÍA JOSÉ POMBO/500PX ©

rendition, on gilt-edged Japanese paper, of her first art book in 1988 in which she followed Henri B around Venice for two weeks, anonymously photographing the enigmatic stranger.

Literary Drama

Courtly Love to Symbolism

Troubadours' lyric poems of courtly love dominated medieval French literature, while the *roman* (literally 'romance', now meaning 'novel') drew on old Celtic tales. With the *Roman de la Rose,* a 22,000-line poem by Guillaume de Lorris and Jean de Meung, allegorical figures like Pleasure, Shame and Fear appeared.

French Renaissance literature was extensive and varied. La Pléiade was a group of lyrical poets active in the 1550s and 1560s. The exuberant narrative of Loire Valley–born François Rabelais (1494–1553) blends coarse humour with encyclopedic erudition in a vast panorama of every kind of person, occupation and jargon in 16th-century France. Michel de Montaigne (1533–92) covered cannibals, war horses, drunkenness and the resemblance of children to their fathers and other themes. *Le grand siècle* (golden age) ushered in classical lofty odes to tragedy. François de Malherbe (1555–1628) brought a new rigour to rhythm in poetry; and Marie de La Fayette (1634–93) penned the first French novel, *La Princesse de Clèves* (1678).

French Romanticism

The philosophical Voltaire (1694–1778) dominated the 18th century. A century on, Besançon gave birth to French Romantic Victor Hugo (1802–85).

In 1857 literary landmarks *Madame Bovary* by Gustave Flaubert (1821–80), and Charles Baudelaire's (1821–67) poems *Les Fleurs du Mal* (The Flowers of Evil), were published. Émile Zola (1840–1902) saw novel-writing as a science in his powerful series, *Les Rougon-Macquart*.

Evoking mental states was the dream of symbolists Paul Verlaine (1844–96) and Stéphane Mallarmé (1842–98). Verlaine shared a tempestuous relationship with poet Arthur Rimbaud (1854–91): enter French literature's first modern poems.

Modern Literature

The world's longest novel – a seven-volume 9,609,000-character giant by Marcel Proust (1871–1922) – dominated the early 20th century. *À la Recherche du Temps Perdu* (Remembrance of Things Past) explores in evocative detail the true meaning of past experience recovered from the unconscious by involuntary memory.

Surrealism proved a vital force until WWII. André Breton (1896–1966) captured fascination with dreams, divination and all manifestations of the imaginary in his autobiographical narratives.

In Paris the bohemian Colette (1873–1954) captivated and shocked with her titillating novels detailing the amorous exploits of heroines such as schoolgirl Claudine. In New York, meanwhile, what would become one of the best-selling French works of all time was published in 1943: *Le Petit Prince* (The Little Prince), by Lyon-born writer and pilot, Antoine de Saint-Exupéry (1900–44), a magical yet philosophical tale for children about an aviator's adventures with a little blonde-haired Prince from Asteroid B-612. After WWII, existentialism developed around the debates of Jean-Paul Sartre (1905–80), Simone de Beauvoir (1908–86) and Albert Camus (1913–60) in Paris' Left Bank cafes.

The *nouveau roman* of the 1950s saw experimental young writers seek new ways of organising narratives. *Histoire d'O* (Story of O), an erotic sadomasochistic novel written by Dominique Aury, sold more copies outside France than any other contemporary French novel. Radical young writer Françoise Sagan (1935–2004) shot to fame overnight at the age of 18 with her first novel, *Bonjour Tristesse* (Hello Sadness; 1954).

The New Generation

No French writer better delves into the mind, mood and politics of France's notable ethnic population than Faïza Guène (b 1985; http://faizaguene.fr), who writes in a notable 'urban slang' style. Born and bred on a ghetto housing estate outside Paris, she stunned critics with her debut novel, *Kiffe Kiffe Demain* (2004), sold in 27 countries and published in English as *Just Like Tomorrow* (2006).

Musical Encounters

Classical

French Baroque music heavily influenced European musical output in the 17th and 18th centuries. French musical luminaries – Charles Gounod (1818–93), César Franck (1822–90) and *Carmen* creator Georges Bizet (1838–75) among them – were a dime a dozen in the 19th century. Modern orchestration was founded by French Romantic Hector Berlioz (1803–69). He demanded gargantuan forces: his ideal orchestra included 240 stringed instruments, 30 grand pianos and 30 harps. Claude Debussy (1862–1918) revolutionised classical music with the music impressionism of *Prélude à l'Après-Midi d'un Faune* (Prelude to the Afternoon of a Fawn).

Jazz & French Chansons

Jazz hit 1920s Paris in the banana-clad form of Josephine Baker, an African-American cabaret dancer. Post-WWII ushered in a much-appreciated bunch of musicians, mostly black Americans who opted to remain in Paris' bohemian Montmartre rather than return to the brutal racism and segregation of the US: Sidney Bechet called Paris home from 1949, jazz drummer Kenny 'Klook' Clarke followed in 1956, pianist Bud Powell in 1959, and saxophonist Dexter Gordon in the early 1960s.

The *chanson française*, a French folk-song tradition dating from the troubadours of the Middle Ages, was eclipsed by the music halls and burlesque of the early 20th century, but was revived in the 1930s by Édith Piaf and Charles Trenet. In the 1950s, Paris' Left Bank cabarets nurtured *chansonniers* (cabaret singers) such as Léo Ferré, Georges Brassens, Claude Nougaro, Jacques Brel and the very charming, very sexy, very French Serge Gainsbourg.

Rap

France is known for its rap, an original 1990s sound spearheaded by Senegal-born, Paris-reared rapper MC Solaar and Suprême NTM (NTM being an acronym for a French expression far too offensive to print). Most big-name rappers are French 20-somethings of Arabic or African origin whose prime preoccupations are the frustrations and fury of fed-up immigrants in the French *banlieues* (suburbs).

Disiz La Peste, born in Amiens to a Senegalese father and French mother, portrayed precisely this in his third album, *Histoires Extra-Ordinaires d'un Jeune de Banlieue* (The Extraordinary Stories of a Youth in the Suburbs; 2005). He later morphed into Peter Punk (www.disizpeterpunk.com) and created a very different rock-punk-electro sound before returning as rap artist Disiz La Peste, releasing a rash of albums culminating in 2017 with *Pacifique*. France's best-known rap band is Marseille's home-grown IAM (www.iam.tm.fr).

Rock & Pop

One could be forgiven for thinking that French pop is becoming dynastic. The distinctive M (for Mathieu) is the son of singer Louis Chédid; Arthur H is the progeny of pop-rock musician Jacques Higelin; and Thomas Dutronc is the offspring of 1960s idols Jacques and Françoise Hardy. Serge Gainsbourg's daughter with Jane Birkin, Charlotte Gainsbourg (b 1971) made her musical debut in 1984 with the single *Lemon Incest*.

Indie rock band Phoenix, from Versailles, headlines festivals in the US and UK. The band was born in the late 1990s in a garage in the Paris suburbs and has six hugely successful albums under their belt, including *Ti Amo* (2017).

Always worth a listen is Louise Attaque (http://louiseattaque.com) who, after a 10-year break, released a new album, *L'Anomalie,* with huge success in early 2016. Nosfell (www.nosfell.com), one of France's most creative and intense musicians, sings in his own invented language called *le klokobetz*.

Marseille-born Marina Kaye (b 1998) won *France's Got Talent* TV show at the age of 13, as well as huge acclaim with her debut single *Homeless,* and released her first album *Fearless* in 2015. Celebrity singer Nolwenn Leroy (b 1982) performs in Breton, English and Irish as well as French; while Paris' very own Indila (b 1984) woos France with her edgy pop and *rai* (a style derived from Algerian folk music).

Electronica & Dance

David Guetta, Laurent Garnier, Martin Solveig and Bon Sinclair – originally nicknamed 'Chris the French Kiss' – are top Parisian electronica music producers and DJs who travel the international circuit. In the late 1990s Guetta, with his wife Cathy, directed Paris' mythical nightclub Les Bains Douches, today a trendy club-hotel in Le Marais.

Algerian Rai to Zouglou

With styles from Algerian *rai* to other North African music (artists include Cheb Khaled, Natacha Atlas, Jamel, Cheb Mami) and Senegalese *mbalax* (Youssou N'Dour), West Indian zouk (Kassav', Zouk Machine) and Cuban salsa, France's world beat is strong. Manu Chao (www.manuchao.net), the Paris-born son of Spanish parents, uses world elements to stunning effect.

Magic System from Côte d'Ivoire popularised *zouglou* (a kind of West African rap and dance music) with its album *Premier Gaou,* and Congolese Koffi Olomide still packs the halls. Also try to catch blind singing couple, Amadou and Mariam; Rokia Traoré from Mali; and Franco-Algerian DJ-turned-singer Rachid Taha (www.rachidtaha.fr), whose music mixes Arab and Western musical styles with lyrics in English, Berber and French.

No artist has sealed France's reputation in world music more than Paris-born, Franco-Congolese rapper, slam poet and three-time Victoire de la Musique–award winner, Abd al Malik (b 1975). His albums *Gibraltar* (2006), *Dante* (2008), *Château Rouge* (2010) and *Scarifications* (2015) are classics.

Scallops served with asparagus and lardo bacon

VISIONSI/SHUTTERSTOCK ©

French Cuisine

French cuisine waltzes taste buds through a dizzying array of dishes sourced from aromatic street markets, seaside oyster farms, sun-baked olive groves and ancient vineyards. The very word 'cuisine' was borrowed from the French – no other language could handle all the nuances.

Cheese

No French food product is a purer reflection of *terroir* (land) than cheese, an iconic staple that – with the exception of most coastal areas – is made all over the country, tiny villages laying claim to ancient variations. France boasts more than 500 varieties, made with *lait cru* (raw milk), pasteurised milk or *petit-lait* ('little-milk', the whey left over after the fats and solids have been curdled with rennet).

Chèvre, made from goat's milk, is creamy, sweet and faintly salty when fresh, but hardens and gets saltier as it matures. Among the best is Ste-Maure de Touraine, a mild creamy cheese from the Loire Valley; Cabécou de Rocamadour from Midi-Pyrénées, often served warm with salad or marinated in oil and rosemary; and Lyon's St-Marcellin, a soft white cheese that should be served impossibly runny.

★ Top Tables

Restaurant David Toutain (p70), Paris

La Côte (p132), Carnac

L'Assiette Champenoise (p150), Reims

La Grande Maison (p254), Bordeaux

Jan (p207), Nice

La Terrasse Rouge (p254), St-Émilion

Canelés (p253), La Terrasse Rouge (p254), St-Émilion

RIVER THOMPSON/LONELY PLANET ©

Equal parts of Comté, Beaufort and gruyère – a trio of hard, fruity, cow's milk cheeses from the French Alps – are grated and melted in a garlic-smeared pot with a dash of nutmeg, white wine and *kiersch* (cherry liqueur) to create fondue Savoyarde. Hearty and filling, this pot of melting glory originated from the simple peasant need of using up cheese scraps. It is now the chic dish to eat on the ski slopes.

Bread

In northern France wheat fields shade vast swaths of agricultural land a gorgeous golden copper, and nothing is more French than *pain* (bread).

Every town and almost every village has its own *boulangerie* (bakery), which sells bread in all manner of shapes, sizes and variety. Artisan *boulangeries* bake their bread in a wood-fired, brick bread oven pioneered by Loire Valley châteaux in the 16th century.

Plain old *pain* is a 400g, traditional-shaped loaf, soft inside and crusty out, and served with every meal. The iconic classic is *une baguette,* a long thin crusty loaf weighing 250g. Anything fatter and it becomes *une flûte,* thinner *une ficelle.*

Charcuterie & Foie Gras

Charcuterie is traditionally made from pork, though other meats are used in making *saucisse* (small fresh sausage), *saucisson* (salami), *saucisson sec* (air-dried salami), *boudin noir* (blood sausage) and other cured and salted meats. Pâtés, terrines and *rillettes* are also considered charcuterie. The difference between a pâté and a terrine is academic: a pâté is removed from its container and sliced before it is served, while a terrine is sliced from the container itself. *Rillettes,* spread cold over bread or toast, is potted meat or fish.

The key component of *pâté de foie gras* is foie gras, which is the liver of fattened ducks and geese. It was first prepared *en croûte* (in a pastry crust) around 1780 by one Jean-Pierre Clause, chef to the military governor of Alsace, who was impressed enough to send a batch to the king of Versailles. Today, it is a traditional component of celebratory or festive meals – particularly Christmas and New Year's Eve – in family homes countrywide, and is consumed year-round in regions in southwest France where it is primarily made.

Sweet Treats

Patisserie is a general French term for pastries and includes *tartes* (tarts), *flans* (custard pies), *gâteaux* (cakes) and *biscuits* (cookies) as well as traditional croissants, *pains au chocolats* and other typical pastries. *Sablés* are shortbread biscuits, *tuiles* are delicate wing-like almond cookies, madeleines are small scallop-shaped cakes often flavoured with a hint of vanilla or lemon, and *tarte tatin* is an upside-down caramelised apple pie that's been around since the late 19th century.

Breton Butter & Crêpes

An ancient culinary tradition has long ruled Breton cuisine. Pair a sweet wheat-flour pancake or savoury buckwheat *galette* with *une bolée* (a stubby terracotta goblet) of apple-rich Breton cider, and taste buds enter gourmet heaven. Alternatively, order a local beer like Coreff or nonalcoholic *lait ribot* (fermented milk). *Chouchen* (hydromel), a fermented honey liqueur, is a typical Breton aperitif.

Cheese is not big, but *la beurre de Bretagne* (Breton butter) is. Traditionally sea-salted and creamy, a knob of it naturally goes into crêpes, *galettes* and the most outrageously buttery cake you're likely to ever taste in your life – *kouign amann* (Breton butter cake). Butter handmade by Jean-Yves Bordier ends up on tables of top restaurants around the world.

Le Gavage

Traditionally, back in the 11th century, local farmers in the Dordogne would slaughter the farm goose then pluck out its liver and soak it in warm milk to ensure a succulent swollen liver. Today, in order to fatten the livers, ducks and geese are controversially force-fed. During *le gavage* (force-feeding), a tube is threaded down the throat into the bird's stomach, enabling 450g or so of boiled corn to be pneumatically pumped into the bird in just a few seconds.

Force-feeding is illegal in 12 countries in the EU, Norway, Switzerland, Israel and the USA; and foie gras imports are forbidden in many countries. Within France itself, there is a growing movement to end *le gavage*.

Normandy Cream & Apples

Cream, apples and cider are the essentials of Norman cuisine, which sees mussels simmered in cream and a splash of cider to make *moules à la crème normande* and tripe thrown in the slow pot with cider and vegetables to make *tripes à la mode de Caen*. Creamy Camembert is the local cow's milk cheese, and on the coast *coquilles St-Jacques* (scallops) and *huîtres* (oysters) rule the seafood roost. Apples are the essence of the region's main tipples: tangy cider and the potent *calvados* (apple brandy).

À la Provençal

Cuisine in sun-baked Provence is laden with tomatoes, melons, cherries, peaches, olives, Mediterranean fish and Alpine cheese. *À la Provençal* still means anything with a generous dose of garlic-seasoned tomatoes.

Yet there are exciting culinary contrasts in this region, which see fisherfolk return with the catch of the day in seafaring Marseille; grazing bulls and paddy fields in the Camargue; black truffles in the Vaucluse; cheese made from cow's milk in Alpine pastures; and an Italianate accent to cooking in seaside Nice.

Bouillabaisse, Marseille's mighty meal of fish stew, is Provence's most famous contribution to French cuisine. The chowder is eaten as a main course with toasted bread and *rouille* (a spicy red mayonnaise of olive oil, garlic and chilli peppers). The fish stew *bourride* is similar to bouillabaisse but has fewer ingredients, a less prescriptive recipe, and often a slightly creamier sauce. It's customarily served with *aïoli* (garlic mayonnaise).

★ Best Bakeries & Cake Shops

Jacques Genin (p68), Paris

Du Pain et des Idées (p67), Paris

La Reine Mathilde (p110), Bayeux

Maison Violette (p187), Avignon

Boulangerie de Mamie Jane (p178), Gordes

Chocolates, Jacques Genin (p68), Paris

MATT MUNRO/LONELY PLANET ©

When in Provence, drink pastis. An aniseed-flavoured, 45% alcoholic drink, it was invented in Marseille by industrialist Paul Ricard in 1932. Amber-coloured in the bottle, it turns milky white when mixed with water.

Piggy Parts in Lyon

All too often Lyon is dubbed France's gastronomic capital. And while it doesn't compete with France's capital when it comes to variety of international cuisine, it certainly holds its own when it comes to titillating taste buds with the unusual and inventive. Take the age-old repertoire of feisty, often pork-driven dishes served in the city's legendary *bouchons* (small bistros): breaded fried tripe, big fat *andouillettes* (pig-intestine sausage), silk-weaver's brains (a herbed cheese spread, not brains at all) – there is no way you can ever say Lyonnais cuisine is run of the mill. A lighter, less meaty speciality is *quenelle de brochet,* a poached dumpling made of freshwater fish (usually pike) and served with sauce Nantua (a cream and freshwater-crayfish sauce).

Equally fine is the Lyonnais wine list where very fine Côtes de Rhône reds vie for attention with local Brouilly and highly esteemed Mâcon reds from nearby Burgundy. In *bouchons,* local Beaujolais is mixed with a dash of blackcurrant liqueur to make a blood-red *communard* aperitif.

The Cheesy French Alps

Savoyard food is justifiably famous, and features in the preponderance of French restaurants in the region. Like all regional French cuisines, it's a product of the *terroir,* and all that grows within it. This means plenty of dairy, cured meats and pasta such as square-shaped *crozets* and *ravioles*.

You can opt for DIY: many *fruitières* (cheesemongers) will lend you the required apparatus, provided you buy their ingredients.

Fondue A pan of cheese is kept warm and melty over a small burner. Diners use skewers to dip in small chunks of bread.

Raclette From *racler,* to scrape, this dish involves melting unholy amounts of cheese over boiled potatoes.

Tartiflette A baked dish of potatoes, *lardons* (diced bacon), onions and crème fraîche, topped with Reblochon cheese.

Perfect Picnics

Baguette French simplicity at its best: buy a baguette from the *boulangerie,* stuff it with a chunk of Camembert, pâté and *cornichons* (miniature gherkins), or a few slices of *rosette de Lyon* or other salami and, *voilà,* picnic perfection!

Macarons No sweeter way to end a gourmet picnic, most famously from Ladurée (p66) in Paris.

Kouign amann The world's most buttery, syrupy cake, aka Breton butter cake.

Fruit Big juicy black cherries from Apt, peaches, apricots and tomatoes from the Rhône Valley, Provence and the Riviera.

Provençal olives or peppers Marinated and stuffed with a multitude of edible sins from market stands.

Champagne From Reims and *biscuits roses* (pink ladyfinger sponge biscuits).

Country produce Pâté, walnuts and foie gras from the Dordogne.

Aperitifs & Digestifs

Meals in France are preceded by an aperitif such as a *kir* (white wine sweetened with a fruit syrup) or a glass of sweet white Coteaux du Layon from the Loire Valley. In southern France aniseed-flavoured pastis is the aperitif to drink alfresco; in the southwest, go local with a Floc de Gascogne, a liqueur wine made from Armagnac and red or white grape juice.

After-dinner drinks accompany coffee. France's most famous brandies are Cognac and Armagnac, both made from grapes in the regions of those names. *Eaux de vie* (literally 'waters of life') can be made with grape skins and the pulp left over after being pressed for wine (Marc de Champagne, Marc de Bourgogne), apples (*calvados;* apple-flavoured brandy) and pears (Poire William), as well as such fruits as plums *(eau de vie de prune)* and even raspberries *(eau de vie de framboise).*

Dining Lexicon

Auberge Country inn serving traditional fare, often attached to a small hotel.

Ferme auberge Working farm that cooks up meals from local farm products; usually only dinner and frequently only by reservation.

Bistro (also spelled *bistrot*) Anything from a pub or bar with snacks and light meals to a small, fully fledged restaurant.

Brasserie Much like a cafe except it serves full meals, drinks and coffee from morning until 11pm or later. Typical fare includes *choucroute* (sauerkraut) and *moules frites* (mussels and fries).

Restaurant Born in Paris in the 18th century, restaurants today serve lunch and dinner five or six days a week.

Cafe Basic light snacks as well as drinks.

Crêperie (also *galetterie*) Casual address specialising in sweet crêpes and *galettes* (savoury buckwheat crêpes).

Salon de thé Trendy tearoom often serving light lunches (quiche, salads, cakes, tarts, pies and pastries) as well as green, black and herbal teas.

Table d'hôte (literally 'host's table') Some of the most charming B&Bs serve *table d'hôte* too, a delicious homemade meal of set courses with little or no choice.

Paragliding, Lac Annecy near Annecy (p270)

THOMAS DEKIERE/SHUTTERSTOCK ©

Outdoor Activities

France takes outdoor activities and elevates them to a fine art. In the birthplace of the Tour de France, the cycling is world-class; in Mont Blanc's backyard, the skiing is second to none. And everywhere the hiking – from Brittany's coastal wilds to the sun-blazed vines and lavender meadows of Provence – is just magnifique.

Skiing & Snowboarding

Just whisper the words 'French Alps' to a skier and watch their eyes light up. The ski season goes with the snow, generally beginning in mid-December, with snow conditions at their height between January and March, and ending in mid-April (sometimes later). The higher you go, the more snow-sure the resort and the longer the season. Crowds and room rates skyrocket during school holidays (Christmas, February half-term, Easter), so avoid these times if you can. The following are useful websites for skiing and snowboarding in France:

Météo France (www.meteofrance.com) Weather and daily avalanche forecast during the ski season.

École du Ski Français (ESF; www.esf.net) The largest ski school in the world, with first-class tuition. Search by region.

France Montagnes (www.france-montagnes.com) Official website of French ski resorts, with guides, maps, snow reports and more.

Hiking & Walking

Hikers have a high time of it in the Alps, with kilometre after never-ending kilometre of well-marked trails. Lifts and cable cars take the sweat out of hiking here in summer. Chamonix is the trailhead for the epic 10-day, three-country Tour de Mont Blanc, but gentler paths, such as the Grand Balcon Sud, also command Mont Blanc close-ups. **Club Alpin Français** (French Alpine Club; www.ffcam.fr) has guides for alpine sports and can reserve beds in *refuges* (simple mountain huts).

Cycling & Mountain Biking

France is fabulous freewheeling country, with routes leading along its lushly wooded valleys and mighty rivers begging to be explored in slow motion. Among the best options is château-studded Loire Valley – **Loire à Vélo** (www.cycling-loire.com) maintains 800km of signposted routes. Provence's 236km **Autour du Luberon** *véloroute* (bike path) links one gold-stone village to another. Or partner pedalling with wine tasting in Bordeaux: bike hire is widely available thanks to the the public bike-sharing scheme (€2 per hour). Regional tourist offices also rent bikes (around €18 per day). **Véloroutes et Voies Vertes** (www.af3v.org) has the inside scoop on 250 signposted *véloroutes* and *voies vertes* (greenways), plus an interactive map to pinpoint them.

Kayaking & Canoeing

Top options include the looking-glass Lake Annecy in the French Alps, the River Gard and Provence's highly scenic Gorges du Verdon. Sea kayakers adore the ragged, cove-indented Parc National des Calanques near Marseille; expect to pay from €35/55 for a half-/full-day kayaking excursion.

Rock Climbing & Mountaineering

Chamonix guide companies organise rock-climbing courses (from €44 for a two-hour lesson to €620 for an intensive granite-climbing weekend workshop) or the incomparable Mont Blanc ascent (€840 to €1650) for the truly experienced. If you aren't experienced but fancy flirting with climbing, *via ferrate* (fixed-rope routes) lace the Alps. Guide companies charge around €50 for half-day escapades.

Paragliding

Many a peak, perfect thermals, and glacier-frosted mountains and forests to observe while drifting down to ground level attract paragliders to Alpine resorts such as Chamonix. Lake Annecy is a favourite. Tandem flights with a qualified instructor cost from €95, depending on location.

Gare de l'Est (p76), Paris

Survival Guide

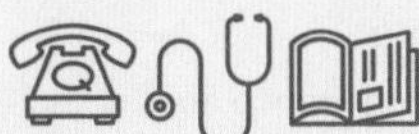

Directory A–Z

Accommodation

Be it a fairy-tale château, a boutique hideaway or floating pod on a lake, France has accommodation to suit every taste and pocket. If you're visiting in high season (especially August), reserve ahead – the best addresses on the coast fill up months in advance.

Reservations

Midrange, top-end and many budget hotels require a credit-card number to secure an advance reservation made by phone; some hostels do not take bookings. Many tourist offices can advise on availability and reserve for you, often for a fee of €5 and usually only if you stop by in person. In the Alps, ski-resort tourist offices run a central reservation service for booking accommodation.

Seasons

- In ski resorts, high season is Christmas, New Year and the February–March school holidays.
- On the coast, high season is summer, particularly August.
- Hotels in inland cities often charge low-season rates in summer.
- Rates often drop outside the high season – in some cases by as much as 50%.
- In business-oriented hotels in cities, rooms are most expensive from Monday to Thursday and cheaper over the weekend.
- In the Alps, hotels usually close between seasons, from around May to mid-June and mid-September to early December.

B&Bs

For charm, a heartfelt *bienvenue* (welcome) and solid home cooking, it's hard to beat France's privately run *chambres d'hôte* (B&Bs) – urban rarities but as common as muck in rural areas. By law a *chambre d'hôte* must have no more than five rooms and breakfast must be included in the price; some hosts prepare a meal *(table d'hôte)* for an extra charge of around €30 including wine. Pick up lists of *chambres d'hôte* (B&B) at tourist offices, or find one to suit online.

Bienvenue à la Ferme (www.bienvenue-a-la-ferme.com) Farmstay accommodation.

Chambres d'Hôtes France (www.chambresdhotesfrance.com) Comprehensive, France-wide B&B listings.

Fleurs de Soleil (www.fleursdesoleil.fr) Selective collection of 550 stylish *maisons d'hôte*, mainly in rural France.

Gîtes de France (www.gites-de-france.com) France's primary umbrella organisation for B&Bs and self-catering properties *(gîtes);* search by region, theme, activity or facilities.

iGuide Rivages (www.iguide-hotels.com) Gorgeous presentation of France's most charming and often-times most upmarket B&Bs.

Samedi Midi Éditions (www.samedimidi.com) Country, mountain, seaside...choose your *chambre d'hôte* by location or theme.

Price Ranges

The following price ranges refer to a double room in high season, with private bathroom (any combination of toilet, bathtub, shower and washbasin), excluding breakfast unless otherwise noted. Breakfast is assumed to be included at a B&B. Where half board (breakfast and dinner) or full board (breakfast, lunch and dinner) is included, this is mentioned with the price.

CATEGORY	COST
€	less than €90 (less than €130 in Paris)
€€	€90–190 (€130–250 in Paris)
€€€	more than €190 (more than €250 in Paris)

Book Your Stay Online

For more accommodation reviews by Lonely Planet authors, check out http://hotels.lonelyplanet.com/france. You'll find independent reviews, as well as recommendations on the best places to stay. Best of all, you can book online.

Camping

Be it a Mongolian yurt, boutique treehouse or simple canvas beneath stars, camping in France is in vogue. Thousands of well-equipped campgrounds dot the country, many considerately placed by rivers, lakes and the sea.

- Most campgrounds open March or April to late September or October; popular spots fill up fast in summer so it is wise to call ahead.
- 'Sites' refer to fixed-price deals for two people including a tent and a car. Otherwise the price is broken down per adult/tent/car. Factor in a few extra euro per night for *taxe de séjour* (holiday tax) and electricity.
- Pitching up 'wild' in non-designated spots *(camping sauvage)* is illegal in France.
- Accessing many campgrounds without your own transport can be slow and costly, or simply impossible.

Websites with campground listings searchable by location, theme and facilities:

Bienvenue à la Ferme (www.bienvenue-a-la-ferme.com)

Camping en France (www.camping.fr)

Camping France (www.campingfrance.com)

Gîtes de France (www.gites-de-france.com)

HPA Guide (http://camping.hpaguide.com)

Hostels

Hostels in France range from funky to threadbare, although with a wave of design-driven, up-to-the-minute hostels opening in Paris, Marseille and other big cities, hip hang-outs with perks aplenty seem to easily outweigh the threadbare these days.

- In university towns, *foyers d'étudiant* (student dormitories) are sometimes converted for use by travellers during summer.
- A dorm bed in an *auberge de jeunesse* (youth hostel) costs €20 to €50 in Paris, and anything from €15 to €40 in the provinces, depending on location, amenities and facilities; sheets are always included, breakfast more often than not.
- To prevent outbreaks of bed bugs, sleeping bags are not permitted.
- Hostels by the sea or in the mountains sometimes offer seasonal outdoor activities.
- French hostels are 100% nonsmoking.

Hotels

Hotels in France are rated with one to five stars, although the ratings are based on highly objective criteria (eg the size of the entry hall), not the quality of the service, the decor or cleanliness.

- French hotels almost never include breakfast in their rates. Unless specified otherwise, prices quoted don't include breakfast, which costs around €8/12/25 in a budget/midrange/top-end hotel.
- When you book, hotels usually ask for a credit-card number; some require a deposit.
- A double room generally has one double bed (sometimes two singles pushed together!); a room with twin beds *(deux lits)* is usually more expensive, as is a room with a bathtub instead of a shower.
- Feather pillows are practically nonexistent in France, even in top-end hotels.
- All hotel restaurant terraces allow smoking; if you are sensitive to smoke, you may need to sit inside.

Which Floor?

In France, as elsewhere in Europe, 'ground floor' refers to the floor at street level; the 1st floor – what would be called the 2nd floor in the US – is the floor above that.

Climate

Bordeaux

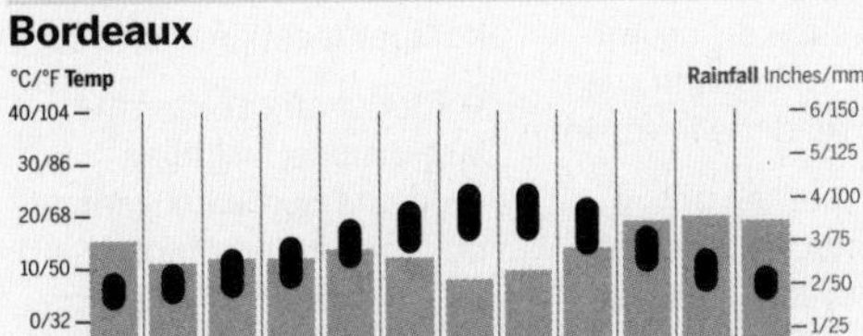

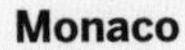

Monaco

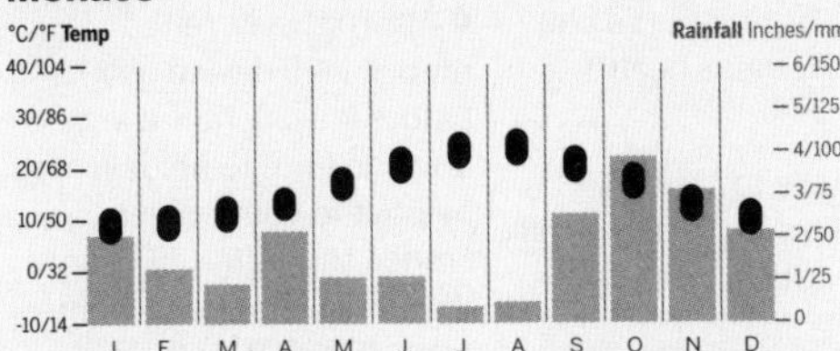

Paris

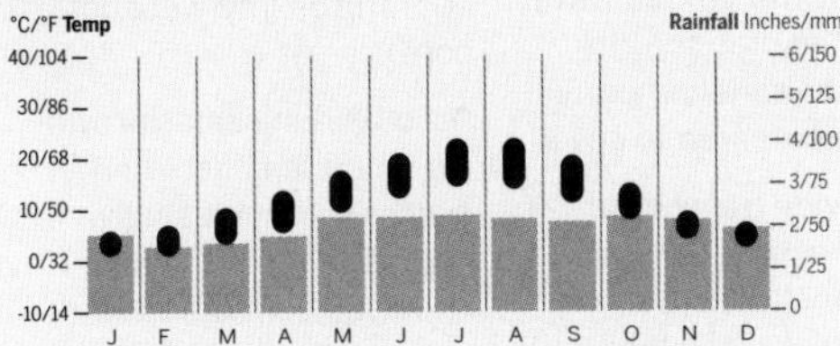

Customs Regulations

Goods brought in and out of countries within the EU incur no additional taxes provided duty has been paid somewhere within the EU and the goods are for personal consumption. Duty-free shopping is available only if you are leaving the EU.

Duty-free allowances (for adults) coming from non-EU countries (including the Channel Islands):

- 200 cigarettes or 50 cigars or 250g tobacco
- 1L spirits or 2L of sparkling wine/other alcoholic drinks less than 22% alcohol
- 4L still wine
- 16L beer
- other goods up to the value of €300/430 when entering by land/air or sea (€150 for under 15-year-olds)

Higher limits apply if you are coming from Andorra; anything over these limits must be declared. For further details, see www.douane.gouv.fr (partly in English).

Electricity

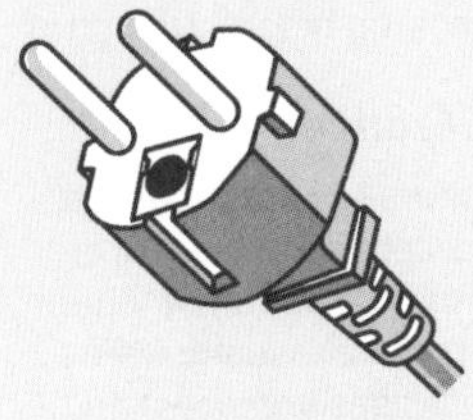

Type E
220V/50Hz

Health

France is a healthy place, so your main risks are likely to be sunburn, foot blisters, insect bites and mild stomach problems from eating and drinking with too much gusto.

Before You Go

- Bring your medications in their original, clearly labelled, containers.
- A signed and dated letter from your physician describing your medical conditions and medications, including generic names (French medicine names are

often completely different to those in other countries), is also a good idea.

- Dental care in France is usually good; however, it is sensible to have a dental check-up before a long trip.

In France

Visitors to France can get excellent health care from hospital *(hôpital)* emergency rooms/casualty wards *(salles des urgences)* and at a doctors' office *(cabinet médical)*.

- For basic requirements, chemists (pharmacies) in France are extremely helpful and sell a wide range of medicines not requiring a prescription *(ordonnance)*.
- As a visitor, you can either make an appointment or sit in line (depending on the doctor's practice) to see a *médecin généraliste* (doctor or general practitioner). Expect to pay between €35 and €50 up front, part or all of which your health insurance will then reimburse.
- If you prove you have valid insurance (ie to reimburse the cost of health treatment), you don't have to pay upfront to receive emergency hospital treatment.

Insurance

- Comprehensive travel insurance to cover theft, loss and medical problems is highly recommended.
- Some policies specifically exclude dangerous activities such as scuba diving, motorcycling, skiing and even trekking: read the fine print.
- Check that the policy covers ambulances or an emergency flight home.
- Find out in advance if your insurance plan will make payments directly to providers or reimburse you later for overseas health expenditures.
- If you have to claim later, make sure you keep all documentation.
- Paying for your airline ticket with a credit card often provides limited travel accident insurance – ask your credit-card company what it is prepared to cover.
- Worldwide travel insurance is available at www.lonelyplanet.com/travel-insurance. You can buy, extend and claim online anytime – even if you're already on the road.

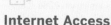

Internet Access

- Wi-fi (pronounced 'wee-fee' in French) is available at major airports, in most hotels, and at many cafes, restaurants, museums and tourist offices.
- Free public wi-fi hot spots are available in cities and many towns. In Paris look for a purple 'Zone Wi-Fi' sign.
- To search for free wi-fi hot spots in France, visit www.hotspot-locations.com.
- Tourist offices in some larger cities, including Lyon and Bordeaux, rent out pocket-sized mobile wi-fi devices that you carry around with you, ensuring a fast wi-fi connection while roaming the city.
- Alternatively, rent a mobile wi-fi device online before leaving home and arrange for it to be delivered by post to your hotel in France through HipPocket Wifi (http://hippocketwifi.com), Travel WiFi (http://travel-wifi.com) or My Webspot (http://my-webspot.com).
- Co-working cafes providing unlimited, fast internet access are increasingly available. Expect to pay about €5 per hour for a desk, plug and unlimited hot drinks and snacks.

Legal Matters

Police

- French police have wide powers of search and seizure and can ask you to prove your identity at any time – whether or not there is 'probable cause'.
- Foreigners must be able to prove their legal status in France (eg with a passport, visa or residency permit) without delay.

- If the police stop you for any reason, be polite and remain calm. Verbally (and of course physically) abusing a police officer can lead to a hefty fine, and even imprisonment.
- You may refuse to sign a police statement, and have the right to ask for a copy.
- People who are arrested are considered to be innocent until proven guilty, but can be held in custody until trial.

Drugs & Alcohol

- French law does not distinguish between 'hard' and 'soft' drugs.
- The penalty for any personal use of *stupéfiants* (including cannabis, amphetamines, ecstasy and heroin) can be a one-year jail sentence and a €3750 fine, but, depending on the circumstances, it might be anything from a stern word to a compulsory rehab program.
- Importing, possessing, selling or buying drugs can get you up to 10 years in prison and a fine of up to €500,000.
- Police have been known to search chartered coaches, cars and train passengers for drugs just because they're coming from Amsterdam.
- *Ivresse* (drunkenness) in public is punishable by a fine.

LGBT+ Travellers

The pride rainbow flag flies high in France, a country that left its closet long before many of its European neighbours. *Laissez-faire* perfectly sums up France's liberal attitude towards homosexuality and people's private lives in general; in part because of a long tradition of public tolerance towards unconventional lifestyles.

- Paris has been a thriving gay and lesbian centre since the late 1970s, and most major organisations are based there today.
- Attitudes towards homosexuality tend to be more conservative in the countryside and villages.
- France's lesbian scene is less public than its gay male counterpart and is centred mainly on women's cafes and bars.
- Same-sex marriage was legalised in France in 2013.
- Gay Pride marches are held in major French cities mid-May to early July.

Money

You always get a better exchange rate in-country but it is a good idea to arrive in France with enough euros to take a taxi to a hotel if you have to.

ATMs

Automated teller machines (ATMs) – known as *distributeurs automatiques de billets* (DAB) or *points d'argent* in French – are the cheapest and most convenient way to get money. ATMs connected to international networks are situated in all cities and towns and usually offer an excellent exchange rate.

Credit & Debit Cards

- Credit and debit cards, accepted almost everywhere in France, are convenient, relatively secure and usually offer a better exchange rate than travellers cheques or cash exchanges.
- Credit cards issued in France have embedded chips – you have to type in a PIN to make a purchase.

Americans, Take Note!

Travellers with credit cards issued in the US should be aware that they might well find themselves occasionally stuck when it comes to paying with their card: certain places in France – notably, Vélib in Paris and bike-share schemes in other cities, self-service toll booths on the autoroute (highway) and garages with self-service petrol (gas) pumps – only accept credit cards with chips and PINs. There is no solution to this bar ensuring you always have an emergency stash of cash on you.

Lost Cards

For lost cards, these numbers operate 24 hours:

Amex (☎01 47 77 72 00)

MasterCard (☎08 00 90 13 87)

Visa (☎08 00 90 11 79)

- Visa, MasterCard and Amex can be used in shops and supermarkets and for train travel, car hire and motorway tolls.
- Don't assume that you can pay for a meal or a budget hotel with a credit card – enquire first.
- Cash advances are a supremely convenient way to stay stocked up with euros but getting cash with a credit card involves both fees (sometimes US$10 or more) and interest – ask your credit-card issuer for details. Debit-card fees are usually much less.

Exchange Rates

Australia	A$1	€0.64
Canada	C$1	€0.66
Japan	¥100	€0.76
NZ	NZ$1	€0.59
UK	UK£1	€1.14
US	US$1	€0.85

For current exchange rates see www.xe.com.

Money Changers

- Commercial banks charge up to €5 per foreign-currency transaction – if they even bother to offer exchange services any more.
- In Paris and major cities, *bureaux de change* (exchange bureaus) are faster and easier, open longer hours and often give better rates than banks.

Tipping

By law, restaurant and bar prices are *service compris* (ie they include a 15% service charge), so there is no need to leave a *pourboire* (tip). If you were extremely satisfied with the service, however, you can – as many locals do – show your appreciation by leaving a small 'extra' tip for your waiter.

Bars No tips for drinks served at bar; round to nearest euro for drinks served at table

Hotel porters €1–2 per bag

Restaurants For decent service 10%

Taxis 10–15%

Toilet attendants 10–15%

Tour guides €1–2 per person

Opening Hours

Opening hours vary throughout the year. We list high-season opening hours, but remember that longer summer hours often decrease in shoulder and low seasons.

Banks 9am–noon and 2pm–5pm Monday to Friday or Tuesday to Saturday

Bars 7pm–1am

Cafes 7am–11pm

Clubs 10pm–3am, 4am or 5am Thursday to Saturday

Restaurants Noon–2.30pm and 7pm–11pm six days a week

Shops 10am–noon and 2pm–7pm Monday to Saturday (longer, and including Sunday, for shops in defined ZTIs (international tourist zones)

Public Holidays

The following *jours fériés* (public holidays) are observed in France:

New Year's Day (Jour de l'An) 1 January

Easter Sunday & Monday (Pâques & Lundi de Pâques) Late March/April

May Day (Fête du Travail) 1 May

Victoire 1945 8 May

Ascension Thursday (Ascension) May; on the 40th day after Easter

Pentecost/Whit Sunday & Whit Monday (Pentecôte & Lundi de Pentecôte) Mid-May to mid-June; on the seventh Sunday after Easter

Bastille Day/National Day (Fête Nationale) 14 July

Assumption Day (Assomption) 15 August

All Saints' Day (Toussaint) 1 November

Remembrance Day (L'onze Novembre) 11 November

Christmas (Noël) 25 December

The following are *not* public holidays in France: Shrove Tuesday (Mardi Gras; the first day of Lent); Maundy (or Holy) Thursday and Good Friday, just before Easter; and Boxing Day (26 December).

Telephone

Mobile Phones

- French mobile phone numbers begin with 06 or 07.
- France uses GSM 900/1800, which is compatible with the rest of Europe and Australia but not with the North American GSM 1900 or the totally different system in Japan (though some North Americans have tri-band phones that work here).
- Check with your phone service provider about roaming charges – dialling a mobile phone from a fixed-line phone or another mobile can be incredibly expensive.
- It is usually cheaper to buy a local SIM card from a French provider such as Orange, SFR, Bouygues and Free Mobile which gives you a local phone number. To do this, ensure your phone is unlocked.
- If you already have a compatible phone, you can slip in a SIM card and rev it up with prepaid credit, though this is likely to run out fast as domestic prepaid calls cost about €0.50 per minute.
- Recharge cards are sold at most *tabacs* (tobacconist-newsagents), supermarkets and online through websites such as Topengo (www.topengo.fr) or Sim-OK (https://recharge.sim-ok.com).

Phone Codes

Calling France from abroad Dial your country's international access code, then 33 (France's country code), then the 10-digit local number *without* the initial zero.

Calling internationally from France Dial ☎00 (the international access code), the *indicatif* (country code), the area code (without the initial zero if there is one) and the local number. Some country codes are posted in public telephones.

Directory inquiries For national *service des renseignements* (directory inquiries) dial ☎11 87 12 or use the service for free online at www.118712.fr.

International directory inquiries For numbers outside France, dial ☎11 87 00.

Practicalities

Laundry Virtually all French cities and towns have at least one *laverie libre-service* (self-service laundrette). Machines run on coins.

Newspapers and magazines Locals read their news in centre-left *Le Monde* (www.lemonde.fr), right-leaning *Le Figaro* (www.lefigaro.fr) or left-leaning *Libération* (www.liberation.fr).

Radio For news, tune in to the French-language France Info (105.5MHz; www.franceinfo.fr), multilanguage RFI (738kHz or 89MHz in Paris; www.rfi.fr) or, in northern France, the BBC World Service (648kHz) and BBC Radio 4 (198kHz). Popular national FM music stations include NRJ (www.nrj.fr), Virgin (www.virginradio.fr), La Radio Plus (www.laradioplus.com) and Nostalgie (www.nostalgie.fr).

Smoking Illegal in all indoor public spaces, including restaurants and pubs (though, of course, smokers still light up on the terraces outside).

TV and video TV is Secam; videos work on the PAL system.

Weights & Measures France uses the metric system.

Time

France uses the 24-hour clock and is on Central European Time, which is one hour ahead of GMT/UTC. During daylight saving time, which runs from the last Sunday in March to the last Sunday in October, France is two hours ahead of GMT/UTC.

The following times do not take daylight saving into account:

CITY	NOON IN PARIS
Auckland	11pm
Berlin	noon
Cape Town	noon
London	11am
New York	6am
San Francisco	3am
Sydney	9pm
Tokyo	8pm

Toilets

Public toilets, signposted as WC or *toilettes*, are not always plentiful in France, especially outside the big cities.

Love them (as a sci-fi geek) or loathe them (as a claustrophobe), France's 24-hour self-cleaning toilets are here to stay. Outside Paris these mechanical WCs are free, but in Paris they cost around €0.50 a go. Don't even think about nipping in after someone else to avoid paying unless you fancy a *douche* (shower) with disinfectant.

Some older establishments and motorway stops still have the hole-in-the-floor *toilettes à la turque* (squat toilets).

The French are completely blasé about unisex toilets, so save your blushes when tiptoeing past the urinals to reach the ladies' loo.

Tourist Information

Almost every city, town and village has an *office de tourisme* (a tourist office run by some unit of local government) or *syndicat d'initiative* (a tourist office run by an organisation of local merchants). Both are excellent resources and can supply you with local maps as well as details on accommodation, restaurants and activities.

Useful websites:

French Government Tourist Office (www.france.fr/en) The low-down on sights, activities, transport and special-interest holidays in all of France's regions. Brochures can be downloaded online.

French Tourist Offices (www.tourisme.fr) Website of tourist offices in France, with mountains of inspirational information organised by theme and region.

Travellers with Disabilities

While France presents evident challenges for *visiteurs handicapés* (disabled visitors) – cobblestones, cafe-lined streets that are a nightmare to navigate in a wheelchair *(fauteuil roulant)*, a lack of kerb ramps, older public facilities and many budget hotels without lifts – don't let that stop you from visiting. Efforts are being made to improve the situation and with a little careful planning, a hassle-free accessible stay is possible. Download Lonely Planet's free Accessible Travel guide from http://lptravel.to/AccessibleTravel.

- Paris tourist office runs the excellent 'Tourisme & Handicap' initiative whereby museums, cultural attractions, hotels and restaurants that provide access or special assistance or facilities for those with physical, mental, visual and/or hearing disabilities display a special logo at their entrances. For a list of qualifying places, go to www.parisinfo.com and click on 'Practical Paris'.

- Paris' metro, most of it built decades ago, is hopeless. Line 14 of the metro was built to be wheelchair-accessible, although in reality it remains extremely challenging to navigate in a wheelchair – unlike Paris buses which are 100% accessible.

- Parisian taxi company Horizon, part of Taxis G7 (www.taxisg7.fr), has cars especially adapted to carry wheelchairs and drivers trained in helping passengers with disabilities.

- Countrywide, many SNCF train carriages are accessible to people with disabilities. A traveller in a wheelchair can travel in both the TGV and in the 1st-class carriage with a

2nd-class ticket on mainline trains provided they make a reservation by phone or at a train station at least a few hours before departure. Details are available in the SNCF booklet *Le Mémento du Voyageur Handicapé* (a handbook for travellers with disabilities) available at all train stations.

Accès Plus (☎03 69 32 26 26, 08 90 64 06 50; www.accessibilite.sncf.com) The SNCF assistance service for rail travellers with disabilities. Can advise on station accessibility and arrange a *fauteuil roulant* or help getting on or off a train.

Access Travel (☎in UK 07973 114 365; www.access-travel.co.uk) Specialised UK-based agency for accessible travel.

Infomobi.com (☎09 70 81 93 95; www.vianavigo.com/accessibilite) Has comprehensive information on accessible travel in Paris and the surrounding Île de France area.

Mobile en Ville (☎09 52 29 60 51; www.mobileenville.org; 8 rue des Mariniers, 14e) Association that works hard to make independent travel within Paris easier for people in wheelchairs. Among other things it organises some great family *randonnées* (walks) in and around Paris.

Tourisme et Handicaps (☎01 44 11 10 41; www.tourisme-handicaps.org; 43 rue Marx Dormoy, 18e) Issues the 'Tourisme et Handicap' label to tourist sites, restaurants and hotels that comply with strict accessibility and usability standards. Different symbols indicate the sort of access afforded to people with physical, mental, hearing and/or visual disabilities.

Visas

- For up-to-date details on visa requirements, see the website of the **Ministère des Affaires Étrangères** (Ministry of Foreign Affairs; www.diplomatie.gouv.fr; 37 quai d'Orsay, 7e; Ⓜ Assemblée Nationale) and click 'Coming to France'.
- EU nationals and citizens of Iceland, Norway and Switzerland need only a passport or a national identity card to enter France and stay in the country, even for stays of over 90 days. However, citizens of new EU member states may be subject to various limitations on living and working in France.
- Citizens of Australia, the USA, Canada, Hong Kong, Israel, Japan, Malaysia, New Zealand, Singapore, South Korea and many Latin American countries do not need visas to visit France as tourists for up to 90 days. For long stays of over 90 days, contact your nearest French embassy or consulate and begin your application well in advance, as it can take months.
- Other people wishing to come to France as tourists have to apply for a Schengen Visa, named after the agreements that have abolished passport controls between 26 European countries. It allows unlimited travel throughout the entire zone for a 90-day period. Apply to the consulate of the country you are entering first, or your main destination. Among other things, you need travel and repatriation insurance and to be able to show that you have sufficient funds to support yourself.
- Tourist visas cannot be changed into student visas after arrival. However, short-term visas are available for students sitting university-entrance exams in France.
- Tourist visas cannot be extended except in emergencies (such as medical problems). When your visa expires you'll need to leave and reapply from outside France.

Transport

Getting There & Away

Flights, cars and tours can be booked online at www.lonelyplanet.com/bookings.

Air

Air France (www.airfrance.com) is the national carrier, with plenty of both domestic and international flights in and out of major French airports.

Climate Change & Travel

Every form of transport that relies on carbon-based fuel generates CO_2, the main cause of human-induced climate change. Modern travel is dependent on aeroplanes, which might use less fuel per kilometre per person than most cars but travel much greater distances. The altitude at which aircraft emit gases (including CO_2) and particles also contributes to their climate change impact. Many websites offer 'carbon calculators' that allow people to estimate the carbon emissions generated by their journey and, for those who wish to do so, to offset the impact of the greenhouse gases emitted with contributions to portfolios of climate-friendly initiatives throughout the world. Lonely Planet offsets the carbon footprint of all staff and author travel.

Bicycle

Transporting a bicycle to France is a breeze.

On Eurotunnel Le Shuttle trains through the Channel Tunnel, the fee for a bicycle, including its rider, is from UK£20 one way. Reserve 48 hours in advance.

A bike that's been dismantled to the size of a suitcase can be carried on board a Eurostar train from London or Brussels just like any other luggage. Otherwise, there's a UK£40 charge and you'll need advance reservations.

On ferries, foot passengers – where allowed – can usually (but not always) bring along a bicycle for no charge.

European Bike Express (☎in UK 01430 422 111; www.bike-express.co.uk) transports cyclists and their bikes from the UK to places around France.

Bus

Eurolines (☎08 92 89 90 91; www.eurolines.eu), a grouping of 32 long-haul coach operators (including the UK's National Express) links France with cities all across Europe, Morocco and Russia. Discounts are available to people under 26 and over 60. Make advance reservations, especially in July and August. A single Paris–London fare starts at €17, including a Channel crossing by ferry or the Channel Tunnel. Book as far ahead as possible to bag the cheapest ticket.

Flixbus (www.flixbus.com) offers low-cost, intercity bus travel between 27 countries in Europe aboard comfy buses equipped with toilet, snacks, plug sockets and free wi-fi.

Car & Motorcycle

A right-hand-drive vehicle brought to France from the UK or Ireland must have deflectors affixed to the headlights to avoid dazzling oncoming traffic. In the UK, information on driving in France is available from the RAC (www.rac.co.uk/driving-abroad/france) and the AA (www.theaa.com).

A foreign motor vehicle entering France must display a sticker or licence plate identifying its country of registration.

Eurotunnel

The Channel Tunnel (Chunnel), inaugurated in 1994, is the first dry-land link between England and France since the last ice age.

High-speed **Eurotunnel Le Shuttle** (☎in France 08 10 63 03 04, in UK 08443 35 35 35; www.eurotunnel.com) trains whisk bicycles, motorcycles, cars and coaches in 35 minutes from Folkestone through the Channel Tunnel to Coquelles, 5km southwest of Calais. Shuttles run 24 hours a day, with up to three departures an hour during peak periods. LPG and CNG tanks are not permitted, meaning gas-powered cars and many campers and caravans have to travel by ferry.

Eurotunnel sets its fares the way budget airlines do: the further in advance you book and the lower the demand for a particular crossing, the less you pay; same-day fares can cost a small fortune. Fares for a car, including up to nine passengers, start at UK£30/€37.

Train

Rail services link France with virtually every country in Europe.

- Book tickets and get train information from Rail Europe (www.raileurope.com). In the UK contact Railteam (www.railteam.co.uk).
- A very useful train-travel resource is the information-packed website The Man in Seat 61 (www.seat61.com).

Eurostar

The **Eurostar** (☎in France 08 92 35 35 39, in UK 08432 186 186; www.eurostar.com) whisks you from London to Paris in 2¼ hours.

Except late at night, trains link London (St Pancras International) with Paris (Gare du Nord; hourly), Calais (Calais-Fréthun; one hour, three daily), Lille (Gare Lille-Europe; 1½ hours, eight daily), Disneyland Resort Paris (2½ hours, one direct daily), Lyon (4¾ hours, one to five per week), Avignon (5¾ hours, one to five per week), Marseille (6½ hours, one to five per week) and Bordeaux (six hours with change of train in Paris, four daily), with less frequent services departing from Ebbsfleet and Ashford in Kent. Weekend ski trains connect England with the French Alps late December to mid-April.

Eurostar offers a bewildering array of fares. A standard, 2nd-class single ticket from Paris to London starts at €44.

For the best deals buy a return ticket, stay over a Saturday night, book up to 120 days in advance and don't mind nonexchangeability and nonrefundability. Discount fares are available for under 26s or over 60s.

Sea

Some ferry companies have started setting fares the way budget airlines do: the longer in advance you book and the lower the demand for a particular sailing, the less you pay. Seasonal demand is a crucial factor (Christmas, Easter, UK and French school holidays, July and August are especially busy), as is the time of day (an early-evening ferry can cost much more than one at 4am). People under 25 and over 60 may qualify for discounts.

To get the best fares, check Ferry Savers (www.ferrysavers.com).

Foot passengers are not allowed on Dover–Boulogne, Dover–Dunkirk or Dover–Calais car ferries except for daytime (and, from Calais to Dover, evening) crossings run by P&O Ferries. On ferries that do allow foot passengers, taking a bicycle is usually free.

Getting Around

Driving is the simplest way to get around France but a car is a liability in traffic-plagued, parking-starved city centres, and petrol bills and autoroute (dual carriageway/divided highway) tolls add up.

France is famous for its excellent public-transport network, which serves everywhere bar some very rural areas. The state-owned Société Nationale des Chemins de Fer Français (SNCF) takes care of almost all land transport between *départements* (counties). Transport within *départements* is handled by a combination of short-haul trains, SNCF buses and local bus companies.

Bicycle

France is great for cycling. Much of the countryside is drop-dead gorgeous and the country has a growing number of urban and rural *pistes cyclables* (bike paths and lanes; see Voies Vertes online at www.voievertes.com) and an extensive network of secondary and tertiary roads with relatively light traffic.

French law requires that bicycles must have two functioning brakes, a bell, a red reflector on the back and yellow reflectors on the pedals. After sunset and when visibility is poor, cyclists must turn on a white headlamp and a red tail lamp. When being overtaken by a vehicle, cyclists must ride in single file. Towing children in a bike trailer is permitted.

Never leave your bicycle locked up outside overnight if you want to see it – or at least most of its parts – again.

Some hotels offer enclosed bicycle parking.

Bicycle Rental

Most French cities and towns have at least one bike shop that rents out *vélos tout terrains* (mountain bikes; around €15 a day), known as VTTs, as well as more road-oriented *vélos tout chemin* (VTCs), or cheaper city bikes. You usually have to leave ID and/or a deposit (often a credit-card slip of €250) that you forfeit if the bike is damaged or stolen.

A growing number of cities – including Paris, Lyon, Aix-en-Provence, Bordeaux, Caen, Marseille, Nice, Rouen and Vannes – have automatic bike-rental systems, intended to encourage cycling as a form of urban transport, with computerised pick-up and drop-off sites all over town. In general, you have to sign up either short term or long term, providing credit-card details, and can then use the bikes for no charge for the first half-hour; after that, hourly charges rise quickly.

Car & Motorcycle

Having your own wheels gives you exceptional freedom and makes it easy to visit more remote parts of France. Depending on the number of passengers, it can also work out cheaper than the train. For example, by autoroute, the 930km drive from Paris to Nice (9½ hours of driving) in a small car costs about €75 for petrol and another €75 in tolls – by comparison, a one-way, 2nd-class TGV ticket for the 5½-hour Paris to Nice run costs anything from €69 to €120 per person.

In the cities, traffic and finding a place to park can be a major headache. During holiday periods and bank-holiday weekends, roads throughout France also get backed up with traffic jams *(bouchons)*.

Motorcyclists will find France great for touring, with winding roads of good quality and lots of stunning scenery. Just make sure your wet-weather gear is up to scratch.

France (along with Belgium) has the densest highway network in Europe. There are four types of intercity roads:

Autoroutes (highway names beginning with A) Multilane divided highways, usually (except near Calais and Lille) with tolls *(péages)*. Generously outfitted with rest stops.

Routes Nationales (N, RN) National highways. Some sections have divider strips.

Routes Départementales (D) Local highways and roads.

Routes Communales (C, V) Minor rural roads.

For information on autoroute tolls, rest areas, traffic and weather, go to the Sociétés d'Autoroutes website (www.autoroutes.fr).

Bison Futé (www.bison-fute.equipement.gouv.fr) is also a good source of information about traffic conditions. Plot itineraries between your departure and arrival points, and calculate toll costs with an online mapper like Via Michelin (www.viamichelin.com) or Mappy (https://fr.mappy.com).

Theft from cars is a major problem in France, especially in the south.

Car Hire

To hire a car in France, you'll generally need to be over 21 years old, have had a driving licence for at least a year, and have an international credit card. Drivers under 25 usually have to pay a surcharge *(frais jeune conducteur)* of €25 to €35 per day.

Car-hire companies provide mandatory third-party liability insurance but things such as collision-damage waivers (CDW, or *assurance tous risques*) vary greatly from company to company. When comparing rates and conditions (ie the fine print), the most important thing to check is the *franchise* (deductible/excess), which for a small car is usually around €600 for damage and €800 for theft. With many companies, you can reduce the excess by half, and perhaps to zero, by paying a daily insurance supplement of up to €20. Your credit card may cover CDW if you use it to pay for the rental but the car-hire company won't know anything about this – verify conditions and details with your credit-card issuer to be sure.

Speed-Fiends, Take Note

When it comes to catching and punishing speed fiends, France has upped its act in recent years. Automatic speed cameras, not necessarily visible, are widespread and the chances are you'll get 'flashed' at least once during your trip. Should this occur, a letter from the French government (stamped 'Liberté, Egalité, Fraternité – Liberty, Equality, Fraternity') will land on your door mat informing you of your *amende* (fine) and, should you hold a French licence, how many points you have lost. Motorists driving up to 20km/h over the limit in a 50km/h zone are fined €68 and one point; driving up to 20km/h over the limit in a zone with a speed limit of more than 50km/h costs €135 and one point.

There is no room for complacency. Moreover, should you be driving a rental car, the rental company will charge you an additional fee for the time they spent sharing your contact details with the French government.

Arranging your car hire or fly/drive package before you leave home is usually considerably cheaper than a walk-in rental, but beware of website offers that don't include a CDW or you may be liable for up to 100% of the car's value.

International car-hire companies:

Avis (www.avis.com)
Budget (www.budget.fr)
EasyCar (www.easycar.com)
Europcar (www.europcar.com)
Hertz (www.hertz.com)
Sixt (www.sixt.fr)

French car-hire companies:

ADA (www.ada.fr)
DLM (www.dlm.fr)
France Cars (www.francecars.fr)
Locauto (www.locauto.fr)
Renault Rent (www.renault-rent.com)
Rent a Car (www.rentacar.fr)

Rental cars with automatic transmission are very much the exception in France; they usually need to be ordered well in advance and are more expensive than manual cars.

For insurance reasons, it is usually forbidden to take rental cars on ferries, eg to Corsica.

All rental cars registered in France have a distinctive number on the licence plate, making them easily identifiable – including to thieves. *Never* leave anything of value in a parked car, even in the boot (trunk).

Driving Licence & Documents

An International Driving Permit (IDP), valid only if accompanied by your original licence, is good for a year and can be issued by your local automobile association before you leave home.

Drivers must carry the following at all times:

- passport or an EU national ID card
- valid driving licence (*permis de conduire;* most foreign licences can be used in France for up to a year)
- car-ownership papers, known as a *carte grise* (grey card)
- proof of third-party liability *assurance* (insurance)

Fuel

Essence (petrol), also known as *carburant* (fuel), costs between €1.48 and €1.65 per litre for 95 unleaded (Sans Plomb 95 or SP95, usually available from a green pump) and €1.35 to €1.60 for diesel (*diesel, gazole* or *gasoil,* usually available from a yellow pump). Check and compare current prices countrywide at www.prix-carburants.gouv.fr.

Filling up *(faire le plein)* is most expensive at autoroute rest stops, and usually cheapest at hypermarkets.

Many small petrol stations close on Sunday afternoons and, even in cities, it can be hard to find a staffed station open late at night. In general, after-hours purchases (eg at hypermarkets' fully automatic, 24-hour stations) can only be made with a credit card that has an embedded PIN chip, so if all you've got is cash or a magnetic-strip credit card, you could be stuck.

Insurance

Third-party liability insurance *(assurance au tiers)* is compulsory for all vehicles in France, including cars brought in from abroad. Normally, cars registered and insured in other European countries can circulate freely in France, but it's a good idea to contact your insurance company before you leave home to make sure you have coverage – and to check whom to contact in case of a breakdown or accident.

If you get into a minor accident with no injuries, the easiest way for drivers to sort things out with their insurance company is to fill out a Constat Aimable d'Accident Automobile (European Accident Statement), a standardised way of recording important details about what happened. In rental cars it's usually in the packet of documents in the glove compartment. Make sure the report includes any information that will help you prove that the accident was not your fault. Remember, if it *was* your fault you may be liable for a hefty insurance deductible/excess. Don't sign anything you don't fully understand. If problems crop up, call the police (☎17).

French-registered cars have details of their insurance company printed on a little green square affixed to the windscreen.

Parking

In city centres, most on-the-street parking places are *payant* (metered) from about 9am to 7pm (sometimes with a break from noon to 2pm) Monday to Saturday, except bank holidays.

Road Rules

Enforcement of French traffic laws (see www.securite routiere.gouv.fr) has been stepped up considerably in recent years. Speed cameras are common, as are radar traps and unmarked police vehicles. Fines for many infractions are given on the spot, and serious violations can lead to the confiscation of your driving licence and car.

Speed limits outside built-up areas (except where signposted otherwise):

Undivided N and D highways 80km/h (70km/h when raining)

Non-autoroute divided highways 110km/h (100km/h when raining)

Autoroutes 130km/h (110km/h when raining, 60km/h in icy conditions)

To reduce carbon emissions, autoroute speed limits have recently been reduced to 110km/h in some areas.

Unless otherwise signposted, a limit of 50km/h applies in *all* areas designated as built up, no matter how rural they may appear. You must slow to 50km/h the moment you come to a white sign with a red border and a place name written on it; the speed limit applies until you pass an identical sign with a horizontal bar through it.

Priority to the Right

Under the *priorité à droite* ('priority to the right') rule, any car entering an intersection (including a T-junction) from a road (including a tiny village backstreet) on your right has the right of way. Locals assume every driver knows this, so don't be surprised if they courteously cede the right of way when you're about to turn from an alley onto a highway – and boldly assert their rights when you're the one zipping down a main road.

Priorité à droite is suspended (eg on arterial roads) when you pass a sign showing an upended yellow square with a black square in the middle. The same sign with a horizontal bar through the square lozenge reinstates the *priorité à droite* rule.

When you arrive at a roundabout at which you do not have the right of way (ie the cars already in the roundabout do), you'll often see signs reading *vous n'avez pas la priorité* (you do not have right of way) or *cédez le passage* (give way).

Other important driving rules:

- Blood-alcohol limit is 0.05% (0.5g per litre of blood) – the equivalent of two glasses of wine for a 75kg adult. Police often conduct random breathalyser tests and penalties can be severe, including imprisonment.
- All passengers, including those in the back seat, must wear seat belts.
- Mobile phones may be used only if they are equipped with a hands-free kit or speakerphone.
- Turning right on a red light is illegal.
- Cars from the UK and Ireland must have deflectors affixed to their headlights to avoid dazzling oncoming motorists.
- Radar detectors, even if they're switched off, are illegal; fines are hefty.
- Children under 10 are not permitted to ride in the front seat (unless the back is already occupied by other children under 10).
- A child under 13kg must travel in a backward-facing child seat (permitted in the front seat only for babies under 9kg and if the airbag is deactivated).
- Up to age 10 and/or a minimum height of 140cm, children must use a size-appropriate type of front-facing child seat or booster.
- All vehicles driven in France must carry a high-visibility reflective safety vest (stored inside the vehicle, not in the trunk/boot), a reflective triangle, and a portable, single-use breathalyser kit.
- If you'll be driving on snowy roads, make sure you have snow chains *(chaînes neige)*, required by law whenever and wherever the police post signs.
- Riders of any type of two-wheeled vehicle with a motor (except motor-assisted bicycles) must wear a helmet. No special licence is required to ride a motorbike whose engine is smaller than 50cc, which is why rental scooters are often rated at 49.9cc.

Travel Conditions

In many areas, Autoroute Info (107.7MHz; www.autorouteinfo.fr) has round-the-clock traffic information for motorists.

Hitching

Hitching is never entirely safe in any country in the world, and we don't recommend it. Travellers who decide to hitch should understand that they are taking a small but potentially serious risk. Remember that it's safer to travel in pairs and be sure to inform someone of your intended destination. Hitching is not really part of French culture.

Hitching from city centres is pretty much hopeless, so your best bet is to take public transport to the outskirts. It is illegal to hitch on autoroutes, but you can stand near an entrance ramp as long as you don't block traffic. Hitching in remote rural areas is better, but once you get off the *routes nationales* traffic can be light and local. If your itinerary includes a ferry crossing, it's worth trying to score a ride before the ferry since vehicle tickets usually include a number of passengers free of charge. At dusk, give up and think about finding somewhere to stay.

Ride Share

A number of organisations around France arrange *covoiturage* (car sharing), that is, putting people looking for rides in touch with drivers going to the same destination:

- Covoiturage (www.covoiturage.fr)
- Bla Bla Car (www.blablacar.fr)
- Karzoo (www.karzoo.eu) International journeys.

Local Transport

France's cities and larger towns have world-class public-transport systems. There are *métros* (underground subway systems) in Paris, Lyon and Marseille and ultramodern light-rail lines *(tramways)* in cities such as Bordeaux, Lyon, Nice, Reims, Rouen and parts of greater Paris.

In addition to a *billet à l'unité* (single ticket), you can purchase a *carnet* (booklet or bunch) of 10 tickets or a *pass journée* (all-day pass).

Train

Travelling by train in France is a comfortable and environmentally sustainable way to see the country. Since many train stations have car-hire agencies, it's easy to combine rail travel with rural exploration by car.

The jewel in the crown of France's public-transport system – alongside the Paris metro – is its extensive rail network, almost all of it run by the heavily indebted, state-rail operator **SNCF** (Société Nationale des Chemins de fer Français, French National Railway Company; ☎from abroad +33 8 92 35 35 35, in France 36 35; http://en.voyages-sncf.com). The SNCF employs the most advanced rail technology, but its network reflects the country's centuries-old Paris-centric nature: most of the principal rail lines radiate out from Paris like the spokes of a wheel, the result being that services between provincial towns situated on different spokes can be infrequent and slow.

Since its inauguration in the 1980s, the pride and joy of SNCF is the TGV (Train à Grande Vitesse; www.tgv.com), pronounced 'teh zheh veh', which zips passengers along at speeds of up to 320km/h.

The main TGV lines (or LGVs, short for *lignes à grande vitesse*, ie high-speed rail lines) head north, east, southeast and southwest from Paris (trains use slower local tracks to get to destinations off the main line):

TGV Nord, Thalys and Eurostar Link Paris Gare du Nord with Arras, Lille, Calais, Brussels (Bruxelles-Midi), Amsterdam, Cologne and, via the Channel Tunnel, Ashford, Ebbsfleet and London St Pancras.

LGV Est Européene (www.lgv-est.com) Connects Paris Gare de l'Est with Reims, Nancy, Metz, Strasbourg, Zurich and Germany, including Frankfurt and Stuttgart. The super-high-speed track stretches as far east as Strasbourg.

TGV Sud-Est and TGV Midi-Méditerranée Link Paris Gare de Lyon with the southeast, including Dijon, Lyon, Geneva, the Alps, Avignon, Marseille, Nice and Montpellier.

TGV Atlantique Sud-Ouest and TGV Atlantique Ouest Link Paris Gare Montparnasse with western and southwestern France, including Brittany (Rennes, Brest, Quimper), Tours, Nantes, Poitiers, La Rochelle, Bordeaux, Biarritz and Toulouse.

LGV Rhin-Rhône High-speed rail route bypasses Paris altogether in its bid to better link the provinces. Six services a day speed between Strasbourg and Lyon, with most continuing south to Marseille or Montpellier on the Mediterranean.

Long-distance trains sometimes split at a station – that is, each half of the train heads off for a different destination. Check the destination panel on your car as you board or you could wind up very far from where you intended to go.

Other types of train:

TER (Train Express Régional; www.ter-sncf.com) A train that is not a TGV is often referred to as a *corail*, a *classique* or, for intraregional services, a TER.

Transilien (www.transilien.com) SNCF services in the Île de France area in and around Paris.

SNCF Fares & Discounts

Full-fare tickets can be quite expensive. Fortunately, a dizzying array of discounts are available and station staff are very good about helping travellers find the very best fare. But first, the basics:

- First-class travel, where available, costs 20% to 30% extra.
- Ticket prices for some trains, including most TGVs, are pricier during peak periods.
- The further in advance you reserve, the lower the fares.
- Children under four travel for free, or €9 with a *forfait bambin* to any destination if they need a seat.
- Children aged four to 11 travel for half-price.

Ouigo

Run by the SNCF, Ouigo (www.ouigo.com) is a low-cost TGV service that allows travel on high-speed TGVs for a snip of the usual price to 17 destinations in France, including Aix-en-Provence TGV, Angers-St Laud, Avignon TGV, Le Mans, Lyon, Marseille, Montpellier, Nantes, Nîmes, Paris, Paris Disneyland's Marne-La Vallée-Chessy TGV station and Paris' Aéroport Charles de Gaulle.

- Tickets can only be purchased online from three weeks until four hours before departure; tickets are emailed four days before departure and must be printed out or readable on a smartphone with the Ouigo app (iPhone and Android).
- The minimum single fare is €10. Children under 12 pay a flat €5 single fare.
- Each passenger is allowed to bring on board one piece of cabin luggage (35cm x 55cm x 25cm), one piece of hand luggage (27cm x 36cm x 15cm) and a child's pushchair for free; an extra bag and/or a larger bag costs €5 (€20 if you rock up at the train without registering the bag online in advance).
- If you want to plug in while aboard, be sure to reserve a seat with electric plug socket for an additional €2.

Discount Tickets

The SNCF's most heavily discounted tickets are called Prem's, available online, at ticket windows and from ticket machines: 100% Prem's are available from Thursday evening to Monday night for last-minute travel that weekend; Saturday-return Prem's are valid for return travel on a Saturday; and three-month Prem's can be booked a maximum of 90 days in advance. Prem's are nonrefundable and nonchangeable.

Intercités 100% Éco can be booked from three months to the day of departure, and offer cheap tickets between any stops, in any direction, on four main lines: Paris–Toulouse, Paris–Bordeaux, Paris–Nantes and Paris–Strasbourg. A single fare costs €15 to €35.

On regional trains, discount fares requiring neither a discount card nor advance purchase include:

Loisir rates Good for return travel that includes a Saturday night at your destination or involves travel on a Saturday or Sunday.

Découverte fares Available for low-demand 'blue-period' trains to people aged 12 to 25, seniors and the adult travel companions of children under 12.

Mini-Groupe tickets In some regions, these bring big savings for three to six people travelling together, provided you spend a Saturday night at your destination.

Discount Cards

Reductions of at least 25% (for last-minute bookings), and of 40%, 50% or even 60% (if you reserve well ahead or travel during low-volume 'blue' periods), are available with several discount cards (valid for one year):

Carte Jeune (€50) Available to travellers aged 12 to 27.

Carte Enfant+ (€75) For one to four adults travelling with a child aged four to 11.

Carte Weekend (€75) For people aged 26 to 59. Discounts on return journeys of at least 200km that either include a Saturday night away or only involve travel on a Saturday or Sunday.

Carte Sénior+ (€60) For travellers over 60.

Language

The sounds used in spoken French can almost all be found in English. There are a couple of exceptions: nasal vowels (represented in our pronunciation guides by 'o' or 'u' followed by an almost inaudible nasal consonant sound 'm', 'n' or 'ng'), the 'funny' *u* sound ('ew' in our guides) and the deep-in-the-throat *r*. Bearing these few points in mind and reading our pronunciation guides below as if they were English, you'll be understood just fine. The markers (m) and (f) indicate the forms for male and female speakers respectively.

To enhance your trip with a French phrasebook, visit **lonelyplanet.com**. Lonely Planet iPhone phrasebooks are available through the Apple App store.

Basics

Hello.
Bonjour. bon·zhoor

Goodbye.
Au revoir. o·rer·vwa

How are you?
Comment allez-vous? ko·mon ta·lay·voo

I'm fine, thanks.
Bien, merci. byun mair·see

Please.
S'il vous plaît. seel voo play

Thank you.
Merci. mair·see

Excuse me.
Excusez-moi. ek·skew·zay·mwa

Sorry.
Pardon. par·don

Yes./No.
Oui./Non. wee/non

I don't understand.
Je ne comprends pas. zher ner kom·pron pa

Do you speak English?
Parlez-vous anglais? par·lay·voo ong·glay

Shopping

I'd like to buy ...
Je voudrais acheter ... zher voo·dray ash·tay ...

I'm just looking.
Je regarde. zher rer·gard

How much is it?
C'est combien? say kom·byun

It's too expensive.
C'est trop cher. say tro shair

Can you lower the price?
Vous pouvez baisser le prix? voo poo·vay bay·say ler pree

Eating & Drinking

..., please.
..., s'il vous plaît. ... seel voo play

A coffee	*un café*	un ka·fay
A table for two	*une table pour deux*	ewn ta·bler poor der
Two beers	*deux bières*	der bee·yair

I'm a vegetarian.
Je suis végétarien/végétarienne. (m/f) zher swee vay·zhay·ta·ryun/vay·zhay·ta·ryen

Cheers!
Santé! son·tay

That was delicious!
C'était délicieux! say·tay day·lee·syer

The bill, please.
L'addition, s'il vous plaît. la·dee·syon seel voo play

Emergencies

Help!
Au secours! o skoor

Call the police!
Appelez la police! a·play la po·lees

Call a doctor!
Appelez un médecin! a·play un mayd·sun

I'm sick.
Je suis malade. zher swee ma·lad

I'm lost.
Je suis perdu/perdue. (m/f) zhe swee pair·dew

Where are the toilets?
Où sont les toilettes? oo son lay twa·let

Transport & Directions

Where's ...?
Où est ...? oo ay ...

What's the address?
Quelle est l'adresse? kel ay la·dres

Behind the Scenes

Acknowledgements

Climate map data adapted from Peel MC, Finlayson BL & McMahon TA (2007) 'Updated World Map of the Köppen-Geiger Climate Classification', Hydrology and Earth System Sciences, 11, 1633–44.

Illustrations pp42-3 and pp48-9 by Javier Zarracina.

This Book

This 2nd edition of Lonely Planet's *Best of France* guidebook was curated by Anita Isalska and researched and written by Oliver Berry, Kerry Christiani, Gregor Clark, Damien Harper, Anita Isalska, Catherine Le Nevez, Hugh McNaughtan, Christopher Pitts, Daniel Robinson, Regis St Louis and Nicola Williams. This guidebook was produced by the following:

Destination Editor Daniel Fahey

Senior Product Editor Genna Patterson

Product Editors Alison Ridgway, Jessica Ryan

Senior Cartographer Mark Griffiths

Book Designers Virginia Moreno, Jessica Rose

Assisting Editors Katie Connolly, Bruce Evans, Victoria Harrison, Kate Mathews, Anne Mulvaney

Assisting Cartographer Hunor Csutoros

Cover Researcher Naomi Parker

Thanks to Imogen Bannister, Andi Jones, Kirsten Rawlings, John Taufa, Juan Winata

Send Us Your Feedback

We love to hear from travellers – your comments keep us on our toes and help make our books better. Our well-travelled team reads every word on what you loved or loathed about this book. Although we cannot reply individually to postal submissions, we always guarantee that your feedback goes straight to the appropriate authors, in time for the next edition. Each person who sends us information is thanked in the next edition, the most useful submissions are rewarded with a selection of digital PDF chapters.

Visit lonelyplanet.com/contact to submit your updates and suggestions or to ask for help. Our award-winning website also features inspirational travel stories, news and discussions.

Note: We may edit, reproduce and incorporate your comments in Lonely Planet products such as guidebooks, websites and digital products, so let us know if you don't want your comments reproduced or your name acknowledged. For a copy of our privacy policy visit lonelyplanet.com/privacy.

A–Z

Index

000 Map pages

000 Map pages

Symbols & Map Key

Look for these symbols to quickly identify listings:

- Sights
- Activities
- Courses
- Tours
- Festivals & Events
- Eating
- Drinking
- Entertainment
- Shopping
- Information & Transport

These symbols and abbreviations give vital information for each listing:

Sustainable or green recommendation

FREE No payment required

- Telephone number
- Opening hours
- Parking
- Nonsmoking
- Air-conditioning
- Internet access
- Wi-fi access
- Swimming pool
- Bus
- Ferry
- Tram
- Train
- English-language menu
- Vegetarian selection
- Family-friendly

Find your best experiences with these Great For... icons.

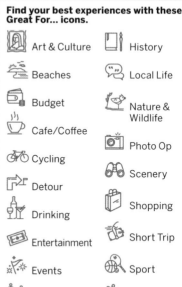

- Art & Culture
- Beaches
- Budget
- Cafe/Coffee
- Cycling
- Detour
- Drinking
- Entertainment
- Events
- Family Travel
- Food & Drink
- History
- Local Life
- Nature & Wildlife
- Photo Op
- Scenery
- Shopping
- Short Trip
- Sport
- Walking
- Winter Travel

Sights

- Beach
- Bird Sanctuary
- Buddhist
- Castle/Palace
- Christian
- Confucian
- Hindu
- Islamic
- Jain
- Jewish
- Monument
- Museum/Gallery/Historic Building
- Ruin
- Shinto
- Sikh
- Taoist
- Winery/Vineyard
- Zoo/Wildlife Sanctuary
- Other Sight

Points of Interest

- Bodysurfing
- Camping
- Cafe
- Canoeing/Kayaking
- Course/Tour
- Diving
- Drinking & Nightlife
- Eating
- Entertainment
- Sento Hot Baths/Onsen
- Shopping
- Skiing
- Sleeping
- Snorkelling
- Surfing
- Swimming/Pool
- Walking
- Windsurfing
- Other Activity

Information

- Bank
- Embassy/Consulate
- Hospital/Medical
- Internet
- Police
- Post Office
- Telephone
- Toilet
- Tourist Information
- Other Information

Geographic

- Beach
- Gate
- Hut/Shelter
- Lighthouse
- Lookout
- Mountain/Volcano
- Oasis
- Park
- Pass
- Picnic Area
- Waterfall

Transport

- Airport
- BART station
- Border crossing
- Boston T station
- Bus
- Cable car/Funicular
- Cycling
- Ferry
- Metro/MRT station
- Monorail
- Parking
- Petrol station
- Subway/S-Bahn/Skytrain station
- Taxi
- Train station/Railway
- Tram
- Tube Station
- Underground/U-Bahn station
- Other Transport

Gregor Clark

Gregor Clark is a US-based writer whose love of foreign languages and curiosity about what's around the next bend have taken him to dozens of countries on five continents. Chronic wanderlust has also led him to visit all 50 states and most Canadian provinces on countless road trips through his native North America. Since 2000, Gregor has regularly contributed to Lonely Planet guides, with a focus on Europe and the Americas.

Damian Harper

With two degrees (one in modern and classical Chinese from SOAS), Damian has been writing for Lonely Planet for more than two decades, contributing to titles as diverse as China, Beijing, Shanghai, Vietnam, Thailand, Ireland, London, Mallorca, Malaysia, Singapore & Brunei, Hong Kong, China's Southwest and the UK. A seasoned guidebook writer, Damian has penned articles for numerous newspapers and magazines, including *The Guardian* and *The Daily Telegraph,* and currently makes Surrey, England, his home. A self-taught trumpet novice, his other hobbies include collecting modern first editions, photography and Taekwondo. Follow Damian on Instagram @damian.harper.

Catherine Le Nevez

Catherine's wanderlust kicked in when she roadtripped across Europe from her Parisian base aged four, and she's been hitting the road at every opportunity since, travelling to around 60 countries and completing her Doctorate of Creative Arts in Writing, Masters in Professional Writing, and postgrad qualifications in Editing and Publishing along the way. Over the past dozen-plus years she's written scores of Lonely Planet guides and articles covering Paris, France, Europe and far beyond. Her work has also appeared in numerous online and print publications. Topping Catherine's list of travel tips is to travel without any expectations.

Hugh McNaughtan

A former English lecturer, Hugh swapped grant applications for visa applications, and turned his love of travel into a full-time thing. Having done a bit of restaurant-reviewing in his home town (Melbourne) he's now eaten his way across four continents. He's never happier than when on the road with his two daughters. Except perhaps on the cricket field...

Christopher Pitts

Born in the year of the Tiger, Chris's first expedition in life ended in failure when he tried to dig from Pennsylvania to China at the age of six. Hardened by reality but still infinitely curious about the other side of the world, he went on to study Chinese in university, living for several years in Kunming, Taiwan and Shanghai. A chance encounter in an elevator led to a Paris relocation, where he lived with his wife and two children for over a decade before the lure of Colorado's sunny skies and outdoor adventure proved too great to resist.

Daniel Robinson

Brought up in the San Francisco Bay Area, the Chicago suburb of Glen Ellyn and Israel, Daniel first saw Europe as a nine-year-old, when family travels brought him to pre-Thatcher London, post-1968 Prague and economic-miracle-era Rome. He first hit the road on his own at age 17 with a trip to Cyprus. Daniel is now based in New London, Connecticut.

Regis St Louis

Regis grew up in a small town in the American Midwest – the kind of place that fuels big dreams of travel – and he developed an early fascination with foreign dialects and world cultures. He spent his formative years learning Russian and a handful of Romance languages, which served him well on journeys across much of the globe. Regis has contributed to more than 50 Lonely Planet titles, covering destinations across six continents. His travels have taken him from the mountains of Kamchatka to remote island villages in Melanesia, and to many grand urban landscapes. When not on the road, he lives in New Orleans. Follow him on Instagram @regisstlouis.

Nicola Williams

Border-hopping is way of life for British writer, runner, foodie, art aficionado and mum-of-three Nicola Williams who has lived in a French village on the southern side of Lake Geneva for more than a decade. Nicola has authored more than 50 guidebooks on Paris, Provence, Rome, Tuscany, France, Italy and Switzerland for Lonely Planet and covers France as a destination expert for the *Telegraph.* She also writes for the *Independent, Guardian,* lonelyplanet.com, *Lonely Planet Magazine, French Magazine, Cool Camping France* and others. Catch her on the road on Twitter and Instagram at @tripalong.

Our Story

A beat-up old car, a few dollars in the pocket and a sense of adventure. In 1972 that's all Tony and Maureen Wheeler needed for the trip of a lifetime – across Europe and Asia overland to Australia. It took several months, and at the end – broke but inspired – they sat at their kitchen table writing and stapling together their first travel guide, *Across Asia on the Cheap*. Within a week they'd sold 1500 copies. Lonely Planet was born. Today, Lonely Planet has offices in Franklin, London, Melbourne, Oakland, Dublin, Beijing, and Delhi, with more than 600 staff and writers. We share Tony's belief that 'a great guidebook should do three things: inform, educate and amuse'.

Our Writers

Anita Isalska

Anita Isalska is a travel journalist, editor and copywriter. After several merry years as a staff writer and editor – a few of them in Lonely Planet's London office – Anita now works freelance between Australia, the UK and any Alpine chalet with good wi-fi. Anita writes about France, Eastern Europe, Southeast Asia and off-beat travel. Read her stuff on www.anitaisalska.com.

Oliver Berry

Oliver Berry is a writer and photographer from Cornwall. He has worked for Lonely Planet for more than a decade, covering destinations from Cornwall to the Cook Islands, and has worked on more than 30 guidebooks. He is also a regular contributor to many newspapers and magazines, including *Lonely Planet Traveller*. His writing has won several awards, including *The Guardian* Young Travel Writer of the Year and the *TNT Magazine* People's Choice Award. His latest work is published at www.oliverberry.com.

Kerry Christiani

Kerry is an award-winning travel writer, photographer and Lonely Planet author, specialising in Central and Southern Europe. Based in Wales, she has authored/co-authored more than a dozen Lonely Planet titles. An adventure addict, she loves mountains, cold places and true wilderness. She features her latest work at https://its-a-small-world.com and tweets @kerrychristiani.

More Writers

STAY IN TOUCH LONELYPLANET.COM/CONTACT

AUSTRALIA The Malt Store, Level 3, 551 Swanston St, Carlton, Victoria 3053 ☎03 8379 8000, fax 03 8379 8111

IRELAND Digital Depot, Roe Lane (off Thomas St), Digital Hub, Dublin 8, D08 TCV4

USA 124 Linden Street, Oakland, CA 94607 ☎510 250 6400, toll free 800 275 8555, fax 510 893 8572

UK 240 Blackfriars Road, London SE1 8NW ☎020 3771 5100, fax 020 3771 5101

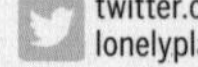 twitter.com/lonelyplanet
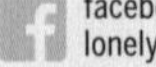 facebook.com/lonelyplanet
 instagram.com/lonelyplanet
 youtube.com/lonelyplanet
 lonelyplanet.com/newsletter